RADIUM OF
THE WORD

THINKING LITERATURE
A series edited by Nan Z. Da and Anahid Nersessian

Radium of the Word

A POETICS OF MATERIALITY

Craig Dworkin

The University of Chicago Press
Chicago and London

The University of Chicago Press, Chicago 60637
The University of Chicago Press, Ltd., London
© 2020 by The University of Chicago
All rights reserved. No part of this book may be used or reproduced in any manner whatsoever without written permission, except in the case of brief quotations in critical articles and reviews. For more information, contact the University of Chicago Press, 1427 East 60th Street, Chicago, IL 60637.
Published 2020

29 28 27 26 25 24 23 22 21 20   1 2 3 4 5

ISBN-13: 978-0-226-74342-4 (cloth)
ISBN-13: 978-0-226-74356-1 (paper)
ISBN-13: 978-0-226-74373-8 (e-book)
DOI: https://doi.org/10.7208/chicago/9780226743738.001.0001

Library of Congress Cataloging-in-Publication Data

Names: Dworkin, Craig Douglas, author.
Title: Radium of the word : a poetics of materiality / Craig Dworkin.
Other titles: Thinking literature.
Description: Chicago : University of Chicago Press, 2020. | Series: Thinking literature | Includes bibliographical references and index.
Identifiers: LCCN 2020018399 | ISBN 9780226743424 (cloth) | ISBN 9780226743561 (paperback) | ISBN 9780226743738 (ebook)
Subjects: LCSH: Poetics. | Literary style.
Classification: LCC PN1042 .D75 2020 | DDC 808.1—dc23
LC record available at https://lccn.loc.gov/2020018399

THIS BOOK IS DEDICATED TO MARJORIE,
MY FIRST READER, FOR THIRTY YEARS.
AND TO ANNE AND MILES,
WHO ENCOURAGED EVERY WORD.

Contents

LIST OF FIGURES ix

INTRODUCTION 1

ONE · The Prosaic Imagination 21

TWO · The Onomastic Imagination 48

THREE · The Logic of the Work (on P. Inman) 79

FOUR · The Logic of Print (on Russell Atkins) 101

FIVE · The Logic of Spacing (on N. H. Pritchard) 143

SIX · The Logic of Registration (on Andy Warhol) 170

ACKNOWLEDGMENTS 189

NOTES 191

INDEX 243

Figures

1. Daniel-Henry Kahnweiler colophon (1907) 54
2. Pablo Picasso, *Daniel-Henry Kahnweiler* (1910) 60
3. Pablo Picasso, *Daniel-Henry Kahnweiler* (1910) (detail) 61
4. Pablo Picasso, *The Poet* (1911) 62
5. Pablo Picasso, *The Poet* (1911) (detail) 63
6. Russell Atkins, "Spyrytual" (1966) 102
7. Russell Atkins, "A Storm Shall Break" (1967) 113
8. T. L. Kryss, "Winter Rain and Purple Rainbow" (1967) 114
9. T. L. Kryss, "monsoooooooooon" (1967) 116
10. T. L. Kyrss, untitled poem (1967) 117
11. Russell Atkins, "Spyrytual" (2016) 125
12. D. A. Levy, from *Plastic Saxophone Found in an Egyptian Tomb* (1966) 128
13. D. A. Levy, untitled poem (1967) 129
14. rjs, untitled poem (1967) 132
15. T. L. Kryss, "i wisht i cd play the beautiful instrument" (1967) 135
16. Don Thomas, "2 Above, 3 Below" and "Homage to Issa" (1967) 136
17. Russell Atkins, from *The Saundaryalahari, or Flood of Beauty* (1967) 138
18. Russell Atkins, from *Spyrytual* (1966) 139
19. Russell Atkins, *Spyrytual* (title page, 1966) 140
20. N. H. Pritchard, "junt" (1971) 144
21. N. H. Pritchard, """ (1970) 147

Introduction

Wenn wir eine Maschine, die Lösung einer mathematischen Aufgabe, die Organisation irgend einer sozialen Gruppe schön nennen, so ist das mehr als eine Redensart.

[If we call a machine, a solution to a mathematical problem, or the organization of some social group "beautiful," it is more than just a figure of speech.]

MAX DESSOIR

In its narrowest sense engineering drawing is a language used for communication. However, languages in general are not only useful for communication.

PETER BOOKER

This book proposes a methodology. The following chapters cumulatively demonstrate that attending to the material forms of language can reveal significations not accessible through conventional reading strategies. Linguistic materiality—the specific forms and configurations taken by the signifier—generates its own nonsymbolic associations; the physical substance of writing highlights similarities between signifiers, establishes connections that cut across grammatic and rhetorical units, and creates patterns that can be significant without communicating any set or preordained message. In short, as Ludwig Pfeiffer has phrased it, "signifiers, in their materiality as a source and support, will produce meanings as their effects."[1]

"To look at signifiers in isolation, one would be interested not in their meaning but in their 'materiality,'" Pfeiffer continues, but they never in fact appear in isolation, and to recognize the pure play of the signifier, free from the reign of any symbolic and ideational functions of language, need not, however, stop at some dehistoricized *locus solus*, segregated from political concerns and social conditions.[2] For the poems under consideration here, the meaning effects of materiality, again and again, draw the works into dialogue with unexpected political topics: the death penalty from opera-queen gossip (in chapter 6), for instance, or civil-rights riots from a set of quotation marks (chapter 4), or homelessness and addiction from the shattered, erratic spacing of the typeset line (chapter 5). My goal with this book has been to take up the challenge of Veronica Forrest-Thomson's admonition that "the best way to restore value to poetic artifice is to find ways of discussing it that do not presuppose the subservience of form to extended meaning." I have tried throughout to let the materiality of texts speak on its own terms, listening to the significations it produces independently of any ostensible thematic content or authorial communication, but always resonating within a particular social space and at a specific historical juncture.[3]

For a brief, concrete example, consider Gwendolyn Brooks's aubade "An Aspect of Love, Alive in the Ice and Fire: LaBohem Brown," the final poem in the triptych series of her chapbook *Riot*. The central stanza of the poem turns its descriptive attention to the lover rising from bed and leaving the privacy of domestic space with a "direct and respectable stride [...] down the imperturbable street":

> You are direct and self-accepting as a lion
> in African velvet. You are level, lean, remote.[4]

Symbolically, the lines offer an encomium, enumerating the lover's attributes; they have been taken by critics, not unreasonably, as ascribing "favorable African characteristics to twentieth century American blacks," portraying the lover "as a proud black man," with the confidence that comes from "fighting back, by standing up against oppression," and adding rounded depth to a portrait of someone who, despite his leonine fierceness, "seems tame, nonetheless, by virtue of the fabric."[5] The figure of the lion, moreover, both evokes and keeps at a safely abeyant remove the related panther (*Panthera pardus* as kin to *Panthera leo*), which might have served a similar symbolic function within the poem.[6] Indeed, "lean" and "velvet" would be more apt associations for a panther. The choice of feline affiliation is perhaps even more surprising given that the Black Panther Party was at the height of its membership when Brooks was writing her poem, and had just opened its Chicago chapter. Indeed, the metaphor was readily available to Brooks, who within a year or two would describe the heroism of her fugitive grandfather "panthering through the woods" in escape from slavery.[7]

"Lion," however, provides linguistic affordances that *panther* cannot. To begin with, the ghost of *lyin'* that echoes behind its pronunciation reinscribes and troubles the structural binary of the poem's narrative scenes, which oppose the initially supine figure who will "rise" from the "level" bed amid the anarchic uprising around him. Furthermore, unlike *panther*, "lion" attracts the collocation *pride*, which as the collective noun for "a group of lions forming a social unit" evokes the collective sociability of the community formed in its resistance to white supremacy, and as a noun denoting "self-esteem" characterizes the emotion portrayed by the description of the lover as "direct and respectable […] and self-accepting"; indeed, the phrase *Black pride* gained currency at precisely the moment Brooks was composing the poem.⁸ Moreover, at a different level of linguistic association, the near-anagram of "velvet" and "level" invites the reader to look closely at the position of the text's words along the chain of signifiers, which immediately reveals a new logic. A synonym for "lean" and graceful is *svelte*. Similarly, while one might expect the metaphorical lion to be found in kente cloth, say, the phrase "in African velvet" is decidedly odd. A more direct route leads to the African *veldt*—the "level" and "remote" (from Chicago) open plains of South Africa. Let me emphasize that none of these words—which come, respectively, from medieval Latin, modern French, and Afrikaans—are etymologically related.⁹ But they forge a tighter textual weave than the subjective associations summoned by the descriptive scene; and while that scene, occurring within the fictionalized narrative of a civil rights protest, can easily accommodate the symbolic figures deployed by Brooks, only the material forms of the words themselves can account for the particular vocabulary ("level," "lean," "velvet") and explain the otherwise strange locution of a cat "in African velvet." The web of the signifier, articulating even words that do not themselves appear in the text, reveals the workable mechanism of the poem in its own right.

The forces produced by that mechanism might of course be reabsorbed by traditional communicative readings, perhaps as further evidence of the level of Brooks's finely tuned craft, or as a prefiguration of the subjects of her later anti-apartheid poems such as *The Near-Johannesburg Boy* and *Winnie*, or even as part of the psychology that would lead to approaching—without explicitly naming—a panther, at a time when tensions between Chicago civic officials and Black Nationalists were reaching a pitch, culminating in the infamous assassination of Fred Hampton, Illinois chief of the Black Panther Party, by Chicago police.¹⁰

In addition to demonstrating the interpretive payoffs that follow from unconventional reading practices, this book intervenes to reconfigure the field of the literary and to broaden what might come to mind when we consider categories like "contemporary poetry" or "avant-garde" or "African American poetry," because new ways of reading make an entire range of works newly accessible. The "materiality of language" might sound passé or carry a musty whiff of 1970s period style, but it is "news that stays news," not only because contemporary literature is still most often discussed (and written) as if it were primarily about thematic content, but also because by making certain works more readable it broadens, complicates, and diversifies what we think of as poetry.¹¹ Some of the works I focus on in this book are by well-known figures (Gertrude Stein, Lyn

Hejinian, Andy Warhol) but remain little read because of their obstreperous recalcitrance; by revealing the patterns at work in a number of exceedingly difficult texts, I hope to end their being dismissed as unreadable or hopelessly opaque. Furthermore, I hope to show how vital and exciting the work of some lesser-known writers (P. Inman, Russell Atkins, N. H. Pritchard) can be, and to make the case that their neglect has been unjust and has impoverished our sense of the literary record.

Two themes govern my focus here: typography and proper names. While these might seem disparate and unrelated motifs, each provides a privileged vantage from which to observe the dynamic interaction of linguistic material and literary meaning. Typography might at first glance appear to be sheer, meaningless material: a neutral form available to hold whatever content fills it. As I will demonstrate, however, typographic particulars—from the shape of glyphs to the kerning between them to the orthography of the lexemes they form—encode and transmit connotations, histories, and the scars of social conflict, or what can be understood as the *ordinatio* of the printed page (the way in which ideological beliefs and the formal structures of a text dynamically construct and support one another).[12] The proper name, by contrast, might initially seem an ideal sign, pointing uniquely to a single individual with a perfect alignment of signified and referent. In order to signify at all, however, the proper name must enter into the same nexus as every other word, so that, as Derrida reminds, it is "toujours pris dans une chaîne ou un système de différences" [always caught in a chain or system of differences].[13]

Chapter 1 looks at the familiar form of the typeset prose page (like the one you are reading now) and argues that we might perceive moments at which it attains the status of a form, rather than a mere format, through the affordances of the new lexical relationships it orchestrates with an inherent logic of chance and determinism, dispersion and consolidation, fixity and flow. This perspective, as it happens, explains some of the most abstract, agrammatical, and restive works of twentieth-century poetry, including Hejinian's most fragmented and abstract work, *Writing Is an Aid to Memory*, with couplets such as "guage means general / will push straction one day to the left." The first line, for instance, come from following the vertical logic that emerges from the typesetting of a particular edition of Jean Piaget's works, in a passage that will resonate with the theories presented later in this chapter: "Actions can be represented in a number of different ways, of which language is only one. Language is certainly not the exclusive means of representation. It is only one aspect of the very general function. ..." Attending to the form of prose in even the most conventional (indeed, *prosaic*) narrative fiction reveals moments at which discursive descriptions figure their own format, that of printed prose, to offer a glimpse of the intersection between the symbolic and material planes of language. These instances of "prose in prose" thus illuminate the dynamic transfers between medium and symbol that take place along the surface of a text, in moments at which noise and message, or signifier and signified, invert themselves in short-circuiting exchange.

Chapter 4 moves from the specific shape of printed characters to the various modes of print itself, including mimeograph, letterpress, and Warhol's beloved silkscreen, to ask what it means to quote a quotation, and whether one mode of production can meaningfully quote another. The chapter focuses on the work of Russell Atkins, a true "unsung master" of twentieth-century American poetry, who served as a hinge between the Black Nationalist poets of Cleveland's Muntu workshop and the counterculture poets of the city's concrete poetry scene in the 1960s.[14] His poems, accordingly, migrated among readerships as well, circulating in different print forms and signifying in different ways, depending on the social context. The same set of ditto marks might signify a contemporary riot in an anthology of protest poetry on the counter at Ahmed Evans's Afro Culture Shop and Bookstore and an abstract visual poem across town in a mimeo 'zine behind the counter of Jim Lowell's Asphodel Bookshop. In each venue, however, it demonstrated the degree to which the most minimal mark, accidental inscriptive trace, or even the technical means of printing itself can open onto the most urgent, heated, and fraught cultural politics.

Traditionally, as these chapters argue, uniformity is one of the hallmarks both of printerly skill and of prose, which is frequently justified (as on this page) to create neat, geometric blocks. Chapter 6 turns instead to the wildly irregular prose and idiosyncratic *mise-en-page* of Warhol's notorious *a: a novel*, with an erratically spaced format that has been of recent interest to poets.[15] Ostensibly the direct, unartificed transcript of a day in the life of Factory regulars, the text was in fact roughly spliced and subjected to processes that produced and amplified irregularities. Warhol, to begin with, sought inexperienced typists and had them work without professional equipment; he then insisted on retaining all of their errors, refused to regularize the typescripts, and added capricious changes of his own during editing and proofing—including haphazard substitutions of names and pseudonyms. The result, a radically indeterminate and unstable work, again affords a revealing glimpse of the moments when material substrate and narrated description short-circuit, as the various technologies of inscription record their own act of recording as well as the loquacious banter of the protagonists, culminating unexpectedly in an evocation of precisely the same instance in one of John Cage's texts. At the same time, the novel's radical artifice and semiotic indeterminacy highlight—with a perspicacity arising ironically from the text's very obtuseness—the ways in which common words can engage in acts of nomination and, conversely, proper nouns must enter into the paronomastic play of the signifier. At one point, for instance, Warhol's own name—some pages after a passage that confuses a "whole house" and a "whore house"—emerges from the typescript as "Warhole," as if the prosopopoeia of his own amoral commercialism and philosophy of emptiness, which he explained by saying "my favorite piece of sculpture is a solid wall with a hole in it."[16]

This logic of the name, compounded by Derrida's specific understanding of the operation of the signature, is the subject of chapter 2, which looks at that ways in which proper names animate, generate, and account for a number of poems from the most experimental phase of early modernism, including interrelated works by Guillaume Apollinaire, Gertrude Stein, Mina Loy, and Blaise Cendrars. The same sense of the Derridean signature—in which authorial name, signature literary style, and the chance association of the signifier align in a series of congruent affirmations—is also seen to operate in texts by Peter Inman and Norman Pritchard, the subjects of chapters 3 and 5, respectively. Inman, a writer associated with what came to be known as Language poetry, exemplified and long sustained the essence of that movement's core, foundational poetics of "diminished reference."[17] Pritchard, who under other social circumstances might have been assimilated to the Language poetry program, worked a decade earlier at the intersection of the most politically vociferous Black Nationalist poetry and the most minimalist concrete poetry. Both poets innovated with typography to create new modes of meter and measure within the poetic line, rearticulating their texts in ways that simultaneously separate and connect words with the logic of Melvin Tolson's *paseq* (a glyph he glossed as the "vertical line that occurs about 480 times in our Hebrew Bible [...] still the most mysterious sign in the literature").[18]

Both poets, moreover, challenge their readers to find ways of deciphering what initially present themselves as nonsensical and even nonlexical texts. In the case of Inman, I argue, decoding requires reading over his entire oeuvre, mapping connections between strings of letters from across disparate books and pamphlets in the ways one might normally pull together words from across poetic lines or stanzas. In the case of Pritchard, it requires understanding the distinctive spacing of his printed text as a formal allegory in relation to what Michael Riffaterre, following Ferdinand de Saussure's anagram studies, characterized as a hypogrammatic *matrix* (the title, perhaps not incidentally, of one of Pritchard's books). In Riffaterre's model, the matrix generates a poem through an acute absence: a word or phrase that does not appear in the text but around which the text weaves its syntagms, approaching without ever explicitly naming the kernel keyword.[19] With a similar structure (what, in fact, Jacques-Alain Miller deduced as "[la] structure de la structure" [the structure of structure] itself), in which absent terms nonetheless organize and determine a text in which they may not themselves appear—as in my reading of the lines from Brooks's poem above—my analyses throughout this book leverage what we might call the transitive property of poetry: a concatenation of terms that generates a network of associations across a text through a series of equations that firmly link words which may themselves never appear together on the same page.[20] If $a = b$, and $b = c$, then $a = c$. The identical principle might be applied at the broader level of the poems as a whole, and seen in the structure of a book that would bring together writers not otherwise commonly considered together: Warhol and Pritchard, Inman and Atkins, Hejinian and Loy (affiliations I will return to at the close of this introduction).

In addition to making a case for such associations, and for expanding the canon of poetry accordingly, I hope that the following chapters will convince readers that the new ways of writing pioneered by the avant-garde require new ways of reading commensurate with its experiments and adequate to its modes of composition. If literary writing has changed radically over the last century, it might be time to change how we read in response. Much more, however, I hope that the methodology elaborated here can provide models for how other unconventional and restive literature might be approached, opening avenues for comprehension and appreciation at the very moments when texts seem most inexplicable, whimsical, refractory, or outright meaningless. Above all, I hope that these modes of reading and describing textual material might find their way back to even the most familiar, conventional, canonical literature—opacifying, confounding, and disorienting it in turn.

For the moment, however, because the methodology advanced here follows from a certain philosophy of language, let me sketch the contours of the loosely associated theoretical tradition from which my approach both emerges and deviates.

* * *

Complaining to his friend Stéphane Mallarmé, Edgar Degas fulminated against poetry. Despite being "plein d'idées" [full of ideas], he could never get the results he wanted when he tried to write a poem.[21] "Ce n'est point avec des idées, mon *cher Degas*, que l'on fait des vers," Mallarmé replied. "C'est avec des mots" [*My dear Degas*, one doesn't write poetry with ideas; one writes poetry with words].[22] The story is worth retelling (I repeat it from Roman Jakobson, who got it from Paul Valéry, who heard it from his artist friend), not just because of its wit but because the point is—paradoxically—

both obvious and prone to being forgotten.[23] The self-evident materiality of language somehow induces a chronic amnesia. Shakespeare had said essentially the same thing three hundred years earlier, when he had Hamlet conflate literary subject and linguistic form, summarizing his reading as "words, words, words."[24] Hamlet's reply blurs the two antithetical senses of "reading matter," which alternately deny and insist on specific material form. On the one hand, the phrase denotes "the subject of a book, speech, etc.; a theme, a topic, a subject of exposition," that is, the summarizable, general conceptual "substance of a book," "the contents of a composition in respect of the facts or ideas expressed, as distinct from the form of words used to express them." On the other hand, it denotes precisely the form of those words: the materiality of language regardless of what it signifies, its physical manifestation as, in the examples considered here, various instances of ink on paper: "printed or written material," "type set up," "manuscript prepared for printing."[25] Hamlet sees words as something to be seen: "language to be looked at," as Robert Smithson telegraphed the two sides of the linguistic sign, "and/or things to be read."[26]

Hamlet's tone is more clearly petulant, even snarky, than Mallarmé's salon repartee, the exact temper of which is difficult to pin down, but despite the punchline logic that risks rendering both responses mere jokes, they make a serious point in favor of literalism through a self-aware insistence on the literal. "Although it is an old insistence, it is one hard at times to remember," as Robert Creeley wrote, taking the realization as a theoretical principle by which to characterize poetry itself: "poems are not referential, or at least not importantly so."[27] The symbolic powers of language are so entrancing, summoning narratives and representing ideas with such mesmerizing, phantasmagoric force, that the physical substance of the words ("… words, words") is hard to keep in focus, or even remember. "Vergiß nicht" [Do not forget], Ludwig Wittgenstein cautioned, knowing how easily the amnesia sets in: "daß ein Gedicht, wenn auch in der Sprache der Mitteilung abgefaßt, nicht im Sprachspiel der Mitteilung verwendet wird" [that a poem, even though it is composed in the language of information is not used in the language-game of giving information].[28]

Contemporaneous with Wittgenstein, Jan Mukařovský leveraged a similar dichotomy as thesis and antithesis to arrive at the very definition of poetry. Poetic language for Mukařovský was not limited to verse, nor was it a euphemism for ornamental or beautiful writing, but rather the result of a dialectic between two aspects of language which take relative prominence according to an inverse ratio. The banausic use of language for some practical goal, or what Mukařovský calls its "sdělovací funkce" [communicative function]—the task of transmitting a message that has some comprehensible meaning prior to its enunciation and separable from the particular form of the text—is demoted in poetic language.[29] In contrast to that quotidian "orientation toward the goal of communication," poetic language instead promotes an "orientation toward expression itself."[30] Roman Jakobson, Mukařovský's colleague in the Pražský lingvistický kroužek [Prague Linguistic Circle], employs similar terms to define poetic language as "the supremacy of the poetic function over the referential function," where "the poetic function of language" is "the set toward the message as such," with a "focus on the message for its own sake."[31] "Poeticity," accordingly,

> is present when the word is felt as a word and not a mere representation of the object being named or an outburst of emotion, when words and their composition, their meaning, their external and inner form, acquire a weight and value of their own instead of referring indifferently to reality.[32]

We can hear an echo here of Viktor Shklovsky's argument that art has the power to defamiliarize what habit renders invisible: "чтобы делать камень каменным" [to make the stone *stony*] or, in this case, to make the word *wordy*.[33] Indeed, the Prague School arguments begin from the same literalist recognition as Mallarmé and Hamlet: in addition to language's symbolic uses, Mukařovský affirms, "je jazyk materiálem literatury, obdobně jako dřevo, kámen či kov materiálem sochařství nebo v malířství barevná hmota a také on" [language is a *material* of literature like metal and stone in sculpture, like pigment and the material of the pictorial plane in painting].[34] Avoiding what Steve McCaffery, sensing a semiotic crisis, sought to demystify as "the referential fallacy"—or ideologies that conspire to distract readers from the material of language through figures of transparence and immateriality—we might learn to look at the opaque materiality of language in the way one might look *at* rather than *through* the pane of a window, registering the artifice of its framing rather than focusing on the scene beyond, repressing glare and smudge, specks and imperfections, reflection and refraction, to the point that the we no longer sense the glass at all.[35]

The present book is an attempt to look right at the glass. It begins from a literalist insistence on material, but proceeds to understand the vitreous surface of the sign as a point at which prospect and screen interact, as opaque material becomes itself fully a part of the view and, simultaneously, the spectator realizes that no scene is possible without its intervention. The point is not to merely substitute the word for the referent, or to neatly invert the hierarchy of the sign's parts, turning over the page that Saussure figured as the relationship between signifier and signified, but to insist, along with Mukařovský, that "znak může mít i funkce jiné, kromě této funkce sdělovací" [the sign may have other functions in addition to the communicative function].³⁶ Once one considers those other functions, the material of language begins to seem less like the handmaid of communication ("words," as we will see Norman Pritchard declare in chapter 5, "are ancillary to content"), or even as subservient to the needs of the message; instead, it comes to seem more like an independent agent in its own right. For instance, as Creeley said of his attraction to poems, "it was never what they said *about* things that interested me," but rather the way they came to exist on their own terms, "which could never be possible as long as some subject significantly elsewhere was involved. There had to be an independence derived from the very fact that words are things too."³⁷

Creeley, who was interested in Wittgenstein and fascinated by his propositions' relevance to literature, would elucidate elsewhere: "Meaning is not importantly *referential*. Reference may well prove *relevant*—but I can make myself clearer by quoting a sense of meaning which [Charles] Olson used [...]: *That which exists through itself is what is called meaning.*" Thus, a poem, from this perspective, "might exist in words as primarily the fact of its own activity."³⁸ With that emphasis on autonomous self-sufficiency, Creeley echoes William Carlos Williams, who argues that the significance of a poem cannot be found in its message, which he says would be redundant: an equivalence of denotation and meaning that Wittgenstein would recognize as a tautology.³⁹ Forrest-Thomson, who again, not coincidentally, explicitly grounds her poetics in Wittgenstein, makes a similar point in order to launch her investigation of poetic artifice: "The poem is always different from the utterances it includes or imitates; if it were not different there would be no point in setting down these utterances or writing these sentences as a poem."⁴⁰ The type of proposition that Wittgenstein rejected as philosophically meaningless is rejected in turn by these writers as poetically meaningless. If Creeley, in dialogue with Charles Olson, equated form and content in a dynamic not unlike Mukařovský's functions—one never more than the extension of the other—Charles Bernstein, directly following from a reading of Forrest-Thomson, sums up the implications of poetic artifice with a succinct counter-equation: "content never equals meaning."⁴¹

In place of the content, message, or ostensible subject, Williams proposes that the significance of a poem can be discovered if one is able to discern its operation as a mechanism; precisely *how* its words work reveals what the poem means. Construing the operation of words as interlocking parts of a poetic apparatus leads to Williams's later, well-known definition of a poem as "small (or large) machine made out of words."⁴² Intrinsic and economical, with a "physical more than a literary character," Williams's poetic machine is not so much a matter of style as of function.⁴³

With a sense not only of enclosed self-sufficiency but of impulse and motivation (the animated parts of machines move and propel one another), Williams's textual engine collapses the message of the poem into its form by equating the machinic network—the logical interrelation of its moving parts, or what could be abstracted as an engineering diagram, flowchart, or circuit schema—with its meaning. A text's "existence as a poem," he declares, "is of first importance, a technical matter, as with all facts, compelling the recognition of a mechanical structure."⁴⁴ He continues:

> It is the acceptable fact of a poem as a mechanism that is the proof of its meaning and this is as technical a matter as in the case of any other machine. Without the poem being a workable mechanism in its own right, a mechanism which arises from, while at the same time it constitutes the meaning of, the poem as a whole, it will remain ineffective.⁴⁵

More could be said about the figure of the machine, but I want to focus here on its connotation of productive energies. In his sinister mechanics of language, Paul de Man calls on the figure of the machine to attribute an active agency to linguistic structures, the radical formalism of which deforms and generates the literary and rhetorical ends which might seek to harness the powers of its internal combustions:

> the anamorphosis of a form detached from meaning and capable of taking on any structure whatever, yet entirely ruthless in its inability to modify its own structural design for nonstructural reasons. The machine is like the grammar of the text when it is isolated from its rhetoric, the merely formal element without which no text can be generated. There can be no use of language which is not, within a certain perspective thus radically formal, i.e. mechanical, no matter how deeply this aspect may be concealed by aesthetic, formalistic delusions.⁴⁶

The material aspects of language, those ways in which it can operate "in addition to the communicative function," do not just gain a measure of freedom from the symbolic functions of language but—as we shall see in the chapters that follow—acquire at times a fully generative agency. In part, this recognition follows from the conceptualizations of "noise" and "writing" in information theory. Norbert Weiner's midcentury work on what he termed "cybernetics," with its overturning of metaphysical hierarchies and its figure of writing in the "program" [πρό + γραμμα (*letter*)], one might recall, is the very origin of Jacques Derrida's *De la grammatologie* and his belief that "tout le champ couvert par le *programme* cybernétique sera champ d'écriture" [the entire field covered by the cybernetic *program* would be the field of writing].[47] From the point of view of the information theory that underwrote cybernetics, there exists "no signification, no meaning or sense that is not accompanied, and disrupted, by a nonmeaning, a non-sense, a finally random noise that no hermeneutics could appropriate."[48] Under such conditions, the material and the message form an interdependent bond, without grounds for giving one precedence over the other, since "what appears as information at one level of observation is, at another level, noise."[49] Translated to linguistics, this understanding fits neatly with the most radical and counterintuitive implications of structuralism; as Claude Lévi-Strauss understood the autonomy of both language and the social, "les symboles sont plus réels que ce qu'ils symbolisent, le signifiant précède et détermine le signifié" [symbols are more real than what they symbolize, the signifier precedes and determines the signified].[50] Or, to return to the principle with which I began, "signifiers, in their materiality as a source and support, will produce meanings as their effects."[51]

If the classical tendency had been to regard the signifier as the necessary but unfortunate form of the sign, merely a required expedient allowing access to the immaterial ideas of "extended meaning," we might instead look back from the reverse perspective and see the whole spectrum of literature—its marshaling of ideas, elaboration of descriptions, spinning out of narrations, reaching toward reference and communication with the world outside the text—and the very aggregation of words into grammatical and rhetorical units as the fortuitous occasions for assembling signifiers in a context in which their own logics can proliferate.

The precedents for reading the materiality of the sign and taking the signifier on its own terms can be located at several junctures. In chapter 2 I will look more closely at Ferdinand de Saussure's speculation on the significance of anagrammatic patterning, which proved to be an inspiration for later theorists' explorations of the implications of the signifier's own production of meaning effects. Julia Kristeva, who more than anyone followed Saussure's more tentative discoveries to their logical extremes, and with whose work my own has the most affinities, conceptualized a paragrammatic condition in which, for any text:

> its organization of words (and their denotations), grammar, and syntax is challenged by the infinite possibilities provided by letters or phonemes combining to form networks of signification not accessible through conventional reading habits.[52]

The excessive, sublime order of those "infinite possibilities" leads to unsettling conclusions about the limits of readers' desires and writers' intentions. Picking up on Saussure's speculation that the significance of anagrammatic patterning proceeds "que le critique d'une part, et que le versificateur d'autre part, le veuille ou non" [whether the critic, on the one hand, or the poet, on the other, wants it or not], Jakobson extended his interest in the poetic function of language beyond the skill of the poet to instances that occurred merely because of "la matérialité du fait, dont le poète lui-même peut se rendre compte ou non" [the materiality of the fact, whether the poet is aware of it or not] and which "reste en vigueur quel que soit le dessein conscient de l'auteur et le jugement du critique" [remains in force regardless of the author's conscious intention or the critic's judgment].[53] More recently, David Wellbery has identified a certain strain of German systems theory as a "post-hermeneutic" criticism, which in contrast to "die Privilegierung der semantischen Dimension" [the privileging of the semantic dimension] of a text would proceed without concerning itself with the intentionality, psychology, or writerly control behind such instances.[54] In that criticism, "the object of study is not what is said or written but the fact—the brute and often brutal fact—that it is said" in the first place (the formulation may remind one of Wittgenstein's aphorism: "Nicht 'wie' die Welt ist, ist das Mystische, sondern 'daß' sie ist" [not how the world is, is the mystical, but that it is]).[55] Similarly, considering "a language completely devoid of any kind of meaning function, language which would be pure signifier, which would be completely devoid of any semantic function whatsoever," Paul de Man dwells with morose delectation on a litany of "linguistic structures, the play of linguistic tensions, linguistic events that occur, possibilities that are inherent in language—independently of any intent or any drive or any wish or any desire we might have."[56] Reconciled to the fact that the "nonhuman aspect of language" is "totally indifferent in relation to the human," de Man resigns himself to admitting that "language does things which are so radically out of our control that they cannot be assimilated to the human at all, against which one fights constantly."[57] As George Oppen summarizes the situation, in a couplet: "Words cannot be wholly transparent. And that is the / 'heartlessness' of words."[58] Or again, with more pragmatism than de Man's dark theology, Creeley succinctly states the problem of intention and semantics from the other side: "words will not say anything more than they do."[59]

Michel Foucault outlined a similar perspective from the discipline of history. In the research program laid out in his inaugural address to the Collège de France (a discourse, ironically, about discourse) he cautioned against presupposing that one could recover a repressed truth beneath the artificial surface of "systèmes de raréfaction" [systems of rarefaction], or that one could gain access to the presence of meanings undeformed by linguistic practices, much less comprehend the fully saturated intention of creative authors.⁶⁰ Skeptical of recovering any semantic revelation from direct representations of some prior truth, Foucault's project would attend instead to the distinct patterns which "il se produit comme effet de et dans une dispersion matérielle" [are effects produced by the dispersion of matter] as "les structures mêmes de la langue mises en jeu et produisant un effet de sens" [the very structures of language put into play and producing meaning effects].⁶¹ As linguistic events measuring the slight discrepancy between communicative intention and the inhuman swerve of language beyond our control, those meaning effects would become the "petite […] machinerie qui permet d'introduire à la racine même de la pensée, le *hasard*, le *discontinu* et la *matérialité*" [small machine which allows *chance*, *discontinuity*, and *materiality* to be insinuated at the very root of thought].⁶² His future research program, Foucault predicted, would entail certain methodological requirements accordingly, including a rule of

> *l'extériorité*: ne pas aller du discours vers son noyau intérieur et caché, vers le coeur d'une pensée ou d'une signification qui se manifesteraient en lui; mais, à partir du discours lui-même, de son apparition et de sa régularité, aller vers ses conditions externes de possibilité, vers ce qui donne lieu à la série aléatoire de ces événements et qui en fixe les bornes

> [*exteriority*: not to go from discourse toward the kernel of its hidden, interior core, toward the heart of a thought or a signification that would manifest itself in discourse; but instead strike out from discourse itself, from its appearance and its regularity, and to head toward its external conditions of possibility, toward what gives rise to the aleatory series of its events and to what sets its limits]⁶³

A literary theory committed to dehierarchizing the regime of the signified over the operations of the signifier might thus look to Foucault's attempt to theorize a set of "systématicités discontinues" [discontinuous systematicities] "permettant de penser les rapports du hasard et de la pensée" [enabling one to think the relations between chance and thought].⁶⁴

In fact, a premonition of the limits of the various depth models of reading—those representational and therapeutic methodologies aimed at recovering repressed truths somewhere beneath the material exterior of discourse—have recently animated debates in literary studies. Echoing the diagnosis made a dozen years earlier, *en passant*, by Pfeiffer in his outline of the nonhermeneutic enterprise opened by a study of the "materialities of communication," Stephen Best and Sharon Marcus made a widely noticed call for a "surface reading" that would abjure revelatory hermeneutics in order to instead reveal the surface that has been hidden by prevailing "symptomatic" reading practices.⁶⁵ With a clever substitution, the concealing surface has become, for them, paradoxically, the very thing concealed by dominant modes of literary criticism. The present study proposes a surface reading as well, but the surface is very different from the one imagined by Best and Marcus; as the example from Brooks above suggests, my readings stand in an oblique relation to their sense of surface. On the one hand, like suspicious and symptomatic readers, I want to demonstrate patterns that the works under consideration do not readily reveal; such relationships are in fact "not immediately apprehensible and may be veiled or invisible" from the perspective of conventional reading practices.⁶⁶ But unlike more semantically focused approaches, which seek to uncover the buried symbolic referents of ideological or psychological repression, my paragrammatic readings here merely retrace structures already inherent in the material surfaces of texts, mapping metonymies of inscription rather than summoning the metaphorics of representation. The analyses are hence more focused on the physical than the literary (in Williams's terms), or on the linguistic rather than the literary (in de Man's terms), offering assiduous descriptions and microanalyses rather than subjective evaluations or sweeping abstractions.⁶⁷

In the process, the case studies here are meant to prove, thicken, and complicate the recent methodological debates in literary studies. In my presumption that literary texts are capable of generating the theoretical, political, and critical structures necessary for their own apprehension, the present book takes up the "critical description" that Best and Marcus mention in passing. With this type of description, "the purpose of criticism is thus a relatively modest one: to indicate what the text says about itself."⁶⁸ Assuming that "texts can reveal their own truths because texts mediate themselves," such readings undertake a patient articulation of the paragrammatic networks of signifiers Kristeva envisaged dispersed across a space in which, in accord with Foucault's "règle de l'extériorité" [rule of exteriority], "depth is continuous with surface and is thus an effect of immanence."⁶⁹

Those dispersals, in fact—and the meaning "effects produced by the dispersion of matter" as the material of language—are what require an analysis of the textual plane in order to reveal its modes of signification. As will be most evident in chapter 3, which draws its evidence from across the decades-long scope of an entire oeuvre, the lateral extent can be broad enough that patterns and structures—even though they remain unhidden and plainly on the surface—are difficult to discern without a view of signifiers unclouded by the grammars, rhetorical divisions, and semantic referents repeatedly structured and summoned beneath their own inky surfaces. In all of the chapters that follow, in fact, signification will be found to emerge only after aggregating terms drawn from across those boundaries that normally divide grammatical units, shape rhetorical structures, or articulate the constituent building blocks of narrative and discursive forms. Identifying the interrelation of those scattered, disseminated terms compels a recognition of the "technical matter" indicated by Williams, and accounting for such matter invites a mode of critical description; it calls for something more like a machine diagram than a rhetorical interpretation. Jakobson, similarly, bases his account of discovering poeticity on a kind of radical description of formal properties, rather than semantic reference. Implying objective observation, he declares:

> Any unbiased, attentive, exhaustive, total *description* of the selection, distribution and interrelation of diverse morphological classes and syntactic constructions in a given poem surprises the examiner himself by unexpected, striking symmetries and antisymmetries, balanced structures, efficient accumulation of equivalent forms and salient contrasts, finally by rigid restrictions in the repertory of morphological and syntactic constituents used in the poem, eliminations which, on the other hand, permit us to follow the masterly interplay of the actualized constituents.[70]

Without sharing Jakobson's mania for doubling (surely part of the rapport he felt with Saussure), and without limiting myself to the particular linguistic categories he names, I hope that the readings embedded in the following chapters will endorse his claim for the often quite startling power of attentive, exhaustive descriptions.

In the process, these descriptions corroborate my conviction, held out in different ways in each of my previous books, that contrary to expectations, the more closely one hews to the sheer, brute materiality of an artwork, the more clearly the social and political come into view. Rather than isolating or segregating literary works from questions of social politics, the formal and linguistic experiments of the avant-garde reveal them to be privileged sites for exploring precisely such issues in new ways, from fresh perspectives, and hence recognize the signifier's ability to perform a politics, rather than merely assist in talking about a political topic. Concurrently, they evince a skepticism toward ideologies that would posit language as a transparent, undistorting, representational medium—including the politics allied with values of efficacy, utility, uniformity, authorial will, and a host of attendant Enlightenment ideals that have found themselves aligned with a certain regime of signs. In brief, they extend a critical positionality familiar from the conventionally recognized realm of social politics to the material foundations of literature itself. That extension was a central plank in the Surrealist platform that promoted the revolution of the word with a faith that the revolution of the world would follow, a position echoed with endearing period slang by John Cage in his *Diary*: "if we could change our language, that's to say the way we think, we'd probably be able to swing the revolution."[71] I'm not so sanguine, but starting from the position that the status quo is unacceptable, and that some sort of change—whether transformation, disruption, rebellion, innovation, intervention, or insubordination—is therefore necessary, the works under discussion in the chapters that follow offer a version of Cage's optimistic transferral; they expand that conviction about the intolerability of the status quo to literary modes, advocating implicitly for a more variegated canon, and then continue more radically to question the fundamental structures of language itself. Texts here are conceived not only as artifacts documenting moments in which writers have undertaken the radical reevaluation of modes of composition but also as sites encouraging readers to proceed in unconventional and innovative ways; they exhibit experimental writing and reward experimental reading. If the world requires new positions and relations, new modes of attention and perception, a refreshed awareness of material conditions, the redistribution of powers, and continually active participation, unscripted by conventions, here are the proving grounds. Those who aspire to change society shouldn't shy from the far less ambitious task of reconsidering what—and how—they read.

To situate these claims within the contours of a specific philosophical argument, consider Jacques Rancière's theses on the relation of politics and aesthetics. Analogous to my focus on the literal rather than the figurative, and my sense of a radical formalism, Rancière advocates for a performative rather than symbolic politics, so that the "politics of literature" is not equivalent to

> the politics of its writers. It does not deal with their personal commitment to the social and political issues and struggles of their times. Nor does it deal with the modes of representation of political events or the social structure and the social struggles in their books.[72]

Instead, the politics of literature can be located in what literature proposes by its particular ways of being, situated in the networks that connect writers and readers.

Literature, under such circumstances, can enact a subversive sort of "cut"—"always ambiguous, precarious, litigious"—that intervenes in politics not through the particular messages communicated but by a material reconfiguration of the very grounds for discourse: by the power of inscription to effect "a suspension with respect to the ordinary forms of sensory experience."⁷³ Rancière imagines that aesthetic cut as intervening in what he calls the "partage du sensible" [distribution of the sensible]: "ce système d'évidences sensibles qui donne à voir en même temps l'existence d'un commun et les découpages qui y définissent les places et les parts respectives" [the system of self-evident facts of sense perception that simultaneously discloses the existence of something in common and the delimitations that define the respective parts and positions within it].⁷⁴ Like the material facts of the systems of signifiers under consideration in the pages that follow, with the self-evident technical matters of the text displaying the interrelation of their respective parts, Rancière's object of analysis is open to patient and meticulous perception, and so it calls, once again, more for the critical description of what is there—right before the eyes, if not always easy to recognize—than for persuasive cajoling or symbolic interpretation. Such descriptions reveal that

> ces formes définissent la manière dont des oeuvres ou performances «font de la politique» quels que soient par ailleurs les intentions qui y président, les modes d'insertion sociaux des artistes ou la façon dont les formes artistiques réfléchissent les structures ou les mouvements sociaux

> [these forms define the way in which works of art or performances are "involved in politics," whatever may otherwise be the guiding intentions, artists' social modes of integration, or the manner in which artistic forms reflect social structures or movements.]⁷⁵

Aesthetic practices, as Rancière understands them (in a gloss added for the English translation), are "'ways of doing and making' that intervene in the general distribution of ways of doing and making as well as in the relationships they maintain to modes of being and forms of visibility."⁷⁶

One of those interventions, as we shall see, is to militate against any easy sort of consumption by obviating passive absorption and the ready exchange of a text for its abbreviated, processed, digestible meaning ("the matter that you read" in the way Polonius intends it). Through the disruption of textual, grammatical, and literary conventions, the works under discussion in the following chapters repeatedly bring readers up short, leaving them unsure of how to proceed, or force them to slow down, blocking their ability to skim.⁷⁷ These unconventional textual forms alienate readers from the conventions of realist representation, deny facile emotional identifications or comforting illusions of psychological coherence and unified subjectivities; above all, their forms frustrate efficient parsing, unsettle certainty, and question the very terms of what might constitute a "productive" reading. Here, accordingly, are Rancière's *coups*, swiping across the types of perception and activity encouraged by the order of things under the regime of contemporary politics, with its commodification of attention, affect, exchange, and the partitioning of time itself.

To disrupt or ignore the order of things, to cut against the organizations that would seek to maintain uniform and familiar consumption, and to disorient readers in the process is to suggest another way of understanding the political potential of the paragrammatic networks that lace their way across texts, refusing to heed the hierarchies of grammar, disregarding the boundaries of rhetoric, and oblivious to the wills of those who would make instrumental use of a document. Arguing for disorientation as a grounds for queer politics, Sarah Ahmed has underscored the degree to which disruptions in one realm unsettle the social more broadly, encapsulating the mechanisms at work with the assertion that "to make things queer is certainly to disturb the order of things."[78] In this equation we can see the grounds for the radical formalism I have argued for elsewhere, and which has recently been taken up in the context of feminist performance:

> The question of formalism often gives rise to well-rehearsed notions of political indifference, autonomy, and ahistoricity. Yet what if a radical formalism was deployed—against these normative understandings—as a contextual practice and subversive method of critique? Mobilized into action, "Radical Formalism" proposes that institutionalized understandings of form may be hijacked from within as an alternative strategy of resistance.[79]

This is a point at which I diverge from a possible extension of the self-sufficiency of poetic language admired by Creeley and Williams: what I propose is neither *l'art pour l'art*, or "an absolute, radical formalism that entertains no notion of reference or of semiosis," however much agency one ascribes to the signifier, nor a supposedly political or social or "real world" realm superciliously insulated from the literary or from the mechanisms of language, above which it fancies itself righteously elevated.[80] Instead, it is a leaky, level, dynamic interpenetration between all of these realms, with each sensitive to how a textual "disorientation slides quickly into social disorientation, *as a disorientation in how things are arranged.*"[81] Once they are seen as performing relationships rather than communicating semantic reference, as enacting more than merely relaying conventional meanings, texts can become "disorientation devices": recognizable in their unrecognizability not "simply as loss but as the potential for new lines, or for new lines to gather as expressions that we do not know how to read. Queer gatherings are lines that gather [...] to form new patterns and new ways of making sense."[82] The political work undertaken by those new patterns and their resultant significations assumes a positive form as well. However singular and unfamiliar, the instances of literary estrangement that I investigate here are not isolated or unprecedented, and in bringing them together as a book "we might allow the moments of disorientation to gather," as Ahmed puts it. In the process, "we might, in the gathering, face a different way" because "queer objects might take us to the very limits of social gathering," leading us not only to marvel at, and wonder about, the technical matter of their material techniques but to realize, in the process, that "to live out a politics of disorientation might be to sustain wonder about the very forms of social gathering" themselves.[83]

I intend for the gatherings here, bringing together writers not considered part of the same movements and groups, to be equally queer. Forrest-Thomson remonstrated against the tendency of literary criticism to subsume the strangeness, non-sense, opacity, artifice, and material patterning of poetic language into the comforting, unchallenging, naturalized, and familiar thematics of semantic reference. There are reasons beyond the canon of poetry to follow her lead.

The Prosaic Imagination [CHAPTER ONE]

Müßen wir eine Handlung, die wir gegen andere ausüben, nicht als eine Handlung der Gütigkeit und Großmuth ansehen, sondern als eine kleine Erstattung deßen was wir ihm durch allgemeine Einrichtung entzogen haben.

[We have to regard an act we perform for another, not as an act of kindness and generosity, but as a small return of what we have taken from him in virtue of the general arrangement.]

IMMANUEL KANT[1]

The time when there are four choices and there are four choices in a difference, the time when there are four choices there is a kind and there is a kind.

GERTRUDE STEIN

Prosaic: "commonplace, mundane." *Prosaic*: "written in prose."[2] The denotations reinforce one another because for the modern reader prose itself is now a commonplace, almost unrecognizable in its familiarity. Unmarked and seemingly unremarkable, the typographic rectangle has become so predictable, ubiquitous, and neutral that it now appears, if we notice it at all, as the natural look of language in books.[3] But what if we restored some of the strangeness to the visual prosody of that layout and took the measures of prose—its staggered spatial distributions and spread—with the same attention traditionally paid to the syllabic meters of certain verse?

To do so, one would first have to recognize prose, but identifying prose with certainty, surprisingly, is harder than one might expect. "The word prose carries little meaning, and taxonomic approaches to it will bring only ridicule," caution Jeffrey Kittay and Wlad Godzich.[4] Alternately indicating subject matter, style, and form, and even a genre, "prose"—like the word "genre" itself—proves too various and indiscrete to helpfully serve any simple self-evident taxonomy. Idiomatically, it sometimes distinguishes a given text from poetry. At other times it designates a special case, as in the so-called *prose poem* ("poetic content expressed in prose form," as Richard Aldington defined it), or a literary-critical distinction, as between prose and meter or prose and verse.[5] The connotations are not only varied, but any given referent stumbles over attempts at a fixed definition; pursued at any length, even the most seemingly obvious descriptions become muddled. As William Wordsworth wrote in a note to his preface to the second edition of the *Lyrical Ballads*: "Much confusion has been introduced into criticism by this contradistinction of Poetry and Prose, instead of the more philosophical one of Poetry and Matter of Fact, or Science."[6] Wordsworth tries to clarify matters by shifting the category from genre to form, but he immediately has to qualify even that seemingly straightforward foil: "The only strict antithesis to Prose is Metre; nor is this, in truth, a *strict* antithesis, because lines and passages of metre so naturally occur in writing prose, that it would be scarcely possible to avoid them, even were it desirable."[7]

As Wordsworth and Aldington understood, prose texts can of course contain poetic language (however that might be defined; recall the several attempts by Slavic formalists which I covered in the introduction). And while it may run counter to expectations, there is no reason why a work in the *genre* of poetry cannot be printed in the *format* of prose. One might think of Old English poetry, for instance, which was composed in metrical units but written out to fill the parchment page (just as the grammatical units called sentences are printed here, running over the right margin and onto further lines); only in modern times has Anglo-Saxon poetry been printed so that its metrical units correspond with a line. The traditions of the *poème en prose* [prose poem], suggest another instance, along with works as varied as Gertrude Stein's *Tender Buttons*, Haroldo de Campos's *Galáxias*, and Pierre Guyotat's later books, which are composed in segments he refers to as *versets* ("verses," in the sense of biblical prosody). Guyotat, that is, writes according to strict metrical patterns and precise internal rhyme schemes, but his texts are metered in units other than the line. Although printed as prose, Guyotat's books, accordingly, are "poetic" in the sense of their artifice and measure.[8] An even better-known instance of identifying a poetic quality inherent in a prose work can be found in William Butler Yeats's infamous proem to the first *Oxford Book of Modern Verse*, where he nominated—as the inaugural work of modern poetry—a passage from Walter Pater's nonfiction prose study *The Renaissance*. Translating between typographic conventions, Yeats deforms the layout of Pater's text, rearticulating one of his signature, long, accumulative sentences into Poundian free-verse units and titling the result "Mona Lisa":

> She is older than the rocks among which she sits;
> Like the Vampire,
> She has been dead many times,
> And learned the secrets of the grave;
> And has been a diver in deep seas,
> And keeps their fallen day about her;

And trafficked for strange webs with Eastern merchants;
And, as Leda,
Was the mother of Helen of Troy,
And, as St Anne,
Was the mother of Mary;
And all this has been to her but as the sound of lyres and flutes,
And lives
Only in the delicacy
With which it has moulded the changing lineaments,
And tinged the eyelids and the hands.[9]

Pater's paragraph, a fantasia on the theme of Leonardo da Vinci's *La Gioconda*, continues, in the original:

> The fancy of a perpetual life, sweeping together ten thousand experiences, is an old one; and modern thought has conceived the idea of humanity as wrought upon by, and summing up in itself, all modes of thought and life. Certainly Lady Lisa might stand as the embodiment of the old fancy, the symbol of the modern idea.[10]

Although Yeats does not include these sentences in his free-verse version of Pater's text, the telos of this section in "the embodiment of the old fancy, the symbol of the modern idea" is all to the point for a project setting out to canonize a *soi-disant* Modern Verse: an embodied idea in which the concept of a genre is recognized through its material form. At both the general level of the anthology's conception and the specific level of typesetting the proem, Yeats is thus exploiting visual format as a kind of literary form. The organizing principle is not just "verse" in general—a typographic format for visually isolating compositional units—but the distinct subcategory of "modern verse." The significance of his version of Pater's sentence, that is, arises not merely from the fact that there are lines, which would always be the case, but that those lines assume the particular kinds of variable mensuration that typify a certain period style of free verse: lines of unequal length articulated in dynamic tension with the sentence's grammar and in support of the rhetorical structure of syntactic anaphora that Yeats's layout further emphasizes.[11]

The fact of lineation, however, is also where the obvious and intuitive discriminations between verse and prose become more complicated and imbricated and interesting. *Pace* T. S. Eliot's assertion that "the distinction between 'verse' and 'prose' is clear," the precise differences are, in the final analysis, "very obscure."[12] To put it bluntly, the typical descriptions of Yeats's practice as dividing, breaking, or chopping Pater's passage "into lines" are spurious.[13] Yeats's publication certainly changes the lineaments of the strange web of Pater's sentence by stretching the warp and shortening the weft of its textual weave, but Pater's prose—to insist on the obvious—was printed in lines to begin with.[14] The situation is a more specific instance of the amnesia surrounding the materiality of language more generally (as we saw in the introduction): however self-evident, this fact of prose is apparently easily forgotten, even when critics are thinking carefully about form. The *Princeton Encyclopedia of Poetry and Poetics*, for instance, differentiates prose from verse because prose, it speciously states, "has no line breaks."[15] "What poetry has that prose does not have," Eve Kosofsky Sedgwick concurs, "is linebreaks."[16] M. H. Abrams, to take another instance, defines prose as "a continuous sequence of sentences without line breaks."[17] Taken at face value, these definitions would result in very long books indeed; they would prove impossible to print in any kind of practical format.[18] I quote the definitions "not for the pedantic pleasure of finding fault with some very bright minds" but to illustrate, by their examples, the pervasiveness of this aporia.[19] To be more generous and refine such formulations, the implied distinction presumably would be between the judgment or whim of the author and that of the typesetter—between *composition* in the sense of "writing prose or verse" ("literary production," as the dictionary has it), on the one hand, and, on the other hand, *composition* denoting "the setting up of type; the composing of pages of matter for printing."[20] Or, if the model of letterpress now seems too quaint, we can contrast the intention of the poet with the algorithm of a digital design program. One might, indeed, understand prose as simply the projection, if not the expression, of the material substrate of writing: a simple ratio of format to font, of page trim to line length. A sheer material geometry has, surprisingly, generated a recognizable, ubiquitous cultural form.

Even that distinction between writing and printing, however, turns out to be far from foolproof. One would probably not, for instance, want to say that a literary composition employing chance operations in order to determine line breaks at random, or a poet's conscious and explicit delegation of choices about lineation to a printer, would thus constitute prose. Or, less speculatively, one would presumably not want to designate *as prose* the many editions of Walt Whitman's poetry that find an anonymous typesetter breaking Whitman's signature long verse lines to fit the format of the page. More complicated still would be the first edition of *Leaves of Grass*, parts of which were set by Whitman himself. To designate some passages in the 1855 edition as prose and others as verse on that account would be manifestly absurd. Indeed, since Whitman "considered himself a book-

maker more than an author" and composed his poetry from the perspective of a professional printer, his literary decisions were fundamentally influenced by his typographic knowledge in a way that would complicate any distinction between prose and verse based on authorial election.[21] "Having been a printer myself," Whitman explained to Horace Traubel, "I have what may be called an anticipatory eye—know pretty well as I write how a thing will turn up in the type—appear—take form."[22] As Ed Folsom argues, accordingly, "Whitman probably never composed a line of poetry without, in his mind's eye, putting it on a composing stick."[23] While Whitman's anticipatory eye may be a special case, his lesson applies more generally: the opposition of poet and printer does not offer a very solid criterion for discriminating between the categories of prose and verse.

Conversely, we do not imagine Jorge Luis Borges's Pierre Menard, author of the *Quixote*, to be composing poetic *verse* when he produces his text of "los capítulos IX y XXXVIII de la primera parte del *Don Quijote* y de un fragmento del capítulo XXII" [the ninth and thirty-eighth chapters of the first part of *Don Quixote* and a fragment of chapter twenty-two].[24] Borges's narrator explains:

> No quería componer otro Quijote—lo cual es fácil—sino *el Quijote*. Inútil agregar que no encaró nunca una transcripción mecánica del original; no se proponía copiarlo. Su admirable ambición era producir unas páginas que coincidieran—palabra por palabra y línea por línea—con las de Miguel de Cervantes

> [He did not want to compose another *Quixote*—which is easy—but *the Quixote itself*. Needless to say, he never contemplated a mechanical transcription of the original; he did not propose to copy it. His admirable intention was to produce a few pages which would coincide—word for word and line for line—with those of Miguel de Cervantes.][25]

The result, the narrator opines after a careful stylistic comparison of seemingly identical passages, "es más sutil que el de Cervantes" [is more subtle than Cervantes'].[26] But a more subtle reading of Borges's own passage discovers the crux that Menard, though not copying, may be composing by the unit of the printed prose page, so that his text coincides with a specific edition of *Don Quixote* and not merely an abstract sense of the work or the novel. Menard's pages correspond "palabra por palabra y línea por línea" [word for word and *line for line*]. The colloquial sense of the phrase is the same in Spanish as in English, indicating a seriatim activity: all the way through in *linear* order, with an implication of exactitude. But the phrase is also the technical term for the unit of composition in certain printing methods, from hand-set letterpress to Monotype to early digital impact printers, all of which order their matrices *línea por línea*. That reading is corroborated by Menard's habit of working at the level of the line in other instances as well; one of his earlier works transposes Paul Valéry's masterpiece "Le cimetière marin" from its heteroclite decasyllabics—a verse meter that accounted in large part for the poem's notoriety to begin with—into the more familiar alexandrines of traditional French verse. I admit that this may be leaning a little too hard on one phrase, however careful a writer we imagine Borges to be, but in the end, whether or not one understands "línea por línea" in its literal or figurative sense, Borges's turn of phrase is a good reminder of the point I want to keep in mind here: that as with the two senses of "printed matter" I considered in the introduction, we both readily know and easily forget that almost all writing, even nonpoetical prose writing, is typically printed in lines.

To insist on prose, and resist the amnesia of repetition and habituation that blinds us to its lineation (to make the prose *prosy*, as Viktor Shklovsky might put it) would be to recognize those lines of prose *as a form* and not merely a format. That insistence would mobilize and motivate the properties of prose: above all, a uniform geometric extension and spatial distribution of language in lines that both disperse and consolidate. Prose, that is, both severs and solidifies. Prose fractures sentences, displacing and isolating certain syntactically neighboring words at the margins, on opposite borders of the prose block; at the same time, prose compresses its texts perpendicularly, establishing new proximities and vertical formations from what would otherwise be discontinuous and semantically unrelated words. The strata of the prose lines short-circuit the sequential ordering of grammatical and rhetorical constructions. Lines of prose, in short, disrupt the linearity of language in Saussure's sense.[27] Furthermore, an insistence on the form of prose might also resist ignoring the telling fact of hyphenation required—all the more urgently with justification—for the compilation of uniform geometric textual strata. Prose, that is, functions at times with a linguistic logic operating below the level of the word and independent of the morpheme. Prose's use of language subordinates local semantic structures to larger rhetorical ones, and hyphenation is one indication that language is put in the service *of prose*, and not the other way around.

In practical terms, moreover, an insistence on prose explains some of the most radical and refractory postwar American poetry. Consider, for example, Clark Coolidge's long poem "Cabinet Voltaire," from his 1968 book *ING*.[28] One passage reads:

tradict

theless

it gether
tastic
for

gin tion

and sarily
and
    sests

In an interview with Ed Foster, Clark Coolidge recalls:

> I remember some of the earliest writing I did was an attempt to do automatic writing under the influence of the surrealist concept of automatism. I had read that Motherwell collection of Dada painters and poets [Robert Motherwell, *The Dada Painters and Poets: An Anthology*, 1951]. But I couldn't figure out how to proceed. I just kind of started writing and it got awful right away, real gooey and either sort of (what would you call it?) substitute-sexual or sentimental or too easy in associative pattern. Nowhere near even something like *Soluble Fish*, which at least has its points of interest here and there.[29]

The point of interest here is not so much what Coolidge says; Motherwell's book was enormously influential for Coolidge's New York School peers, including John Ashbery, Ted Berrigan, and Frank O'Hara—any of whom might have said much the same thing. The point of interest is instead what he does *not* say. Coolidge refrains from mentioning that he did indeed "figure out how to proceed" directly from Motherwell's book. As he explains in a later statement, the poem "came from a scanning of Motherwell's *Dada Painters and Poets*."[30] Motherwell's book—*as a book*, as a specific, printed textual object—provides the structured source material for "Cabinet Voltaire." Even the oversized pages of *Dada Painters and Poets*, with their print closely set in an exceptionally small font, required occasional hyphenation to accommodate the uniform strata of prose. The typesetter for the press fragmented, for instance, Hugo Ball's "Dada Fragments," where the words "contradict" and "nonetheless" supply the first two lines in the excerpt above. Coolidge often reads straight down the margin, taking the first word or word-fragment in a series of consecutive lines. The compositional rules—with only one or two exceptions in Coolidge's entire thirty-page poem—seem to be that he may only take words from the margin and must take them in the order they appear. The contingent format of Motherwell's printed prose thus discloses the logical sequential order behind Coolidge's seemingly disjunctive, inexplicably nonsensical verse. The words in "Cabinet Voltaire" evince a linear order, in the sequential sense, even as they nonetheless contradict the linear sequencing of Ball's original syntax; their linearity simply proceeds along a vertical rather than a horizontal axis.

Seen from this perspective, the odd title "Cabinet Voltaire"—in place of the expected "Cabaret Voltaire," the name of the Dadaists' Zürich venue—makes a certain descriptive sense. Coolidge has replaced the indiscrete and promiscuous flow of the vaudeville cabaret with the constrained geometric container of the prose block: the *cabinet* of found linguistic curiosities. So where the 1921 manifesto *Dada soulève tout!* announced, "The cabinet has been overthrown," Coolidge reinstates it by leveraging the very spirit of the Dadaists' revolutionary textual experiments.[31] Recognizing that the interplay of rule and chance was not only a key Dada principle discussed by the essays and manifestos included in Motherwell's collection, but that they were also demonstrably enacted through the format of the book, Coolidge takes the defining dynamic of the prose-block format—the simultaneous pull of chance and necessity—as a form that reveals poetic vocabulary. The seemingly static format of prose, in Coolidge's procedure, is recognized as an active structure that can be put in the service of a genre: the avant-garde lyric.

Nor was Coolidge alone in mortising this kind of avant-garde cabinetry. A decade later, in 1978, Lyn Hejinian's long poem *Writing Is an Aid to Memory* engaged in similar tactics. Like "Cabinet Voltaire," Hejinian's decidedly recalcitrant text is so disjunctive that it at first appears to be all but nonsensical. Restlessly built from fragmented phrases, often incomplete or ungrammatical, the poem offers only sporadic glimpses of isolated images and tantalizingly remote hints at referents. Snippets flicker swiftly, fleeting without context, refusing to assimilate and failing to cohere. The poem opens: "apple is shot nod / ness seen know it around saying."[32] Clarifications, over the book's forty-eight pages, are not forthcoming. A typical passage, from the fifth section, reads:

> guage means general
>   will push straction one day to the left
>   carried out on the pebbles
>   drops of water of light off of abstraction in the other

>   way
> but the order

The section continues in this vein, "but the order" is merely occult, not entirely absent. Like "Cabinet Voltaire," much of the seemingly alogical syntax of *Writing Is an Aid to Memory* evinces the crystalline, rectilinear logic of prose. Like Coolidge, Hejinian bases her poem on the contingent, idiosyncratic disposition of print in specific editions of other books, from Herman Melville's *Piazza Tales* to the 1898 compilation of *Curiosities of Popular Customs and of Rites, Ceremonies, Observances, and Miscellaneous Antiquities* by William Shepherd Walsh. The section just quoted, for instance, draws heavily from one particular edition of Jean Piaget's *Genetic Epistemology*, in which the format and design—a relatively large 12-point Garamond type set across a four-inch block and heavily hyphenated—accounts for some of the most mysterious and memorable passages in Hejinian's poem. The line "guage means general," for example, derives from the layout of the following sentences in Piaget's treatise:

> [...] Actions can be represented in a number of different ways, of which language is only one. Language is certainly not the exclusive means of representation. It is only one aspect of the very general function that Head has called the symbolic function [...].[33]

The final line of the preceding section of Hejinian's poem—"(genre find two of gence object screen object ble)"—has its origins on the margins of another page from Piaget's book, where two paragraphs are set like so:

> In other words, we find here, in a sensory-motor intelligence, a certain logic of inclusion, a certain logic of ordering, and a certain logic of correspondence, which I maintain are the foundations for the logical mathematical structures. They are certainly not operations, but they are the beginnings of what will later become operations. We can also find in this sensory-motor intelligence the beginnings of two essential characteristics of operations, namely, a form of conservation and a form of reversibility.
>
> The conservation characteristic of sensory-motor intelligence takes the form of the notion of the permanence of an object. This notion does not exist until near the end of the infant's first year. If a 7- or 8-month-old is reaching for an

object that is interesting to him and we suddenly put a screen between the object and him, he will act as if the object not only has disappeared but also is no longer accessible.[34]

In other words, we find here a certain logic of inclusion, a certain logic of ordering, and a certain logic of correspondence, which I maintain are the foundations for the logical poetic structures of Hejinian's seemingly illogical and disordered verse. As Hejinian, in an account from 2007, explains the origins of *Writing Is an Aid*:

I opened books at random, scanning the left margin for suggestive words or phrases and writing them down on sheets of paper or index cards, along with phrases of my own that came to mind. There was no conceptual motive for restricting myself to the phrases along the left margin of the pages, but it had the practical benefit of keeping my attention on phrase units rather than on larger semantic units (the ideas being articulated in the books). It's because I was scanning only along the left margin of the pages that *Writing Is an Aid to Memory* includes a number of part words, many of the suffixes: "ness," "civious," "glish," "cerns," "duce," "mena," etc., and morphemes like "deed," "chant," and "poses," that are words as well as possible word-ends.[35]

With its carefully inflected verse form, in which each line is indented according to its first letter's position in the alphabet, *Writing Is an Aid to Memory* attends to its own left margin with a symptomatic meticulousness that recalls its mode of composition. Pushed "to the left" by the prose form of its previous contexts, much of the language in *Writing* is abstracted in a procedure that at the same time, paradoxically, refuses abstraction. Drawn off and withdrawn, separated and removed from its original source, the unattributed and largely untraceable phrases are disengaged from their original contexts in a way that connotes even the euphemistic use of "abstract": "to take away secretly, slyly [...]; to purloin."[36] At the same time, with Hejinian's attention to her source texts clearly abstracted ("diverted") to their margins, she was apparently not consulting them primarily for "the ideas being articulated." She did not, that is, *abstract* her sources by considering a "mental conception [...] apart from the material embodiment" and the "particular instances" of their original typographic setting in prose.[37] As a symbolic communicative system, language means in a general way, permitting allusion and reference and conceptual use, but the physical fixity of printed texts can never be truly abstract, however pervasive the ideology of a transparent language might be. The particularity of printed texts requires citation and encourages collage. Or, in short, proving both propositions at once: "guage means general."

Now, to be precise, one should note that although Hejinian describes her compositional procedure as "restricting" her "to the phrases along the left margin of the page" so that she read "only along the left margin," in practice she is not as consistent as Coolidge, and phrases are frequently drawn from the interior of her source texts' pages. In the passage quoted above, for instance, while "straction" and "one day" do indeed occur on the left margin of a verso page, with "drops of water" on the left margin of the facing recto, all of the other phrases—"carried out on the pebbles," "of light off," "of abstraction," "in the other / way," and "but the order"—occur haphazardly in the middle of the page.[38] Nor is Hejinian always strictly linear in her transcriptions; she sometimes interpolates phrases rather than following their occurrences in sequence either up or down the page. That said, the poetics of *Writing Is an Aid to Memory* nonetheless reveals an acutely prosaic imagination.[39] Hejinian's collage of phrases is always more visual and material than allusive, and even when not restricting herself to the left margin, she frequently allows the typography of the source pages to suggest her poetic line, producing a verse that relies on the formal arrangement of language under the regime of prose. With a minor variant on her stated procedure, for example, she reads up the right margin of a prose page to assemble the line "something edible to his nose like an ape," which reveals its source in Leonardo da Vinci's notebooks:

> [...] Often when I see one of these men take this work in hand, I wonder whether he will not put it to his nose like an ape and ask himself whether it is something edible.[40]

With an echo of the etymology of "poetry" (the appropriative "work in hand" of the Greek ποίησις) and the question of mimesis ("like an ape": in imitation of an imitator), the passage is suggestive of Hejinian's abstract poetics, which refers directly to other texts while abjuring the symbolic references of conventional narrative and expository genres. The passage, in fact, is suggestive of her detailed copying of fragments of others' language in more explicit ways as well, given the pertinence of the passage's immediate context; Leonardo is arguing, in this section, about the relation of textual authority to creative invention and critical interpretation, including a parable of collecting and redistributing the works of others. Ironically, given Hejinian's practice, Leonardo begins this section by inveighing against the abridgement and abbreviation of source texts. He defends his own practice with the following apologia:

> If I do not quote from authors as they do, it is surely more worthy of the reader for me to quote from experience, the instructress of their masters. They strut about puffed up and pompous, adorned and clothed not in their own labors but in those of others, and will not allow me my own. But if they scorn me for being an inventor, how much harsher a judgment do not they deserve who are not inventors but trumpeters who can only recite the works of others?[41]

If Hejinian seems able to "only recite the work of others" in *Writing*, she does not "quote from authors" in the conventional manner; instead, she negotiates a way out of Leonardo's opposition between the Scylla of originality and the Charybdis of citation. With a creative plagiarism, *Writing* relentlessly copies without citation, innovating signature verses that "require the words of others for their expression."[42] The maneuver is telling. One of the starkest changes in poets' discourse over the last half century has been their position toward appropriation. With works such as *Writing Is an Aid*, or Charles Bernstein's "Ballet Ruse," from the same year (the language of which is drawn entirely and sequentially from *The Diary of Vaslav Nijinski*), the mode of appropriation leads directly to the distinctive styles that set these works apart from the deep-image, creative-writing workshop poems of the period; in fact, the very act of appropriation would have underscored their opposition to the ideologies of authentic voice and personal experience that dominated poetics at the time. And yet, in the extensive correspondence and coterie reviews among poets of Hejinian's generation, writers do not see fit to mention their sources or procedures (and at times even actively *deny* such borrowings). For decades, Hejinian would refrain from divulging the appropriations, and even flatly denied them. Hejinian's 2007 statement, made following the rise of Conceptual writing, when the fact of appropriation and the source text used have become the first thing noted when introducing a poem or framing it for discussion, describes the poetic process in detail.

In the case of *Writing Is an Aid to Memory*, part of what is being quoted—perhaps more importantly than any particular author or work—is prose, in all its typographic logic. Even when those "words of others" are not drawn from the margin, Hejinian's lines typically rely on other properties of prose, such as its division into columns and paragraphs or its arrangement of stratified lines. The couplet "rarity cination in nervous scenes by condemning / straight colors," for instance, traces a ruler-straight 45-degree path across the three-column layout of the Orion edition of Leonardo's writings, taking its words from the corners of paragraphs.[43] Starting at the left margin of the third column of page 214 she selects "rarity" and, immediately below it, "cination" (the result of an hyphenated *fascination*); "in" marks the top right corner and "nervous scenes" the bottom left corner (and last line) of a paragraph in the middle column; and "by" appears on the right margin at the bottom of the first column, just above the final line: "[roundly] condemning straight colors."[44] Again, the context of the passage bisected by Hejinian's protracting sample is apposite: notes on Leonardo's optical theories and the path of the eye in perspective geometry, ray tracing, foreshortening, and plotted angles. Hejinian's lines, in short, are both the residua of Leonardo's text and the result of enacting its thematic concerns.

The path of the eye, in fact, is one of the themes of her poem, where "motion is debate to the eye" and one line reads, with a punning aside on the first-person pronoun, "I glance toward what the eye can pronounce aside."[45] In *Writing Is an Aid to Memory* eyes fix, hang, and return, so that "the action of looking" remarked in the poem also describes a fundamental aspect of its composition.[46] The words, fragments, and phrases in *Writing* record the physical itineraries of the reading eye as it scans the field of prose: skimming, saccadic, erratic in its restless skip and wander over the page, with unfocused sweeps and momentary stays of attention, refreshing and restful. Rather than a disembodied assimilation of content conceived "without reason of the eyes," Hejinian attends to both the visual drift—whether from distraction or a momentarily relaxed conscious control—that can compass words in a vertical arrangement down the page rather than along the horizontal line, as well as to the ciliary and extraocular muscular work of the return sweep required by the line breaks and wide margins of prose.[47] The verse line "in a single day what is called whole is brick," for example, follows the oscillating pitch of the reading eye as it negotiates the margins of the prose page.[48] The words are drawn from a prose-block wall that frames the following paragraph in *The Book of English Trades and Library of the Useful Arts*:

> A Bricklayer and his labourer will lay <u>in a single day</u> about a thousand bricks, in <u>what is called whole</u> and solid work, when the wall <u>is</u> either a brick and a half or two bricks <u>thick</u>; and since a cubic yard contains 460 <u>bricks</u>, he will lay above two cubic yards in a day.[49]

With "the wall part a legible space," as Hejinian writes elsewhere, the "frame around" that space requires extra effort from the muscles involved in reading, so that initially "only spots seem to frame a plan" to the reading eye.[50] Individual words and couplets—discrete spots at the margin of the plane of prose—silhouette the fixed, flat level "block of material" typeset with an even spread and spatial distribution.⁵¹ As we saw Andy Warhol profess in the introduction, "my favorite piece of sculpture is a solid wall with a [w]hole in it."

Demonstrating a similar reliance on the aleatory but necessary disposition of prose to generate a poetic line, the same section of the poem finds Hejinian taking words in a perpendicular formation, as they happen to fall one on top of another in the prose layout from the *Book of English Trades* chapter on carpentry. "When beauty is vertical," as one reads elsewhere in *Writing*, "a coincidence touches / a random more."⁵² Reading down the page, like Tom Phillips in *A Humument*, so that "intensity in its little place is vertical," Hejinian cuts across the grain of the original text to generate the verse line "commonly this pitch its second name":

> to England. The Norway fir produces the *white* deal, <u>commonly</u> used by Carpenters; from <u>this</u>, <u>pitch</u> is also drawn; whence it takes <u>its second name</u> of the *pitch* fir. There is also the *red* deal which is very much used.⁵³

Rather than follow the conceptual logic of the essays' arguments, Hejinian's lines thus follow the visual paths of eyes as they observe the material logic of prose. At the same time, the subjects of those essays, as we have seen, are not entirely irrelevant. While Peter Nicholls has argued that "it is not a matter of being able to clarify Hejinian's text by adducing contexts for particular references and allusions," the themes of those sources are far from coincidental. Indeed, the sections scanned in *The Book of English Trades* speak not only to Hejinian's poetics, or to questions of "craft" in American poetics in the period, but also to the very nature of prose itself: the accumulative horizontal strata of bricklaying, the squaring and plumb framing of carpentry, the cutting and joining of craft construction.⁵⁴

In page after page, Hejinian recognizes the potential for the material aspects of prose to generate traditionally poetic effects of language oriented away from the communicative function (as we saw Jan Mukařovský define it in the introduction): artificed arrangement, estrangement, alogical associations, *et cetera*.⁵⁵ Format, once again, is construed as a significant form in the service of the genre of the avant-garde lyric. The genre informed by prose, however, would not need to be poetry. Another instance of putting prose in the service of a genre can be found in John Baldessari's 1967 canvas of uninflected primer and the sign painter's careful block lettering, which reads, "A TWO-DIMENSIONAL SURFACE WITHOUT ANY ARTICULATION IS A DEAD EXPERIENCE." That sentence's ironic and de-aestheticized linguistic interrogation of the viewer functions as part of the genre of conceptual art, but it derives from the prose format of Baldessari's unattributed source text: György Kepes's art-theory textbook *Language of Vision*. The play of Baldessari's work, and what surely suggested the quotation to him in the first place, is that in its original printed form the sentence, by chance, appears typeset intact, at the very top of a page, perfectly composed across one full line of the block of prose. That sentence, it happens, in its materiality, is the typographic measure of the oversize format of Kepes's book.[56] On the canvas, however, Baldessari has wittily allowed it to be articulated and enlivened through line breaks:

A TWO-DIMENSIONAL
SURFACE WITHOUT ANY
ARTICULATION IS A
DEAD EXPERIENCE.

Prose operates not only at the level of the line, but also through the unit of the page, filling from the top down and then beginning again on the next page. For readers, this format requires a repeated visual itinerary, down and back up, in continual laps of equal measure. William Carlos Williams's *Kora in Hell: Improvisations* thus enacts a kind of formal allegory, placing its attenuated account of the myth of Persephone (Kore)—who descends to Hades for half of each year and returns for the other half, in endless cycles—in a self-consciously chosen prose form. The work, indeed, is a landmark of experimental prose, repeatedly cited along with Gertrude Stein's *Tender Buttons* and John Ashbery's *Three Poems* as the foundational texts of a certain genre (for Ron Silliman, it is the "sole precedent" he can find for the paratactic prose of the "new sentence").[57] With the conflation of Kore and *Kora*, Williams collapses character and text, its print flowing up and down like the annual cycles of Kore's descent and return: "by virtue of works of art the beauty of woman is released to flow whither it will up and down the years," as the gloss to section VI summarizes.[58] Williams reiterates this cyclical movement of ascent and descent in other sections, in both literal and figurative phrases: "odd ramblings up and down, over and over"; "driven up one street and down another"; "where does this downhill turn up again?"; "a man's desire is to win his way to some hilltop [...] the man being half a poet is cast down"; "having attained the mountaintop [...] the descent proffers its blandishments quite as a matter of course"; "often when the descent seems well marked there will be a subtle ascent over-ruling it so that in the end when the degradation is fully anticipated the person will be found to have emerged upon a hilltop."[59] The hill, in fact, offers the path for up-and-down motion even when the actors are not tied to the terrestrial: "the cackling grackle that dartled at the hill's bottom have joined their flock and swing with the rest over a broken roof."[60]

Broken lines and oblique flight are a recurrent theme in *Kora*, which figures the poetic imagination as what cuts against regimentation and laminar flow with an improvisatory and unpredictable syncopation. In works like *Kora in Hell* and *Spring & All*, Williams, like Mukařovský, did not define "poetry" based on a distinction between verse and prose, and one can see him recognizing the typographic equivalent of his early poetics in prose, with its dynamic of a continual fluidity cut by the chance geometry of the right-hand margin and the footer of the page, which are continually "breaking the back of a willing phrase," as an early phrase puts it.[61] In that dynamic of fixity and flow one can see "the spectacle of two exquisite and divergent natures playing out one against the other," as when "between two contending forces there may at all times arrive that moment when the stress is equal on both sides so that with a great pushing a great stability results giving a picture of perfect rest."[62] Throughout the book, the rested, calming regularity of rank and file, like lines of type on a printed page, establishes a stable background against which poetic mastery can be achieved through "the brokenness of composition."[63] For the most part, the car runs smoothly past "rows of celery" and "long beet rows," the driver thinking of "clean raked fields" "plowed" with "furrows"; the lull of easy motion along these parallel lines takes on the fluid dynamics of breeze and stream as the "car" is dreamily transformed into the "caress of the low clouds—river lapping at the reeds."[64] In contrast, the poetic imagination interrupts these soothing striations. "Here's the way! and—you're hip bogged," as one sentence enacts its logic of diversion; at other moments, the "pace leads off anew," or turns "off from the path into the field" (where the "path" in *Kora* comes to be linked with the aberration of "pathology").[65] "Queer how a road juts in," Williams exclaims, picking up on the repeated vocabulary of "oblique," "sidelong," and "twisted" trajectories.[66] Equating the "lack of imagination" with "an easy lateral sliding," like the fluent line across the page, Williams laments that "the attention has been held too rigid on the one plane instead of following a more flexible, jagged resort."[67] Similarly, with figures of fluidity ("stream") and lineation ("wiry strands"), Williams returns to the fundamental dynamics of prose in order to describe his poetics: "the stream of things having composed itself into wiry strands that move in one fixed direction, the poet in desperation turns at right angles and cuts across current with startling results."[68] In the context of this poetic skew, certain scenes begin to take on an allegorical weight; "when you hang your clothes on the line you do not expect to see the line broken," the third section opens, drawing attention to the line of print and prefiguring later constructions of interrupted rows:

"lath-strips" cut "on a diagonal" and a "cracked window blind" where "the blinds are down."[69]

If, in the context of these repeated figurations, the flight of the grackle over the line of the rooftops acquires a certain significance, those birds are also an instance of the way in which Williams orbits *Kora* with a web of homophones in a manner not unlike the Riffaterrian matrix we will encounter in chapter 5: asymptotically approaching but not quite naming the various definitions not only of κόρη [kore] but of χορός [choros], χῶρος [khoros], ὄρος [horos], ὥρα [hora], and κοράκας [korakas]. The latter, sounding by onomatopoetic reason something like *grackle*, is the ornithonym designating the European equivalent of the American corvid. In *Kora*, the grackle hews to the contour of the hill, and the specific use of ὄρος in classical Greek to designate a chain of mountains or line of hills corroborates the suspicion that Williams may be working from the Greek when he writes of "the long unbroken line of the hills there," repeating the phrase later: "that long unbroken line of the hills there."[70] Related to the root of the English *horizon*, the word also denotes a boundary or limit, which occurs in *Kora* as the "world's edge," the city seen "at the horizon," and—with a specifically cyclical sense of repeated up and down motion—"when the wheel's just at the up turn it glimpses horizon."[71] More generally, "edge" recurs frequently, including in two moments determined by prose, which neatly enacts that boundary limit of the text-block border with the hyphenated "knowl-edge" and "acknowl-edge" ("again the words break," as one reads in section XIII).[72] As a defined period of time, marking everything from hours to seasons, and specifically denoting just the right moment—as when a musician comes in precisely on the beat—ὥρα translates the sense not just of the poem's themes of youth and old age, in analogue to the seasons governed by Kore's ascent and descent, but also the specific phrasings of "this day of all others," "there may at all times arrive that moment," and "childbirth follows in its time."[73] Each of these would translate ὥρα exactly. Finally, Williams goes out of his way to mention a "chorus" [χορός], and the dance, rhythm, and poetic measure that the Greek word connotes are a central theme of the book.[74]

Let me be clear that I do not find the correspondence of the more general themes to be especially significant here; one might well expect a work about gynecology with Greek mythic overtones to include references to maidens, virgins, brides, and daughters (the very denotations of κόρη which gave the goddess her name), just as poets might be concerned with metrical feet and the metaphor of dance without having a particular Greek word in mind. But the exhaustive inclusion of more precise denotations is striking.[75] In ancient Greek, κόρη also denoted the kind of sleeve cut to extend over the hand, and Williams not only mentions "hearts on sleeves" (with a possible macaronic pun between the Latin *corda* [hearts] and *Kora*), but also their extension: "Oh I'd hold my sleeves *over* the sun awhile."[76] Similarly, κόρη is also an ocular term, denoting the pupil of the eye, which Williams specifies with an odd doubling as "one sees only eye pupils," and by extension it is the form taken by the imperative of "to look," which appears in *Kora* with the commands "look at his hands" and "look at it."[77] Finally, the denotations of ὅρος that indicate a boundary or frontier (which occurs in *Kora* as "it's our frontier you know," and "despite vastness of frontiers, which are as it were the fringes of a flower") begin to merge with the senses of χώρα: the "field" from which Kore was abducted but also specifically the extra-urban territories that designate the outskirts of a city, as when Williams indicates the "outskirts of a mill town" or allows his imagination to repeatedly return to the *terrains vagues* of railyards and vacant lots.[78] The same word, as it happens, also denotes "sieve," which appears in two different sections, deliberately modified, as "mirror sieve" and "wire sieve," evoking in their turn the twin symbolic (mimetic) and typographic (linear) faces of print.[79]

In philosophy, χώρα is also a key term in Plato's metaphysics in the *Timaeus*, and many of the connotations he draws on are relevant to a reading of Williams's obstetric reimagination of the Kore myth: womb, mother, midwife, the winnowing baskets of harvested grains. Here we can perhaps see why Williams insisted on the unusual spelling of the epithet for Persephone, rather than her more familiar name. In particular, as an abstract receptacle or space, the term marks the intervalic locus between forms—an unformed material arena that receives the stamp of pure ideation as part of the process of creation in Platonic thought. Williams seems to refer directly to this sense when he speaks of the "alchemy of form" and "the empty form" of poetic creation that drops from the heavens.[80] Moreover, as elaborated through critical readings by Julia Kristeva and Jacques Derrida, the χώρα itself offers ways to understand the dynamics of prose I am arguing for here. The analogies are not strict but are highly suggestive (which accords with the very description of the χώρα itself by the two French philosophers). For Kristeva, the *chora* embodies a dynamic—like prose's logic of dispersal and consolidation—between "la condensation et le déplacement" [condensation and displacement].[81] These inherent tensions result in the contradictions of a space of heterogeneity (it can take any form, just as prose serves novels and philosophical treatises equally well) emerging from uniform, undifferentiated homogeneity. A space both bounded and fluid, regulated and chaotic, the *chora* is defined by the very kinds of dynamic contradictions that define the logic of prose. Furthermore, where Plato figures the χώρα as a passive receptacle, Kristeva figures it as unpredictably eruptive and able to provide an "articulation provisoire" [provisional articulation] that is modulated but motile, with a fluidity that forms in ways other than the hard geometric rule of the carpenter's square or the bookmaker's ruler.[82] Although not itself subject to laws of meaning, the *chora* describes the condition that makes those representations of the symbolic and semantic possible in the first place. It is the condition by which inscription can be understood as semiotic: as signifiers ready to disseminate themselves in a system of signs. For Derrida, similarly, the *khôra* is the space, like the text block of a page, ready to receive an imprint: a "porte-empreinte" [print-bearer] that encompasses the "lieu d'inscription" [place of inscription].[83] Figured as the gutter of the book— that thing which is not itself a page but makes the page, rather than a mere sheet, possible as such—the Derridean *khôra* is "un abîme, un chasme" [an abyss, a chasm] in which material and meaning arise in the indeterminate relationship of a "τρίτον γένος" [third genre] not unlike the provisional articulations of the dynamics whereby prose transforms between format and form.[84] With χώρα figuring the prose of the page that Kora (as *Kora*) figures, in her cycles of descent and ascent, the *mise-en-abîme* is thus itself placed *en abîme*—a figure of its own figuration: not only is *abîme* the synonym for *enfer* [hell], but Kora is led there, of course, by the opening of a χάσμα [chasm].[85]

From another direction, the format of prose can be put in the service of a genre without regard to its articulation or even any specific sense of the line. So where Yeats mobilized the form of modernist free verse to underscore the poetic nature of Pater's prose, and Hejinian—inversely—used the fragmenting arrangements of the prose form to construct a postmodern verse lyric, I want to continue to think through the "τρίτον γένος" of prose by considering passages where the narrative genre of descriptive fiction figures the format of its own printed prose. The ultimate twist for such works comes from the recognition that such self-reflexive, autoreferential, concretely visual writing would—by many definitions, such as Mukařovský's—transform the genre of these prose fiction passages into poetry, even though they do not transmogrify into verse. Such scenes are instances of what Aaron Fogel calls "the image of prose in prose."[86] That image is the shadow cast by the quadrilateral planar geometric units of the paragraph and the two-dimensional surface of the page, with their paradoxical combinations of fixity and flow: the constraint of the page space's typographic area against the discrepant extension of grammar and the rigid orthogonal forms of the prose block imposed by an invisible perimeter. As Robert Hodge puts it, "The conventions of prose in print format present a rectangle of print surrounded by a blank margin. […] The uniformity of the black of print on page after page is a transparent signifier of mechanical uniformity imposed on the flow of sense."[87] The dynamic between the fluent and the orthogonal, diversity and uniformity, is amplified by the widespread use of the prose format; for centuries, every nonverse story or argument printed—occasional experiments and gimmicks only proving the rule—has taken the same physical form regardless of style or content.

For one example of the image of prose in prose—of a text figuring its own form—consider the fifth chapter of Joseph Roth's 1932 novel, *Radetzkymarsch* [*The Radetzky March*], which opens with a scene in which the central character, Carl Joseph, returns to his regiment's station on the Moravian marches of the Hapsburg Empire:

> Whenever he returned home to the barracks in the afternoon, and the huge double gate closed behind him, he felt trapped; never again would the gates open before him. His spurs jingled frostily on the bare stone staircase, and the tread of his boots echoed on the brown caulked wooden floor of the corridor. The whitewashed walls clung to a bit of vanishing daylight, radiating it now, as if making sure in their bleak thrift that the government kerosene lamps in the corners were not lit until evening had thickened completely, as if they had collected the day at the right time in order to dole it out in the destitution of darkness.
>
> Carl Joseph did not turn on the light. Pressing his forehead against the window, which seemed to separate him from the darkness but was actually the cool, familiar outer wall of the darkness itself, he peered into the bright yellow coziness of the troop rooms.
>
> […]
>
> They kept playing their harmonicas there nonstop. He could clearly see sporadic glints of the metal and the movements of the coarse brown hands pushing the metal instruments back and forth in front of red mouths. The vast melancholy of these instruments poured through the closed windows into the black rectangle of the parade ground, filling the darkness with vague inklings of home and wife and child and farm.
>
> "Switch on the light!" Carl Joseph ordered without looking around. Across the square the men were still playing harmonicas.
>
> Onufrij switched on the light. Carl Joseph heard the click of the switch on the door molding. Behind him the room lit up. But outside the window the rectangular darkness was still gaping, and across the square the cozy yellow light of the troop rooms was flickering.[88]

In this scene set behind "the huge double gate," an enclosure doubled like the boards of a book, the reader encounters a series of rectangular surfaces—whitewashed like bleached stock or yellowed like the acid paper pages of a popular novel—containing further rectangles in reversible plays of opacity and transparency, visual blackness and expressive narrative sound: "The vast melancholy of these instruments *poured* through the closed windows *into the black rectangle* of the parade ground." The sense of print in that dark rectangle is corroborated by both the ranked *lines* of soldiers who repeatedly fill and empty the parade ground in other scenes and the fortuitous *ink* in "inkling" in the English translation. Moreover, the activity of pouring figures the liquidity of fungible content filling the container of the page: the sense that text assumes a form that defines it but is not its own; that fluid content adapts itself to inflexible form; that text runs up against an invisible container—the flow into the "blank margin," as Hodge puts it. Or, in Roth's terms, that typographic blank margin matches a description of the solid but invisible glass pane "which seemed to separate him from the darkness but was actually the cool, familiar outer wall of the darkness itself." Print, in prose, gives the impression of a strictly defined rectilinear form that nonetheless does not have a hard outline. Prose, one might say, seeks its own level.

My point is not just that Roth gives us images of dark and light rectangles, but that their paradoxical play of opacity and transparency corresponds to the ideology of referential narrative being momentarily undone here. As the summoned images of the imagined scene come too close to describing the printed page—when descriptive passages approach the figuration of their own material forms—they risk unveiling the ideology of the transparent page by drawing the reader's attention back to that surface, to a focus on the page itself, rather than allowing the reader to look imaginatively through the page with the mind's eye to the scenes its words describe. The literal image of the dark ink in the prose block gives us the words that summon a mental image, but the framed block of prose is meant to be a transparent window onto the world of its *histoire*, in the way that Alberti figured the panel painting of the Renaissance as an *aperta finestra* [open window] onto the depicted perspectival scene (recall that Roth, in this scene, specifies a "closed window," one which only "seemed" to separate Carl Joseph from the speculative scene but which is itself, in fact, a dark wall). When the reader looks at the patterned and pigmented surface of the page—at "the wall of the darkness itself"—the narrative illusion of fancied scenes collapses beneath the physical imposition of immediately present, proximate ink. Carl Joseph enacts this moment when he has the light in his room switched on at night, obviating the transparency of the window and transforming it into a mirror reflecting the room back on itself: a moment when he knows both that the cold rectangular darkness is still there *and* that the comforting scenes from which he is separated can still be imagined. The illuminating moment nicely captures the mutually dependent dialectic of story and text with a dizzying recursion; initially, the textlike blackness of the window in the darkened room is transparent, an ambivalence paralleled by the reader who must simultaneously remember the look of the page and comprehend its content in order recognize the self-reflexivity of this passage; then—with a figure of mimesis figuring a mimesis—the mirroring reflection of the window in the illumined room turns back on the fictional character whose resemblance can only be fully imagined by the reader who has also rendered the block of material type invisible.

Another instance of a description that risks disrupting its diegetic projection occurs in a chapter of Stephen Crane's 1893 novel *Maggie, A Girl of the Streets*, "In Darkest New York." Crane describes a scene in which Maggie heads outside to Tompkins Square, "that dreary, house hemmed, overcrowded, electric lighted square," to lounge and hear "da band."[89] But the passage, which again figures the play of light and dark on a flat surface, also simultaneously describes the typographic shape of that description itself as it appears on the prose-formatted page. "Streams" of humanity "poured into the square [...] meandered aimlessly along the paths and overflowed the benches"; they then "danced shadow dances on the grass plats where the hissing electric lights cast fantastic figures for them."[90] As in the audible black rectangle of Roth's dark harmonic square, Crane does not just summon the closely bordered square, a flat rectilinear receptacle form being filled with overflowing patterns and figures, but also hints at the prose page's visual organization of phonetic signs in the simultaneously audible and visible "hissing [...] lights." Crane's scene also suggests the dynamic tension in prose between the rigid container of its geometric forms and the fluidity of its grammatical content, the varied and variable words and subjects that are always poured into the same mold: from page to page, the same set of blocks, regardless of narrative development. Or—pitched at another level—the sublime realization that from book to book, novel to novel, an endless variety of stories are always told in the same visual format. Accordingly, one again finds the sense of contained fluid forms that fill and empty a space: the figures in *Maggie* "*poured* into the square" just as the sound in Roth's scene "*poured* [...] into the black rectangle."

Precisely the same language recurs in Eugène Ionesco's *Le solitaire* (*The Hermit*), his only novel, and so a work in which he may well have been thinking about the format of prose in contradistinction to the dialogue lines of drama. As the narrator describes the dreamlike town of his surroundings, a mass of figures "continuaient de déboucher des quatre rues" [continued *streaming into the square* from all four streets], where "des boîtes invisibles de verre [...] des cars chargés de policiers arrivaient des quatre rues qui débouchaient sur la place. Eux aussi étaient entourés du cercueils de verre" [invisible from all four streets that emptied into it, vans packed with police *poured into the square*. They too were encased in invisible glass coffins].⁹¹ Indeed, everyone, the narrator discloses, seems "enfermés dans des cercueils transparents […] à la fois enfermé et trop ouvert. Le cristal est invisible" [locked in glass coffins … Locked up and at the same time too free. The crystal is invisible].⁹² Contained within invisible forms that lack a hard-edged outline, the characters of the novel are figured like the printed characters of its prose-set type. Moreover, one might recall that "coffin" is a printing term: "that part of a printing machine on which the forme of type is laid."⁹³ Not directly visible on the printed page, yet defining its contours, that coffin is the punch line to Laurence Sterne's bibliographic jest in *Tristram Shandy*: a funereal "black page" which both announces the death of Yorick and also, in the original edition, fills out precisely the area of the prose block. In essence an image of every prose-set page, the black page in *Tristram Shandy* lays bare the coffin buried beneath each impressed sheet in the books whose printing Sterne so actively oversaw. The very parameter of prose, Sterne's coffined page appears like an illustration to David Antin's claim that under the right circumstances "prose is a kind of concrete poetry with justified margins."⁹⁴

With this denotation of "coffin" in mind, consider the similar role of the casket in William Faulkner's *As I Lay Dying*, where the box's geometric form—presented in one chapter as a line drawing interrupting the lines of the text—insists on the mute, visual physicality of print in contrast to the sounds of speech.⁹⁵ As Michael Kaufmann has argued, Faulkner had both a "fascination with print" and an "apprehension about the effect that the intricate print box he prepared for his largely oral tale might have on it."⁹⁶ One of those effects, as we have seen, is the risk that imagined speech will disappear in the face of the visual immediacy of the page. Accordingly, one of Faulkner's characters stands motionless before a building as if he were a surrogate for the printer looking at the press bed or the reader looking *at*, rather than through, the page; he sees "the square orifice of doorway broken only by the square squat shape of the coffin" as it "comes into relief."⁹⁷ "Relief," moreover, describes the type of printing at issue. Elsewhere in the novel, the coffin moves through space "like a sled upon invisible snow, smoothly evacuating atmosphere in which the sense of it is still shaped."⁹⁸ Shaping sense—constructing meaning—without the benefit of sound, the printer's coffin set with engraving "relief" type produces a geometric arrangement of phonetic characters, each a "grave, composed face" as Faulkner puns, and each, as the novel's final page names it, a literal "graphophone."⁹⁹ In a corroborating scene, the diegetic square of the town and the physical square of the prose page are both filled with a fluid seriality and a disorienting play of deletion and manifestation. As in the passages from Roth and Crane, summoning the silent image of prose with an overflowed square seems to require a compensating insistence on narrative sound:

> I hear the cow a long time, clopping   on the street. Then she comes into the square. She goes across the square, her head down   clopping. She lows. There was nothing in the square before she lowed, but it wasn't empty. Now it is empty after she lowed. She goes on, clopping   . She lows.[100]

Given the congruence between the animal's motion across the square and the procession of type across the text block, Faulkner's cow flirts etymologically with the boustrophedonic imagination that still haunts the ideology of prose, which requires the illusion that the format is a continuous and uninterrupted precession of text rather than an assemblage of discrete and discontinuous lines.[101] The paradox of Faulkner's square, simultaneously emptied and replete, resolves when one separates the two homonyms and distinguishes the rectangle of the novel's prose page from the civic space its text describes; the passage both depicts and enacts the logic of conservation between the two. The materiality of print disrupts descriptive illusion, which in turn works to suppress the intervention of print; the page, its inked surface always present before any scene can be read, recedes and nearly vanishes when one vividly imagines the cow and its lowing. In this case, the play of tangibility and disappearance is refracted by the fact that the page itself—highlighted by Faulkner's calculated spacing—is so palpably present. While any printing is legible only because of the dependent balance between ink and substrate, Faulkner's paragraph reminds one that the justification of prose depends especially on the adjustment of uninked spaces as well as on type; the *khora* of the page, too, plays a requisite role in establishing the uniformity of the text block that it frames.

"Trop matérielle et immatérielle à la fois. Ce monde, en carton pâte, ce décor de théâtre pouvait se substituer n'importe quand à un autre" [Too material and yet immaterial, too. This world made out of *papier-mâché*, this particular theatrical setting could be substituted for any other at any time], says Ionesco's narrator, moving his description closer to that space of the page, a paper terrain that might record any sort of narrative world in the same format.[102] He continues, with a vocabulary that should by now be familiar: "Je regardai par la fenêtre et contemplai quelque temps les silhouettes fuyantes qui semblaient sortir de la brume pour s'y enfoncer à nouveau et disparaître" [I gazed out the window and for some time watched the fleeting silhouettes which seemed to emerge from the thick fog only to plunge back into it again and disappear].[103] Then, further courting the collapse of the *histoire* into the printed text by gesturing to transparent and opaque quadrilaterals, he adds, "Il n'y a peut-être rien derrière tout ça, dis-je en montrant de la main les fenêtres, les murs, la rue" ["You know, there may be nothing beyond all that," I said, pointing to the windows, the walls, the street]. His companion replies: "Que voudriez-vous qu'il y ait derrière? C'est ça, c'est tout" [What do you want beyond them? They're there, that's all].[104]

That blunt presence of the form of the page, its "brute and often brutal fact," is both less heavy-handed and even more pervasive in Andrei Bely's 1916 novel, *Petersburg*.[105] As with Faulkner's "square," Bely's title charts an unquiet congruence of diegetic and literal space at a one-to-one scale, conflating the geometric layout of the city and the pages of the book itself, public squares and prose blocks, cartography and typography. Ultimately, the clear distinction between the name of the city and the eponymous title of the novel collapses completely: "Петербургом же—ничего нет" [Beyond Petersburg, there is nothing], Bely writes with the hyperbole of fiction and the literalism of text.[106] "А там были—линии" [And what was there, were lines].[107] In that simultaneous textual urbanism of *Petersburg* the reader once again finds not only the same images of fluid containment ("everyone *poured* into the streets, gathered in crowds, and then dispersed") but also a thematized recurrence of rectilinear forms in scenes explicitly contrasting an attention to black rectangles with an incompatible state of narrative reverie. As with the windows of Roth and Ionesco, in Bely's *Petersburg* one cannot look both transparently through a figurative structure and simultaneously at its material surface. "I cannot," as Hejinian writes, "imagine a glass prose."[108]

Two parallel scenes present each possibility in turn, positing a dialectic of materiality and mimeticism, of the tain and the reflective glass. In the first, near the beginning of Bely's novel, Senator Apollon Apollonovich rides within the "четырехугольными стенками" [four perpendicular walls] of his carriage, a "черного [...] куба" [black cube] of perfect, confining quadrangular planes that moves among the "черновато-серыми домовыми кубами" [blackish gray cubes of houses] in rank after rank of parallel, linear, rectilineal prospects.[109] Like the assimilation of lines to paragraphs, paragraphs to chapters, and chapters to books, he sees the "пересеченная сетью проспектов, в мировые бы ширилась бездны плоскостями квадратов и кубов" [network of parallel prospects expand into the abysses of the universe in planes of squares and cubes]: where "есть бесконечность в бесконечности бегущих проспектов с бесконечностью в бесконечность бегущих пересекающихся теней. Весь Петербург—бесконечность проспекта, возведенного в энную степень" [there is an infinity of rushing prospects with an infinity of rushing, intersecting shadows. All of Petersburg is an infinity of the prospect raised to the Nth degree].[110] The senator, enamored of that "государственной планиметрии" [plane geometry], loves the lines of stratified architectural rows because they differ from "the line of life" and its narrative entanglements.[111] "Рожден для одиночного заключения" [completely isolated and cut off from] others' lives by the square black walls of the carriage and fixating on the shaped components of prose—the line and the square—the senator is lulled into a momentary reprieve from the need to identify or interact with anyone else.[112] Bely presents the senator as if he were a reader unable to look beyond the visual geometry of the surface of the page: "он, бывало, подолгу предавался бездумному созерцанию" [at times, for hours on end, he would lapse into an unthinking contemplation] of geometric forms.[113]

The second scene, nearly identical to the first, opens with all the hallmarks of the logic of prose, including a compensatory emphasis on sound ("тротуары шептались" [the sidewalks of the square conversed in whispers]) and a suggestion of the fluidity of type and print ("же серые проходили там токи людские [...] побежали там лица" [gray human streams of people passed by there ... Faces ran by there]).[114] As in *Le solitaire*, where one of Ionesco's recurrent themes is the absorption of difference in the same "grand-place" [big square]—"un mélange de plein et de vide" [a mixture of void and fullness] in which "tout finit pareil" [everything comes out the same in the end]—Bely underscores the assimilation of diverse content within duplicate forms. Although radically different lives play out within their walls, Petersburg is composed of line after line of "такие же точно там возвышались дома" [exactly the same kind of houses]: "черновато-серыми [...] кубами" [blackish gray cubes] arrayed along "сеть параллельных проспектов" [the network of parallel prospects].[115] Unlike the first scene, however, the senator here is involved in a romance that dissolves the stark material forms of his earlier focus, replacing them with the daydreams of narrative absorption and psychological identification:

Аполлон Аполлонович не глядел на любимую свою фигуру; квадрат; не предавался бездумному созерцанию каменных параллелепипедов, кубов; покачиваясь на мягких подушках сиденья наемной кареты, он с волненьем поглядывал на Анну Петровну

[Apollon Apollonovich was not looking at his favorite figure: the square. He did not lapse into an unthinking contemplation of the stone parallelepipeds and cubes. Gently rocking on the soft seat cushions of the hired carriage, he stole an occasional agitated glance at Ann Petrovna.][116]

As Viktor Shklovsky writes in *Theory of Prose*, Bely does not semanticize or symbolize, but rather he "transfers the attributes from one metaphor leitmotiv to another."[117] In these two framing scenes, Bely transfers the attributes of prose itself.

One of those attributes, indeed, is prose's transferability. Both a format and a device, prose, in the case of *Petersburg*, is thus recursively embedded. But even standard prose is *mise-en-abîme*. The rectangle of the prose block—a sable billet charged as a bearing and borne at the fess upon the field of the page—forms an inescutcheon ordinaire doing duty as the banner of many modern genres. But prose, as we have seen, is far from parsimonious in its allegiances. Prose heralds its format from afar, but its true allegiance to any given genre requires a closer inspection. The structural dynamics that define prose—fluidity and containment, strict rectilinear geometry without hard outlines, uniform stratification, chance distribution and determinate placement—permit prose to be enlisted in the service not only of those genres with which it is popularly associated, such as the novel and the essay, but also of those its very presence would seem to forefend. As in the case of Coolidge and Hejinian, the particulars of prose can generate lyric verse; as in the case of Bely or Roth, it can transform passages of narrative fiction into poetry. That ability to transfer the attributes of a genre between forms, to function as a sort of literary *lapis philosophorum*, marks the incredible generosity of the kindness of prose.

The Onomastic Imagination

[CHAPTER TWO]

> Qu'est-ce qui fait du nom propre une sorte de surnom, de pseudonyme ou de cryptonyme à la fois singulier et singulièrement intraduisible?
>
> *[What is it that makes the proper name a sort of surname, a kind of pseudonym, or cryptonym at the same time singular and singularly untranslatable?]*
>
> JACQUES DERRIDA[1]

Blaise Cendrars left us a snapshot, from 1924, of all of the ramifications of the literary name—versions, in every case, of what comes down to linguistic propriety. His book *Kodak*, a collection of short lyrics in a direct, matter-of-fact style that seemed to chime with the portable, popular, modern photography named by the book's title, compiles an album of verse as if the poems were a series of travelogues, or quick, postcard-ready verbal pics. Indeed, the poems were taken as pioneering works in a new modernist style of vernacular immediacy, countering the high academic style of Parnassian verse with the linguistic equivalent of an amateur photograph: instantaneous, fragmentary, improvisatory, touristic souvenirs of Cendrars's own publicized travels to the Americas. Specifically, critics saw *Kodak* as revealing the same "playfulness and taste for adventure," as well as the same documentary observations, evinced by Cendrars's famous *La Prose du Transsibérien et de la petite Jehanne de France* (a collaboration with the painter Sonia Delaunay) and books such as *Panama (ou les aventures de mes sept oncles)* and the descriptively titled *Feuilles de route [Travel Notes]*.[2] John Dos Passos, for one, wrote that in *Kodak*, "Blaise Cendrars seems to have rather specialized in America, in the US, preferring the happier Southern and Western sections to the Bible-worn hills of New England."[3] "Happier," of course, is a suspect adjective with relation to the Jim Crow South, but problems with perspective are all to the point for Dos Passos's assessment of Cendrars's book. For Dos Passos, the camera reference of the book's title signaled the poems' ontological veracity, the "photorealist," "camera-eye" objectivity of the foreign author's distanced insights. In his translation, the poem "Mississippi" opens:

> At this place the stream is a wide lake
> Rolling yellow muddy waters between marshy banks

> Waterplants merging into acres of cotton
> Here and there appear towns and villages carpeting the bottom of some little bay with their factories with their high black chimneys with their long piers which advance quite a way into the water on their stakes[4]

Assessing Cendrars's poems from this collection, Paul Auster similarly singles out the "snapshot realism of his travel poems," seeing the snapshot as the solution to the modernist poet's realization that "everything around me moves." "In *Kodak*," Auster writers, "it is as if each of these poems was the record of a single moment, lasting no longer than it takes to click the shutter of a camera."[5] Furthermore, although critics frequently note the similarity of the signature style of *Kodak* and Cendrars's first novels, arguing that the prose works extend the direct, plain mode of his travelogue poems, after forty-five years no one had yet noticed what Cendrars finally confessed in his 1970 memoir *L'homme foudroyé* [*The Astonished Man*]:

> J'eus la cruauté d'apporter à [Gustave] Le Rouge un volume de poèmes et de lui faire constater de visu en les lui faisant lire une vingtaine de poèmes originaux que j'avais taillés à coups de ciseaux dans l'un de ses ouvrages en prose et que j'avais publiés sous mon nom! C'était du culot.
>
> [I was cruel enough to take Le Rouge a volume of poetry and make him read, and confirm with his own eyes, some twenty original poems which I had clipped out of one of his prose works and had published under my own name! It was cheeky.][6]

Cendrars goes on to caution the curious with a parenthetical demurral and warning:

> Avis aux chercheurs et aux curieux! Pour l'instant je ne puis en dire davantage pour ne pas faire école et à cause de l'éditeur qui serait mortifié d'apprendre avoir publié à son insu une supercherie poétique.
>
> [Note to researchers and the inquisitive: for the moment I can speak no more about it, so as not to attract imitators and for the sake of the publisher, who would be mortified to learn that he had unwittingly published my poetic fraud.][7]

As investigators and the inquisitive now know, *Kodak* was sourced from Gustave Le Rouge's pulpy genre novel *Le mystérieux Docteur Cornélius* [*The Mysterious Doctor Cornelius*], which had been published serially between 1912 and 1913. Accordingly, the subtitle added to the second edition of

Cendrars's book, "(Documentaire)," begins to sound like a parenthetical index less to the genre of the travelogue, or even to the stylistic mode or ideological register of the "snapshot record" of the portable camera, than to the previously published textual documents Cendrars recorded, with the flat literal realism of direct quotation, in his plagiarism.

In any case, Cendrars's poetics point neatly back to the poems' source. In Le Rouge's novels, Doctor Cornelius is a sort of mad scientist allied with the secret criminal organization Le Main Rouge [the Red Hand]. As an evil plastic surgeon, he has the ability to disguise the appearance of others, sculpting their visages with a scalpel to the point they might pass as someone else. Cendrars, analogously, cuts and sculpts Le Rouge's texts to the point that they passed, for decades, under another identity, as the distinctive lineaments of Cendrars's own signature style. He emphasizes the sharp tool of his appropriation: "j'avais taillés à coups de ciseaux" [I had clipped out with scissors]. Cendrars mimics Doctor Cornelius's unethical surgery on the text of the novel itself, literalizing its narrative in a sort of formal allegory.[8]

First plagiarizing the signature style of Gustave Le Rouge [*le main de La Rouge*, as the metonymic idiom would have it], and then aligning himself with the criminal disguises of Le Main Rouge, Cendrars cheekily returns to Le Rouge with the proof of his crime: "et de lui faire constater de visu en les lui faisant lire" [and make him read, and confirm with his own eyes]. With both his cruel social visit and, decades later, the publication of his confessional memoir, Cendrars ensures that his plagiarism, however crafty and devious, will be discovered: that he will be caught, as it were, red-handed—*avec un main rouge*, to translate that idiom literally, or *en flagrante* to be more idiomatically precise, which brings us, via the Latin *flagro*, to the still burning blaze that has not yet left the sooty fingerprint trace of its own cinders: the hand (as one might "show" or "play" a hand) of Blaise Cendrars.

And here we can start to see the uneasy strangeness of the boldest bluffed assertions in his claims for revealing "poèmes originaux" [original poems] published "sous mon nom" [under my own name]. The potential scandal, of course, or what would have mortified Cendrars's publisher, is that the poems are not "original," and he had not, in any event, published them under his own name, since the blatantly punning *Blaise Cendrars* was only ever a *nom de plume* for Frédéric Louis Sauser. An echo of the given name remains, however, through a sort of annominatic displacement that we shall see throughout this chapter. Henri Morier defines *annominatio* as an "allusion qui consiste à évoquer un nom au moyen d'un autre aux sonorités analogues" [allusion that consists of evoking a name (which is not fully pronounced) through another word with analogous sounds] or as "interprétation qui tire d'un nom propre la valeur exprimée par un nom commun de même sonorité" [interpretation that draws from a proper name the meaning expressed by its common noun homophone].[9] In the picturesque opening of "Mississippi," for one instance of such homophony, the riparian plants might well be weeping willows, suggesting the homonym of his patronym: *saussaie* [a place planted with willow trees], like the aquatic flora along that Mississippi, "entre deux berges marécageuses / plantes aquatiques qui continuent les acreages des cotonniers" [between marshy banks / waterplants merging into acres of cotton]. Elsewhere in *Kodak*, Cendrars explicitly names a "saule rabougri" [stunted willow], specifies where waterfowl seek refuge "sous le couvert des joncs des réseaux des saules" [under the cover of the rushes of willow branches], and singles out "saules arctiques" [arctic willows] bordering a heath.[10] Similarly, in the poem "Golden Gate," Cendrars seems to countersign his *nom de plume* with the punning implications of the "vieux grillage" that gave a name to the San Francisco tavern that is the poem's setting ("le vieux grillage qui a donné son nom à la maison" [the old grillwork which gave its name to the public house]) with a antanaclastic transfer of *bar* (metal rod) to *bar* (tap room). The obvious sense of *grillage*, of course, is ironwork, but the word also denotes, as the nineteenth-century French dictionary Littré confirms, the result of grilling: in a culinary sense, "to char," or, more generally, to transform material to ashes via the intense heat of direct flame. In other words: the cinders from a blaze (or, homophonically, in *other* other words: *Blaise* [Cendrars]). With a further paronomasia, we might note that "the result of burning" and "the mark made by burning with a hot iron," like the iron of the grill, would be a brand (*tison, cendre*). So with an appropriation of Le Rouge's text as his own, Cendrars transfers his own invented proper name to the trademarkable *brand* name of the Vieux Grillage.

The transferable property of a name, as a signature, is precisely what the poems in *Kodak* call into question: from the mystery of how Cendrars's signature style can possibly be the result of another writer's words to the status of the book's title itself. After its first printing, Cendrars's publisher was required to add the subtitle "(Documentaire)" [(Documentary)] to avoid a lawsuit by the Eastman Corporation, the owner of the *marque propriétaire* [brand name] *Kodak*. George Eastman and the company had discussed the word repeatedly over the years, from 1888 onward, telling and retelling the same stories in various venues. As one example of many, in a letter from 1906, Eastman writes, "In regard to the word Kodak I can say that it was a purely arbitrary combination of letters, not derived in whole or part from any existing word, arrived at after considerable search."[11] Indeed, *The Oxford English Dictionary* endorses this account with its etymology: "an arbitrary word invented by Mr. G. Eastman for trade-mark purposes" (Saussure, to be sure, would find the idea of an "arbitrary word" redundant).[12] As Eastman explained to the English Controller's Office, seeking to register the name as a trademark in England:

> This [*Kodak*] is not a foreign name or word; it was constructed by me to serve a definite purpose. It has the following merits as a trade-mark word: First, it is short. Second, it is not capable of mispronunciation. Third, it does not resemble anything in the art and cannot be associated with anything in the art except the *Kodak*.[13]

That *Kodak* tautologically recalls only itself is a point which Cendrars, in his eponymous collection, seems to set out to disprove.[14] The word does of course resemble others, particularly "foreign" names (foreign, that is, to English speakers), and it draws in their associations accordingly. To begin with, the word is a single, epenthetic letter away from *Kodiak*, one of the Aleutian Islands—and itself the title of a section of *Kodak*, which also includes the similarly formed "Klondyke" [Klondike].[15] More pointedly, Cendrars singles out "Kankal-Oysters," quoting from a passage in *Docteur Cornélius* but retaining the Breton spelling in place of the more academic *cancle*. At the same time, he includes "Canaques" [Kanaks] among the ethnicities catalogued in the closing line of "Victuailles" [Victuals], and tellingly alters Le Rouge's source text in order to repeat the distinctive collective name when he sets the scene in the Old Grillwork Bar by enumerating its clientele.[16] Where Le Rouge writes of "un certain nombre de Papous, de Maoris et de types d'autres races océaniennes" [some number of Papuans, Maoris, and other sorts of Oceanic races], Cendrars substitutes an indiscriminately colonizing "quelques Canaques" [some Kanaks].[17] *Kodiak, Klondike, kankal, Canaques*: against the aspirations of the proper name, Cendrars aggregates all of these "foreign" words with their doubled, framing voiceless velar stops in a single book, and so parades the "malheur de son arbitraire" [misery of its arbitrary nature] foretold by Jacques Derrida, a misfortune I will consider in greater detail later in this chapter.[18]

Not coincidentally, the other origin myth reiterated and propagated by Eastman was his love of the hard consonant *k*. In *System Magazine* in 1920 he confesses, "The letter K had been a favorite with me. It seemed a strong, incisive sort of letter."[19] In in a 1938 press release, the company avers, "philologically, the word Kodak is terse, abrupt to the point of rudeness, literally bitten off by firm and unyielding consonants at both ends, it snaps like a camera shutter in your face."[20] The word is thus the phonetic opposite, in the sense of a photographic negative, of Cendrars's own pseudonym, with its initial soft voiceless alveolar sibilant (under other circumstances, the *c* might too sound a firm, unyielding *k*) and near silent terminal consonant, reiterating the softness of its first and the slur of interior nasals and liquids. Moreover, where Eastman hoped that Kodak could not be mispronounced, Blaise Cendrars's pseudonym depends for its punning force precisely on its easy mispronunciation and its invitation to slippage, from the proximity of *blaise* and *blaze*, *cendre* and *cendrar*. In fact, the name itself encodes the technical description for its own vocal production. Such confusions perform the doubled signatory effect of the *nom de plume*, since *blaise* (as a proper dictionary lemma, though not a proper name), derives from *blaisement*, which it turn descends from *blésité*: a wounded diction, or miswording—the technical term for an improper enunciation or the solecism of a slight mispronunciation.[21] Specifically, the term describes the "vice de prononciation qui consiste à substituer une consonne faible à une plus forte" [the mispronunciation that consists in substituting a hard consonant with a weak one], precisely like the framing sibilants that replace the stops of *Kodak* in *Cendrars*.[22]

* * *

Although they had never met, Cendrars wrote to Guillaume Apollinaire in 1912 entreating the older poet to post his bail (he was in jail for shoplifting a copy of Apollinaire's *L'hérésiarque et Cie.*).[23] Cendrars was released before he could send the letter, but the two would meet a few months later, challenging and inspiring one another to create the "simultanéisme poétique" [poetic simultaneity] of a new literary cubism. Previously, Apollinaire had been working in rather different modes. After the clandestine publication of *Les onze mille verges; ou, Les amours d'un hospodar* (a pornographic novel signed simply "G. A."), in 1907, the first book under his name, *L'enchanteur pourrissant* [*The Putrefying Magician*], was issued in 1909. A hallucinatory, gothic prose-poem dialogue between the decaying Merlin and a nymph, interrupted by an assortment of animals which come to converse with him, the book was a debut thrice over. In addition to being the first openly acknowledged book by Apollinaire, it was the first book illustrated by André Derain (in this case, with stylized woodcut prints) and the first published by the avant-garde art dealer and champion of cubism Daniel-Henry Kahnweiler. As such, it carried a publisher's vignette, cut by Derain, which takes the form of a rebus. The device presents the HK monogram (Kahnweiler began using "Daniel" only later) positioned between two seashells, flamelike drops of water, and a diminutive set of Derain's own initials (figure 1). Not merely decorative, with a vibrant rusticity filling the tightly bordered space, the emblem hinges on a pun, since *coquille* ("shell" in French) is also a *terme de métier* denoting a kind of printer's error or

1 Daniel-Henry Kahnweiler colophon. From the title page of Max Jacob, *Saint Matorel* (Paris: Henry Kahnweiler, 1911), after a woodcut by André Derain (1907). Reva and David Logan Collection of Illustrated Books. Photograph: Fine Arts Museums of San Francisco.

typo. Specifically, it refers to what compositors term a paragramme: "toute faute consistant dans la substitution d'une lettre à une autre" [any error consisting of the substitution of one letter for another], as the *Littré* defines it. As Kahnweiler embarked on his new publishing career, the story goes, Apollinaire admonished him that "un bon éditeur ne doit pas tolérer plus de deux coquilles typographiques dans un livre" [a good editor ought not tolerate more than two typos per book].²⁴ So in an apotropaic attempt to ward off any typos in the text of the book that followed, Kahnweiler got them out of the way from the start by advertising those *deux coquilles* as part of the book's very imprint.

However anxious Apollinaire may have been about production standards for the publication of his first book, he knew that the *coquille* was a device that could be exploited rather than studiously avoided. A few years earlier, he had written a poem that elaborated the logic of the paragram. Formally, the verse rehearses a series of constrained and intentional typos, substituting one letter for another in a sort of shell game, as it were, and shuffling the resultant terms in a series of dizzying and distracting prestidigitations. The first of the poem's three columns, staggered beneath an oversize wood-type "A," reads: "Linda / Ilnda / Nilda / Indla / Indal / Lnida / Lndia / Lndai / Lidna / Lidan." The other columns continue accordingly. The poem was published in the Italian Futurist journal

Lacerba in 1914, and in that context it might be read as a proto-Dadaist sound poem (across the Alps, Hugo Ball's *lautgedichte* would be incanted in just a couple years' time) or as an example of the *distruzione della sintassi* [destruction of syntax] F. T. Marinetti had advocated the year before.[25] The poem originates, however, as an obsessive anagram of the first name of Apollinaire's teenage crush: Linda Molina da Silva. As much adolescent fixation as avant-garde experiment, the oversize letter *A* is not merely the free-floating glyph of *una parola in libertà* [a word in freedom] but the dedicatory "to": a poem to Linda, in all her permutations. When Apollinaire first began publishing poems in *Lacerba*, they appeared under the collective title "les banalités" [small talk, chitchat], the self-deprecating epithet he used to describe the manuscripts he had submitted to the journal's editor Ardengo Soffici. But with the poem to Linda, however, Apollinaire altered the title to "Quelconqueries" [Whatnots]. The word is an obvious synonym of sorts to *banalités*—both signify something diminutive, quotidian, inconsequential, and ephemeral—but the displacement from one word to a synonymous term is all to the point. *Quelconqueries* also, at a certain remove, reintroduces the printing pun that describes the formal, structural poetics of the poem "To Linda." If Derain had envisioned the homographic misprints as bivalves, *coquilles Saint-Jacques* or *pétoncles* [scallop shells], Apollinaire reimagines the shell as a *conque* [conch shell], as if to say "what anagrams!" "what shells!": *quel conqueries*. The pun may be goofy, but the homologies are neat (or *linda* [tidy, neat]): a word hidden inside another substitutes itself for what was a hidden word substituting for another to begin with: *deux coquilles*. Apollinaire would have known that the coquille was associated not only with the deformation of orthography but with a private language, through Marcel Schwob's "Glossaire du jargon de la coquille" and his studies into *Le Jargon des Coquillards*, the thieves' cant of the fifteenth-century Burgundian freebooters made famous by François Villon's use of the argot in his "ballades en jargon."[26]

Encrypting names by hiding words inside other words continues in Apollinaire's poetry, as one can see in his landmark "Lundi Rue Christine," which was published at the end of 1913 in the journal *Les Soirées de Paris*. The poem opens:

La mère de la concierge et la concierge laisseront tout passer
Si tu es un homme tu m'accompagneras ce soir
Il suffirait qu'un type maintînt la porte cochère
Pendant que l'autre monterait

Trois becs de gaz allumés
La patronne est poitrinaire

Quand tu auras fini nous jouerons une partie de jacquet
Un chef d'orchestre qui a mal à la gorge
Quand tu viendras à Tunis je te ferai fumer du kief

Ça a l'air de rimer

[The concierge's mother and the concierge will let anybody in
If you're a man you'll go with me tonight
All we would need is one guy to watch the main door
While the other one goes up

Three lit gas jets
The boss has TB
When you're done we'll play a round of backgammon
An orchestra conductor with a sore throat
When you come to Tunis I'll make sure you get a bowl of dope to smoke

That almost rhymes]

The verse is the epitome of what Apollinaire called his "poèmes-conversation" [conversation-poems], a collage of scattered, telegraphic impressions of Christine Street in Paris one Monday, as the title captions, interpolated with snippets of overheard café conversations—often highlighting the sense of eavesdropping by amplifying the personal and private, or even conspiratorial and secretive, aspects of colloquies taking place in public spaces.[27] The poem opens, for instance, with what sounds like the planning for some illegal scheme, a trespass at the very least, and continues throughout with less nefarious gossip about personal finances, health, and sexual relationships.[28] Whether the lines are truly unedited documentation of idiomatic speech or merely simulated with careful craft to appear as such, the effect is achieved because Apollinaire withdraws as speaker, serving less as the traditional enunciatory subject of romantic poetry and more as a mute recording mechanism or orchestrator. Indeed, the "chef d'orchestre" [conductor] may be a figure for this new poetic agency in the conversation-poem: controlling the various independent musical voices but not himself able to speak—at least not in his usual voice or with full expressive force—because of the "mal à la gorge" [sore throat]. However oblique the identification of poet and conductor, and even without speaking as an identifiable speaker in his own voice, Apollinaire still appears in the poem, quite literally, with those three lit gas jets and the tubercular boss. In a fragmented onomastic self-portrait, like a reflection in the window glasses of a city street, the name *Apollinaire* has been skewed like the planes of a cubist painting:

> Trois becs de gaz allumés
> La patronne est poitrinaire

Shunting, off-kilter, in a zigzag between the lines, the two end-words provide *a-po-ll-inaire*.[29] Far more than any other candidate (*Tunis* and *kief* are distant possibilities), "ça a l'air de rimer" [that almost rhymes, it rings a bell], as Apollinaire writes a few lines later, perhaps prompting the attentive reader to look back and consider just what has echoed in lines without any apparent proximate vocalic pairing.

The assertion is pointedly ironic in a poem that derives its energy not from correspondence, but from discrepancy. In his consideration of the disjunctive fragments in "Lundi Rue Christine," David Sweet wonders, "would any collage element have produced the effect of a non sequitur, or is this particular one necessary as a suggestive link to some other theme in the poem"? Thematically, perhaps not, but the suggestive link is instead alphabetic. "If the order of the phrases is necessary for the poetic effects Apollinaire wants to produce," Sweet continues, "those effects may indeed be so subtle as to be indistinguishable from those produced by some other, purely chance arrangement he might have made."[30] Apollinaire's effect may be subtle, but it is indeed distinguishable if one is looking for elements below the level of the referential word.

Apollinaire was pioneering his modernist lyrics at the very moment Ferdinand de Saussure was abandoning his investigations into encrypted names in poetry—in part, ironically, because he could not find confirmation of the practice by contemporary poets. Saussure's research into what he termed "hypogrammes," to indicate a signature inscribed below (*hypo-*) the level of the text, or "cryptogrammes," to indicate the hidden presence of a name, began with his conviction "that Latin poetry was structured by the coded dispersal (or dissemination) of an underlying word or proper name."[31] Exemplifying the "action du signifiant" [action of the signifier], for Julia Kristeva, herself one of the theorists directly influenced by Saussure's hypogram notebooks, "Saussure découvre la dissémination de ce qu'il croit être un nom de chef ou de Dieu à travers le texte" [Saussure discovers the dissemination throughout the text of what he believes to be the name of a leader or god].[32] That name was reconstituted from patterns of phonic elements articulated (or disarticulated, as it were) below the level of the word and irrespective of morphemes. A species of paragram or anagram (Saussure used these words as well, proliferating terminology as he grappled with the exact nature and extent of the phenomenon he thought he had uncovered), these cryptograms took the form of dismembered and disarticulated phonemes scattered in discrete fragments through lines of verse, but adding up—when reassembled—to a dedicatory name that the poem did not otherwise mention. The patterns, perhaps apophenic, involved complicated rules often governing multiple lines to encompass a doubled doubling of phonemes, but the basic idea is easy to grasp; the god Apollo, to take one of Saussure's more succinct examples of an unnamed name, and one that serves as the source for Apollinaire's own *nom de plume*, might be reconstituted, twice over, from the syllables in Titus Livy's oracular line from the *History of Rome*: "*Donom amplom victor ad mea templa portato*" [let the winner convey an abundant offering to my temple].

In chapter 5, I will discuss Michael Riffaterre's development of Saussure's cryptogrammic project as a theory of poetic composition more generally, but for now I want to argue for the reasons that Apollinaire's encryption of his name countersigns his poem with a double signature. To begin with, in a text composed with the kind of collage technique we have already noted, the arranged fragments of the poet's name operate as a sort of formal allegory of the poetics that would make Apollinaire a literary celebrity of the avant-garde. One could quote from any number of suggestively worded critical commentaries to make the point, but I will draw from Hans Robert Jauss's touchstone essay on the poem, which I quote more or less at random but in order to demonstrate, above all, that I am not weighting the evidence in my favor by describing the poem in ways that will lead, circularly, to my own conclusion. In Jauss's account of Apollinaire's poem, "it is up to the reader to search for the lost subject, dissolved in the pure contingency of an alien speech."[33] Jauss continues to observe that with the kind of verbal collage advanced by the conversation-poem against the conventions of the romantic lyric which it challenged, in which Apollinaire orchestrates found demotic material rather than generating expressive, discursive utterances in a personal, subjective voice, "the poet himself is now no longer quite tangible as a stable reference point or as a privileged perspective" and the "the lyrical 'I'" accordingly comes to be "dismembered and dispersed."[34] Jauss's words could be describing the unstable inscription of *Apollinaire*, which is no longer quite coherent and can only be perceived from multiple, shifting viewpoints in motion vertically between adjacent lines. With a similar aptness, the lyrical persona of the poet himself, in the metonymic form of his proper name, is indeed "dismembered and dispersed" in alphabetic fragments through *allumés* and *poitrinaire*. "It follows," Jauss continues, "not only that the reader can interpret the poem in various perspectives, but that he must do so, seeking possible consistencies and repeatedly forming different shapes out of the 'broken images.'"[35] The encryption of *Apollinaire* by Apollinaire performs a literalization of the way in which his poetics is figured.

Fracturing the word as a painter might break an image into kaleidoscopic parts, Apollinaire pursues a linguistic version of the ruptures and spatial displacements that characterize painterly cubism as one of the key gestures in its compositional repertoire. Specifically, the frequent series of shunted refractions that are part of the grammar of analytic cubism provide a salient analogue to Apollinaire's cryptonomy. Recall, for a specific example, Pablo Picasso's famous 1910 portrait of Kahnweiler (Art Institute, Chicago; figure 2), where a series of stepped bracket forms about a third of the way up the central right of the canvas ascend in an incremental arc on the edge of the illuminated cone that may correspond to the sitter's sleeve (figure 3). Such "canting and tilting is Cubism's lifeblood" as T. J. Clark writes, understanding these series of series—the repetition of "straight repetitions of the surface further back"—as the symptomatic outbreak of an irrational logic: the "mad internal multiplying" of a "lunatic redundancy."[36] Those multiplications can also be clearly seen in Picasso's *Le Poète* from the following year (1911, Solomon R. Guggenheim Museum; figure 4), with the slight seesaw of right-angle brackets in stair-step behind and slightly to the left of a less clearly delineated sweep of similar forms pitched at varying angles (figure 5).

Such effects are part of the fundamental idiom of cubism, and not limited to Picasso's compositional repertoire. The visual logic of an abstracted form that is fragmented but shifted in a replicating series, continuing the form in a stair-step manner, is evident as well in the final panel of Sonia Delaunay's illustration in *La Prose de la Transsibérien*, where the top of the figure representing the Tour Eiffel is broken by the embracing sweep of the Grande Roue de l'Exposition de 1900, in the guise of an orange arc; the tower figure then skews slightly to the right before continuing upward into the blue. An arc itself is broken in Delaunay's 1913 *Simultaneous Contrasts* (Museo Nacional Thyssen-Bornemisza, Madrid), which manifests the same logic of rupture and displacement, as the orange and purple bands in the center right of the canvas continue, following the interruption of a yellow swell and green field, but in a way that suggests either an upward lateral repositioning, to maintain the perspectival logic, or a downward repositioning of the cut and pasted forms. Or again, for one more example, from Robert Delaunay's *Fenêtres ouvertes simultanément (1ère partie, 3ème motif)* [*Simultaneously Open Windows (First Part, Third Motif)*], dated 1912 (Tate Modern, London), the salient form of the image, a curved triangular horn, both refers to the riveted iron silhouette of the Tour Eiffel and also, separately, takes part in the geometric design

2 Pablo Picasso, *Daniel-Henry Kahnweiler* (autumn 1910). Oil on canvas, 100.4 × 72.4 cm. Gift of Mrs. Gilbert W. Chapman in memory of Charles B. Goodspeed (1948.561). © 2019 Estate of Pablo Picasso/Artists Rights Society, New York. Photograph: Art Institute of Chicago/Art Resource, New York.

3 Pablo Picasso, *Daniel-Henry Kahnweiler* (detail of figure 2).

that balances chromatic units of curved and rectilinear shapes in a gridded screen. The green curve of the tower's flank is articulated and continued at one step's remove in the central left. And so on, across canvases from any number of artists from the period. The stepped repetition of a fragmented form is such an integral compositional move in cubism that its instances are ubiquitous. The viewer of such works, by habit, mentally reassembles these images by imaginatively realigning the jigsawed composition in order to account for a cumulative composition of assimilated parts, and precisely the same readerly technique is required to fit the neatly disarticulated *Apollinaire* back together into a lexical gestalt from its vertical and horizontal stair-step displacements in "Lundi Rue Christine." Apollinaire's dissemination of the letters of his name thus moves with more than merely a general sense of fragmentation; it moves with the very geometry of "canting and tilting" familiar to the cubist imagination.

That fragment and fracture, moreover, is the signature poetic mode pioneered by Apollinaire in his simultaneous, urban poèmes-conversations, and so when his own name is fragmented the couplet countersigns: it inscribes the signature of a signature in the fullest sense of the term

4 Pablo Picasso, *The Poet* (*Le Poète*) (August 1911). Oil on linen, 131.2 × 89.5 cm. Peggy Guggenheim Collection, Venice, 1976. © 2019 Estate of Pablo Picasso/Artists Rights Society, New York. Photograph: Solomon R. Guggenheim Foundation/Art Resource, New York.

5 Pablo Picasso, *The Poet* (*Le Poète*) (detail of figure 4).

elaborated by Jacques Derrida in his essay on Francis Ponge (a writer to whom I will turn in chapter 5). To begin with, a signature in the most conventional sense of the identifying and authenticating name of a writer—what might be autographed at the end of a manuscript, or inscribed in a dedication copy of a book—obtains as usual.[37] But in special cases like those of Ponge, two postscripts are addended, each with their own "sigle énigmatique" [enigmatic sigil].[38] First, a signature in the sense of "a distinctive technique, attribute, product, etc. which is identified or associated with a particular person," as in a *signature style*.[39] For Ponge, that style includes a poetics of absorption and cleansing: incorporating dictionary definitions into his poems in a series of revised versions which repeatedly polish and clarify the phrasing. Second, that style is named in turn by words related to the author's name as a material signifier among others. Ponge's poetics, for instance, perform the absorptive and clarifying work of *l'éponge* [the sponge]—a neat paragram of *ponge*. Words, as Saussure cautioned against naïve beliefs about language, are not the names for things, and Derrida reminds us in turn that names are themselves things:

material signifiers just like every other word in the sign system of a language. Indeed, for proper names to function as words, to be comprehensible at all in language, they must take their place along the chain of signifiers to the point where "il n'y a pas de nom propre. Ce qu'on appelle du nom commun générique 'nom propre' doit bien fonctionner, lui aussi, dans un système de différences" [there is no proper name. What is called by the generic common noun "proper name" must function, it too, in a system of differences].⁴⁰ As Derrida explicates elsewhere:

> Le nom propre, en son aléatoire, devrait n'avoir aucun sens, et s'épuiser en reference immediate. Or le chance ou le Malheur de son arbitraire (toujours autre dans chaque cas), c'est que son inscription dans la langue l'affecte toujours d'une potentialité de sens; et de n'être plus propre dès lors qu'il signifie.
>
> [The proper name, in its aleatoriness, should have no meaning and should spend itself in immediate reference. But the chance or misery of its arbitrary character (always other in each case), is that its inscription in language always invests it with a potential for meaning, and for no longer being proper once it has meaning.]⁴¹

In the case of "Lundi Rue Christine," the disarticulation, dissemination, and recombination of the constituent elements, graphemic and phonemic, of *Apollinaire* countersigns as the signature of a signature. On the one hand, the inscription is a signature move of Apollinaire's fragmenting poetics pitched at the level of the word rather than the phrase. At the same time, it is an example of how signatures themselves, in the Derridean sense, regain the meaning lost to proper names through the endless enmeshment of the signifier in its network of substitutions and differences. Apollinaire's application of his signature technique to his own signature calls attention to the recombinatory network of differences which threaten the proper name in what Derrida termed "dissemination": the ways in which the trace of the signifier moves in order to generate and multiply meaning, always contingent and unstable, because the same movement in turn leads back to "la force et la forme de sa disruption crèvent l'horizon sémantique" [the force and form of its disarrangement puncturing the semantic horizon] of any text.⁴² Uncontrollable and contingent chance, like the proximity of a name to some other common noun, announces the generating florescence and disintegration that define Derridean dissemination and that, for Derrida, defines the name: "la structure du nom propre en elle-même engage ce processus. Le nom propre est fait pour ça" [the structure of the proper name sets this process (of dissemination) in motion.

That's what a proper name is for].⁴³ So by signing in the mode of the signature, and in his own signature mode, Apollinaire affirms the final codicil which names the process of dissemination itself through its synonym *polliniser* [pollinate].⁴⁴ Let me be immediately clear that while I do in fact suspect the deliberate interpolation of the poet's name in the adjacent "allumées" and "poitrinaire," I do not mean to suggest that Apollinaire was consciously encrypting *polliniser* in that same poem at some hidden remove (although he does in fact proffer the kernel as the keyword in the final line of his famous "Tristesse d'une Étoile," where Apollinaire explicitly identifies "pollen" as his inner essence).⁴⁵ Instead, my claim here is that the same procedure can be at once encoded and unintended, and in both cases made available through sheer chance, and that the two eventualities are all to the point, given that both together illustrate the very definition of dissemination at issue here. "A name of coincidence meets," as Lyn Hejinian has written.⁴⁶ *À polliniser en l'air*: to be pollinated by the breeze; to disseminate through a lyric, through the series of individual notes that go to make up the melodic line of a song in the way that individual letters make up a line of text.⁴⁷ The poem thus exhibits "toutes les manières de faire ça, toutes les operations par lesquelles on peut faire de sa signature un texte, de son texte une chose et de la chose sa signature" [all the operations by which one can make of one's signature a text, of one's text a thing, and, of the thing, one's signature].⁴⁸

* * *

Apollinaire was not alone in making a poetic text from his name. Gertrude Stein also exploits the near rhyme of his name in order to generate the first line of her "Guillaume Apollinaire," a sort of epigraphic encomium to her fellow poet.⁴⁹ Stein was an early advocate and promoter of Apollinaire—she had been urging galleries to carry *L'enchanteur pourrisant* since its publication—and in 1913 she composed her portrait, which reads in its entirety:

Give known or pin ware.
Fancy teethe, gas strips.
Elbow elect, sour stout pore, pore caesar, pour state at.
Leave eye lesson I. Leave I. Lessons. I. Leave I lessons, I.

Guillaume Apollinaire obviously provides the phonic maquette for "Give known or pin ware"; not quite strictly homophonic, but "ça a l'air de rimer," and the resemblance—one of Stein's totem words in her thinking about portraiture—is unmistakable. However, his name also underwrites other lines in less obvious way, even as the status of his exact name is not itself obvious or stable. The gallicized "Guillaume Apollinaire" was the *nom de plume* adopted to coincide with a move to Paris just before the turn of the century, where he was legally registered as "Guillaume de Kostrowitzky" (as Apollinaire would write, in the final line of his poem "La Victoire": "Et que tout ait un nom nouveau" [may everything have a new name!]). But even his mother, in fact, recorded inconsistent versions of his name throughout his youth. Born something like Wilhelm Apollinaris Albertus de Kostrowitzky, the onomastic series brings together a babble of national origins: the aristocratic Slavic family name from his Polish mother, the Latinate *Apollinaris Albertus*, and the Germanic *Wilhelm*. His grandfather was a member of the Vatican's Pontifical Swiss Guards and his father—although Guillaume encouraged the rumor that he had been sired by the pope himself, if not a high-ranking cardinal—was probably also in the Guards, a Swiss soldier from Grisons, where German, Italian, and Romansh are all spoken. Indeed, Apollinaire grew up speaking Italian, and before moving to Paris and adopting French (though never fully mastering which direction the accents went) he learned Walloon, even writing his first poems in the Belgian dialect. In the army, he was called Kostro L'Exquis [Top Shelf Cointreau].[50] Throughout, his mother and brother called him "Wilhelm," like the Kaiser. But the translation went both ways. As Stein recounts, with mannered obliquity, in *The Autobiography of Alice B. Toklas*:

> Olga Picasso, the wife of Picasso, told us that the night of the armistice Guillaume Apollinaire died, that they were with him that whole evening and it was warm and the windows were open and the crowd passing were shouting, à bas Guillaume, down with William and as everyone always called Guillaume Apollinaire Guillaume, even in his death agony it troubled him.[51]

The refrain "à bas Guillaume" was, of course, chanted on 11 November 1918 not against the famous poet but against Kaiser Wilhelm ("Guillaume," to Gallic speakers). "Poor Guillaume," as Stein christens Apollinaire in the *Autobiography*, mistaken for Kaiser, *pour César*, or here, "pore caesar," balancing the confused names against the epithets, *pore* for *poor*, as a close reading (*pore*: "to study or read earnestly or with intense concentration") across Stein's texts reveals. Names, in fact, seem to be at issue from the very first words of Stein's portrait, where "Give known," given in place of *Guillaume*, suggests not only what can be assumed, as in science or math—the datum or axiom that is "given or known," as the hendiadys has it—but also the given name, or *nom* [name] in French, in opposition to the alias of an assumed name (to take the other sense of assumption).⁵² Some decades later, Stein herself would learn the treacherousness inherent in the logic of the signature, and the stakes of having a given name become known, when a jealous Alice B. Toklas learned of Stein's earlier affair with May Bookstaver and insisted on purging most of the instances of the words *may* and *May* from the manuscript of *Stanzas in Meditation*, replacing them with *can* and *April*.⁵³

Whether on cubist canvases or in cubist poems, we find the same semiotic understanding: marks both refer and pattern; they can construct semantic messages, but they also always form material arrangements. Or, to put this slightly differently, words are doubly referential: pointing to concepts as well as pointing to other, perhaps semantically unrelated, words.⁵⁴ The rest of Stein's portrait poem exploits this doubled referentiality to invite associations that it refuses to confirm. "Elbow" perhaps yields the homophonic *elle est beau* [she is handsome], in the same way a reader might be able to grasp the macaronic sounds of *pour saisir* [in order to grasp] behind "pore caesar" or even *fantaisiste* behind "fancy teethe." However fantastic such a translation might sound, we might recall that at precisely the moment Stein was writing her portrait, Apollinaire was popularly associated with writers like André Salmon, Francis Carco, and Max Jacob as part of an *école fantaisiste*; indeed, Amy Lowell, in denouncing the "extreme fad" of the movement, erroneously identified Apollinaire as its "chief priest."⁵⁵ If sound leads across languages from "fancy" to *fin* ("end," in French), it might also lead the eye toward the look of *enfants*, or those who, without language (Latin *in* [privative] + *fans* [from *fari*, to speak]), have nonetheless, as Ulla Dydo suggests, begun to "teethe."⁵⁶ By the same token, "sour stout," beyond the sense of a poured bitter beer, gives the look—but not the sound—of *surtout*: an "eye lesson," or visual reading (*leçon*) that leaves (*laisson*) above all the lasting impression of the word for "above all" (*surtout*) in French. A surtout, as a noun, however, is a word in both French and English denoting a particular type of greatcoat or overcoat (what goes "above all" other clothing)—precisely the kind of garment one might wear ("ware") if it pours ("pour state"). And in fact, in all weather, and whether in a state of war ("ware"), in which one would fight patriotically *pour l'état*, or not, a surtout was the signature sartorial accouterment of Kaiser Wilhelm, becoming a key metonymic part of his iconography. Taking the shared given name as establishing a correspondence between the two men, and with *poor* and *pour* facilitating exchange through the porous border between their appellations, Stein transfers the popular imagination's association of the greatcoat with Kaiser Wilhelm to Apollinaire. Making connections with clothing, finally, is itself one of the possible connections invited by Stein's poem, with its language of vestiary fasteners: "pin," "teeth[e]" (as in the "strip" of a clasp locker, or what would come to be called a zipper), and the "eye" of hooks and grommets. If these leave the reader of this radically indeterminate poem with the sense that they are highly tenuous textual connections, the final lesson of the poem may be that they are all themselves points of tenuous and easily undone textile connection—temporarily pinned but not sewn shut.

* * *

About a decade after writing "Guillaume Apollinaire," Stein was herself the subject of a portrait poem by Mina Loy. Hailing her as the Marie "Curie / of the laboratory / of vocabulary," Loy pictures Stein extracting powerful elements below the level of the word and beyond "consciousness" to release a language working independently of human intentions and free from the psychologies of its speakers.[57] Loy would introduce Stein, on another occasion, in similar terms as "la madame Curie du langage" [the Madame Curie of language].[58] Where Curie crushed and proved pitchblende to extract radium, Stein blended pitches to unleash the generative semantic heat of phrases such as "give known" beneath *Guillaume*. Loy had undertaken similar experiments in her "Songs to Joannes," the very title of which marks the instability of proper names as they enter into language. A variant of *Johannes*, the translation of the Italian *Giovanni*, the poem dedicates itself to Giovanni Papini, with whom Loy had an affair while in Florence in the mid-1910s, and who had already been given an alternate pseudonym in Loy's "Giovanni Franchi," where he is derisively rechristened "Giovanni Bapini" (Loy's cognomina, if obvious, are hardly frank [*franchi*] at all).[59] The play with proper names continues, as Loy was given to what her literary executor has termed a "pseudonymania."[60] The subtitle of her *poème à clef* "Effectual Marriage," for example, transparently names and entwines the two lovers with the spooneristic "Gina and Miovanni," while in an unpublished manuscript titled "Mi and Lo" she split herself into two, according to the syllabic logic of her given and surname, to produce the speakers for a philosophical dialogue.[61] Like the "Alphabet That Builds Itself," a spring-loaded, magnetic toy that Loy later designed for F. A. O. Schwarz, in which letters are animated and self-motivating, her anagrams evince an alphabetic imagination "of language as kinetic [...], recombinant, and open to mutation."[62] In "Lions' Jaws," another account of her time in Florence, a series of recombinant and mutating monikers veil with an equally thin set of disguises and satirical sobriquets; Loy scrambles to do "secret service" as "Nima Lyo, alias Anim Yol, alias / Imna Oly," while Filippo Tommaso Marinetti, one of her other lovers from the period and an apex in the erotic triangle that disillusioned

Loy and irreparably fractured the Futurist movement, masquerades as "Raminetti," with connotations of boorish virility.⁶³ Marinetti makes a cameo in "Songs to Joannes" as well, in a line which can be read somewhere between a taunt to incite Papini's jealousy and an exhausted, ironic, tell-me-about-it acknowledgment to the reader: "I know The Wire-Puller intimately."⁶⁴ *Pace* Matthew Hofer, who finds the "Songs" to be "without anagrammatic name play," we can see precisely such play in action here, if at a remove.⁶⁵ Capitalized as a proper name, the phrase depends on synonymy and paragram to move from *marionetter* to *Marinetti*.⁶⁶ The link is overdetermined and the irony is cutting, since Marinetti sought to associate himself with "l'immaginazione *senza fili*" [the *wireless* imagination]. Rather than be freed from wires, like the new telegraph, here he pulls them (in parallel to the porcine figure of the opening song who "pull[s] a weed" and the boy "pulling [the wires of Edwardian-era] door bells" to disturb the complacent).⁶⁷ "Songs" may announce the presence of "uninterpretable cryptonyms" (in poem XXIX) and "something that has a new name" (in XIII), but its encrypted renominations can be decoded, if not definitively interpreted, with the right procedures for reading.⁶⁸

Equipped with that methodology, we can see ways in which Papini is also named in "Songs," even more obliquely, but with the same logic of substitution and translation. Just as *mari+* works to summon the specter of Marinetti from an etymologically unrelated word, the fragmentation of Papini's name, transmuting across languages, continues to indict the subject behind the emotionally charged fragments that account for the stages of his affair with Loy.⁶⁹ In the process, what we might call the "*pap+* effect" explains some of the poem's oddest and most stilted phrasing. For example, in contrast to the hypothetical lepidopterous offspring of the third song ("we might have given birth to a butterfly"), one of the protagonists in the fourth song "bore a baby / In a padded porte-enfant."⁷⁰ The parallel alliteration, analogues to the doubled *p* in *Papini*, account in part for the shift to French, with the antanaclasis of "bore" (which returns in poem XXV in the sense of "drill into") hinged between "give birth to (offspring)" and "carry" (*porter*).⁷¹ But the more familiar English word for a child-carrier at the time would have been *papoose*. Conversely, the introduction of the French term (like the closing "litterateur") invites the reader to consider that the "butterfly" in the previous poem would be a *papillon*. Loy had lived for several years in Paris before moving to Florence, and she confessed that she thought in "a subconscious muddle of foreign languages."⁷² The macaronic connection would corroborate Tim Hancock's conclusion, arrived at through an entirely different reading strategy, that the butterfly—an image "that Papini uses several times in his autobiography," which Loy had been reading at the time—is a reference to Papini, via *Lacerba*, the "war-mongering newspaper with its red masthead" that he had been editing as an organ for the Futurist cause.[73]

The literal "eclosion" of names "from their incognitoes" continues with "flowered flummery."[74] At one level, the phrase points to the language of decoration in the poem. Denoting "trifles, useless trappings or ornaments," flummery is to fashion what florid is to language. In "Songs," those ornaments appear directly in such details as the trimmings of "a sarsanet ribbon" and the "tassels" on "the fringe of the towel"; but they would also be the accouterments of "the prig of passion."[75] A "prig," in the sense that indicates "a dandy, a fop," connotes a person arrogant with affected precision and strutting with preening finesse.[76] A synonym for "prig," in that sense, and a word idiomatically paired with it, is *papinjay* or *popinjay* (as in the popular nineteenth-century comic song "Mister Timothy Popinjay Prig"), named "with allusion to the bird's gaudy plumage [...]: a shallow, vain, or conceited person."[77] "Feathers," as song X drily concludes, "are strewn."[78] Moreover, the word in Italian (famous from Mozart's variants as characters in *Die Zauberflöte*) is *pappagallo*, which beyond its literal avian meaning serves as the antonomastic "wolf" of a man, figuratively: "a sexually aggressive male, a would-be seducer," a man who makes sexual advances to many women (precisely as Loy paints the Futurists in "Lions' Jaws," who aspire to emulate Gabriele D'Annunzio, a "fancier of lyrical birds" with "fashions in lechery" that make him the "conquerer" of an "abandoned harem").[79] Vain and predatory, the popinjay-vain "Bapini is popular in Vanity Fair," as a line from "Lions' Jaws" puts it, referring to his article "Don Juan's Lament."[80]

The theme is clear enough, but the word "seduce" itself, significantly, occurs in song XXIX; its etymology (*se* + *ducere*, literally to lead astray) appears in XIX as "leading astray," and with a calembour picking up on the star (Greek άστρο, Latin *astrum*, French *astre*), "seduce" explains the "star-topped" weed pulled by Pig Cupid in the opening scene.[81] That weed, specifically, is likely *Aster subulatus*, from the Latin *suere* [to sew], since the plant plucked by Pig Cupid is found "among wild oats   sewn"—in this case, moreover, it is picked by a swine related to a *sow*.[82] Additional echoes follow in later songs in the "starry ceiling" of the room of assignation, a move from "star to star," and the "stars in a stare."[83] This repetition spins a web of words that explain why in song XVI "cob-webs" (French *toiles*, a paragram of *étoiles* [stars]) would be in parallel to "the sea," given the striking image of the opening poem's "constellations in an ocean."[84] The pun is itself a trope in modern French poetry, but the connections continue at another remove, explaining curious phrasings elsewhere in the "Songs."[85] Reinforced by the placement of the ocean's constellations in parallel to a firework's "eye" (or, in other words, what would *see* [sea]), the visual emphasis of the "stars in a stare" and "Wisdom's eyes" vaulted to the "starry ceiling" (pronounced *see*-ling) is then displaced to other instances of *toiles* such as "Hide and seek in love and cob-webs," and the scene led to by the interminable "steps" or stairs [*stares*] that connect the apartments of the star-crossed lovers to a scene of blinding whiteness:

> White   where there is nothing to see
> But a white towel
> Wipes the cymophanous sweat
> —Mist rise of living—
> From your
> Etiolate body[86]

If "towel" echoes *toile* phonetically (as well as being itself likely made of linen, or toile), the association also explains the stanza's most distinctive vocabulary and accounts for the "homophonous" mysteries ("mist rise") of the technical and scientific terms "cymophanous" (denoting "opalescent, chatoyant"—the brand name, not coincidentally, that Loy proposed for the plastic she invented) and "etiolate" (of plants, to bleach from lack of light, here from the "withdrawal of your sun").[87] But *cymophanous* also denotes something "having a wavy, floating light," and it derives from the Greek κῦμα [wave], like those of the sea, while "etiolate" is of course an anagram of the unwritten but nonetheless ubiquitous *etoile*. The logics here indeed evince poetic thinking in a "subconscious muddle of foreign languages," and they are a good reminder that readers of Loy's poetry should not stop at just the most obvious wordplay. Like the overdetermined "wire" and *marionette* that work in tandem to triangulate *Marinetti*, "star" and "stare" are entwined in the logic that links vision to stars, via "ocean" and *sea/see*, over and above their obvious anagrammatic pairing.

Finally, "flummery" simultaneously inscribes Papini's name in the "Songs" by an entirely different route, or root, as well. If the pig among the oats points doubly to the homograph *sow*, those oats also tie back to the ingredient and synonym of flummery: "'a kind of food made by coagulation of wheatflower or oatmeal' (Johnson). Cf. *sowens*."[88] As Tobias Smollett provides the interchangeable terms in *Humphry Clinker*: "at night they sup on sowens or flummery of oat-meal."[89] The synonymous *sowens*, as Johnson and Smollett knew, denotes:

> an article of diet formerly in common use in Scotland (and some parts of Ireland), consisting of farinaceous matter extracted from the bran or husks of oats by steeping in water, allowed to ferment slightly, and prepared by boiling.[90]

Once again, however, the more common Anglo-English word for such "semi-liquid food, such as that considered suitable for babies or invalids, usually made from bread, meal, etc., moistened with water or milk," to bring us back to Papini, is *pap*.[91] Ultimately, this *pap*+ logic would have continued and concluded on the final page of the poem, as Loy envisaged it printed, with the summation of the entire poem as sheer *paper*: "one whole entirely blank page with nothing on it," as Loy's unrealized instructions for the typographic layout of the poem specified.[92] Reading symbolically, to adduce his reincarnation as the Mozartian Don Giovanni and the generic womanizing Don Juan, Suzanne Churchill finds that "Papini's name is encoded in 'Songs to Joannes' through a series of translations and disguises."[93] But, as I hope to have demonstrated, his name is also encoded in more literal and less figurative ways, via material inscription rather than literary allusion, refracted through the text of "Songs" in a kaleidoscope of repeated fragments.

Loy countersigns the poem, in the Derridean sense, with her own name as well, which should come as no surprise; not only did she rechristen others, but "she wrote under an elaborate system of anagrammatically and numerologically derived pseudonyms."[94] To begin with, we can note obvious sets of contrasted themes: on the one hand, a set that includes "virginity" (and the "virginal"), "clear carving," "pure white," and "a haloed ascetic"; on the other hand, "erotic garbage," an "irate pornographer," "pestilent / Tear drops," the "muddled" and unwashed.[95] The dyad is neatly summed by the metaphoric couplet "One wing has been washed in the rain / The other will never be clean any more." The diametric poles, in other words, set the scale for a "comparative purity," the definition of *alloy*, which also describes the ideal admixture of the "inseparable" melding of lovers "together [...] / Into the terrific Nirvana."[96] In contrast to the "inviolable" and "inviolate" egos kept separate by sex without communion, the poems posit a "laughter in solution" as bodies "solve in the humid carnage" (where the elided link between the parallel of "solution" and "[dis]solve" seems to be the synonym for "carnage": s<u>laughter</u>).[97] Such dissolution "melts some of us," setting up the pun on "smelt" in song XXVIII, which points with a wink to the odiferous (foregrounded in the poem as "pollen smelling," "disheartening odour," and "scum" stuffed into "nostrils").[98] But "smelt" more directly denotes the fusion of metal ore into an alloy, or a *loy* as the word is aphetically formed.[99] Loy further corroborates that identification of herself with admixture when she owns the "mongrel" identity described in her long biographical poem "Anglo-Mongrels and the Rose." Indeed, Loy's own hypocoristic simultaneously enacts and refers to alloying. Acquired during her studies in München (a city which derives its name, coincidentally, from the Bavarian *Minna*), but answered to long after, the nickname was a doozy. As "Dusie" or "Ducie" Loy signed her confession to the fact that she often hesitated in conversation between using the familiar and the formal, a lack of boundaries and adherence to hierarchical conventions that extended even to her grasp of German grammar and the difference between *Du* [you (familiar)] and *sie* [you (polite)].[100] With yet further possibilities "for a much more radical degree of distancing," Sarah Hayden notes the numbers and genders that *sie* (or *Sie*) leave undifferentiated when the word is incorporated into the portmanteau moniker.[101]

With a poetic style defined by amalgamations—of recherché and slang lexicons, classical literary allusions and contemporary avant-garde references, the elevated and the vulgar, *et cetera*—and monikers that enact (*Dusie*) or denote (*Loy*) fusion, Loy collapses signature and signature style. "Songs to Joannes," in particular, with its narrative of marital infidelities, is a work of adulteration in all senses of the word. Moreover, Loy's technique of encoding "uninterpretable cryptonyms" ultimately destabilizes the enigmatic crux of the final poem, a concise appositional assertion, defining and personifying: "Love—the preeminent litterateur."[102] The affectation, or merely the shift to French, draws attention to the artifice of the final word and the work it does to balance the series' opening reference to "erotic garbage" with the *litter* that emerges from it.[103] The technique has already been offered as a protocol for reading by Loy's earlier extraction, with a gleeful frisson, of "cock" and "door" from *shuttlecock* and *battledore* in song X. With a similar fragmentation of "litterateur," the series proposes a ratio: the "erotic" is to "Love" as "garbage" is to *litter*. The precarious progression from literature to litter was in fact how Loy figured history itself: "the cultures of all societies are composed of such debris as might litter the floors from an evacuated printing house."[104]

In the process of generating *litter* from "litterateur," the final line of the series recalls the conclusion of song IV: "—Sweeping the brood clean out."[105] The emphatic, colloquial sense of "clean out" as signifying something done entirely or completely underscores the finality of the gesture; at the same time, cleaning out in the sense of cleansing not only enters into the songs' linked themes of purity and garbage but brings out the unwritten *broom* triangulated by its idiomatic association with "sweeping" and its graphemic proximity to "brood." On the face of it, the idea would seem to be that romantic love—the inherited Victorian convention critiqued by Loy for its patriarchal manipulations and something to be swept clean in the new world of the New Woman in the twentieth century—has been the clichéd subject of the lyric tradition.[106] In general, certainly, "Songs" appears to attack both the antiquated misogyny of Victorian "Love" and the new misogyny of the Futurists' indifferent sexual conquests. Specifically, the last poem has been read alternately as a recognition of the failure of language to substitute for lived experience, "an ironic dismissal" accompanying the "repudiation of any possibility of transcendence through language," or, in contrast, a celebratory recognition of her poem's linguistic buoyancy and a reclamation of poetic agency; but Loy's onomastic imagination renders it somewhat less clear and perhaps even more bittersweet.[107] Following her earlier instances of cryptonomy in "Songs to Joannes" the conclusion aligns Loy with Love itself, evincing "the anagram's power to disperse as much as concentrate authority."[108]

With the suggestion that Loy, by any other name, would have been as free, Mabel Dodge proposes a demonization: "Lilith her name might have been. But in reality it was Minna. Minna Levi. Then Minna Lowey."[109] Dodge gets at the spirit, if not quite the letter, of Loy's onomastic transformations. In fact, she began life with the patronymic Mina Löwy, a variant of the ornamental name Löwe [lion], which she dehebraicized to "Loy" on moving to Paris, just as Apollinaire had streamlined his own moniker. Before disappearing briefly behind the married name Haweise, Mina's reemergence as Loy coincided with her eclosion as an author, *une littérateuse*, among the Florentine Futurists.[110] If Loy's mother pointedly slurred the pronunciation of *Lowy*, eliding the *w* to avoid its telltale marker of Central-European Jewishness, her father "could not—or would not—lose his accent."[111] Recalling that *w* is pronounced as a voiced fricative in Hungarian (as in German), the sound of Loy's original surname would have echoed in both *love* and the saccharine affectionate form of address in the Anglo-English *lovey*. Beneath the blended pitches of *Love*, we can hear the ghost of Loy's own appellation. Moreover, with the same ease that Dodge slips from *Mina* to *Minna*, Loy, after her time in München, would have heard *Minne* (from the Old High German *minna*) behind her given name: the German word for courtly love, a synonym of the more modern *Liebe*, but used in its archaic sense, with the same poetic or humorous tone as "littérateur," to denote romantic love with a modern wink. As she writes in song XIII: "it is in my ears   Something very resonant / Something that you must not hear / Something only for me."[112] "More than to read poetry we must listen to poetry," Loy advised in her essay on "modern poetry," which she defined as "a music made of visual thoughts, the sound of an idea."[113] "It is necessary to stay very unknown," Loy proclaimed, divulging her strategy: "to maintain my incognito the hazard I chose was—poet."[114] The revelation illuminates the apposition of song XXXIV; Loy is to poet as Love is to litterateur. The phonetic link between Loy and Love via *Löwy*, or *Minne* and Mina, may be by "hazard," by sheer chance, but the consequences are allegorical for the most oblique of Loy's pseudonymaniacal cryptonyms. In lyric, the literary genre of love, Loy cannot escape her patronym and the mongrel admixture of her own sense of self to which she would have genuine love aspire in its ascendancy over patriarchy and with which she would destabilize conventional lyrical traditions with artifice, anagram, and wordplay.

In Loy's poetics, the cryptonymy of *annominatio* is not merely a local effect, and the scene evoked with its punning in "Songs to Joannes" is the foundation of the power of poetry for her more generally; sweeping away the "litter" is what allows the modern poet to get to the "radium" of the word, as Loy praised Stein for achieving in her own blending of pitches. Loy compared Stein's language to "polished stone" (knowing, of course, that *Stein*, in German, means "stone") and she continues with the language of cleaning and burnishing when she elaborates that the stone is not mere surface, but a "polished nucleus."[115] In her other comments on Stein, Loy again uses the language of detritus and core to describe the "incoherent debris [...] littered around the radium that she crushes out of phrased consciousness."[116] She did not choose her words carelessly. At the end of the 1920s, when the *Little Review* surveyed its authors about what they most looked forward to, Loy responded: "the release of atomic energy."[117]

* * *

Let me conclude by clarifying the scope of my claims here with two brief examples. First, if the materiality of the signifier attracts other words, metonymically, as related things (in addition to the associations made by the related concepts of what linguistic signs signify), the converse holds as well: objects attract the signs associated with them. For instance, following the Surrealist interpretation of Hans Holbein's 1533 *The Ambassadors* (National Gallery, London), in which an anamorphic skull inscribes a skewed signature of the artist, rendering *Holbein* as *hohles Bein* [Hollow Bone], Creighton Gilbert reads the letter D next to a bone in a painting by Dosso Dossi (Giovanni di Niccolò de Luteri) as a rebus of the possessive *d'osso* [of the bone] (one assumes he refers to the painting of St. Jerome, Kunsthistorisches Museum Wien). Gilbert further recalls Lorenzo Lotto's proposal for a panel depicting Sodom as an allegorical signature, since it would have permitted him to paint the figure of *Lot*.[118] Similarly, for an example from the moment of modernist portraiture we have been considering, Marcel Duchamp's 1913 assisted readymade *Bicycle Wheel* takes a vaguely anthropomorphic form, with the wheel inverted and affixed to a wooden stool to suggest an oversize round head and thin torso.[119] Beyond suggesting a generic human form, however, it attains the status of a specific portrait by constructing a rebus; a wheel (*roue*) and stool (*selle*, also the word for bicycle seat) add up to *Roussel*.[120] The brief run of Raymond Roussel's stage-play version of his novel *L'impressions d'Afrique* [*The Impressions of Africa*] was attended by Duchamp, together with Francis Picabia and Apollinaire, who had introduced them to Roussel's strange work. The spectacle made a profound impact on Duchamp, who on numerous occasions acknowledged Roussel's influence. "In the works of Raymond Roussel [...] I found the source of my new activity in 1911 or 1912," he noted in retrospect, signaling works such as the *Moulin à café* [*Coffee Grinder*] (1911) and *Nu descendant un escalier* [*Nude Descending a Staircase*] (1912, both Philadelphia Museum of Art).[121] With similar candor, he divulged, "it was fundamentally Roussel who was responsible for my glass," referring to *La mariée mise à nu par ses célibataires, même* [*The Bride Stripped Bare by Her Bachelors, Even*] (1915–1923, also Philadelphia).[122] And, in general, he explained elsewhere, "Roussel me montra le chemin" [Roussel pointed the way]—but it's a pointing, like Stein's "pin" or Delaunay's tower spire, that is wonderfully oblique.

Roussel's work, which Duchamp regarded as pure poetry, was built from similar-sounding word pairs: either words that differed in only a single letter (*coquilles*, in the typographic sense) or homophones that denote different things. So, for example, in Roussel's later drama *L'étoile au front* [*The Star on the Forehead*], one scene builds from a "coquille à poulet" in the sense of an egg shell given to a sweetheart as a billet-doux (in the play, John Milton cherishes a shell kissed by the girl he once admired), while another scene builds from the same phrase to indicate a rotisserie spit (another denotation of *coquille*) for roasting poultry.[123] Such ambivalences, Duchamp would marvel, were not difficulties of the type found in Stéphane Mallarmé or Arthur Rimbaud, but "une obscurité d'un autre ordre" [an obscurity of another order].[124] The fanciful contraptions, elaborate mechanisms, and automated machines that emerge in Roussel's work by virtue of such verbal constructions and their attendant contortions, or what Michel Foucault would describe as "les machines [...] fabriquées à partir du langage" [machines built from language], provide a model for Duchamp's own machine, with its paired and interlocking parts "built from language": thanks to *Roussel* a bicycle wheel and a stool are brought together and conjoined. Reflecting the basic tenet of a modernist poetics, Duchamp enthuses: "I like words in a poetic sense. Puns for me are like rhymes. [...] For me, words are not merely a means of communication."[125] Those punning words, as with *roue* and *selle*, can be artistically generative. Duchamp continues: "You know, puns have always been considered a low form of wit, but I find them a source of stimulation [...] because of unexpected meanings attached to the interrelationship of disparate words."[126] Furthermore, Duchamp was impressed with Roussel's ability to disassociate a paronomastic language from the images and narratives it summoned—and then to require their recombination, holding text and image in tandem, in order to fully understand the work.[127] Accordingly Duchamp's *Bicycle Wheel* requires the viewer to move from image to language and back in order to recognize the subject of its portrait, or even, in fact, its status as portraiture. With an allonymic transfer of the Derridean sense of the signature, Duchamp's sculpture—mechanical, nonsensical, and constructed by the chance affiliations of homophonic play—is a thoroughly Rousselian portrait of Roussel.[128]

Second, despite my focus here on the signature, the effect need not be limited to personal names (or even to proper names at all).[129] In Aimé Césaire's poetry, for example, one finds two instances in which hairless dogs appear, with strikingly similar descriptions. "Le coup de couteau du soleil dans le dos des villes surprises" [The Sun's Knife-Stab in the Back of the Surprised Cities], mentions, as if common knowledge, "les chiens pelés que l'on voit rôder autour des volcans dans les villes que les hommes n'ont pas osé rebâtir" [the hairless dogs one sees prowling around the volcanoes in cities that men have not dared to rebuild]; and in "Rachat" [Redemption], one encounters the "Touffeurs de tas d'assiettes ébréchées / de ruines de chiens pelés" [Sweltering pile of chipped plates / of ruins of hairless dogs].[130] The effect is vaguely surreal, though—as often in Césaire's poetry, the estrangement arises not from fantasy but rather from the precision of his naturalist description and his fidelity to the specifics of his locale; on the face of it, he is merely describing one of the distinctive aspects of the fauna of Martinique, noted in the nineteenth century by British traveler and collector Greville John Chester, who was startled by "a perfectly hairless dog" and "saw afterwards in Martinique many other specimens of these curious dogs. They are of a kind of terrier breed, and have not a single hair upon their bodies, their black skins being perfectly smooth."[131] Almost a century later, René Étiemble, discussing Michel Cournot's description of Martinique, focuses on "les chiens-fer, ces pauvres bêtes affligées de pelade et dont la peau prend en effet un reflet de métal" [the chiens-fer, those poor beasts afflicted with hairlessness and whose skin takes on a metallic cast].[132] Similarly, Édouard Glissant recalls, "Je vois les chiens en bande qui parcouraient naguère les rues des bourgs et les traces des campagnes de Martinique" [I can still see the packs of dogs that used to run the streets in the small towns in Martinique]; the memory marks a certain past, since after a government campaign to poison them, "les chiens sans poil, que nous appelons chiens-fer, ont disparu du paysage" [the hairless dogs that we called *chiens-fer* have now disappeared from the landscape].[133]

And yet, in both instances in his poems, Césaire uses, not the local idiomatic epithet *chiens-fer* [literally "iron-dogs"], or the more common *chauve* [bald], but rather *pelé* [bald; literally "peeled"]. The geologic setting of each poem—from the explicitly noted volcano in "The Sun's Knife-Stab" to its metaphoric return in "Redemption" as the "virgin umbilicus of the earth" in a scene of sweltering piles and fractured ruins—explains the rationale. In 1902, the dramatic, pyroclastic eruption of Mount Pelée, the deadliest seismic event on earth since the eruption of Krakatoa, destroyed the capital city of St. Pierre, which was in fact never restored (and the name of which may in turn inform the "pierres du volcan mal refroidies qui renaissent précieuses" [ill-cooled stones of the volcano reborn as gems] in Césaire's poem "À la mémoire d'un syndicaliste noir").[134] Césaire's repeated adjective *pelé* (fem. *pelée*), linking the local canines to their volcanic terrain, is thus the converse of what Salvador Dalì would call "la méthode critique-paranoïaque" [the paranoid critical method], or "une méthode spontanée de connaissance irrationnel fondée sur l'objectivation critique et systématique des associations et interprétations délirants" [a spontaneous method of irrational knowledge based on the critical and systematic objectification of delusional associations and interpretations].[135] Rather, the rational and systematic application of a metonymic logic, transferring a proper name back to the adjectival form from which it once originated, leads to the nightmarish and dreamlike phenomena of hairless dogs amid a devastated landscape.

C'est serré [it's "compact, logical; constricted by grief or emotion"]. Both connotations hold true for Césaire's poetics. C'est la serre de langage [it's the bank vault of language]. Even the encrypted name reveals, flaunting as it conceals. Indeed, although one could continue to adduce examples of modernist cryptography—encompassing everything from Walter Arensberg's studies into Shakespeare and Dante to Tristan Tzara's study of François Villon to Unica Zürn's obsessive anagrammatic verse—there is another direction in which the onomastic imagination leads.[136] Exemplary in its dissemination, the proper name—whether pseudonym or *senhal*, given or known, and whomever it might designate, by whatever obliquity—is always naming the movement of Writing.

The Logic of the Work [CHAPTER THREE]

Le travail: ce qui fait oeuvre, sans doute, ce qui oeuvre—et ouvre, ce qui *ouvrage* et *ouverture*: le travail de l'oeuvre en tant qu'il engendre, produit et met au jour.

[Labor: that which makes a work; no doubt, that which works, and which works to open: book and overture; stitching and opening. Labor: the work of the work in as much as it creates, produces, brings to light and puts into play.]

JACQUES DERRIDA[1]

Peter Inman came to Language poetry late, and from out of town.[2]

Although Language poetry is often tidily divided between San Francisco and New York, a kernel of key writers first emerged from the Washington, DC, area, a mid-Atlantic periphery that was necessary to the foundation of the New York City core, even as its origins have been casually forgotten.[3] Inman first published as part of that DC scene, which had come to be centered, in the early 1970s, around DuPont Circle. The writing was manifest in venues such as *Everybody's Ex-Lover* (a journal edited by Inman), S.O.U.P. (Some of Us Press), *Mass Transit* (the magazine of a publishing collective which also hosted readings at the Community Bookstore), and, slightly later, a reading series at P Street Folio Books.[4] Hair was long, consciousness was raised, and the era's tension between individual personal expression and coöperative identification is legible not only in the nature of those collaborative DuPont community events and periodicals but also in the poetry they promoted, which frequently combines colloquial intimacy, sensitive self-examination, and offhand vignettes of relationships fraught by an awareness of the social politics of gender and sex.

Inman's first two books, *What Happens Next* (Some of Us Press, 1974) and *P. Inman USA* (Dry Imager, 1975), are direct products of this context.[5] They feature poems in a mode of outré surrealism: short sentences in a direct style of grammatically unobtrusive dream-narration within which a calculated crudeness—credentialed by the bohemian counterculture of the DuPont Circle scene—bids for attention. Bodily fluids are copious, as is copulation; hallucinatory metamorphoses manage the transitions between episodes; a physically and psychically uncomfortable world repeatedly menaces, though usually from a safely distanced nightmarish irreality. The poems are peppered with proper names, and the writers mentioned sketch Inman's loosely surrealist aesthetic background in broad strokes: Rimbaud, Rilke, García Lorca, Vallejo, Cortázar.[6] Accordingly, one section of a poem from the period, "Solo Ridge," published in Michael Sappol's *Personal Injury Magazine*, obliquely references Max Ernst by performing the language of a passage from Uwe Schneede's monograph on the artist in much the way we saw Clark Coolidge perform the Dadaist poetics of Tzara by cutting and collaging his manifesto from Robert Motherwell's anthology. Inman's stanza begins:

> The principle of collage is the choice of an original, which then invites modification, then incorporation, till the process rebounds Elsewhere, the repetition of which rips a toenail ... (lacked exposition, too eclec. otherwise) so the ego puts on alot of weight, alot of pills in a white hand.[7]

The source, highlighted for comparison, reads:

> The so-called artistic process consists in <u>the choice of an original which invites modification and thus incorporation</u> into art [...] By its very nature, the <u>collage</u>—here as <u>elsewhere</u>—keeps its various levels of reality intact.[8]

By collaging, modifying and incorporating a text about the incorporation and modification of collaged material, without exposition and perhaps too eclectically for coherence, this section of "Solo Ridge" offers a kind of "composition as explanation" (to adopt Gertrude Stein's term). Inman enacts precisely the process Uwe goes on to describe:

> the creative procedure is therefore identical with the changes undergone by the initial material, once adopted. The process of individual artistic creation through formal invention is replaced by the principle of modification of objects taken from reality.[9]

"Wagon Box Fight," a poem from *P. Inman USA*, applies the same procedure to itself. Inman rewrites the first section of the poem in subsequent sections, offering a spaced erasure in part II and a condensed rearrangement in part III. The first section, which provides a good example of his writing from this period, concludes:

> At one point Willie's head cracks open & all the yolk spills out.
> He feels much better after that & starts thinking about getting on
> with the story. The whole room begins to fill up with a warm & milky
> light. Wilma thinks she's just on the edge of a flat earth. Slabs
> of human beef hung drying just outside the cabin door. Some blue
> dots float about. Squish went the urine between their legs.

The corresponding passage from the second section, looking like a stanza of John Ashbery's "Europe," writes through the first, leaving the last line intact as a kind of refrain:

>   At one   yolk spills
>   starts   ing about
>   fill
>   W(van)il(L)ma   on the edge of a
>   beef   dry—   Some blue
> dots float about. Squish went the urine between their legs.

Along with the prose poem "Michael Mantler," a bop-prosodic transcript of auditioning the 1968 *Jazz Composer's Orchestra* album, "Wagon Box Fight" is the most linguistically adventurous poem from the early books. They skirt the outer edges of the New York School's purview—crossing paths with Coolidge's extensions of Kerouac and Ashbery's *Tennis Court Oath* respectively—but they do not give any hint of how the writing in Inman's next book will look. *Platin* opens:

> leans tain clack. cilk   ,   tasp. blosset
>   … leam of visible nephew
>
> writ tilen.   libble.   cuzc …
> leath fews about smoke. tayer,millan. groi.
> trowblur.   (ribble tithe?)
> … view cray. limsit tasp[10]

To be sure, a handful of transitional works, published individually, marked a more graduated shift. In addition to poems such as "Colloam" and "Lotioning," Inman's contributions to the magazine *So & So* (Fall 1978) had signaled the change. Titled "Imagination Lace" and "David," these poems retain the scaffolding of surrealist dream-narrative, but agrammatical phrases and disjunctive word pairs increasingly replace the normative syntax of declarative sentences: "vergul mandate"; "imagination lace"; "gouache pie"; "my cracked attentive"; "omen deal"; "gauge lesion." In this "grammar dissolve" (as one sentence from "Imagination Lace" puts it), one can start to see "the observations of surface freaks spelling out strange grams," even as "meaning intrudes to aerate" those pockets of lexical density (to continue with the poem's own language).

By the time of the books *Platin* (1979), *Ocker* (Tuumba, 1982) and *Uneven Development* (Jimmy & Lucy's House of Knowledge, 1982), the proportion of "meaning" and "dissolve" has inverted. No longer occasional abrasions to the narrative surface of the poem, the "strange grams" now overwhelm the few familiar words that remain. In the stanza quoted above, for instance, common words make up only a third of the poem's vocabulary: "of," "about," "leans," "visible," "view," "nephew," "smoke"—plus the medieval common-law terms of "writ" and "tithe." The less common or hapax words confound grammatical categories (are "tain" and "fews," for instance, to be taken as verbs?), and when they do not turn out to be variants of northern British and Scottish dialects—obsolete or archaic denotations of which Inman may not even have been cognizant—those disjunctive elements do not appear to be recognized words at all.[11] They hint at fragments ("leam" for *gleam*; "cuzc" for *Cuzco*; *written* as "writ tilen"; "groi" for *groin*, *et cetera*), phonetic spellings ("cilk" for *silk*); errors (a barely legible, perhaps scribbled, "libble" for *ribble* or *liable*; "cilk" for *click*, especially in the context of "clack"; "limsit" for *limit*, and so on), compounds ("trowblur"), and neologisms. Inman's poems in this mode are among the most linguistically drastic writing to have emerged from a period of notoriously radical lexical experimentation. They are classically indeterminate, in the sense identified by Marjorie Perloff: neither simply meaningless nor capable of meaning anything whatsoever, but suspended between irresolvable possibilities.[12] *Trowblur*, for instance, seems to be a portmanteau of *trow* and *blur*, or a blurring of *trowel* and *burr* (perhaps the hand tool used to ribble the soil down to the burr of siliceous rock, or simply one with a burred edge). At the same time, the word suggests both *true-blue* and *troubler* (which, semantically, indeed it is), or even, perhaps, the deliberately obscure and cryptic *trobar clus* of the Troubadours. Similarly, "leath fews about smoke" might suggest the mistyping of a topical headline (*Health Fears about Smoking*), or alternately, given that "leath" is an obsolete term for cessation or pause, the phrase might be read as a baroque indication that reduction makes for fewer things (given as the misapplied plural for more than one *few*)—perhaps the whole in tenuous reference to quitting smoking or candlewicks going out. At the same time, the phrase equally suggests the curing of smoked leather buckskin, or a smoking *fuse* (as the phonetic "fews") to a lethal explosive; and it invites a phonetic metathesis yielding *leaf* (perhaps a tobacco leaf to be smoked) and "thews" (as synonym for sinews, but also as the verb *to thew*: "to instruct in morals or manners; to discipline, train, instruct, chastise").[13] More active paragrammatic readings produce only further possibilities, but no definitive resolutions.

That failure to fully resolve, regardless of how much hermeneutic pressure is applied, combined with a refusal, from the other side, to ever give entirely over to sheer asemantic formalism, accounts for the desperately restive status of Inman's texts. The textual details, of course, transform from book to book and from poem to poem—complete phrases become somewhat more prevalent; idiosyncratic punctuation intrudes; Inman explores structures based on lettristic metrics and merged parentheticals; and so on—but the fundamental irresolvability persists: the various parts cannot be assimilated into a coherent whole, and the tension between abstract "dissolve" and referential "meaning"—between the grams and the grammar—is maintained with an astonishingly steady balance. Indeed, what I want to emphasize here is the degree to which, contrary to what one might expect, balance is what makes Inman's poems even stranger than a more seemingly extreme poetics would permit. On the one hand, the severity of the nonsemantic elements bluntly interrupts the communicative work of the standard passages, frustrating grammar, countermanding the clarity of any referential message, and obviating a readerly absorption into an illusionistic narrative. On the other hand, the familiar phrases simultaneously forestall a lapse into sheer, nondiscursive material inscription. With a continually reversing dynamic, unrecognizable inscription hinders paraphrase, while standard language impedes the free play of the signifier.[14] One branks while the other baffles in turn.

For all their disruptive strangeness, that is, Inman's works are never merely abstract compositions. Passages of phonemic density featuring the deliberate clash of consonantal blends offer a facture of sonic interest and frisson, but the poems do not give over to mellifluous patterns or continued rhythms in a way that leads readers to stop worrying about sense and lose themselves in a wash of auditory play. Similarly, Inman's varied modes depart from the several traditions of avant-garde abstraction that may have inspired his neologisms: Futurist *заум'* [transratio]; Dadaist *Lautgedichte*; the occasional clinamina with which more conventional poets have swerved into asemantic territory, such as Jean Toomer's two "Sound Poems"; the kinds of invented languages on display in David Melnick's PCOET or Claude Gauvreau's *Jappements à la lune*, or any of the anomalous, now largely forgotten poems resulting from similar experiments by a number of writers in the 1970s, including Ron Silliman, Ray DiPalma, and Dave Morice (publishing as Joyce Holland).[15] While the invented languages of such works are thrilling in their extremity, their pervasiveness paradoxically allows for a certain alibi: however hard it is to account for an invented language, that's all there is to account for; its interaction with the foil of conventional language does not have to be reckoned. In contrast, the counterbalance of standard language in Inman's poems keep them from being appraised as mere instances or examples. The same holds true for a comparison with the nonce words of a certain minimalist tradition in American poetry. Individual words or lines from

Inman's poems share a family resemblance with poems by writers such as Aram Saroyan, Robert Grenier, and John Marron, but because those words are incorporated into Inman's varied and heterogeneous texts rather than isolated on the page, his poems as a whole do not have the same focused torque of those other more minimal lexical deformations.[16] Similarly, the variety of nonstandard usage, demonstrated in the example from *Platin* above, differentiates Inman's "grammar dissolve" from the more consistently antistheconic verse of a book such as David McFadden's *The Ova Yogas*, or the more concretist disruptions of a writer such as Norman H. Pritchard (whom we will focus on in chapter 5), or the more ironic misprisions of counterculture flaunting by a writer like Bill Bisset.[17] The variety also sets Inman's poems apart from Maggie O'Sullivan's incantatory performance verse, Gail Sher's mongrel transliteration, or, frankly, anything else that I can think of.[18] And while Bruce Andrews had been advancing a poetics of grammatical sabotage throughout the 1970s, the force of his poems depended on the nonce pairing of *standard* words, often according to a poetic logic of microphonemic internal rhyme. In fact, the absence of a motivating or generative system is another key factor in keeping Inman's poems from settling into a digestible whole; his texts are not, in the final analysis, about their own structure or explained by their procedure. This absence of a discernable structural logic is also what distinguishes them from the precedents that they most resemble: those sections of Lyn Hejinian's *Writing Is an Aid to Memory* and Clark Coolidge's *Ing* which we looked at in chapter 1. In those books, moreover, the prose layout of their source texts explains the textual particulars of their nonce vocabulary.[19] And yet, Inman's use of constructivist visual forms, such as the scrolling spiral of "nimr" or the modules of "Roscoe Mitchell [nonaah]," argues against reading his work as the record of extemporaneous free-form improvisations or the streaming of a spontaneously expressive consciousness.[20]

The poems, in the end, do not yield. They do not give themselves wholly over to any of the recognizable values—melopoeia, phanopoeia, logopoeia, *et cetera*—that might justify the sum of their textual specifics or account for their larger project. Nor do they engage in exchanges, either internally (trading grammar for some different system, say) or as a whole (offering themselves as examples or experimental results). As a glance at any page from any of his later books shows, his poetry is obviously not narrative in the conventional sense, but this is true in a more profound sense as well. Inman's poems are not *about* anything—even in the way one might say that David Melnick's *Men in Aida*, for example, is "about" the semantics of homophony or "about" translation. Similarly, his poems do not seem to be means toward any end; one does not read them *for* something else. The experience of the poems, that is, does not produce the usual dividends: insight, ideas, arguments, psychological identification, varieties of lyrical pleasure, comic humor, and so on—no gains against which the poems are bartered or after which they can be discarded. Having read the poem, one is left merely with the poem: a text undiminished, unaugmented, adamantine, resolute. As Inman himself has said, "the words (or non-) don't point outside or beyond themselves as much as they just name themselves."[21] Giving nothing but itself, getting you nowhere, noncommunicating, unenlightening—there is, in brief, no payoff in his pages.

In that absence of profit, paradoxically, lies the exceptional value of these poems, and their political force. Politics, one should remember, is not something a poem does or does not have—all poems are political—but rather the set of arguments that can be made about the relations of power encouraged and impeded by certain facets of a text. Here, three primary facets of the poems' textual politics immediately present themselves. First, Inman's writing resists not only the substitutions and exchanges that underlie most of the systems with which we are familiar—economic commerce, linguistic communication, representative politics, pedagogy—but also those systems' values of instrumental functionality. As Inman sees it:

> One word does not equal another. Language is not a medium of equivalence. Words are not denominations. Or shouldn't be. Language is not (shouldn't be) immediately "convertible". Every unit of the written or spoken needs to be recuperated via its own particularity. The signal's valence rethickened. Obstinacy & discreteness as defense mechanisms.[22]

Even beyond refusing the familiar regimes of representation—a whole host of mechanisms for veiling and illusion—these poems, as I have just argued, are not good *for* anything else; they thwart any easy consumption, including the easy consumption of themselves as tokens of poetic abstraction.[23] Poetry here presents "language which is too difficult to be seamlessly incorporated."[24] Unprofitable, unrewarding, unassimilable to systems of exchange, unavailable for any sort of banausic purpose, insubordinate and unsubordinated: Inman's poetry demonstrates the astonishing, confounding power—and the tragically surprising rarity—of something that is not already being used by an established, institutional order for some foregone end. Atelic, Inman's poems suggest the possibility of a future whose conclusion has not yet been imagined, a state in which the dominant system has not yet destroyed absolutely everything than cannot be coöpted for profit. "Writing," in Inman's terms, is seen "as an attempt to create a negative, insubordinate space within the administered space we're all daily subjected to."[25] His poems are, in other words, utopian. Inman writes books that Hollywood cannot option.

Second, following from that unfamiliar anti-instrumental poetics, Inman's poems ask one to imagine what it means to read when one is not reading *for* some kind of totalizing comprehension. They open a textual field in which whatever might count as "reading" clearly requires sustained concentration and focused labor, but where precisely what kind of activity would constitute a proper or successful reading is not at all clear. How (or even whether) one is to move from the physical to the cognitive, from the recognition of words to their synthesis, is far from certain when there is "a negation of any cues in terms of how one is going to make the connections between the units."[26] The possibilities for language in his poems remain possibilities: linguistic effects which have not been accounted for in advance and for which a predetermined discourse does not yet exist. Accordingly, to talk honestly and accurately about these poems requires exploring a discursive space in which the discussion about poetry has not yet devolved into reflexive formulae, self-insulating maneuvers in the guise of sanctimonious proclamations, or papier-mâché inaccuracies that ring as hollow as the claims a *soi-disant* oppositional poetics would seek to fight against.

Third, the obdurate materiality of Inman's language—its recalcitrant, rebarbative, insurrectional relation even to the rest of its own poem—asks only for a sustained attention to language in a non-instrumental state. In a world where everything else, including literature, slips increasingly into the rapid flash and flush of disposable, discardable, ephemeral signs—a world in which words and images stream in speeding amnesiac cycles of ever briefer duration, where one sign is not only impatiently replaced by the next but where the very operation of communication always already depends on analogous transformations and substitutions—Inman's poems stay, momentarily, the conversion of language into something else, staving off its replacement by some symbolic meaning that encourages the disappearance of the word and a disregard for the word as such.[27] By refusing to commute, the poems thus stand in fundamental opposition to the impulse of all those oppressive contemporary powers that would eagerly channel everything, including their most strident resistance and their own demise, into packaged sound-bites of flickering symbols, palatable morsels of predigested content, takeaway sentiment, and readily consumable cliché.

More surprisingly, Inman's poetry foils narrative even at the level of a career. Contrary to the dramatic differences between his first two books and what followed (between the period of *What Happens Next* and what did in fact happen next), readers have been struck by the subsequent consistency. Mark Wallace, ventriloquizing one response to this apparent congruity, offers a forthright assessment:

> His [Inman's] writing has consistently refused to develop over time in any of the obvious senses of development; his writing hasn't grown if one means by grown that he has gone on to new principles or new problems as times have changed. To some this fact might make Inman a case of arrested development.[28]

Ron Silliman, similarly, says that Inman's style was so uniform, for over a quarter century, that a recognizable poetic "voice" emerged, naturalizing the poetry until it became fully familiarized, in the Slavic formalist sense of the word.[29] Such readings may be missing unusually nuanced adjustments from one poem to another, but their general point is borne out by a comparison with the changes that took place in the work of the other writers associated with Language poetry. The following excerpts, for just a few instances, will also help to situate the poem above, from *Platin*, in its original literary landscape. Here is the opening page of Charles Bernstein's 1979 poem "Parsing":

> the reach, the middle, endless, drift, sway, hold, belie
> unfold and furl, it makes, smack, abated,
>
>   against at top
>
> what, and frap
>   jimmie, ice blue,
>
>   the. It sat
>
>   sometimes, among
>
>   who on
>
>   could, semblance
>
>   of narrow
>
>   land, larger, riddling
>
>   axe, they[30]

And here, thirty years later, is the opening of Bernstein's "Thank You for Saying Thank You":

> This is a totally
> accessible poem.
> There is nothing
> in this poem
> that is in any
> way difficult
> to understand.[31]

In Clark Coolidge's second book, published in 1967, one of the decidedly "difficult / to understand" poems, in its entirety, reads:

> tapes
>   no and mangrove
>   gas trim marl key
> obsidian
>   douse[32]

Forty years later, a poem picked at random from a recent book opens with these sentences:

> Just to think about Providence and I have to let it lag. There is nothing to consult. Bray at things then shut up like. Providence melts into a pinprick with nothing shining on it to let me in. I don't hardly know the place any more. Did I?[33]

A few lines from Bruce Andrew's 1979 "True Flip To" gives a sense of one of his earlier styles:

> *H* ypnosis   landgrant
> *M* arriage   blocks
> chintz   clasp
> *S* wing   completed
> door   donor
> result   *O* bjet-d'art
> heart   maniac
> *R* otogravure   tenor
> tension   styptic
> *M* aniac   heart[34]

Compare those words, paired in suggested anthimeria, with the no less opaque but nonetheless more soundly categorematic, sentence-based opening of a poem in one of his most recent books:

> Tiffany puncture service. Bouffant wetlands, gigglers on the left: 'oh, nothing.' Slur touts vita headlock, to irrigate the useful content-haunted dial-a-fib. Sieve in a shutdown. Hard rock guam = bachelor lizard but vows barbecue the jury. Says zsa zsa. I stabbed my hand because it was gay. Posse peers heartache liquidators, stoolie smash-up egghead autobody ratio flaps. Use your lips as a hamper. Here's a sentence worth reading out loud.[35]

One final example, from Lyn Hejinian, juxtaposing lines from 1978 and 2006 respectively, reveals a similar shift to more grammatically complete, discursive, sentence-based writing. First, a section from *Writing Is an Aid to Memory*, a book I discussed in chapter 1:

> curtain while the roll each play
>   solo
>   kettle lastly mendous prising
> delve
>   sume but dom or another
> duce
>   thumbing
>   knowing seems years
>   now which pery ground folly
> and more of it for a long time[36]

A section from one of Hejinian's ongoing projects (with thematic relevance to the topic of change over time) begins:

> constant change figures
> the time we sense
> passing on its effect
> surpassing things we've known before
> since memory
> of many things is called
> experience
> but what of what
> we call nature's picture
> of the many things we call
> since memory

> we call nature's picture
> surpassing things we've known before[37]

Points of connection certainly persist across all of these paired examples, each of which still bears its author's unmistakable stylistic stamp; by the same token, I do not mean to imply that Inman's poems are somehow indistinguishable, as even a casual glance from book to book would refute. The differentiating features of his poems, however, do tend to seem less salient. For example, compare a page from the 2000 poem "lake. aside"—

(neach. edges.

écois.   utter.[38]

—with one from the 1984 book *Uneven Development*, where it would not appear out of place:

> hatter drobe.
> quotb.

---

                                        drith black
---
[39]

Inman may have come to Language poetry late—writing, in the 1980s, works that looked more like the textual experiments of the early 1970s than like the increasingly phrasal new-sentence prose of his peers—but he stayed on far longer than anyone else. Looking back, Marjorie Perloff singled out Inman's work as exemplary of a certain "period style."[40] Remarkably, that style has persisted even as the period has passed. Throughout, Inman has continued, with considerable stamina, in an unrelentingly hardcore mode while his cohort's work has taken aim at new targets, changed tactics, moved restlessly on, or sadly attenuated to the softly vitiated pose of a diluted status quo. And here is where Silliman's charge of naturalization requires some qualification. While it may have looked more common in the period of its "period style," and while it may seem familiar compared to his previous publications, decades later, against the background of the very different poetics of the twenty-first-century avant-garde, Inman's poems—and the distinctive techniques of his restive texts—now look even stranger than ever. Indeed, Viktor Shklovsky's redefinition of остранение as the effect of the displaced writer applies especially well to Inman, who is now doubly estranged from both the mainstream *and* the coterie vanguard. Inman is the "person out of place" in both cultural period and locale: arriving, tardy, from out of town, but abiding long after everyone else has abandoned a fashion they could not sustain.[41]

Merely noting a continued poetic style, however, risks both overstating and underestimating the constancy of Inman's poetry because it misses the extraordinary workings of his assembled works. One of the most interesting aspects of Inman's writing, considered as a single body of work, is the fluctuant recurrence of words moving through an unusually fluid and unstable oeuvre, with myriad changes and drastic discrepancies between the versions of poems in typescript, periodical publication, and book form. Inman's texts transmogrify far more often than the expected correction of occasional errors or the small revisions irresistible to most writers: formats reshape from verse to prose; poems are merged in midline mashups or repurposed as spare parts for later poems; titles are recycled; lines excised from one poem reappear in another, and so on.[42]

Ultimately these transformations call into question what we might consider to be a discrete poem. On the one hand, Inman has explicitly differentiated poems that would normally be thought of as versions or drafts of the "same" work. For example, he designates the poem "Roscoe Mitchell," itself identified as "a variant of a multivocal piece" performed at the Kootenay School of Writing, and not be confused with the similarly titled but apparently unrelated "Roscoe Mitchell [nonaah]," as "a different but closely related piece" from the poem "now/time."[43] That relation, however, is very close indeed; the two poems share not only identical stanzas but closely overlapping textual connections. Here is a section from "now/time":

    some.
    sound.
    put.
  grammarian. opened. of. creek. pelt.
    withers.

Compare that stanza with these two paired sections from a page of "Roscoe Mitchell":

> book. sauk. tine.
> opened.
> of.
> creek.
> pelt.

* * *

> a.
> sound.
>   too. mind. that. put. it.
> of.
> withers.[44]

On the other hand, less obviously related texts issue forth under uniform titles. A typescript of the poem "backbite," opens:

> men's ilmh, odor of darning.
> thigh drail, lessness critch
> zero all tinvh
>
> oments
> allow pplen, mile press.
>   seine larner probabilities[45]

In the *Paris Review* "Language Sampler," however, "backbite" opens:

> tract wrote school, arm nane of reddening.
> self all in evenlies, most of language looking for a
>   [landscape.
>   wriit ence hoar
>
>   never mind that decide
>   protrud ure horizon, tlanth nettle mensity.
>   "for our next entitle " pores[46]

When it was published as the very first number of the Potes and Poets Press periodical *A*bacus*, the poem opened with a line recalling both "Waver," which shares the line "never mind that decide," and the eighth section of *Platin*, which contains the lines "(… crumped / quinals …)":

never mind that decide (crump / quant.)
iodine lotion wasn't what he meant,
the wider dims the end to a beer

The second line of the typescript "backbite," meanwhile, returns in the poem "Red Shift" (with a stop replacing the comma), while the poem "quogue" (the title seems to have been taken from one of the words in "Decker") has absorbed the word "pplen" (as "pplenf"), and so on.[47]

Reading across the corpus by following the movement of lines and words in this way provides an analogue to reading across the page, which is the very definition of writing for Inman. Responding to Eric Wirth's notice of the motility suggested by titles such as "Waver," "Vagabond," and "Shift," Inman explains: "writing is linked to motion. Words moving across the page, the reading eye following them."[48] Given the motion of words not just across the page, but from one text to another, Inman's writing is a perfect illustration of John Bryant's argument that the literary work ought to be conceived of as a process rather than a product, as flows of energy rather than things—*work*, that is, not in the sense of *oeuvre*, but rather of *travailler*: as the scientific measure of force over a distance.[49] But Inman's work goes further than Bryant's proposal by challenging the boundaries of those energy flows, so that the textual labor takes place not just between clearly demarcated versions or editions of discrete and identifiable works but across an entire corpus. Perhaps the ostensibly static style of Inman's books arises not because he has failed to change from poem to poem, but rather because he has been engaged in one long continuous *work*.

Regardless of how one defines (a) literary work, such mutations are symptomatic of a more chronic and pervasive textual nomadism in Inman's writing, where phrases drift and migrate, decamping from later drafts and then unexpectedly returning, so that specific words and patterns repeat—verbatim, across different books, over decades—with a statistically astonishing frequency. At times, as we saw with "backbite," these repetitions seem more like the recycling of material from earlier, essentially abandoned poems. For instance, the lines "'waxed rice'" (in quotation marks both times) and "a whited beer by," which first appear in the poem "Plainsong," return in "Brim" (an earlier version of the poem "Landscape")—the latter as "its whited beer by."[50] The phrase "eyehorn at the same dime," also from "Plainsong," resurfaces in the poem "hackensack," just as the phrase "minuses of Arctic women," although it is *not* found in "Landscape," crops up again in "Sunders," while the phrase "creek brass," from "Plainsong," recurs in "Kilter," and so on. At other times, however, phrases seem to be merely, if inexplicably, reiterated from poem to poem. For instance, both the poems "land's end" and "now/time" include the line "brook of edges in a dictionary," while the line "could be prose turned to footsteps," from the poem "delft" is echoed as "turned to footsteps" or "turned to footstep" in the three poems "Less of One," "glimpse," and "Across."[51] Appropriately, the line itself suggests the poetic transformation of language, moving from prose to verse: traditionally in modern prosody progressing with the "footsteps" of metrical feet and etymologically from the Latin *vertere*, via *versus*, something "turned."

In other cases, pairs of words are linked in more varied environments. For instance, those footsteps echo back as the Spanish "passos," which is always paired with "Montauk" when it occurs in Inman's writing.[52] The words "riced" and "still" are similarly linked, always with some connection to economics; in "brim" one reads "a lined face / riced still. who defends wealth" and in "now/time" one finds "as Marx said as sight riced still."[53] The words "steach" and "skin" occur in proximity with one another, as do "beer" and "croft," as well as countless others.[54] More complexly, series of words come to concatenate through something like a transitive property of poetic vocabulary. "Harvard," "typewriter," and the sounds of $p+ain$ ("plain"; "pain"; "paint"), for instance, are linked through the following: "was typewriter said, pained in harvard"; "harvard did nothing / as far as paint"; and "a typewriter blank of plain."[55] At times the catenations are more conceptual than strictly verbal, as when "nostril" is paired with "ocean" and "waves": "Dust Bowl" includes "fog nostril inside smooth, ocean to chord powder," while a line from "hackensack" reads "the waves resemble nouns / nostril damage on a pin / Harry Bridges." The name of the legendary labor union leader, who was nicknamed "the Beak" on account of his prominent nose, clarifies the explanatory logic. A bridge is associated with both water and noses ("bridge of one's nose at a time," as "Think of One" records), and the given name, in this context, evokes nostril hairs, an association corroborated later in "Dust Bowl" with "hairs bridged in," a phrase that occurs, not coincidentally, in a line also referencing collective leftist politics: "the shape of the kolkhoz by 1935." Proximity in these poems carries special weight given the absence of extended narrative or developed themes; Inman's poetics foregrounds metonymy, trumping logic with contiguity, grammar with sheer syntax.

Through a similarly transitive logic, Inman links landscape and vision to a complex of other terms. In lines such as "her eye- / sight as it remained landscape" and "stopped short by the sight of his own landscape," the basic association is not surprising, given that landscape is a genre of visual art, but it continues even with the word "landed": "should i be looking at the intervals instead. / or the midst in their likeness her peers landed from a page."⁵⁶ That last quotation, through a rhyming paragrammatic move from *page* to *age*, recalls the lines "age landed / on bare trees" and "age landed on. / what can't be" (from the poems "hackensack" and "kilter," respectively), but it also reveals a persistent connection between landscape and class, as *peers* in the visual sense of intent "looking" shades into the social peers of sociological class: "where the working class ranked in the landscape"; "where the (about sculpture / working class (length / ranked in the landscape / (of eyesight"; and "painting / landscape from his headache surface: / his river grist whether the underclass."⁵⁷ Perpetuating the visual connotations of "painting" and "eyesight" in those lines, a number of other poems continue to link social class and land not only with sight but also with beer, apparently under the +*eer* influence of *peer*. From "Science Fiction":

> (a croft.
> of beers) amounts of underclass drape bricks.
> sight metis amounts of women to Tuckahoe.
> the land where i think to subtraction.

From "Vagabond 1," which repeats "croft":

> Stray cave paints
>
> each brook of a code mixture. Temperature with beers. Hair croft course. What'd her job been like written about. The dunes behind her slashed out to stillness sight out of prairie

From "Vagabond 2":

> The ending changed by her wearing sunglasses [...]
>
> a beer blank of proletariat
>
> the dunes by their hatband solve nerves outside her

This kind of cumulative textual logic can also unfold to triangulate seemingly isolate, nonsensical words. "Bledge," for instance, appears to be a portmanteau of *bled* and *edge*, eliminating the border between those common words as if enacting the definition of printing that is "bled," so that it extends to the edge of the sheet or "the end of the page," as Inman repeats in more than one poem.⁵⁸ Indeed, he writes of a "bled book" and a "thick book blooded," suggesting both printing and paper cuts, or what a "book cracks open" when a "hold arrives at bleed": the salty sting of blood from a "small epsom. of papercut."⁵⁹ Printing can be bled to the edge of the page, but the thin edge of the page can be bled upon as well when it cuts the hand that holds it. The "thumb. hurts" and the "thumb limps" when it has been a "thumb bladened."⁶⁰

A paper cut, moreover, explains the recurrent link between pages, hair, skin, brooks, and the edges of books. First, one finds "skin," what is threatened by a paper cut ("skin / but missed papercut"), in proximity with +*edge*: "skin's. / edge"; "fledge to the skin"; "wedge shapes / from content. Black drybed / in the print, skin but missed."⁶¹ Second, hair is also equated with the page. Both are stereotypically thin, as in the sense of "hairline tracks" or the paper-thin "thinnest, / paper" (and hair, notoriously, thins with age), but more specifically the edges of books and brooks in Inman's oeuvre are repeatedly noted for their finely measured extension, as what are "ended, / in, width," or with a "width. by. some. of. the. / edges": a "widthed brook"; or paper, as reams and leaves, "divided" at the edge of a book: "widths.) how. on. paper. [...] (meters. to. one. of. a. / side.) each. book. [...] side. meter. of. a. book.) divided"; "each. ream. breadth. [...] the. sided. brook. on"; "side. amounts. (shape. only. where. it. leaves.)."⁶² In addition to their thin borders, book edges and hairlines are collapsed in the striking figures of the "mane of / book" and the "hair's book meant in rips" (where "meant" is a paragram of "mane"), as well as through the parallel constructions "pages piling up into a broken book" and "hairs piling up / into broken books," where the collocation of piling may derive from the sense of "piling" as nap, from *pile*: "hair, *esp*. fine soft hair or down" (from the classical Latin etymon *pilus*).⁶³ Breaking and ripping, dividing, parting and cracking, those books might lead to "thinking of her scar as some number of books" when their "edges rub off on her hands."⁶⁴

These connections between skin and hair and blood and the edges of paper, furthermore, are reinforced by the idiomatic ties of both blood and hair to *cut* as well as to *line*, via *bloodline* and *hairline*, an association underscored by the frequently repeated "red hair" specified throughout Inman's poems. Similarly, blood, of course, is *red* while the pages of books are *read*. Cementing this unexpected nexus of transitive associations even further, "dictionary," "hair," "thinness," and "skin"—as well as "arm" and a "creek," both synonyms for *brook*—are all "parted" in Inman's work.⁶⁵ Indeed, "bloodstream" and "shoreline," words that recur a dozen times across his oeuvre, explain the "brook," or stream, repeatedly located, as we have already seen, at the margin of its paragram: *book*. Inman twice repeats "brook of edges in a dictionary," recalling the "pinstripe glean of french dictionary edge" and the "rouge. at. ends. / of. someone. / else's.

dictionary," as well as the "wash. / on. a. page."⁶⁶ As it happens, "brook" and "edge" do appear together frequently in dictionary pages, given the proximity of the lemmata *brook* and *brow*, *burn* (a Scottish brook) and *burnish* (etymologically from *bryn*, an edge), *burn* and *burr*, and most commonly *rill* and *rim*, which often directly follow in a dictionary's alphabetic layout.⁶⁷ In at least one French-English dictionary, *affront* ("digérer un affront: to brook an outrage") is set to front the facing column's definition of *agacé* ("set on edge").⁶⁸ And recalling Inman's line "brookle limelies," the *World Book Dictionary* defines *brooklime* as "a plant growing on the edges of brooks." More striking still, the synonym section for *rim* in one dictionary brings "brook" and "book" directly together with a set of terms that include Inman's privileged use of "brim" and "brink": "the *rim* of a vessel; the *brim* of a cup or goblet; the *brink*, *verge*, or *edge* of a precipice; the *margin* of a brook or book."⁶⁹

At other times, as the *+eer* effect or the move from *bledge* to *wedge* to *fledge* suggests, the pairings and patterns in Inman's oeuvre seem to be organized by sound structures rather than identical or conceptually related words. Compare, for example, "g l a y s husk" and "husk glaze," or the *-sh* + *drome* combinations of "amish / dromeda" and "ash / drome," or the coupling of *we-* and *nog* in "weakener nog" and "weep nog."⁷⁰ Similarly, "limsit tasp," from the end of that first poem in *Platin* echoes back as "lipst. tass." in the poem "Mel;nick's," as if the *p* from "tasp" were conserved in "lipst" and with the *limp* resulting from the averaging of "limsit" and "lipst" refracted back as "lame" when the word "tass" returns in "kilter" in the pairing "lamed tass."⁷¹ The coincidences are uncanny, and unaccountable: "limsit tasp"; "lipst tass"; "lamed tass."

That limp also returns, with the same phonemic logic, in the following set of lines, where *inkle* presents a kind of broken *ankle*, or "bone drake anklet," perhaps one limping with "hunched paces" because it has tripped over a "rim"—a broken edge of "brim" that in the context of "inkle" suggest the steep decline of a *brink*: "limpse / ankle"; "limpse / brim / ankle"; "limpse brims"; "hunched. paces. // rim inkle."⁷² Each stuttering transformation—of "rim" to "brim," "ankle" to "inkle," and the ghost of *brink* or the suggestion of *brake* (*break*) from "bone drake"—enacts the sort of tripping stumble the lines seem to describe. Moreover, the "brink" is linked not just with feet and falling in Inman's work ("brinked feet"; "where does her brink as thin rainfall") but with writing and language.⁷³ Reinforced by the *ink* in "brink" and "inkle," the stammer at the "brink of mouth" in "vagabond" returns in the poem "amagansett #1," where it occurs, broken across the line, "on paper," in a sort of "footfall between pages": "stam / mers (flat brink / instincts (on paper)."⁷⁴ In the context of a passage about falling, the "footprint" that precedes this stanza brings the two spheres together in one word: the stumbling *foot* and the stuttered *print* of writing, or "stumbles in penmanship" as the poem "Dust Bowl" has it, because the "thumb limps" too.[75] The two terms return, with the *limp* contained in "glimpse," in a line from "pluper": "the well glimpse at a letter's foot."[76] The etymology of *stammer*, like *stutter* (a word that repeats in the poem "i.e.") has long been bound with both language and walking.

And here is where we can begin to glimpse the operation of the signature underwriting this entire oeuvre. From one side, the collected works reveal a recognizable lexical landscape, one characterized by categories of proper names (Anabaptist sects, baseball players, labor leaders and Marxist theoreticians, painters and jazz musicians, First Nations), as well as a score of unexpectedly repeated words, both standard ("rice," "nose," "decimal," "ocean," "cattle," "calve," *et alii*) and nonstandard (which is why most of the invented words here are not, strictly speaking—and contrary to the claims of some critics—nonce words).[77] Moreover, as we have seen, even beyond a favored vocabulary, identifiable phonemic combinations reiterate across the oeuvre. For just one example from some dozen or so, readers can trace the relay of what we might call the +*cc* effect: "occludes"; "ecclure"; "occlay"; "icclose"; "iccler"; "clode"; "occusp"; "occue"; "occlu"; "occliffed"; "occl"; "occlam"; "occlud"; "occupe"; and several times, expectedly, "occur."[78] Such signature repetitions, ironically, are precisely what Inman has sought to avoid. Valuing an ephemeral, ad hoc bricolage of linguistic fragments over the foundation of an invented language with sustainable neologisms, he explains: "one of the reasons I eventually moved back to using 'dictionary words' was that I found myself repeating 'made up' words, falling into patterns, developing a repertoire of 'vocabulary tics.'"[79] Elsewhere, he laments the process by which "an extremely non-representational technique, [Jackson] Pollock's overall dripping, becomes signatory. Through which a radical formal approach to figuration is turned into a trademark, something to peddle the goods with."[80]

From the other side, and with that becoming-signatory in mind, the various "thumb limps," "stumbles in penmanship," and even the paper cuts that might make writing painful offer a connotative rewriting of Peter Inman's distinctive *nom de plume* "P. Inman": the *penman*, via the yoked and elided stick-figure *pinman*, ghosting behind his pen name.[81] Readers are encouraged to consider that very elision with phrases such as "name at the quotient put too close together," "the shortening between to the word," and what a "surname [...] does to letters."[82] More explicitly, Inman is conscious of the moniker and "the difference in / a name" when you have a "real name frozen for the sake of publication"; his writing returns to the topic, frequently with freighted connotations: "the victim over pen name"; "king's men filled up against pen name"; "pen.

names"; "pen, name"; "made up of names"; *et cetera*.[83] In general, in fact, onomastics—the "name. of. names"—and "proper naming," or the "inside / of a proper / name," is a concern from the beginning of Inman's career; in *What Happens Next* he writes: "your name, signature bled its own obsessive, tiny light."[84] Specifically, one might note that *penman* names "a person skilled in writing; one who writes a good hand, a calligrapher."[85] "Penmanship," accordingly, is explicitly mentioned at least a half-dozen times in the collected poems, along with an attendant anxiety about its failure: a "penmanship inside out" of "faint marks," "childish script," and the "scratch & gill of pen stroke" (with an echo of the *plume* of the *quill* behind "gill").[86]

Moreover, Inman's poetry repeatedly links these two concerns—the onomastic and the orthographic—yoking "name" directly to descriptions of the cacographic: dots; blots; stubble and specks; scratch and skew and scrawl; spelling mistakes and wrong symbols; lapses and collapse; the sketched and murmured and stuttered.[87] If "P. Inman" sounds the marred approximation of *penman*, then the signature of the signature will be legible in a deformed calligraphy, deskilled orthography, and the marking of a poor hand: what will appear to be typos, misspellings, and, ironically, illegibilities. Or, as the poem "i.e." puts it, plainly, "limped notes to say pierre," which is to say, of course, in French: *Peter*.[88] These oblique nominations thus countersign the signature in the ways we saw in chapter 2: a signature style affirmed by the entry of the proper name into the signifier's system of spacing and paragrammatic measure: "a writing out of names," "entirely out of names," in which the recurrent concern with the materials of writing, with the facture and fracture of its physical form, coupled to its "own obsessive" focus on names, rewrites Inman's own pen name 'in other words,' through his signature style of cacographic combinations and what appear to be errata, corrigenda, and scriptorial faults that worry the very status of lexemes themselves in his most radical writing.[89] Phrases, throughout, suggest the operation: "a name out of / marks"; "my. name's. effects"; "my name / as crayon arithmetic"; *et cetera*.[90] Note, for one final example, the "quill" and misspelled *pencil* of "pencit" that frame the lines in *Platin*:

> ... pencit drake ...
> namely blotter nominatives , quill,fluie[91]

The writing here both refers to and simultaneously enacts the wandering inky bleed of fluid ("fluie") error and fluke ("fluie") by or in need of a "blotter" ("a scribbler, a sorry writer," "one who stains or defiles," or a "thing used for drying wet ink marks; as a piece of blotting paper or a blotting-pad"). It does so, moreover, while encircling the naming of names ("namely [...] nominatives") as a signature of signatures, so that whatever else it may be doing, the lines point discursively to its author, whose euphemistic name, a "signature bled," a "name turned," in turn, gestures directly back to writing itself, never quite ever "leaving names behind."[92] Indeed, even that *pencil* (etymologically from *peninculus*, Latin for a "small paintbrush"), in the sense that it was used through the nineteenth century, originally denoting "a paintbrush made with fine hair," or what came in the twentieth century to be designated as a "hair-pencil," in the context of "drake" (as the twentieth-century colloquialism to denote "unruly hair"), may bring the cut and colored hairs that recur in Inman's poetry into the orbit of his onomastics.[93] But one not need follow the web of connections so far from the pen or pencil or platen of the typewriter; ultimately, *a penman*, in general, designates anyone who simply writes, who gives up the written—inscription regardless of any message, signifiers in whatever disarray, the trace of spacing, the violence of the letter, the incisive incising mark the gram—as Inman, in his oeuvre, in fact, has.

The extraordinary effect of that oeuvre is the extent to which, even still, it works.

The Logic of Print [CHAPTER FOUR]

*The voice of Mahalia Jackson
came through the ether.*

VAN MORRISON

*the world's apostrophes collapse
into the oneness of all ditto marks*

WALTER LOWENFELS[1]

In a 1963 review of Robert Hayden's poetry, Russell Atkins—polymath editor of the *Free Lance*—lauded its "relief from an exaggerated preoccupation with 'content'" in contemporary African American poetry.[2] A few years later, Atkins's own poem, "Spyrytual," would seem, at first glance, to be similarly relieved (figure 6).[3] Published as a single-page chapbook by Darryl Allen (D. A.) Levy's 7 Flowers Press, the poem features clusters of marks—whether quotation marks, apostrophes, or ditto marks (or the quotation of ditto marks, or the ditto reiteration of quotations) is a central question posed by the poem's interrogative—that interrupt a single, repeated phrase: "oh didn't it / rain." But if Atkins's text relinquishes most of its "content," it does not escape signification. Indeed, this chapter will argue that the most abstract elements in Atkins's poem—those marks that would seem, in fact, to be the signs of refusing to say anything at all—speak directly to the racially fraught politics of current civic affairs and the sociability of texts taking an active, voluble part in the construction of explicitly activist communities.

Despite its idiosyncratic spelling, the title of the poem indicates the source of the language it quotes: an African American spiritual, the title of which Atkins articulates down the page with a spatial distribution reminiscent of Stéphane Mallarmé's *Un coup de dés*. In the first decades of the twentieth century, folklorists and sociologists traced the song's origins to African American "work songs" with more extended narratives about Jonah and Noah.[4] Howard W. Odum finds that "the present-day song that apparently originated" in the "plantation and slave" spirituals "is less elaborate, having only portions of the old song, and not being much in demand."[5] He quotes the opening of the more recent version:

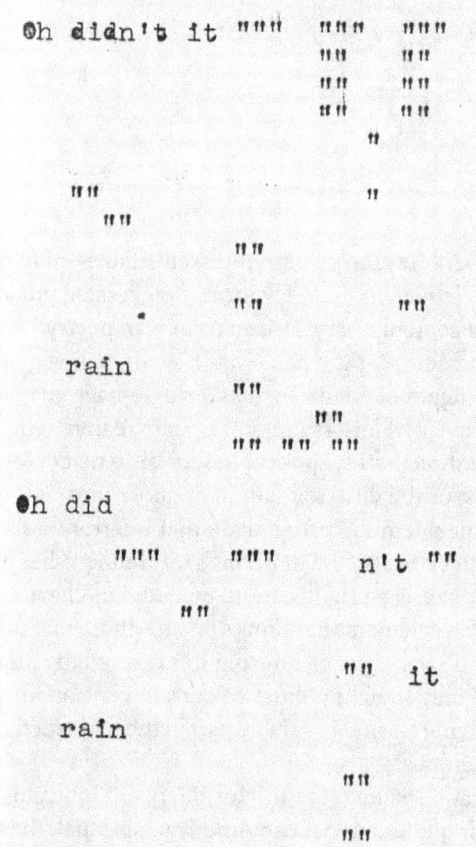

6 Russell Atkins, "Spyrytual." From Russell Atkins, *Spyrytual* (Cleveland: 7 Flowers Press, 1966). By permission of Kevin Prufer and Bob McDonough, for Russell Atkins. Author's photograph.

God told Noah 'bout de rainbow sign—
Lawd, did n't it rain?
No more water but fier nex' time—
*O did n't it rain? Halleluyer.*⁶

Atkins's redactions, in which quotation marks seem to replace the missing lyrics, might be read as a literalization of Odum's textual history: "Spyrytual" quotes only portions of the old song. The song's central line, the one cited by Atkins's poem, is deceptively simple. Structurally, it encodes a linguistic analogue to the call-and-response mode of the spiritual; while colloquially familiar, the phrase takes the form of a grammatically unusual construction: an interrogative that anticipates its own answer in order to make sense. Indeed, Atkins's poem quotes not just the spiritual's title but what is also its refrain, and thus makes a repetition of a repetition. Together with the responsorial structure inherent in the grammar of the phrase and implicit in the musical form it quotes, the poem suggests thematic analogues to its formal structures. Furthermore, the *idem* denoted by what might be ditto marks could well refer to the relentless sustain of the biblical rain both named and mimicked by the spiritual's reiteration of the quadragesimic period: "forty days and forty nights" sets the anaphoric meter in some versions of the song, while it serves as "the first line of eight successive stanzas" in others.⁷ In all cases, the levels of repetition performed by "Spyrytual" set subject and form into resonant echo: "[ref]rain."

At the same time, the visual prosody of the poem is striking, with its glyphs spaced in deliberate but enigmatic arrangements across the page. Taking precedence over any grammatical coherence, those nonlexical marks invite visually iconic or pictorial readings. Given the cue of the legible word "rain," raindrops come immediately to mind—a pattern of patter against the pane of the page—but in the broader context of a song about the flood, they might be read as inch marks, measuring the cataclysmic rainfall, or even the hoof tracks of paired ruminants queuing for the ark: "sets of inky two-part punctuation units" in a field that "suggests sets of paw or hoof-prints—the imprint of a geometrically minded deer."⁸ In the context of an old-time song, further reveries might see the page design reflecting the punched roll for a piano-player (I will argue later in this chapter that the poem calls up its own modes of printing in various ways, and so imagining its duplicator master cycling around the metal drum of a mimeograph machine with a rhythmic clatter might make the image of a piano roll less fanciful). Indeed, among the new music rolls advertised in an industry journal in 1926 one finds an offering from the Aeolia Company: "Deep River (Key of F); Oh, Didn't It Rain (Key of G) (Burleigh)—Negro

Spirituals."⁹ In Atkins's own musical imagination, moreover, *spiritual* carried a musical (rather than, say, religious) association; it was the title he was also giving to a number of contemporaneous music scores.

Even without these associations, however, the poem exploits a dynamic tension between the written and the heard, the literary text and the musical performance, sight and sound. To begin with, the prestandard orthography of the title ("I used Chaucer's Middle English," Atkins explains) recalls the precarious relation of print and pronunciation in English and the warp of letters required to signal sound.¹⁰ At the same time, the archaic spelling draws out a visual pun on a visual register: *spy* ("to look at, examine, or observe closely or carefully," from the Old French *espier*, but with Germanic parallels; to "discover, to notice, or observe").¹¹ To recognize the *spy* in *Spyrytual* is thus precisely the sort of close attention and discernment implied by the word itself: a specific ritual of reading. In Aldon Nielsen's assessment, most of the poem that follows is visibly written at the expense of the spoken; "Atkins' cloudburst of quotation marks," he argues, "can only be transcribed and read, it can't be recited at all." An imaginative performance in the tradition of graphic scores or sound poetry could surely find a way to recite the marks, *pace* Nielsen, but the impassive glyphs do certainly contrast with the easy decoding of the conventional words. That contrast is heightened by the degree to which the song's original phrasing is given, discursively, to emphasizing spoken language. In the most famous recording, Mahalia Jackson describes and instructs: "God *told* Noah about the rainbow sign"; "*talk* about the rain"; "just *listen* to it rain"; and so on.¹² Other versions emphasize the characters crying out, as well as the desperate entreating percussion of knocking on windows and doors.¹³

Jackson's performance, at the same time, underscores another tension between the written and the sung, as the song charts a pivot from transcription to score. The song as Atkins and his audience would have known it in 1966 was a gospel standard.¹⁴ While it may have originated as a folk spiritual, Jackson provides a useful reminder: "a lot of folks don't know that gospel songs have not been handed down like spirituals. Most gospel songs have been composed and written by Negro musicians like Professor [Thomas] Dorsey."¹⁵ Elaborating the spiritual's late development of choral harmony, and adding musical instrumentation, gospel music was notated in musical scores; it is a written form. In contrast, spirituals, as true folk songs, are products of anonymous, community performance traditions, passed on by practice through oral imitation and reiteration. Originating in work songs, and inflected by Protestant hymnal modes, the monophonic African American spiritual was unaccompanied by musical instruments other than incidental percussion (perhaps continuing the corporeal claps and stomps of ring rituals—sounds echoed in this particular song's recollection of knocking on windows and doors). Following the arrangement of these folk songs by ethnographers and performers, and their incorporation into notated genres, from Western concert music to blues and jazz, spirituals were absorbed into the new performance styles and musical genres that proliferated in the twentieth century under the influence of African American culture—a "cultural intermingling" that in contrast to European culture, for Atkins, led to "American *spiritual* vitality."[16]

Throughout Atkins's writing on aesthetics, the written and the heard were freighted concepts. Inverting the terms of a dynamic discerned by Brent Hayes Edwards in the work of Duke Ellington, we might say that for Atkins the musical is less an *analogy* for poetry than an inherent element in his conception of literature itself, and a key formal bridge or instigating spur in his compositional process.[17] In the resulting "literature of music," or musicating of literature, however, the conventional distinctions invoked by remarking that "Spyrytual" makes use of musical forms folds in on itself.[18] In Atkins's theoretical writing on music, the visual and the aural are put into a reorienting—if not disorienting—parallax, or what Cameron Williams has described as a "defamiliarization of aesthetic practices via the mutation of the senses."[19] Atkins's prose, somehow both convoluted and curtailed, is obfuscatory (to put it politely), but as one critic has summarized the basic terms, "Atkins draws a sharp line between music and composition; he claims in fact that they are contradictories."[20] The communicative power of music, for Atkins, "lies outside of the very element that transmits it," which is to say, its power comes not from sound. Atkins decouples music from sound because he understands "composition" as a structure or patterned arrangement grasped cognitively rather than heard.[21] Composition, accordingly "is not a binaural art but a VISUAL ART. In short, so-called 'musical composition' is a VISUAL ART."[22] Because Atkins proposes an intellectual rather than an auditory basis for composition, the brain rather than the ear becomes the locus for his musical activity. Rather than writing "FOR THE EAR," with composition as the means to organize sound, the "psychovisualist" composer arranges sound—as a kind of script taking the medium of vibrational frequencies—in order to produce a compositional structure, or formation of material relationships, to be cognitively apprehended.[23] The purpose of a psychovisualist work is thus "to be seen psychovisually [i.e., in the mind's eye] and 'heard' only intermittently, finally not to be 'heard,' but comprehended by a feeling of relationships in object formations."[24] "Spyrytual" obviously gestures toward a decidedly visual poetry, and with its formations of printed characters in unusual arrangements on the inked object of the page it elicits the very terms of the debate taken up in Atkins's essays on aesthetics: the written quotation of a song which was itself the written transcription of a traditional oral practice.

Dramatizing this historical pivot from folk spiritual to written gospel, with its marks of omission and quotation, each like a doubled apostrophe, Atkins's poem both literally and figuratively reduplicates what Edwards has identified, with respect to the blues lyric, as the "unresolved tensions between transcription (the 'musical' apostrophe) and score (the 'discursive' apostrophe)."[25] Following Edwards's explication of the apostrophe's ability to serve both formal and discursive ends, we can see the glyphs in Atkins's poem asserting a mute formal index of the absent (or silenced, or silent) words for which they substitute as placeholders while simultaneously volunteering positive declarations, in their own voice, as part of the poem's own eloquent statement.[26] Furthermore, the grammatically strange phrase at the heart of "Spyrytual" signals excess via negation. Despite the negative verbal construction, the point, of course, is that it *did* rain—a lot: oh did it rain! In the same way, the ciphers of the quotation marks, indicating redacted text, or standing in as placeholders for implied text, do not so much negate signification as solicit an excess of possible meanings, and if read as ditto marks they double down on that bargain: indicating more of the same by removal and replacement.

Atkins's poem "Narrative," in part an imagined account of John Brown's assault on Harper's Ferry, deploys apostrophes so that they begin to edge toward the reiterative sign of the ditto mark while simultaneously functioning within the formal orthography of the text. The marks, in this poem, both represent and enact the confusion and loss that takes place in the narrated episode. Rhetorically, moreover, they intimate a diminuating "*et cetera*"—as if to say: more of the same, *ad terminus*. The poem concludes with the swift violence of the skirmish's thunderous clash; Atkins transforms the description of the charge—"in a rush / passed swift fierce"—into the moment of the arsenal's breach: a fracas which dissolves "in a dust" that replicates the confusion of the mêlée (and perhaps the sortie's failure):

' 'ft passed 'ierced
' 'if's, in, ss'd
shsh 'erced
' 'ft
' 'isk[27]

Here, in this mimetic sketch of the instant of the arsenal's breach, Atkins submits those four words describing the celeritous intensity of the approach—"swift," "passed," "fierce," and "rush"—to permutation and apostrophized elision. The reader is then asked to reverse the process in order to reconstruct the meaning of the final word: "'isk." An earlier line contrasts the thunder of the charge with the "whist," or silence, of the surrounding trail—a word that in a subsequent line transforms to "w'isk'," giving a flash of *whisking*, a synonym for the kind of brief rapid fleeting movement described by the other key words. But the apostrophe opens the possibility as well of *brisk*, an alternate synonym, as well as *risk*, the very condition of the raid. With that literal figure of a failed risk, the final line strikes a tone of elegiac consolation and concludes the "narrative" with a moral to the story: nothing ventured, it reminds the reader, nothing gained.

The apostrophe, indicating the contraction of a verbal participle, would become a signature tic of Atkins's style, which often foregrounds anthimeria—using one part of speech as if it were another—as he deforms nouns, adjectives, and prepositions into past participles: "Euclid'd," "nosferatu'd," "furious'd," "around'd," and so on.[28] In such instances, the punctuation draws attention, visually, to words that have already been grammatically estranged; they signal not so much orthographic contraction as artifice itself. Atkins employs quotation marks to similar effect; a dozen years before the publication of *Spyrytual*, he had premiered the use of the punctuation as a device insisting on its own presence, rather than serving any obvious discursive function:

/the fourth in wrath the tall 1
flames S s staggers s s S s upon
crashes) th'/'xo .x/ " " " " " " " " " " ![29]

Rising and falling between upper- and lowercase form in uneven permutation, the letter *s* in the second line breaks from the end of *flames*, surges and recedes, reattaches to the beginning of *staggers* and then itself staggers through the line in sibilant imitation of the clichéd hiss of flames—a convention Atkins had used to conclude what is perhaps his most famous poem, "Trainyard at Night," where the steam engine of the "great Limited" rolls to a stop thus:

hiss insists upon hissing insists
on insisting on hissing hiss
hiss s ss ss sss sss s
ss s s
s[30]

In "Lisbon," the possibility of onomatopoeia gives way to unpronounceable combinations, punctuation marks, and graphic glyphs of parenthesis and slash. Abby and Ronald Johnson quote these same lines to illustrate their claim that Atkins "was so experimental […] that it was often difficult to trace his ideas."[31] While the quotation marks here do indeed remain restively opaque and hermetic, or at least irresolvably indeterminate in their signification, they may again indicate falling, as in "Spyrytual"— though here, in a poem that takes the massive 1755 earthquake in Portugal as its subject, they would remark the stones of a collapsing tower rather than the salving drops of summer rain. "What I relate in this poem is of a large city that fell to pieces"; the verse opens with a grand sweep, before implicitly comparing the devastation of the eighteenth-century city with the urban decay of neglected inner-city infrastructures two hundred years later: "Something very much as now in some places." After setting the scene with the liturgical celebrations of All Saints' Day ("a reverential day in Portugal," Atkins glosses), the "pious murmurs" of "hymns" ascend from chanting choirs in contrast to the collapsing architecture that will follow the collective screaming at the sudden catastrophe:

    Ten thousand ! ! x/ .!' 'go scrEa

EameaEamEaeEam I ng i nn nnnn

    n n n n n

               nnn nnn g!
!! (

)

    (LIS/ BON

    LIS/ BON

With a fracturing pun on its title (and the possibility of a shift to French), the poem reveals the words hidden within the city's name: "LIS/BON" [read/good]. Asking for a good reading of broken words, the poem itself ends by breaking the French word for *words*: "mot / s." At the same time, that final *s* also appears as the last residual drop of a wash of letters that in the previous stanza had remotivated the staggering hiss of flames in overdetermined figuration: the unrecoupable excess of mass fatalities; the sound of the quake-surged surf; the pictorial visual notation of eviscerated entrails; and the missing initial letter of *strewn*, which had been compensated for by the transegmental stretch between "is" and "trewn":

with boats the sea is trewn
with multitudes the shore

the mul lllllll llll llll t
i tudes sssS s SSSS
   s s sssS S s s
   s   ssss   S
       the guts of
       men
       in ruts
            lie up

In a "trance of horror" which literally and figuratively arises from the "En / trance of horror" that blocks escape from a collapsing building, the singular words "one" and "each" are impacted ("upon each") in "up OnE ach" when the very language of the poem itself condenses and distends to mimic the confused jostle of the crowd it describes trying to find an exit:

Gre At h' shock f all s udden
one e very huge to WerE dged
C On vents an K ill'd
multituDes per at En
trance of horror up OnE ach
o theRu sh

As in "Narrative," the lines both describe and provoke confusion, but the sense here seems to be that at the great shock of the tremor which comes "all sudden" with everyone in the vicinity ("one e very") threatened by the sudden fall ("f all") of the very huge tower ("very huge to WerE") which had been pictorially figured as "the tall 1" in the stanza's first line.[32] As it "staggers" and "crashes," the convent bordered (or "E dged") by that tower—perhaps the famed Carmo convent—has also collapsed at the edge of fissured vents ("On vents"), and victims (who are wedged ["WerE dged"]? and harmed ["ill'd"]?) give vent to their own emotional shock in the interjections of the immediately preceding lines: "Oh for Christ's sake! Good God! / Good Lord! Misericordia ! !."[33] In the context of these exclamations, we might read the earlier sequence of quotation marks as indicating the expression of speechless stupefaction, something like the comic-strip convention of representing unspoken or unspeakable emotional outbursts with a jumble of punctuation marks. At the same time, their ditto function, indicating more of the same, augments the sense of scale and the mass of casualties. Reminiscent of roman numerals, the "x/" in "Lisbon" might be read as shorthand notation for 10,000, in apposition to the written form: "Ten thousand !! x/ .!"; accordingly, the "th'" preceding the line of quotation marks suggests an abbreviation of *thousand* and a restatement of the count: th'/'xo .x/, or a thousand multiplied ten times—precisely the number of the ten quotation marks which follow.

In contrast with the panicked agitation of the nonverbal marks in "Lisbon," which skitter in excessive exclamation along the line, the quotation marks in "Spyrytual" riot over the page with a more deliberate insistence, but both poems refer—with differing degrees of discursivity—to historical events of public violence. While one might not expect a gospel refrain fragmented amid a field of punctuation to speak to topical local politics, precisely that distance between cool abstraction and the heat of the moment is what makes *Spyrytual* such a powerful publication. The standard bibliographic information on the book's title page—"1966 / Cleveland,Ohio"— is resonant, indicating that the poem was printed at a particular moment of mass political violence. Following smaller episodes of unrest in New York, New Jersey, and Philadelphia in 1964—and the iconic Watts rebellion in 1965—Cleveland set the precedent for the hundreds of instances of civic summer turmoil that would simmer through the following year, including the 12th Street riot in Detroit, all in advance of the protests that would erupt following the assassination of the Reverend Martin Luther King Jr. and the chorus of those speaking "the language of the unheard."[34] In Cleveland, the rough music was raised in the racially segregated Hough neighborhood, a roughly two-mile-square sector just north of the city's urban center. By the time of the riots, it was "one of the nation's most economically depressed African American communities" and was the epitome of the postwar American racial ghetto.[35] Protest began on Monday, 18 July, and by the end of the week four bystanders had been murdered by vigilantes and white police, who also arrested hundreds of protestors. If the Watts rebellion was symbolized by depredation, the Hough riots were specifically marked by targeted arson. Some 240 fires were reported to authorities, resulting in millions of dollars of damage, with almost a hundred fires set on Thursday night alone.[36] Charles Lucas (then the pastor at Greater Avery AME Church) recalls, "Hough was on fire. I don't how many fires, I couldn't remember [...] and it burned down; Hough burned down that night."[37]

Those fires, and the violence they illuminated, were cooled by tardy rains that arrived on Sunday night, after two and a half weeks without precipitation under abnormally high, sweltering summer temperatures.[38] But water had also been the origin of the riots. Against a "reservoir of grievances" (the liquid metaphor is suggestive, in the context) and a "massive tangle of issues and circumstances" that mired relations in a segregated society, America was primed for the hundreds of outbursts of concentrated violence that flared in cities in the late 1960s.[39] In Cleveland, that violent protest was sparked by a glass of water. An African American customer who had bought a bottle of wine at the Seventy-Niners' Café was refused a glass of water by the white proprietor. The dispute over whether takeaway purchases entitled one to a glass of water turned on the suspicion that frugal customers attempting to evade state liquor laws would purchase cheaper packaged bottles but then use the water glass to drink on the premises. Summoning images of Jim Crow water-fountain signage, the angry customer affixed an ad hoc sign to the café's door, reading "No Water for Niggers." It attracted an increasingly enraged neighborhood crowd, which turned violent by nightfall.[40]

By the light of these vivid particulars—how the Cleveland riots progress from drought to flood, by way of fire—we can begin to see the resonance of *Spyrytual* in its particular historical moment. The spiritual quoted by Atkins refers not only to the biblical flood but to God's postdiluvian covenant with Noah: "Never again will all life be destroyed by the waters of a flood; never again will there be a flood to destroy the earth."[41] The lyrics of the song continue with the veiled threat made famous as the title of a James Baldwin collection (and a phrase that Pete Seeger considered "one of the greatest lines in all of American folk music"): "no more water, but the fire next time."[42] With the wit of just the right allusion at just the right moment, Atkins calls attention to the irony of the narrative reversal in Cleveland: no (more) water, so the fire this time—followed by torrential rains.[43]

The Hough riots and the history of the mimeograph networks in Cleveland are inextricably intertwined in ways more direct than Levy's printing of *Spyrytual*. Later that same year, Levy edited *46¢: An Anthology of Cleveland Poets*, which featured a reprint of Atkins's 1958 poem "Lakefront, Cleveland." It also included Joel Friedman's "Black Revolt (Hough, July, 1966)," which praised the arson of urban protest over and above the napalm the military was using in Southeast Asia at the time, and elevated an angry human mob above the "methodical fascist machine" of concealed social violence:[44]

> My young eyes shine
>   As i see i
> Fighting forces of motherfucking complacency
>   Blowing those assholes off theirs
>   Fighting for imagined mine black cock & cream.[45]

Although Levy's own pacifism kept him from sympathizing with the rioters ("black power doesnt mean black violence," he would write to a friend at the time), he admired the force of the sentiments expressed by a white teenager.[46] Friedman's parents were less enthralled with their son's attitude, and filed a complaint with the police when they discovered a copy of Levy's *Marrahwannah Quarterly* in Joel's bedroom. In response, the police were secretly taping when Levy read "Black Revolt" during an open mic literary event at The Gate, a coffeehouse in the basement of the Cleveland Trinity Cathedral, which modeled itself on New York's Café Le Metro (Friedman was too shy to read the poem out loud himself).[47] Levy was arrested for contributing to the delinquency of a minor—through obscenities, ironically, written by the minor himself—and his mimeograph machine was confiscated.[48] It was the beginning of the end of his publishing career.

To be sure, as "Lakefront, Cleveland" evinces, rain and storms and turbulent water are part of the luridly gothic mise-en-scène to which Atkins's poetry returns—long before the Hough riots—and "Spyrytual" reads easily into this personal style. Atkins repeatedly depicts a lowering "sepulchral sky" above the local lakefront, with whirlwinds and lightning over a "lake in a storm," "a squall," a "tempest," a "winter storm," "thunder and lightning," and rains in "strange fluences" with the "gust'd" blows of "no ordinary wind" in "furious weather" and "flood."[49] In the poem "A Storm Shall Break," for one visually marked example (figure 7), Atkins breaks the words of the title into a snaking agitation of repeated letters above a frantically sputtered "hysterical"; the page, moreover, includes a fall and flurry of double quotation marks that in isolation might be seen as the flicker of leaves quivering in the wind of an impending gale ("a rush of miserabled leaves" or the "woe of shuddered leaves," as other of Atkins's poems put it), but for those who recall "Spyrytual" they might be understood as the answer to the alternatives introduced by the punning conjunction that homophonically brings together atmospherics and possibility:

" " " .
" "

is in the leaves
a strange whether

A STORM SHALL BREAK[50]

Indeed, the fall of rain figured on the page as repeated punctuation marks develops into its own trope in the '60s small-press periodicals of the Cleveland concrete poetry network. In "WINTER RAIN AND PURPLE RAINBOW" (figure 8), for an instance, T. L. Kryss conveys the relentless, fatiguing monotony of seasonal precipitation with repeated lines set to negative

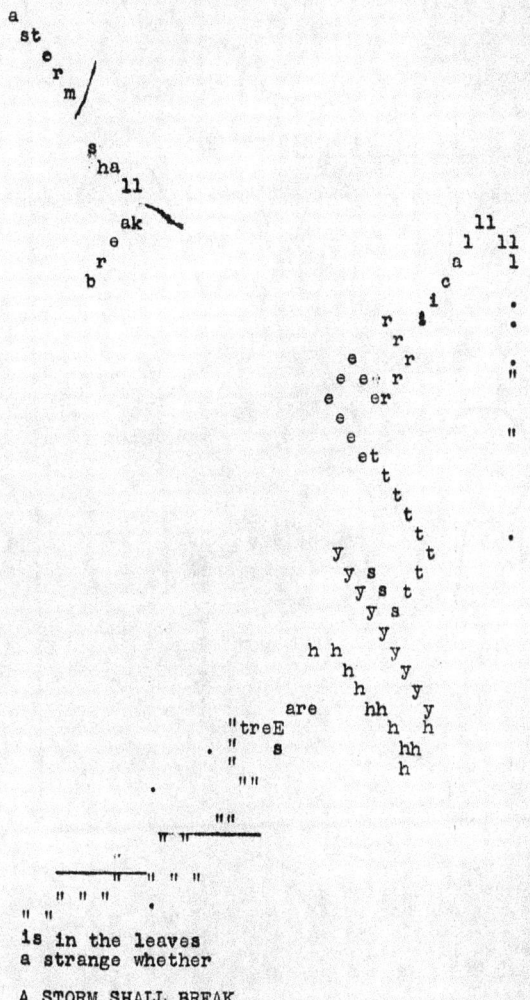

7 Russell Atkins, "A Storm Shall Break." From *Marrahwannah Quarterly* 3.3 (1967). By permission of Kevin Prufer and Bob McDonough, for Russell Atkins. Photograph: Special Collections, Michael Schwartz Library, Cleveland State University, Cleveland Memory Project.

```
                    WINTER RAIN AND PURPLE RAINBOW
                 WINTER RAIN AND PURPLE RAINBOW
         i am tired of the curse
                                 PURPLE RAINBOW
     WINTER RAIN AND PURPLE RAINBOW PURPLE RAINBOW
         i am tired of the curse      PURPLE RAINBOW
         i am tired of the curse        PURPLE RAINBOW
         i am tired of the curse          PURPLE RAINBOW
         i am tired of the curse            PURPLE RAINBOW
                                              PURPLE RAINBOW
         FOOTPRINT NAILED TO THE WIND
                                      WINTER RAIN AND PURPLE RAINBOW
         i am tired                  WINTER RAIN AND PURPLE RAINBOW
         i am tired                 WINTER RAIN AND PURPLE RAINBOW
         i am tired                WINTER RAIN AND PURPLE RAINBOW
     iamtirediamtired              WINTER RAIN AND PURPLE RAINBOW
         i am tired FOOTPRINT NAILED TO THE WIND
         i am tired FOOTPRINT NAILED TO THE WIND
         i am tired FOOTPRINT NAILED TO THE WIND
         i am tired FOOTPRINT NAILED TO THE WIND
                    FOOTPRINT NAILED TO THE WIND
                    FOOTPRINT NAILED TO THE WIND
                   FOOTPRINT NAILED TO THE WIND
                  FOOTPRINT NAILED TO THE WIND
                 FOOTPRINT NAILED TO THE WIND
                FOOTPRINT NAILED TO THE WIND
               FOOTPRINT NAILED TO THE WIND
              FOOTPRINT NAILED TO THE WIND
             FOOTPRINT NAILED TO THE WIND
            FOOTPRINT NAILED TO THE WIND
                                      i am tired of the curse
                                      i am tired of the curse
              i am tired             i am tired of the curse
              i am tired             i am tired
                  i am tired  of the curse i am tired
                     i am tired of the curse   of the curse
                                 of the curse
                                    of the curse i am tired of the curse
              i am tired of the curse  i am tired
              i am tired of the curse  i am tired
              i am tired of the curse  i am tired
              i am tired of the curse  i am tired
                                       i am tired
                                       i am tired
         FOOTPRINT NAILED TO THE WIND  i tired am
         i am tired of the curse       am tired i
         FOOTPRINT NAILED TO THE WIND  i am tired
         i am tired of the curse       i   am
         WINTER RAIN AND PURPLE RAINBOW  i
         i am tired of the curse
         FOOTPRINT NAILED TO THE WIND
         i am tired of the curse
         i am tired of the curse
         WINTER RAIN AND PURPLE RAINBOW

         i am tired
         WINTER RAIN
         i am tired  of the curse
         WINTER RAIN                              T.L. Kryss
                     of the curse
         i am tired
         WINTER RAIN
                     of the curse
         i am tired
                        PURPLE RAINBOW
              PURPLE RAINBOW
```

8 T. L. Kryss, "Winter Rain and Purple Rainbow." From *Marrahwannah Quarterly* 4.1 (1967). By permission of Tom Kryss. Photograph: Special Collections, Michael Schwartz Library, Cleveland State University, Cleveland Memory Project.

leading, in a cascade down the page. The compositional repetition prefigures the exposition of tedium: "I am tired of the curse / WINTER RAIN," the speaker eventually confesses under the low clouds of unrelenting overcast and downpour.[51] Similarly (figure 9), his poem "monsoooooooooon" overlays the cloudlike puffs of the letter *o*, striating the page in horizontal banks that extend across the width of the sheet as they reiterate the distended spelling of the title, all crossed by the descent of a vertical series of slash marks that sweep like sheets of wind-driven rain diagonally down the page. Closer yet to "Spyrytual," another of Kryss's untitled poems in *Marrahwannah Quarterly* describes the great biblical flood and Noah's ark (figure 10), with punctuation (possibly commas, or single quotation marks) dropping in looping torrents to justify and redeem his shipbuilding while a stifling weight of densely packed letters—x, c, z, m, a—pools at the bottom of the page to drown the mocking skeptics' cries of "help."[52] In its local publishing context, that is, "Spyrytual" looks less like an anomaly and more like the familiar model for a subgenre.

These conventions, however, are not isolated; they extend a general cliché of the midcentury genre of concrete poetry, which often positions repeated words to indicate vectors of motion within the fluid dynamics of atmospheric systems. In general, these shaped compositions perpetuate the legacy of Guillaume Apollinaire's iconic work of visual poetry, "Il Pleut," from his 1918 *Calligrammes*, a poem which "Spyrytual" immediately brings to mind.[53] The most cited versions were written by Eugen Gomringer and Ian Hamilton Finlay. Finlay's 1966 *Wave Rock* collides the two title words until the particles of the spray of letters from the first cover the second, merging with (or "avec," as the central portmanteau of the poem reads) one another.[54] One of Gomringer's 1953 *konstellationen*, similarly, scatters the letters of the word *wind* so that they intersect in shifted apices.[55] Like Gomringer's poem, a page from Ronald Johnson's *Songs of the Earth* maps the four corners of the compass rose from which the *wind* comes to lift a *wing*, but the trope is a commonplace in concrete poetry from the late 1950s and early '60s: Augusto de Campos's rain to river transformation of "pluvial" into "fluvial"; Pedro Xisto's "Autumn" (which alternates the words "vento" [wind] and "folha" [leaf] in staggered lines of bold and regular typeface); multiple meditations on the word [*wird*] (as) wind by Heinz Gappmayr and a lofted extension of the vowel breath in *vitr* [wind], with the acute dot of the *i* blown forward by the force in the Czech typeface chosen by Bohumila Grögerová and Josef Hiršal.[56] Significantly, Ivo Vroom's 1966 "Winden" [Winds], in which the title word gusts up the page in a sweeping arc, was republished in the same special Concrete issue of *Marrahwannah Quarterly* as Atkins's "Storm" and Kryss's "monsoooooooooon," alongside works by D. A. Levy (which we shall examine

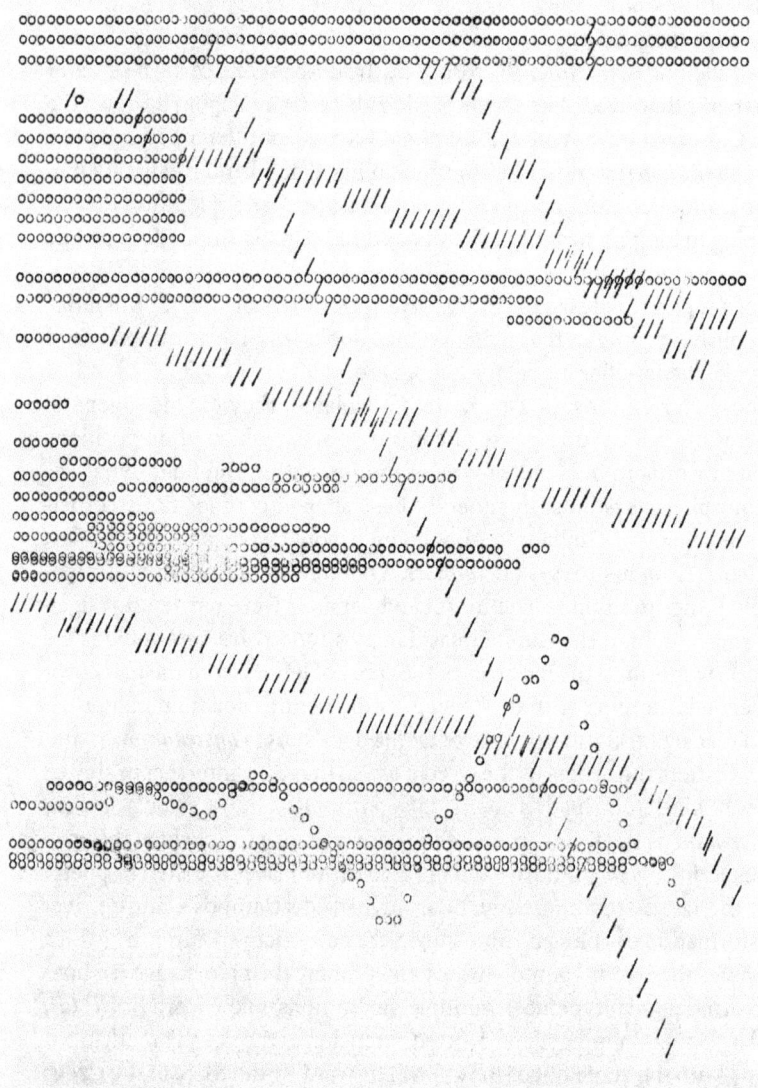

9 T. L. Kryss, "monsoooooooooon." From *Marrahwannah Quarterly* 3.3 (1967). By permission of Tom Kryss. Photograph: Special Collections, Michael Schwartz Library, Cleveland State University, Cleveland Memory Project.

(TL Kryss)

```
noah spent building the tribes the four of the to see great
a lifetime the ark  came from  corners wind  this  ship
in the mid the desert not look  old man  not look they said
dle of    & it did   like rain it does  like rain hahah ahaha
& the sea is miles to hahahaha  but the old & did not second
two hundred  the west they said man smiled  for one   lift
his hands  task hahahahhahahchahahahahchahahahahahahah ahahaha
from the  hahahahahahahahah ahah ahah ahahahahahah ahah ahahaha
          one day noah last chink & sat down little animals
          calked the   in the hull to wait   & big
 ,  ,     animals came  caroused   castles  feasted on
  ',,,    the people   in their    noah    bread & black
   ,  ',,,,wine        & saved
    ,     the last     crumbs      it was
     ,    for the      bedlam                   hahaha
      ,,,,       ',,,     on     ,  ,
              ,  ',,,     the      ,  ,       ,,,,             ,
           ,,     ',    boat,'                         ,
         ,   ,,     ',,                  ,   ,           ,
noah pulled      'plank' with    ', as the skies'     ,, ,
up the gang      his wives &       '& the boat    ',    ,   ,
          ,,     lowered            into the skies  ,,    ,
          ,,,    rose into          so 'sudden  ,,          ,
     ,,,,        it was all         had time to          ,
       ,         that no  ',        moment  ,     ,     ,
                 one       ,,,      ,  ,,          , ,,   ,
see of    ,      mans         ,,,,     ,  ,     ,  ,,    '
the glory ',     ,,,  ,             ,  ,           ,,  ,
old       ,              ,,,  ,     ,',,,          ,,,
    ,              ,,        ,       ,   ,      ,,
,,,       ,                ,,     ,   ,,   ,,,  ha
  ,,            ,           ,,
     ,      ,     ,,   ,   ,,     ,,    ha '
ha             ,,     ',,   ,          ,, ,   ,,,
    ,,,    ',,   ha  ,,   ',    ,           ,
        ,    ',,,             ,,  ,,,'       ,
      ,              ,,      ,    ,'helphelp     ,
hahahahahahaha    ,,,       ,     ,  ,          ,
        , hahahahahaha  xcxcxcxcxcxcxcxcxcx. xcxcx xcxcxc
             xmxmxmxmxmxmxmxm xmxm xmxmxmxmxmxmxm xmxmxmxmxmxmxmxm xmxmxmxmxmxm
xmxmxmxm xmxmxmxmxmxmx mxm xmxmxmxmxmxm xmxmxmxmxmxmxmxmxmxmxmxmhe
     xmxmxmxm xmxmxmxmxm xm xmxmxmxmxmxm xmxmxmxmxmxm xmxmxmxmxmx he
zmzmzmzm zmzmzmzmzmzmzm zmzmzm zmzmzmzmzm zmzmzm zmzmzmhelph
smsmsmsmsmsmsmsmsmsm smsmsmsmsmsmsm smsmsmsmsmsmshelphel
xmxmxmxmxmxmxmxmxmxmxmxmxmxmxmxmxmxmxmxmxmxmxmxmhelphelp
zm zmzm zm zmzmzmzmzm zmzm zmzm zmzmzm zmzmzm zmzmhelphelphe
amam amamamamamamamamamam amam amamamam amam amamhelphelphel
am aamamamamamamamamamamamamamamamamam amamxm huxlphelphelphe
smsmsm sm smsmsm smsmsmsmsmsmsmsmsmsmsm smsmhelphelphelphe
xmxmxmxmxmxmxmxmxmxmxmxmxmxmxmxmhelphelphelphelphelphelph
zszszs zszszszs zhelphelphelphelphelphelphelphelphelphelph
helphelphelphelphelphelphelphelphelphelphelphelphelphelp
```

10 T. L. Kryss, untitled poem. From *Marrahwannah Quarterly* 3.4 (1967). By permission of Tom Kryss. Photograph: Special Collections, Michael Schwartz Library, Cleveland State University, Cleveland Memory Project.

shortly).⁵⁷ In brief, one can see the poets in Cleveland developing their own native sense of concrete poetry while also entering into dialogue with the international networks documented by Mary Ellen Solt.⁵⁸ One might, in fact, read the stylistic affiliations and dissemination of these tropes as a textual reflection of the institutional function of Jim Lowell's Asphodel Book Shop, which both cultivated community and imported books and journals featuring visual poetry, such as Finlay's *Poor Old Tired Horse* (Edinburgh) and David Holmes's *Link* (Cheltenham), from across the Atlantic to the shores of Lake Erie.⁵⁹ In a piece referred to as "an antitled [*sic*] CONCRETE POEM," D. A. Levy explicitly maps these geographic and cultural connections in a poem that figures the columnar logic of ditto repetition as a kind of "rain," even without the figural pictoriality on display in Atkins's punctuation poem. Lamenting the complacency and reactionary politics of those in the vicinity of "swamp erie"—a lackluster lacustrine scene from which the concrete poetry that "began in Switzerland in the early 50s" would find an equally amenable culture of bland neutrality—Levy tallies a demographic accounting:

THE PEOPLE OF	CLEVELAND	ARE APATHETIC & INDIFFERENT & FULL OF SHIT
THE PEOPLE OF	NEWBURGH	ARE APATHETIC & INDIFFERENT & FULL OF SHIT
THE PEOPLE OF	SOLON	ARE APATHETIC & INDIFFERENT & FULL OF SHIT
THE PEOPLE OF	BAY VILLAGE	ARE APATHETIC & INDIFFERENT & FULL OF SHIT
THE PEOPLE OF	WESTLAKE	ARE APATHETIC & INDIFFERENT & FULL OF SHIT
THE PEOPLE OF	ROCKY RIVER	ARE APATHETIC & INDIFFERENT & FULL OF SHIT
THE PEOPLE OF	PARMA	ARE APATHETIC & INDIFFERENT & FULL OF SHIT

And so on, for three-quarters of the page—all the way to Cuyahoga Heights. "It looks," Levy writes in a headnote, "like an amphetamine rain."⁶⁰ I will argue later in this chapter for why Levy might associate the reiterative logic of the *idem* with rain, but for now I want to note the wit of Atkins's own rain of ditto marks in "Spyrytual" (remembering that "clever, smart, witty," as it happens, is one of the nineteenth-century denotations of *spiritual*).⁶¹ Atkins's insight was that the formal devices of international concrete poetry had something to say to local Cleveland politics as engaged by the activist neighborhoods of Hough and Glenville—both notably absent from Levy's census of apathetic enclaves—and to recognize the eloquence with which the idiom used by one community could speak to another.

Wind and water, as we have seen, are explicit tropes in the concrete poetry of the period, and there is something elemental in the spiritual as well. Not only is the spiritual a sung work from an oral tradition, but the word's own etymology points to the origin of speech in the respirated air piloted from the larynx through the various structures of the buccal cavity. Early denotations of *spiritual* included meanings "relating to breathing; respiratory," with *spirit* arising directly from the Latin *spiritus* [breath], from *spīrāre* [to breathe]. In the context of Atkins's spiritual, we might remark that *Hough*, pronounced *huff*, encodes its own history of rough breathing; an obsolete intransitive, *hough* denotes clearing the throat or breathing hard (as in *to huff and puff*).[62] But the spirit itself is also a sign of rough breathing: the written mark used to indicate the type of aspiration that leads to certain pronunciations. In classical grammar, *spirit* (short for *spiritus asper* or *spiritus lenis*: rough and smooth breathing, respectively) is the mark conventionally used to indicate an aspirate "in the writing or printing of Greek."[63] Like Atkins's erratic punctuation, these diacritics enlist the mutely visible as a score for specifically inflected—one might say, thus, musically *sung*—speech. Moreover, in accordance with Atkins's theory of a visual music understood intellectually but not necessarily sounded, Roman Jakobson designated the *spiritus lenis* as the "zero phoneme," because it "occurs linguistically only as an absence of all occurrence"; it is "neither necessarily phonetically silent [...] nor ever, even when silent, inaudible."[64] With a further serendipity, those diacritic spirits take the form of marks resembling apostrophes, differentiated by the direction of their swerve. Written over a vowel or *r* to indicate *spiritus asper*, the rough breath marking takes the form of a single curved stroke concave with its ellipsis to the left. Conversely, when turned in the other direction, like the coronis (from the Greek κορωνίς, curved) which is placed over a vowel as a mark of crasis in ancient Greek, the diacritic indicates smooth breathing.

I do not mean to suggest that the punctuation in "Spyrytual" and the diacritics of the *spiritus* lead to the same etymology and similar shapes by routes other than the happy chance of sheer coincidence, but the forms of the spirit offer an important lesson about technology and signification to which the reader of Atkins's poem would do well to attend. On the typewriter that produced the stencil from which *Spyrytual* was printed, the strictly vertical, or neutral form of the typeface would be unable to differentiate between the marks for smooth and rough breathing. In typescript, the sign cannot effectively function diacritically, and it must also stand in for all of the other characters that might indicate apostrophes, single quotation marks, prime signs, or even the גֶּרֶשׁ [Geresh] (used in Hebrew to mark cantillations, loans, transliterations, and certain initializations). The straight quote thus poses a paradox: a diacritic (directly from the Greek διακριτικός, "that which distinguishes") that does not distinguish. Readers might make do, with more or less guesswork and trouble, but the distinguishing performed by curved forms is a difference that makes a difference. When used as a diacritic, as we have seen, the curve of that mark signifies pronunciation, and depending on the cultural context the stakes can be high when that notation is ignored. For just one example: despite the exigencies of famine and Nazi occupation, the Arts Faculty at the University of Athens took the time in 1941 to put Ioannis Kakridis on trial for publishing monotonic Greek—a demotic without the diacritics of classical Greek. He was found guilty of disseminating orthographic heresy and suspended from his post.[65]

Typically, the consequences are less dire. When used as punctuation, the curves of the letterform signify professional competence, design sophistication, and modes of print technology. Professional typographers have traditionally spoken in terms of "quote sophistication" and "proper quotes," but the condescension carries over into the realm of personal computing, desktop publishing, and social media as well.[66] "The first tip-off that someone is green behind the ears in desktop publishing," as one instructional manual explains "is his or her use of straight quotes instead of proper 'printer's quotes.'"[67] Or, similarly:

> One of the sure giveaways that something was printed on the Macintosh rather than being professionally typeset is the lack of true quotation marks. Real quotation marks, known as curly quotes, curved quotes, true quotation marks, printers' quotation marks, and smart quotes, curve around the text.[68]

As with "proper" in the previous quotation, "real" here establishes the standard of value that explains the shame of the counterfeit implied by "giveaways," but the passage also reminds us that the style of the quotation mark is not just a matter of visual sophistication but of technological capability. The quotation mark is a typographic shibboleth. Even with the advent of personal computers, this glyph remained a vestige of typewriter design, where the premium on keyboard real estate meant that a single, unidirectional sign freed at least an entire key. Technology, of course, is not always determinant, but its agency should not be underestimated. The form of written Navaho, for one relevant example, emerged as the standard from a number of competing scripts because it was the version most easily approximated on a standard typewriter.[69] More recently, the small but measurable labor required to engage the shift key on the computer keyboard has been identified as the motor behind a recent trend toward using single in place of double quotation marks.[70]

The parsimonious practice of typewriter keyboard design was codified in 1870 by Émile Baudot, who developed a 5-bit code similar to Morse code for use in telegraphy. Baudot's code served as the basis for Donald Murray's turn-of-the-century International Telegraph Alphabet 2 (ITA2), which was in turn absorbed into the American Standard Code for Information Interchange (ASCII) for digital communications in 1963. The straight quote is thus a legacy of the typewriter, perpetuated because numerical limits persist in computing, even when the character set is freed from the set tiles of a keyboard.[71] Initially, the most reliable cross-platform encoding scheme, the 7-bit ASCII developed for use in teletype, was constrained to fewer than a hundred glyphs, the selection of which was keyed to national language needs, imagined certain hardware, and omitted curved quote marks.[72] Indeed, taking his analysis of the absence of any markers for representing "dialect or language shifts" to a logical extreme, C. M. Sperberg-McQueen concludes that "there is no real way to represent French or German texts [in ASCII], because ASCII has no standard method for representing the necessary diacritics."[73] Even with the introduction of 8-bit ASCII, which could support a curved apostrophe, different proprietary programs used the same data ranges for different purposes, so that local attempts to indicate printers' quotes and other "special" symbols often triggered glitches when attempts were made to move document files between the programs, platforms, or machines manufactured by different corporations.[74] Rather than the elegant look of commercial print that users aimed for by specifying curved quotation marks, these misalignments often produced nonsense dingbats, or simply blanks.[75] Additionally, even when not translating between different software programs, software attempts to automatically determine the direction of the quote's curve (as with the "smart quotes" of Microsoft Word) can be baffled by misleading contexts and a confusion between apostrophes and quotation marks. Digital quotation marks, in short, are often too smart for their own good.

The repercussions are not merely practical, and they can reveal the sometimes discordant theoretical presumptions of linguistics, politics, and technology.[76] The Unicode code point U+0027, for example (for the straight mark formerly known as the "apostrophe-quote" and now simply as "apostrophe"), is especially freighted. Although since 2003 "the preferred character for apostrophe is U+2019," Unicode recognizes that

> U+0027 is commonly present on keyboards. In modern software, it is therefore common to substitute U+0027 by the appropriate character in input. In these systems, a U+0027 in the data stream is always represented as a straight vertical line and can never represent a curly apostrophe or a right quotation mark.[77]

When signaling diacritics, or what Unicode refers to as "modifier letters," the character indicates part of a coherent lexical unit, such as the Breton trigraph (denoting a voiceless velar fricative), the unicameral consonants in certain Polynesian languages like Tongan and ʻŌlelo Hawaiʻi

(Hawaiian), or even the transliterated soft sign in Cyrillic.[78] But when signaling punctuation, U+0027 indicates the division or fracture of a word. In Greek, for instance, the smooth breathing mark of the ψιλή [*psili*] not only resembles the apostrophe, with which it might be easily confused, and which might lead to contextual problems when one quotes a word that begins with the diacritic, but the apostrophe itself in Greek, unlike the orthography for other languages, is followed by a nonbreaking blank space.[79] Unicode conventions for diacritics, in short, reveal a visual rather than a semantic logic, organizing signs by their morphology rather than by language, linguistic function, or meaning. Accordingly, visually identical marks are not differentiated even when they are in fact different signs.[80]

As far from Atkins's poem as we may seem to have swerved, these histories of technologies bear directly on the interpretation of *Spyrytual*, which might well depend on whether one reads the poem's glyphs as quotation marks or ditto marks (or possibly as a series of paired apostrophes), even when the form of the text itself cannot differentiate between them. In practical terms, the impediments to information interchange built into those histories are legible in the different textual versions of the poem that have been published. The textual history of "Spyrytual" evinces how difficult it can be to quote a quotation. For instance, in the version presented by Aldon Nielsen in the anthology *Every Goodbye Ain't Gone*, the apostrophes are contextually curved, but the double quotation marks remain uninflected. However, when the poem is adduced in an essay by Nielsen as "a concrete sign of citation, visually glossing the spiritual's lyric," he quotes the first half of the poem as an inset quotation, introducing various changes in spacing (*cf.* lines 7, 9, 10).[81] More striking, however, are the visual impression and semantic implications of the form of the quotation marks themselves. When quoted in the essay, even the straight typewriter face of the original's quotation marks are converted to printer's curly quotes. The change in form might be seen to diminish the iconic sense of the marks as raindrops, but it also invites questions about what, exactly, is being enclosed between the paired sets.[82] The first line of the poem, for instance, no longer reads as the repetition of a figure and seems instead to be quoting a triplet of opening quotation marks:

"""   """   """

While the next quatrain seems to be quoting the blank of the page, or an unspoken pause, or marking off silence itself:

""   ""

Long before its quotation in a scholarly essay, the poem as a whole changed both its publishing contexts and its forms. Shortly after the appearance of the 7 Flowers Press pamphlet, "Spyrytual" was republished in *The Muntu Poets of Cleveland*, an anthology showcasing the work of members of a workshop Atkins had founded a few years before. Derived from a Bantu word for "Black person," the name of the collective reclaimed what had become a derogatory South African slur as a marker of ethnic pride.[83] In the tradition of other mid-'60s institutions such as Chicago's Organization of Black American Culture, the Watts Writers Workshop, Rapa House (Detroit), and Spirit House (Newark), the Muntu Poets worked at the intersection of spiritual jazz, modern poetry, community organizing, and Black Nationalist politics. Characterized by "raw, stinging poetry as voices of black awakening and dissent," the direct, declamatory, speech-based poems in the anthology look little like "Spyrytual."[84] Sababa Akili's hortatory "Black Women, Black Men (If We Had Been Stronger)," for instance, entreats "Beautiful Black Women" to "Come Back / To Black Men," confessing: "If we had been / Stronger / You wouldn't have to / imitate miss ann / you would have been / freed from slavery / long ago."[85] An untitled poem by Jon Hall, for another example, concludes with a paraphrase of the famous order attributed to William Prescott at the battle of Bunker Hill, recasting the sclera with a racial tinge: "let your words / be bullets and your mind / the gun and blast / when you observe / the whites of / their eyes."[86] Like Atkins himself, who moved between the social worlds of Levy's counterculture mimeo networks, headquartered in Lowell's Asphodel Bookshop (which had been raided by police under the pretext of a drug search), and the Black Nationalists who met at (Fred) Ahmed Evans's Afro Culture Shop and Bookstore (which had been raided by police under the pretext of sanitary inspections), the poem was able to move between the overlapping communities of readers. In the process, different facets of the text came to be highlighted. If "Spyrytual" announces itself as more formally daring than the other texts collected by the Muntu poets, for instance, its tone also sounds less militant and more cerebrally clever by comparison.[87] At the same time, the political valence for which I have been arguing may have been more immediately obvious when Atkins's poem appeared among poems that more forthrightly "reflected the rage, dissent, and rebellious nature of the community," as part of a collective chorus of woke, urgently contemporary commentary (the workshop, as it happens, was meeting on the night the Hough riots broke out—providing a handy alibi for several of its members).

In the process of its anthologization, Atkins's poem underwent some formal transformations as well as semantic recontextualizations. Conforming to the collection's overall style sheet, the title is set flush left, aligned with the first line, but more significantly, sets of quotation marks are eliminated altogether (as in the line above "oh did," which retains only four of the six double quotation marks from the earlier versions). The second section of three sets of stepped quotation marks, reminiscent of the measure of William Carlos Williams's late triadic line, is shifted up to become part of the opening stanza, integrating its form into the space around the two vertically aligned quote marks that make up the fifth and sixth lines in the 7 Flowers Press version. The spacing in the penultimate section has been similarly adjusted to close the line-leading of the double quotation mark pair preceding "it" and bring it up to abut the line with "n't." The poem, in short, is vertically compacted—a reflection of the change from the eccentrically elongated format of the 7 Flowers pamphlet to the squatter and more standard Free Lance trim adopted by the United Black Artists of Cleveland Press to print *The Muntu Poets*.

More substantial metamorphoses accompanied the poem's layout in a republication of *The Muntu Poets of Cleveland* in 2016 (figure 11).[88] There, the lineation and spacing clearly follows from the earlier anthology version, but with additional inversions, skews, and shifts introduced. The apostrophe in "n't," for example, appears in a glaringly slanted form, as does the second pair of quotation marks that follows it. The mélange of smart and straight quotation marks reflects the desktop publishing program that allowed the born-digital manuscript to be sent directly to a print-on-demand machine without the technical uniformity and human copyediting once standard in marking up a manuscript for commercial offset. This promiscuity of type founts condenses, in miniature, the medley of visual styles in the book as a whole, which mixes bold and regular founts, incongruous typefaces at dramatically different sizes, and images of astrological signs (presumably identifying the birth month of each author), which are enlarged from interpolated jpg files at such low resolution that they and the text of their bit-mapped captions were pixelated when embedded in the preproduction PDF.

At the same time, the most obvious variation in the anthology text, when compared to the earlier versions of the poem, recalls the original mode of production for *Spyrytual* in the same way that its straight quotation marks recalled their typewriter origins in the 7 Flowers pamphlet. The anthology version reverses the block of quotation marks that immediately follow the opening phrase, almost as if they were reflected in a mirror. Although one assumes this discrepancy is unintentional, merely the result of a transcription error, it nicely encrypts a ghost of the duplicators used by Levy and other small-press publishers of the '60s "mimeo revolution." With mimeograph, the master is a stencil, oriented like the print it

```
SPYRYTUAL

    Oh didn't it    " " "     " " "     " " "
                        " "       " "
                        " "       " "
                        " "       " "
    " "
    " "                 " "               "
                " "               " "      "

        rain
                    " "
                        " "
                   " "       "    "

        Oh did
            " " "      " " "    n't       " "
                " "               " "

                                            it
        rain                        " "
                            " "


                    -- Russell Atkins
```

11 Russell Atkins, "Spyrytual." From *The Muntu Poets of Cleveland*, vol. 1, ed. Sababa Akili and Mutawaf Shaheed (Cleveland: Uptown Media Ventures, 2016). By permission of Kevin Prufer and Bob McDonough, for Russell Atkins, and by permission of M. A. Shaheed. Author's photograph.

will produce; during printing it is flipped and ink is forced through perforations in its surface. With duplicators evolved from hectographic processes, by contrast, such as the Ditto machine, the master is a mirror image of its product, typically a slickly sized ceraceous sheet with a thick impasto of aniline dyed ink debossed from the transfer of the typewriter's strike or the press of a stylus. The Ditto master, that is, carries its own ink, which is transferred to a copy in a solvent bath, whereas the mimeograph relies on an external, replenishable store of ink. Despite these differences, both processes required a reversal at some stage of the printing.

Indeed, we should remember that not only are the glyphs that proliferate through *Spyrytual* known as *ditto marks*, but the Ditto machine, in the precise terminology of midcentury print technology, is a type of *spirit duplicator* (so-called because of the mix of alcohols used as transfer solvents—possessing a volatility that also fueled the Molotov cocktails used by Hough arsonists). That Atkins's spiritual would name the spiritous thus enacts a double pun that might begin to explain Levy's substitution of ditto marks for the slashes Atkins had originally imagined. The conflation was exact: since at least the 1950s, the Ditto Corporation had used as its logo an encircled typewriter double-quote, with the right-hand mark raised slightly higher than the left (and sometimes the entire circle set as the dot over the *i* in *Ditto*).

Levy, in fact, explored the reversible logic of print in other projects from the period. Consider, for one example, *Plastic Saxophone Found in an Egyptian Tomb*, which he published the same year as *Spyrytual* and which played on the same punning "spirit."[89] To begin with, the work figures media as spectral. Metaphorizing the Holy Spirit as a television, the poem exhorts the photons of its cathode, in the name of the "Spirit behind the 21 inch third eye of America," with the mock elevation of a jussive prayer: "may the vibrations of the cosmos flow thru yr channels for eternity." That "spirit of T.V." is then followed by "a mandala to free the spirit" and "a charm to free the spirit." With an implicit pun on "tomb" and *tome*, *grave* and *engraved*, Levy describes the book itself—a "Book of the DEAD" transcribed from "NECROPOLIS, OHIO"—as "sound and light rays retranslated." "The letter killeth," as the Bible claims, "the spirit giveth life."[90] Similarly, with its insistence on the spirit of television, the ghostly glow of the cathode scanning rays brings together the senses of electromagnetic spectrum and the phantasmagoric specter that *spectral* can equally possess. Furthermore, and in contrast to a mimeograph, Levy's book manifests the look of "spirit" duplication, with its distinctive mauve ink, the soft blur of lines that results from the bulge of the waxy master and the wash of solvent onto dampened paper, along with the hallmark forms of its affordances: the combination of holographic text and freehand drawing in the same frame space, direct frottage (the design of one page is built from rubbings of coins), and the mix of multiple ink colors that could be printed in a single run. One line sums up the possibilities of this new kind of duplication paper with an emphatic invocation of "the mixture—from the papyrus of New." In fact, the text itself seems aware of its own material specificity at several junctures. In Levy's foreword, the purple of the aniline tint of the master not only colors the text but seems to seep into the form of the word *propose*, deforming its orthography to the quasi-purple "purpose": the book, Levy announces, will "purpose to provide an introduction to the wisdom and knowledge of the ancient master through the one media americans can understand." *Master* and *media*, of course, are all to the point in a Ditto-duplicated page. Moreover, following the cover sheet and an introductory edition notice, the first page of the book is followed by the same text printed in faded reverse (figure 12). The subject of the page is not coincidental; it captions itself as coming "from the papyrus" and is titled with its subject: "of the INK-POT & PALETTE." Calling attention to its fictional scene of inscription—a self-referential "SCRIBE" has "COPIED" it with the "tools of THOTH" on an excreted substrate ("I have the shit of Osiris & I wrote on it")—the page makes visible its own scene of production: the mirrored page in purple palette that would be visible to Levy, as duplicating scribe, even as its reversals typically remain hidden to the uninitiated reader.[91] Indeed, taking the proof from the rotated cylinder, Levy would have seen what the reader sees in contemplation of the opening: two images, in mirror, hinged: the sheet to be pulled and its inverse in curve along the drum.

The Concrete issue of *Marrahwannah Quarterly*, published the following year, offers another example of Levy's deliberate play with chiral reversals (figure 13). There, the inked cylinder of the duplicator has been permitted to print a partially legible text in a mirrored block, with only a retyped attribution in all caps sitting easily readable at the bottom of the page: "JULIAN KALLANDER." Above this punning pseudonym the fragile facture of the partially transferred letterforms scrumble the ink in uneven twinkles of macled black and fade.[92] If one takes the trouble to decipher it, the didactic text, presumably penned by Levy himself, sermonizes about the relative dangers of social repression when compared with the harmlessness of drug use. Thematically, the editorial sits squarely in the anti-square rhetoric of Levy's counterculture advocacies, and it complements the collage of fragments on the preceding page, which contains unattributed transcriptions of passages from Aldous Huxley's *Texts and Pretexts* reformatted into broken free-verse lines. A discrepant inclusion among the visual poems and permutational texts of the rest of the Concrete special issue, the notebook page presents a duplicator-printed instance of a duplicated genre: transcribing selected passages from Huxley's book, which was itself largely an assembly of diverse literary passages. Although the single notebook page draws from only four pages of *Texts and Pretexts*, it manages to quote Huxley quoting from a sonnet by Cavalier poet John Suckling, one of Hector's speeches from William Shakespeare's *Troilus and Cressida*, and lines from William Blake's *The Marriage of Heaven*

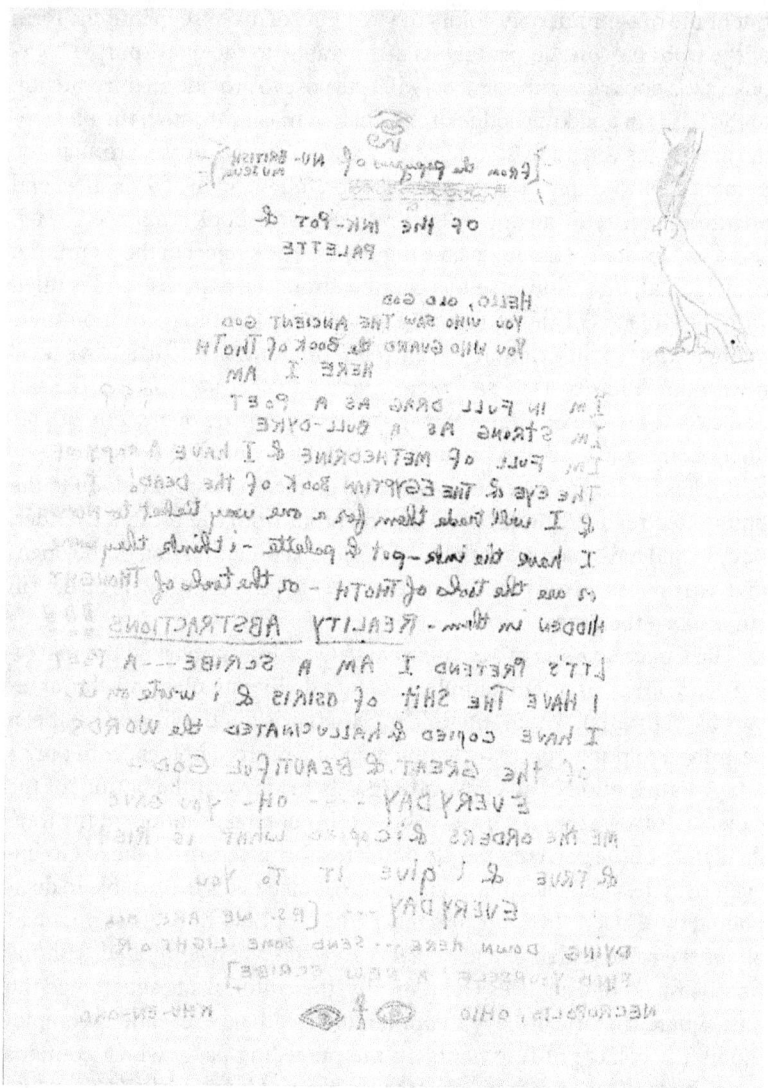

12 D. A. Levy, from *Plastic Saxophone Found in an Egyptian Tomb* (Cleveland: n.p., 1966). By permission of Jeff Maser. Photograph: Special Collections, Michael Schwartz Library, Cleveland State University, Cleveland Memory Project.

and Hell—in a passage where Huxley would later find the title of the book for which he became a celebrity to Levy's cohort: "if the doors of perception were cleansed every thing would appear to man as it is, infinite."[93] Indeed, Huxley's championing of mescaline in *The Doors of Perception*, and his enthusiasm soon after for lysergic acid diethylamide, implicitly

13 D. A. Levy, untitled poem. From *Marrahwannah Quarterly* 3.3 (1967). By permission of Jeff Maser. Photograph: Special Collections, Michael Schwartz Library, Cleveland State University, Cleveland Memory Project.

endorses the editorial page that follows, which argues that although "LSD could be dangerous to he who would not know himself," "this generally does not include the young." Moreover, the passages from Huxley's commonplace book appeal to precisely those stakes of epistemology and the metaphysical aspirations of altered states.[94] The page opens, "He imaginatively apprehends—these / within certain limits, are continuously changing," and while the authors and sources that follow are indeed continuously changing, the text reiterates the theme of enlightened awareness of reality behind a veil of appearances: "melting apparent surfaces away" so that "the whole will be consumed and appear infinite and holy," "whereas [it] now appears finite and corrupt," because the collective voice seeks to be "free / to create imaginatively a / world other / than that in which / we find ourselves."

One of the constraining "objects" recognized as "absolute and things […] in themselves" is the particular typographic disposition of the edition of Huxley's text from which the notebook quotes. The first line of the notebook entry, for instance, picks up—midphrase—from the first line of page 54 of *Texts and Pretexts*; the complete sentence, beginning on page 53, reads:

> Nature, then, does not change; but the outlines that man sees in Nature, the tunes he hears, the eternities he imaginatively apprehends—these, within certain limits, are continually changing.

Similarly, one can trace the transcribing reader-writer moving up the vertical layout of one paragraph and then later completing the broken word *sen/-sual*, hyphenated at the edge of the prose block in the 1933 edition of Huxley's book, as if the transcribing pen were moving faster than the return sweep of the reading eye, writing instead: "this comes by an improvement of / sensed / enjoyment."[95] If the mirrored page that follows in the *Quarterly* can be read as a literal example of the "finite and corrupt" appearance that needs to be seen through newly cleansed doors of perception, or conversely as a simulation of altered visual perception itself, its printing also recalls the very process described by Blake in the passage quoted by Huxley: "writing in the infernal method by corrosives." One might even go so far, looking at the pool and clog of ink around those letterforms with larger counters, as to see the apertures of the stencil—what permits the perception of the text at all—as needing to be cleansed (with solvents, if not corrosives). Although the exact details of Blake's process have occasioned surprisingly heated controversy, the idiosyncratic relief etching or "illuminated printing" he developed would have required either writing backward or etching a conventionally written script in intaglio which would then be printed (producing a reversed text) and counterproofed.[96] In either case, the "infernal method" confronted the inherent logic of all press printing: the reversal of the initial design at some stage in the process. Levy's own innovative page thus reënacts the innovative textual procedure described in the preceding notebook passage, setting up a dynamic between an awareness of the fixed, literal, physical objecthood of print and the infinite vision revealed by the salutary corrosion of the world as it is given. Once again, Levy stages an image of the text not usually considered by the reader but always in front of the printer as seen in its moment of production: the mirrored matrix on the cylinder of the duplicator.

A reversed text would usually betray an error in setting up the duplicator, inadvertently positioning the matrix so that it, rather than the print, were legible. Fittingly, *The Cleveland Manifesto of Poetry*, a key document in the mimeograph revolution to which Atkins and Levy both contributed, begins with a mirror-printed statement as its header, just above the title: "Mimeographed courtesy of Jim Lowell, The Asphodel Bookshop / 465 The Arcade, Cleveland, 14, Ohio." A more decisive use of inversion comes in a poem by rjs (Robert J. Sigmund), who motivates the orientation of printed text as an integral part of its crystalline form (figure 14): a symmetrical, lattice-like meander that enacts a dialogue between the visible and the legible and offers a concrete illustration of the poem's central assertion: "yr / eyes / R / a / necessari / part / ov / this / conversation." When Levy retains the chirality of texts, they become part of the formal development which pushed his printing from spontaneous immediacy toward obsessive reiteration—each pole of which expressed urgency and immediacy in its own way. Like Andy Warhol with silk-screening, Levy embraced what most mimeographers shunned; he permitted rather than corrected what the mode of production was prone to create: overinking, smearing, blurred and nebulous borders, bleeds and offsets, misregistration, editioning variations, and the ghostly trace of the faint impression of cylinder and screen. In contrast to the clean ideal of mimeo aspired to by institutional uses (small business, schools, and churches), Levy pursued a deskilled, proto-punk aesthetic that sought a visual manifestation of the DIY and counterculture virtues espoused discursively in the works he printed. In the printing of *Spyrytual*, for example (figure 6), notice how the counters have overinked where the stencil covering has detached (as at the capital *O* in both instances of "Oh" and the *d* that repeats in the first line), as well as a stray mark, slightly larger than the size of a full stop, that floats tantalizingly—with meaningful significance or mere accident?—above "rain."

Levy's experiments with reversals expand on the smudges and wet transfers that advertised a hasty, improvisatory, deskilled aesthetic, and

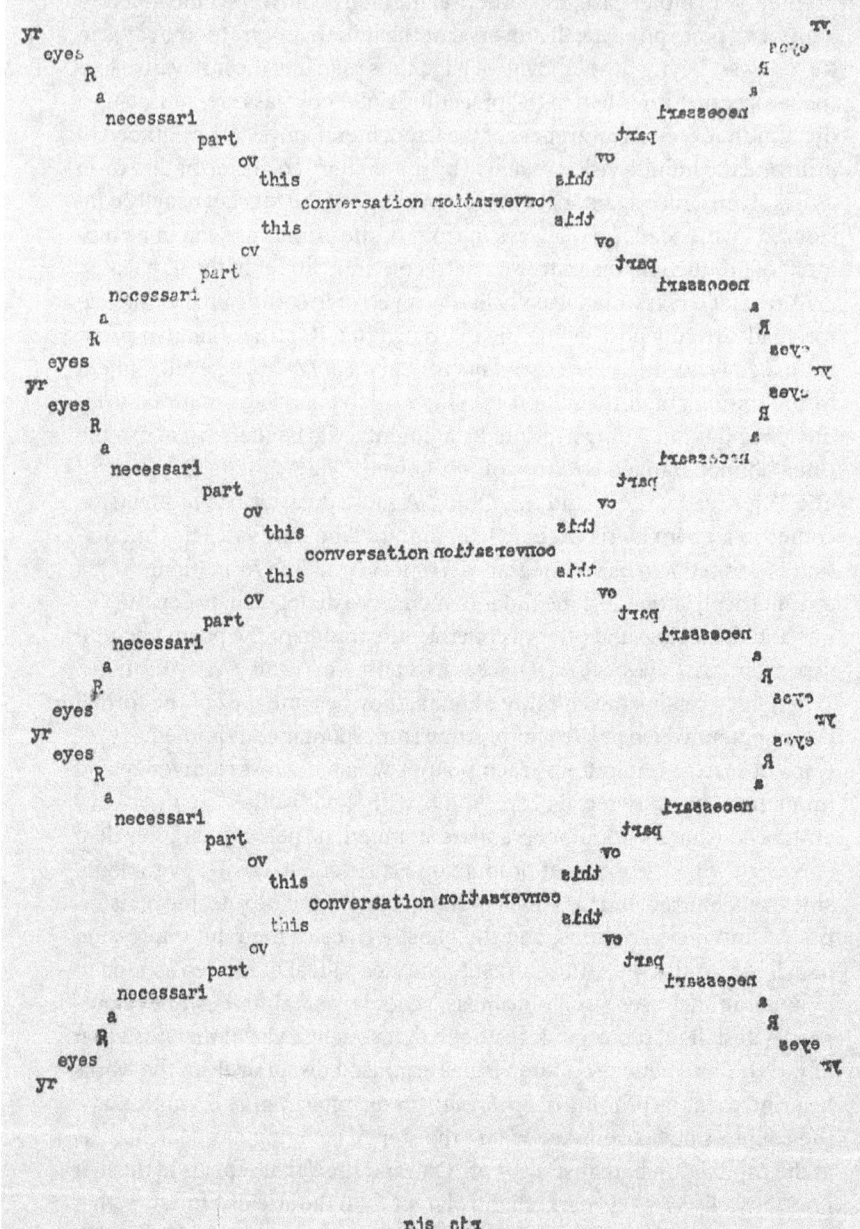

14 rjs, untitled poem. From *Marrahwannah Quarterly* 4.1 (1967). By permission of rjs. Photograph: Special Collections, Michael Schwartz Library, Cleveland State University, Cleveland Memory Project.

their retention as part of the published text gestures toward the calculated illegibilities that he would pursue at even greater lengths.[97] That illegibility, furthermore, might be seen as a means for figuring the logic of the duplicator process itself, and the way in which the stencil, from whatever direction, makes print present and visible by occlusion and counter-opacity. Levy, in turn, visualizes this means of visualizing with patterns of cancellation and obfuscation; he essentially stencils stenciling.[98] The poem "Religious Acid," for another instance, brackets the space of the page with a similar dialectic between presence and absence, framing its visual patterns in Blakean terms of visual and visionary revelation.[99] Moving from the statements

>   There are no   (   )
>   There are no non   (   )

the poem tests verbal against visual restatements:

>   (nothing)   (nothing)
>   (   )
>   nothing (   ) nothing
>   (   )

Ultimately, with the regular rhythm of a periodic motor, the penultimate stanza punctuates its visionary scope with the word "electric," ending, not coincidentally, on the word "mirror." Later in the issue, that *mirror* is itself literally mirrored in Levy's "Comment on Acid Landscape."[100] With the same directional reversal of text, an earlier poem in which the "trip flips" flips the direction of print for the words "innerspace" and "mushrooms," as well as the poem's title ("Psychedelic Information Center") and the signature line (d.a.levy / 1967). Recalling the "doors of perception," the poem describes awaking "AT THE DOOR," and the title in its inverted form appears as a literal depiction of public window signage when seen from inside an office. The reader experiences this line not so much mirrored as from the back. The reversals available through cylinder printing thus allow Levy to provide a literal visualization of the dissolution of interior and exterior that characterizes hallucinatory experience and to approximate for the reader an extraordinary mental experience that is the quintessential example of the uniquely intimate, personal, and incommunicable. With a reorientation of type and a disorientation of reading, the flipped text of the trip literalizes and provokes rather than describes. The result is what Atkins might have termed "egocentric phenomenalism," which eschews subjective insights in favor of "*non-representationalism*," creating an experience "through ARTIFICE" and "CONSPICUOUS TECHNIQUE" rather than recounting one.[101] Those conspicuous techniques are not put in the service of meaning, "but rather meaning must not only *be* but SERVE technique."[102]

A related maneuver simulates the stencils of screen printing—whether the halftone available to skilled mimeographers or the silkscreen used to print some of the covers for *Marrahwannah Quarterly* and related publications from the Cleveland underground—themselves modes of simulating photography and other previously reproduced prints. For example, in the second movement of T. L. (Tom) Kryss's poem "i wisht i cd play the beautiful instrument" (figure 15), also from the special Concrete issue of the *Quarterly*, upper- and lowercase x's—a bilaterally symmetrical letterform, significantly—are typewritten repeatedly in an occasionally smudged and faded chain-link scrim. The section not only insists on the opacity of print—irregular windows permit the reader to glimpse disarticulated iterations of the word *paranoia*—but it simulates the metal mesh of a screen. A prominent figure in the concrete scene in Cleveland, Kryss made repeated single letters—in shearing strata, drifting clouds, or schooling masses—a signature part of his repertoire. In at least one instance, moreover, he explicitly aligned the grid of repeated glyphs with the metal screen of a cage.[103] The conceit, however, was a familiar part of the local period style more broadly.[104] Two of Don Thomas's typewriter poems (figure 16), printed in *Marrahwannah Quarterly* in 1967, for example, elaborate repeated figures in order to construct patterned blocks that suggest printing screens, each with inevitable clogs of deposited accumulations, ink-logged lint, and abraded fades from the smear and lift of their own mimeo printing. The first, titled "2 Above, 3 Below," overprints narrowly angled glyphs to approximate the links of wire mesh, as in a silkscreen ("the only [predigital] print process in which the final image does not reverse the composition on the matrix," as Jennifer Roberts perceptively notes), while the other, titled "Homage to Issa," nestles oval zeroes into what might be seen as the unmarked blank of a halftone master.[105]

Levy also makes a similar alignment of the screen and the print block. Following the poetics of illegibility and print that we have already seen him explore through reversals, the pages of his *Saundaryalahari*, a hymn to beauty modeled on the eighth-century Sanskrit text सौन्दर्यलहरी [*Flood of Beauty*], are embellished with abstract patterns from alternating punctuation marks that distract and entrance like bejeweled tantric mandala miniatures.[106] By overprinting the poem proper with little regard for any ease of legibility, Levy's pages pulse with lozenges and shifting diagonals, stream like the painted beads of a hanging door curtain, and construct a

15 T. L. Kryss: "i wisht i cd play the beautiful instrument." From *Marrahwannah Quarterly* 3.3 (1967). By permission of Tom Kryss. Photograph: Special Collections, Michael Schwartz Library, Cleveland State University, Cleveland Memory Project.

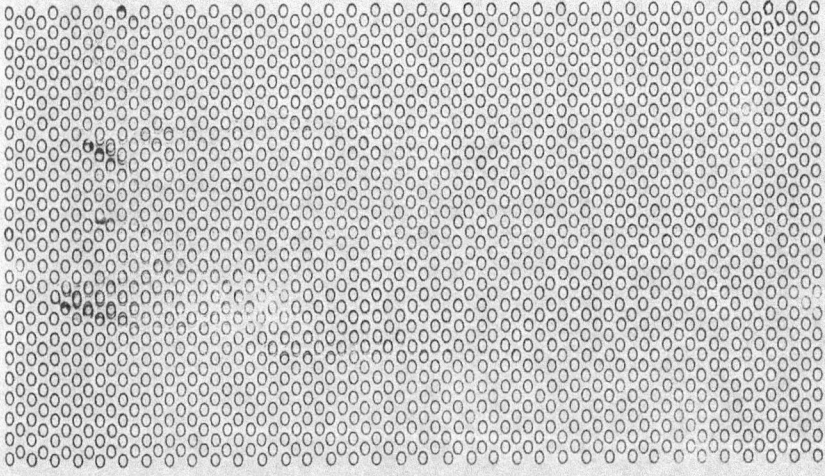

16 Don Thomas, "Two Poems": "2 Above, 3 Below" and "Homage to Issa." From *Marrahwannah Quarterly* 4.2 (1967). Photograph: Special Collections, Michael Schwartz Library, Cleveland State University, Cleveland Memory Project.

fractal expanse of checkered grids—as if a screen were seen up close, or magnified and enlarged. The first page (figure 17), moreover, figures rain with both the virgules Atkins originally imagined for "Spyrytual" and the quotation marks that were ultimately used ("La pluie," as Francis Ponge recognized in a poem figuring precipitation as punctuation marks, "ne forme pas les seuls traits d'union entre le sol et les cieux" [rain is not the only hyphen linking earth and sky]).[107] If the patterns on other pages seem to illustrate the beads of the "rosary" and the links of the "tinkling girdle" mentioned discursively in the poem, the vertical fall of punctuation marks on the first page gives concrete expression to the "flood of beauty" that the poem eulogizes as it describes a perfumed deity "streaming with showers" that "dissolve" into an "Ocean." By forming a screen, however, the "waterfall" of glyphs in their "streams" and "sprinkling" also recalls the liquidity of the duplicator process that printed them. The religious (spiritual) subject of the poem emerges from the spirit (duplicator) process. And here we can begin to see why Levy might associate his "amphetamine rain" with the ditto logic of repetition and might substitute ditto marks for Atkins's virgules. As the smudges still attest, duplication—whether mimeo or spirit—was a relatively damp and humid affair, and printers would have been aware of the unfixed ink of the mimeo with every carefully handled sheet as it came from the machine ready to smear on contact; indeed, they would have felt the saturated moistness of every limp and spirit-logged page taken from the duplicator. In the current age of thermal toner, we might forget how remarkably arid photostatics was in comparison with other printing methods, but the etymology of *xerox* (from the Greek ξηρός, "dry") is a good reminder of the novelty of dry printing in the age of mimeo.[108]

Corroborating Levy's suggestion of the humectance behind the screen of duplicator printing, Don Thomas's proto-manifesto on concrete poetry conflates the printers' term for the binding margin of the codex and the common cloaca of industrial waste in the single word "gutter." Part machined metal industrial hardness (concrete) and part viscous chemical mix, a mirroring liquidity forms the very definition of concrete poetry for Thomas, who sees the art of mimeographed typewriter forms "reflected in the slime-ooze waters of the Great Errie [...] swamp."[109] According to Thomas, the genre is "a mind-photo recreation of / mass-mechanical submission to / the sluck mire muck, ingrown-toe-nail jam, dia)rea/lity (drip / pings) all nice and bleedy"—the "oil-sleek rainbow sludge" of industrial swamp. The assessment of print's essential viscosity need not be so lurid; Roberts, importantly, recognizes that printing's "physical transfers and replications rely on pressing, squeezing, rolling, smearing, and various species of oozy surface contact."[110]

```
TANTRIC              THE SAUNDARYALAHARI              sTROBE
                                                     strobe
                            or                       strobe
                                                        BY
                      FLOOD OF BEAUTY                d.a.levy
                                                       1967
         /:/:/:/:/:/(Traditionally Ascribed to Sankaracarya)

/:/:/:/:/Siva is united with sakti, he is able to exert his /:/:/:/
         powers. As Lord; if not, the god is not able to stir.
         Hence to you who must be propitiated by Hari Hara, Viranci,
         and the other (gods)
         how can one who has not acquired merit sufficient to offer
         reverence and praise?
                                                                       0
         The tiniest speck of dust from your lotus feet.          0
         Viranci (Brahma) collects and fashions into the worlds in
         their entirety;
         Hari (Vishnu, serpent) himself supports it, with his thou-
         sand heads;
         Hara (Siva) takes it and uses it to dust himself with ashes.

         For the ignorant you are the island city of the sun;
         for the mentally stagnant you are a waterfall in streams
         nectar (flowing) from bouquets of intelligence;
         for the poor you are a rosary of wishing jewels; for those
         who in the ocean of birth are submerged you are the tusk
         of that boar (Vishnu incarnare)
         who was the enemy of Mura, your ladyship.

         Others than you the rest of the gods grant freedom from
         danger and gifts with their hands;
         you alone make no overt gesture of gift and immunity.
         For to save from danger and to grant reward even beyond
         desire, to the world are the refuge of the world, your
         two feet alone are adequate.

         Hari, after propitiating you, who are the mother of welfare
                  for folk bowed in worship,
         once became a female and agitated him (Siva) who is the
         enemy of the cities;
         Smara (Kama) himself, after bowing to you with his body that
         is worthy of being carressed by the eyes of Rati,
         has the power to produce illusion within even mighty sages

         His bow is made of flowers, the bowstring of bees, five are
         his arrows,
         Vasanta (Spring) is his adjutant, the Malaya breeze his
         wind chariot,
         and yet, by himself, O daughter of the snow mountain, when
         born a bit of compassion
         he has got from a side glance of yours, the Bodiless One
         /:/:/:/:/ (Kama) conquers this world entire./:/:/:/:/:/:/:/:/:/
```

17 D. A. Levy, from *The Saundaryalahari, or Flood of Beauty* (1967). By permission of Jeff Maser. Photograph: Special Collections, Michael Schwartz Library, Cleveland State University, Cleveland Memory Project.

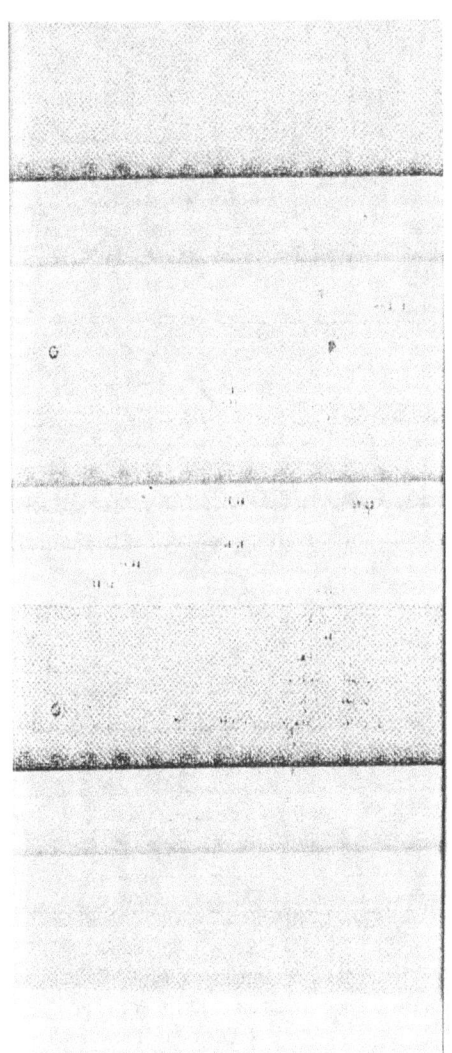

18 Russell Atkins, page from *Spyrytual* (Cleveland: 7 Flowers Press, 1966). By permission of Kevin Prufer and Bob McDonough, for Russell Atkins. Author's photograph.

Against the backdrop of these concrete typewriter grids and their screens of abstract glyphs, and with the further association of Cleveland's distinct species of concrete poetry with the liquidity of the duplicator process, we can start to see the specific performance of the design decisions Levy made with the 7 Flowers edition of *Spyrytual*. On the booklet's endpaper (figure 18), the pattern of a print screen has been allowed to ink its form, along with revenant fragments of a few of the poem's quotation marks, which have transferred before the wet ink of an impression had dried or the cylinder been wiped clean. The streak and drizzle of that

Spyrytual

by Russell Atkins

first printing
200 Copies

7 flowers preſs—1966
Cleveland‚Ohio

19 Russell Atkins, title page from *Spyrytual* (Cleveland: 7 Flowers Press, 1966). By permission of Kevin Prufer and Bob McDonough, for Russell Atkins. Author's photograph.

endpaper screen-print corroborates the association of Atkins's poem with its mode of production: a spiritual imagining the spirit duplicator, and a concrete rain printed with its own mode of fluid expression.

That fluidity is prefigured on the title page of the booklet (figure 19), which is printed letterpress, and where an inverted open quotation mark does duty as an unspaced separating comma in the place of publication ("Cleveland‚Ohio"), looking like a leaking drop seeping from the region Levy and his fellow poets referred to as "swamp erie."[111] Another vertical inversion occurs on the previous line, where the spelling of *press*—with an inverted, ligatured double-f stereotype pressed into service as a substitute for archaic long-s letterform—evokes a print tradition harkening back before the nineteenth century (although historical usage, to be punctilious, would not have employed two medial-s forms at the end of a word). Such vertical rotations are easy in hand-set letterpress printing; indeed, because an inverting mistake is so easy to make, foundry-cast pieces of lead type typically contain a groove to help compositors check that they are correctly and uniformly oriented. In contrast, the inversion of an isolated glyph is impossible or tediously difficult to effect with other processes (even digital tools are cumbersome; to perform the feat in Microsoft Word requires inserting a text box, positioning the box precisely, selecting a 3-D rotation tool, changing the y-axis setting, accepting the change, and resizing the box to fit the page layout while somehow keeping the glyph itself at the proper size). The inverted *ff* thus doubly indexes letterpress, first through its visual evocation of an earlier moment in print history and then, like the apostrophe *cum* comma, through the exploitation of one of the mode's affordances. If Levy's eccentric, ad hoc, bricolage orthography makes a blunt, conspicuous gesture toward the legacy of letterpress, picking up on the archaic spelling of Atkins's title, his title page edition notice—"first printing / 200 Copies"—speaks with elegant understatement to the fine-press and rare-book conventions with which letterpress would come increasingly to be associated. As offset and photostatics became less expensive and more widely available to commercial printers over the course of the second half of the twentieth century, letterpress became proportionally associated with antiquarian craft traditions. And yet, at first glance, the page suggests not so much letterpress as spirit duplication; the lightly inked blue chosen by Levy nods to the distinctive Perkin's mauve of Ditto.

Thus, we can read a deliberate confusion and conflation of media in *Spyrytual*, which elaborates a series of technological displacements between the various modes of production used by Levy in his publishing enterprises. In general, Levy's printing career moved from letterpress to Ditto and then to mimeo (before the government confiscated his machine, at which point he adapted to offset). In various other publications, Levy also mixed media within a single publication, but by recalling one duplication mode through the means of another print process in *Spyrytual*—a poem fundamentally and explicitly about the act of quotation—he essentially *quotes* various modes of small-press production.[112] Employing letterpress to evoke spirit duplication, mimeograph to recall typewriting, and pressure proofing to recall screen printing, Levy's remediations add variety to the booklet, creating a visual texture analogous to the haptic texture of the tissue wraps with their flaked inclusions, and they establish a distinct rhythm to the few turnings of the codex, which moves to new genres and media with each page.[113] Beyond laying bare the mode of production, however, these moments make the process of printing part of its product, folding means into ends and blurring the distinction usually maintained between printer and reader.

"In the beginning," to lift a line from *Plastic Saxophone*, "was the screen." Indeed, as with the reversed printing in *Plastic Saxophone* and *Marrahwannah Quarterly*, the presentation of the screened endpaper brings the scene of printing into view for the reader, aligning two phases in a text's history with an uncanny simultaneity. At the same time, the book's self-aware gestures extend the self-reflexive aspect of concrete poetry beyond the signifier, as conventionally conceived, to the sign's material production. In the process, by transforming the literal, concrete pictographs of the visual poem into a metaphor for their printing, Levy manages a clever reversal between the abstract and the concrete. Specifically, by figuring the literal in these ways in *Spyrytual*, his practice restores the metaphoric aspect of the spiritual through material means. The Middle English senses of the word include the aesthetic ("of transcendent beauty or charm") and the poetic ("applied to material things, substances, etc., in a figurative or symbolical sense"), with *spirit*, in both cases, carrying a connotation of immateriality in contrast to the fleshy material. In the case of *Spyrytual*, however, we find dynamic reversals: the symbols (printers' glyphs) as material things seen literally rather than symbolically but rendered symbolic of their literal inscription.[114] For readers who attend to these reversals and relays, and try to follow them through their mirroring infinities—especially when encountering the poem on a "screen" digitally reproduced from a digital scan in files copied and assembled *ad libitum* with uncanny fidelity—"nous nous prenons sans fin dans le réseau des guillemets. Nous ne savons plus comment les effacer ou les accumuler les uns par-dessus les autre. Nous ne savons même plus comment citer" [we are endlessly ensnared in the network of quotation marks. We no longer know how to cancel them or how to multiply them, stacking one on top of the other. We no longer even know how to quote].[115]

The Logic of Spacing [CHAPTER FIVE]

Les choses sont toujours déjà inscrites dans la différance, tissées à partir de son espacement, inscrites dans une matrice différentielle

[Things are always already inscribed in their difference and deferral, woven from their spacing, inscribed in a differential matrix].

RENÉ MAJOR[1]

Following a centerfold cover-story feature in *Liberator* magazine, the *soi-disant* "Voice of the Black Protest Movement" in the early 1960s, N. H. (Norman Henry) Pritchard published two collections of poetry in quick succession—*The Matrix, Poems: 1960-1970* and *eecchhooeess*—before making a fugitive remove from the downtown avant-garde communities of Manhattan's Lower East Side in which he had flourished in the previous decade.[2] In addition to the intellectual institutions in which he studied and taught (including NYU, Columbia, and the New School), that network of overlapping communities included the imaginative spaces for new dance and poets' theater opened by Al Carmines at the Judson Memorial Church, Richard Kostelanetz's impresario editing and editorializing, sound poetry, jazz poetry, underground cinema, the experimental performances of the Living Theatre, concrete poetry, minimalism, the intermedia happenings that grew out of Fluxus, and the proto-Black Arts Umbra poets' workshop, in which he was a core member. Given this nexus, the range of Pritchard's poetic modes comes as no surprise.

One of those methods involved arranging neologisms in the tradition of Russian Futurist *заум'* [transratio] poems of heightened sonic facture and diminished reference. A contemporary account describes one reading of these texts, in which "handsome poet Norman Pritchard chanted nonsense words in sequences in groovy repetitions like a stuck record."[3] The pun conflating the hipster's jazzy swing style and the locked grooves of a phonograph underscores the dynamic between sound (phone-) and writing (-graph) in poems such as Pritchard's "junt" (figure 20).[4] On the one hand, the broad kerning with which the letters are set draws attention to the visual layout of the text, while the doubled "oio" suggests both a pictographic image of two eyes and the sound of the Spanish *ojo* [eye]. "Cence," recalling the ending of Latinate nouns originally ending in *-entia*

junt

mool oio clish brodge

cence anis oio

mek mek isto plawe

20 N. H. Pritchard, "junt" (1971). From *Eecchhooeess* (New York: New York University Press, 1971). Author's photograph.

(a reference corroborated by the Latin pronoun *isto* [this] in the last line), plays similarly on written spelling and voiced sounding as the reader seeks its sense or meaning. "These poems," as one critic put it, "decompose the reader by sight and sound."[5] Other words highlight the further play of sound and sense. "Clish," for instance—echoing the context of a "plawe," a version of the Middle English *plaze* [play, sport, or fight], from the Icelandic *plaga*, with the sense of romping or simmering and their attendant noises—also brings fighting and noise together while modeling the poem's paromoion and repetition of entire words. Clish-clash, a reduplicate formation of clash, specifically denotes "the reciprocal or alternate clash of weapons," as well as "idle chatter," as in the clish-ma-claver of gossip or foolish talk—all versions of the sound and fury of language signifying nothing with empty words.[6]

Whether the language of "junt" itself is meaningless clish, however, depends on the reader's cultural perspective. For instance, a reader sensitive to racialized vernacular in New York City in late 1960s and early 1970s—precisely when and where the poem was written—might find it hard to read "mool" without hearing the echo of moolie and moolinyan (derived from the Calabrian *mulignana* [eggplant]), derogatory Italian American epithets for African Americans.[7] On the other hand, readers with recourse to a good dictionary (or those versed in regional Northern English and Scottish dialects) quickly note that "mool," an etymon of "mould" under the influence of "mull" ("something reduced to small particles" such as dust or ashes, and in particular "a suspension of a finely ground solid in a liquid"), denotes "to crumble; esp. to crumble (bread) into a bowl in order to soak it in liquid."[8] The word thus affiliates with the poem's title, which denotes "a lump or large piece, esp. of meat or bread; a chunk; also, a large quantity of liquid." Similarly, in Jamaican English (Pritchard's father, one might recall, was Jamaican), "mek mek" describes something "with too much liquid; messy, sloppy; muddy"; the phrase, "used mainly about food," denotes the hash of "a liquid mess."[9] Even unaware of these meanings, the reader who pronounces the poem's weave of nasal consonants and licking liquid blends that follow the final *l* of "mool" ("clish," "plawe"), while working their mouths around the sibilants brightening the center of each line ("clish," "cence anis," "isto"), imitate the mouth-work of gumming mek mek from a junt to a mool.

With the regional language of mek mek in mind, "anis" might be understood to refer not to "a liqueur or wine flavoured with aniseed," but rather (as the plural of *ani*) to a species of cuckoo native to the West Indies. Indeed, the fastidious reader annoyed by the poem's deliberate frustrations might note that in West Indian English "mek mek" connotes both fastidiousness and indecision, as well as repetition, to the point of nagging irritation.¹⁰ Repeated in Pritchard's poem, the word thus performs and displays its own meaning. Indeed, the deliberately reiterated "mek" also speaks to its own poiesis (from ποιεῖν, "to make") and the constructivist artifice of the poem: "mek mek" derives from the iterative of *mek*, "to make." In the pregnant sense of the word, furthermore, mek mek conveys the connotations of "making trouble" and "making noise"—precisely what the word does in Pritchard's difficult sound poem.¹¹

Another of Pritchard's poetic modes involves deploying typography in striking ways, further emphasizing the visual forms hinted at by the eyes of "oio" and the unusual kerning of "junt." As Stephen Henderson characterizes the development:

> Pritchard's poetry in the seventies veered toward the visual, the abstractly visual at that, toward a kind of essentialist or reductionist linguistics, where the aesthetic object becomes one or two capital letters composed of subtly placed smaller letters engaged in subliminal dialogue. [...] Pritchard thus becomes a kind of concrete poet.¹²

"His work," in Anthony Reed's assessment, "makes people like E. E. Cummings seem very primitive."¹³ Not all readers have been so perceptive; a condescending review by Helen Clark lumps Pritchard's typographic experiments together with shaped poetry and flipbooks, dismissing *The Matrix* as "203 pages of cute configurations" and a belated entry in a genre of poems that were already "kind of cute when they first appeared."¹⁴ On the contrary, rather than diminishing the value of his poems, Pritchard's elaboration of a tradition of avant-garde interventions is a key part of what makes his work so important.

Specifically, Pritchard seems to have been one of the most acutely discerning readers of Russell Atkins, expanding on the signifying potential of the older poet's most radical gestures. Atkins's "Spyrytual," the focus of the previous chapter, for instance, serves as a striking companion to Pritchard's poem " " " " (surely, one of the pleasures of titling the piece was imagining the awkward absurdity of the conventions for quoting the titles of poems) (figure 21).¹⁵ Both poems posit geometric patterns of syncopated terms—minimal, familiar words and spaced quotation marks—with a deliberate calculation that magnifies the distance between the incisive impression of their typographic disposition and the opaque indeterminacy of their signification. In "Spyrytual," the monospaced typewriter face projects the logic of an underlying grid across the expanse of the page, implying a metric—even where the page is blank—as the words and glyphs irregularly cluster and disperse. In contrast, Pritchard's poem, as printed in *The Matrix*, is set in a version of Baskerville, a neoclassical

```
                      ”
  ”   ”   ”   ”   ”
  ”   ”   ”  red  ”
  ”   ”   ”   ”   ”     ”  red  ”   ”
  ”   ”   ”   ”  red    ”   ”   ”  red
 red red  ”   ”   ”    red   ”   ”   ”
  ”   ”  red  ”   ”    red   ”  red  ”
 red  ”   ”   ”   ”    red   ”   ”   ”
  ”  red  ”   ”   ”     ”   ”   ”   ”
  ”   ”   ”  red  ”     ”   ”   ”   ”
  ”   ”   ”   ”   ”     ”  red  ”   ”
 red  ”   ”   ”   ”     ”   ”   ”   ”
 red  ”   ”   ”   ”    red  ”   ”   ”
 red  ”   ”  red  ”     ”   ”   ”   ”
  ”   ”   ”  red  ”     ”   ”  red  ”
  ”  red  ”   ”   ”     ”   ”  red  ”
  ”   ”   ”   ”   ”
 red  ”   ”   ”   ”
  ”   ”   ”   ”   ”
  ”   ”   ”   ”   ”
```

21 N. H. Pritchard, "". From *The Matrix: Poems, 1960-1970* (New York: Doubleday, 1970). Author's photograph.

typeface associated with university presses.[16] Without the monospaced lattice, Pritchard's grid depends on the insistent uniformity of filling every nodal position in its matrix (as it were); the words of the text—twenty-five instances of "red"—are centered in vertical alignment with equally spaced glyphs. Moreover, the solidity of the typographic structure is reinforced by nesting quadrilaterals within the rectangular frame of the page; the poem is set in two columns (attentive readers will note the leading between them is slightly greater than between the nodes of the grid of words generally), with a left-hand rectangle of 5 × 19 units abutted by a smaller 4 × 13 rectangle situated slightly above its midpoint.

Like "junt," " " " " simultaneously invites and frustrates the reader. The poem flaunts its indeterminacy and the distance between the deliberate clarity of its precisely placed minimal terms and the range of significations that it fails to resolve. With its closing quotation marks gesturing toward ditto marks, the poem doubles its display of excessive repetition. Accordingly, Pritchard's poem might triangulate Robert Burns's famous simile, in the opening line of his late eighteenth-century lyric, "O my luve's like a red, red rose," and Gertrude Stein's modernist revision into the infinitely looping insistence "Rose is a rose is a rose is a rose."[17] As Stein explained:

> Now you have all seen hundreds of poems about roses and you know in your bones that the rose is not there. All those songs that sopranos sing as encores about "I have a garden; oh, what a garden!" Now I don't want to put too much emphasis on that line, because it's just one line in a longer poem [...] I know we don't go around saying "is a ... is a ... is a ...".[18]

Stein hoped that with her poem, "the rose is red for the first time in English poetry for a hundred years"; Pritchard's poem tries to reincarnate it again fifty years on.[19] If Stein ultimately set her famous phrase in a signet circle, Pritchard's layout insists on its lines, translating the implicit *rose* into the homophonic *rows* of the rectilinear text, "the double facet / cementing the grooved / columns" of the page.[20] Furthermore, when viewed as a kind of concrete poem, the quotation marks might be seen as thorns among flowers' red petals, so that the poem materializes, or concretizes, the proverb "no rose without a thorn." From the fifteenth century, with John Lydgate ("there is no Rose / Sprigyng in garde[n], but there be sum thorne") to James Joyce ("Queer the number of pins they always have. No rose without a thorn"), the saying signifies, in other words (to bring us back to color terms) that every silver has a cloudy lining.[21] Indeed, if the stormy weather of Atkins's poem suggests that the quotation marks represent drops of water, here they might start to seem like drops of blood. As Lydgate continued the theme: "the thorne is sharp, kevered with fresshe colours."[22]

Then again, imagining the fresh color of the red, the quotation marks might appear as painterly brushstrokes. If the similarity to Atkins's "Spyrytual" calls into question Maxwell Geismar's claim that Pritchard's "poetry is absolutely original," with "nothing else like it," it also validates his endorsement that "Pritchard's poems [...] can be compared to the best abstract painting."[23] Reed—placing Pritchard in dialogue with painters, following his degree in fine arts—concurs, appraising that Pritchard "was able to bring the techniques of the visual arts to the page."[24] Indeed, the measured geometric patterning of the poem's rectangles, and its single stated color, recalls canvases of monochrome abstraction. At the same time, the discrepancy between the black ink and the color named opens an abstractionist twist on Andy Warhol's *Do It Yourself* series of paint-by-numbers works—themselves a retort to the ideology of abstract expressionist painting—which Pritchard would have known from Warhol's major exhibition at Stable Gallery in 1962. A less pointed reference might be Jasper Johns's contemporaneous Wittgensteinian investigations into indexicality, in works such as *Map* (Museum of Modern Art, 1961) or *False Start* (1959, in lithographic series in 1962), where he stenciled the names of colors in hues other than the one indicated. Yet other artworks could be considered, and in greater detail, but whatever the associations to the visual arts, Pritchard's poem calls attention to the relation between the visual and the linguistic, to what is seen and what is understood, to what—in short—is "red" and what is *read*.[25]

Or, alternately, the poem proposes the distance between what is read and what is heard. Quotation marks, visible but inaudible, originally indicated the transcription of speech, in which the difference between *red* and *read* cannot be heard but which must be resolved when rendered in print. Throughout his poetry, in fact, Pritchard experiments with print's ability to make trouble and make noise, including a series of poems which Aldon Nielsen has nicely described as "ventilated" texts.[26] In these poems, Pritchard extends Atkins's occasional tactic of nonstandard spacing into a strategy for typesetting entire texts. Recalling moments we saw in Atkins's poem "Lisbon," or his "nigh)th'cry,pt," with lines such as "I stum Ble D amlOn g / one's h and grasped grisly," Pritchard often reprinted poems in both erratically stretched and standard versions, depending on the venue.[27] For example, "Alcoved Agonies," as printed in Adam David Miller's anthology *Dices or Black Bones: Black Voices of the Seventies* (published, anticipatorily, in 1970), opens:

Below
Cooper Square
the January lateness
lies cold in doorways.
Men alcoved in agonies
sprawl
    their lives
outwardly upon
an inward
    World

as if bottled
in a dream preferred.[28]

When it appeared in Pritchard's collection *The Matrix*, the poem, now titled "AGON" and printed upside down, as if from the perspective of one of the supine sprawlers, or one of their bottles, inverted to be drained to the dregs, opens:

```
b low C oo p e r sg n are
         the fun era r y late n e s s
       lies c old in or ways
     men a l coved in agon i e s
   s p raw l t heir lives
 in war d l y
up on an out war d
w l or d
as if bo tt l e d
in a d r e am p refer e d
```

Much, obviously, could be said about Pritchard's downtown revision of Langston Hughes's uptown "dream deferred" as a "dream prefer[r]ed," with the sun-dried raisins of the latter's Harlem replaced by the wintery, sousing, rotgut wine grapes of the Bowery. For now, however, I merely want to call attention to the way that Pritchard's typographic revision of his poem draws out the root of "agonies." Derived from the Greek ἀγών, which carries both the senses of a public viewing (here recast as the "outward world" and the public space of doorways), the word specifically denoted the spectatorship of a contest, as well as the contest or struggle itself, including the militaristic sense of "battle"—a connotation heightened by the *war* that emerges from "inwardly" and "outward" as a palindrome of the *raw* from "sprawl"—a word that the *Matrix* version accentuates by having both the Bowery bums and the text itself "s p raw l."[29] The military valence of ἀγών will be key to understanding another of Pritchard's poems, which I discuss below, but for now let me simply note that the Bowery first became a location associated with destitution and addiction in the 1870s, following the dispersal of veterans from the Civil War; the ranks of its homeless swelled again following the First World War, and again in the 1960s—while Pritchard was writing his poems—when the demographics of skid row were dramatically transformed by an increased population of Vietnam veterans and younger African Americans.[30]

The sprawling typographic spacing in poems like "AGON," one presumes, are among the "cute configurations" to which Clark objected, and I suspect that many readers may in fact be put off by what could seem a gratuitous impediment to reading the poem in the first place. Is the struggle to merely comprehend the text worth the effort of what is decoded? Taking the poem "N OCTUR N" from *The Matrix* as an example, I hope to make the case for both the subtle precision of Pritchard's writing and the degree to which his typographic experiments can become, and even *enact*—rather than mask or distract from—the themes of his poetry. The scene is set in the opening stanza, where "@ / fi rst / th e whi sper of c at s a l arm s" and the "nigh t s eeks ou t / in lig ht s / f used / e yes / a mbe rl y / beco ming / s him mere d / ai r / g rope s / w her e c ar's b right s prea d / fo gho vers." The mist and darkness, with their respective glare and shrouding, offer impediments to vision, and the following stanza introduces the beggared protagonist as "a rag gedw it hh alf a neye" (he later views his blurry environment with "eyes half open"). Distorted vision, in short, is an issue in both the work and the confusingly spaced text itself.[31] For readers with even two unfused eyes accustomed to conventional spacing, the visual comprehension of this text poses an immediate challenge; seeking and groping, they must eke out the right way to read ("prea d") this verse ("vers"), as words are fused and fragmented, becoming mere agglutinations of letters and resolving into words as the reader mentally reassembles the text into a comprehensible form as their eyes teeter forward and backward across the lines. As in "junt," the negotiation between clustered clumps and small particles is central to the poem. In "N OCTUR N," however, the estranging typography places the reader in the same position as the poem's protagonist; the eccentric spacing provokes, at the level of the reading process, what the fictional character experiences in terms of physical mobility. As in Atkins's difficult-to-decrypt line from "nigh)th'cry,pt," in Pritchard's poem "The Harkening," which describes one "sear chin g th rough d plai ns of m ist," both reader and protagonist grope, tentatively advance, stumble, stagger, occasionally trip, and make their way with dysfluent difficulty—one through the narrative and one through the text that conveys that narrative.[32] Neither is likely to remain "not shaken by the pat h / t h at s t r e t c h e s forth," as Pritchard sets two lines in another poem.[33] Even the brief passage above should give those unfamiliar with Pritchard's poetry a sense of the obstacles to reading, but the cumulative difficulty ("N OCTUR N" runs to seven pages) should not be underestimated. As one reader has described the experience, perhaps with an unconscious recollection of "AGON," the progress is "agonizingly slow, a process of reading and sounding out that emphasized the differences between what you see and what you hear, and how you hear what you see," as "ASI DUO S L L Y EARS UN FOLD" (though assiduous readers will note how the cacographic gemination of the *l* and the singularization of the *s* and *u* in this line from Pritchard's poem "EPILOGUE" add another obstacle to decryption, even as the sound remains the same to the sedulous ear).³⁴ Similarly, in "N OCTUR N," the initial "@," which betrays the typewriter provenance of the poem, clearly translates to "[at] first," but in the context of the comments on vision that follow it also begins to assume the status of a hieroglyphic eye. Even without such glyphs, however, the visual and aural negotiations in Pritchard's poetry, as his poem "via," from *eecchhooeess* has it, are "ark   eni   n   g": *darkening* (visually obscured), *harkening* (requiring keen auditory attention), and cryptically enclosed in a spiritual—indeed, at times specifically theosophical—coffer, an *arkening*, awaiting a readerly awakening.³⁵

Even in his most conventional poems, Pritchard's affected style—grandiloquent and replete with anthropomorphized abstractions undertaking concrete actions, nominalized adjectives, neologisms, and archaisms—further hampers the reader's decoding. "Amberly," in the lines above, for instance, might conceivably be familiar as a proper name or place name associated with West Sussex (a stretch, admittedly, and one that would, in the event, be a false lead); but in the context of the passage here it both slows the reader and thematizes that very retard. Given the stanza's description of automobile lights under hazardous driving conditions ("fog hovers," as the first stanza concludes, "where car's bright spread"), "amberly" suggests some adverbial form of the amber glow of a traffic light, or what would signal the temporary halt of forward motion—perhaps foreshadowing what is to come in the poem's fatal conclusion, given that *amber*, as the *Oxford English Dictionary* defines it, can mean, more generally, "an indication of approaching change or danger." As the sign for traffic to slow with caution, it might also announce the "pause" in the poem's fourth stanza, which opens: "a   cro   ss   th   est   reet / f   ate / w   alk   s / inpoi   sedpa   use" on a traffic "is   l   and" with "ca   r   s / p   ass   in   g" (additionally, with the even tread of softly alliterating plosives, the "poised pause" may also make a pun on the homophonic *paws* of the padding "c   at   s" that open the poem with a whispering hiss). Pritchard, perhaps not coincidentally, was involved in a serious automobile accident, from which he never fully recovered.³⁶

Whatever the exact relation of the pedestrian to the traffic in these stanzas, the description of walking with a "poised pause" accords with the poem's especial attention to modes of locomotion and to the *ambulation* approached by "amberly." In addition to the general "walking" recounted in the poem, Pritchard specifies more descriptive verbs—"stalks," "drift," "wanders," "struts"—and he repeatedly emphasizes hesitant, tentative, uncertain, and ungainly motion: as the "night / seeks out," things "grasp" and "cling" and "grope" (a word repeated four times over the course of the poem)—with a resultant "tripped," "floundering," and "sprawling" (which occurs twice). As evinced by that last word, Pritchard's usage is both casually colloquial and historically precise, and the text of "N OCTUR N" activates the same self-referential potential of the word we saw in the *Matrix* version of "AGON." Originally, before the more prevalent sense of "stretched out on the ground"—like the inebriated, or the dead—to *sprawl* denoted legs flung "in a convulsive effort or struggle," and specifically "to crawl from one place to another in a struggling or ungraceful manner." Idiomatically, furthermore, "to sprawl one's last" refers to making a last convulsive struggle in death, so when Pritchard describes "bodies sprawling" in dank gutters and "sprawling tatters" he foreshadows the agonized death throes of the intoxicated tatterdemalion described in the poem's final stanzas (a passage I will examine in detail). For now, I want to remark that here again "sprawling" also summons the extended, barely legible, typographic form of the lines' own spacing; the word specifically denotes, "of handwriting or written matter," "to spread or stretch out" (as in Robert Louis Stevenson's use: "The blind man in these sprawled lines sends greeting").[37] "The difference," as Gertrude Stein might write, "is spreading"—which makes all the difference for [sp]reading, and for what (as Pritchard puts it in another poem) is "sp read."[38] Indeed, when time is stretched, in the poem—both in terms of the temporality of reading and the word *time* itself—it approaches the "unreadable" condition by which it is described adjectively and typographically: "str etches o ftim e / u nre ada ble."

The same doubling logic pertains to the poem's inclusion of "pass" and "passing," which may be part of what prompts Anthony Reed to conclude that "N OCTUR N" "evokes both alcoholism and the Middle Passage."[39] In addition to forward motion and making one's way, the difficulty of which the poem underscores, the word specifically denotes the final journey narrated in the poem's conclusion: "of a soul or spirit: to go to one's spiritual destination" (as in *pass to heaven*), and hence to die (*pass over*, or *pass away*, as we still employ the euphemism).[40] Once again, moreover, the word brings form and narrative together; its etymology passes back, in part, to the Latin *passus* [step, pace] and the ambulation detailed in the poem's narration, via the past participle of *pandere* [to stretch, extend]: precisely what has happened to the text itself in Pritchard's typesetting and what will befall its sprawling protagonist.[41]

With this vocabulary in mind, we can begin to see the logic which underwrites the poem's conclusion. Ambulation not only conveys the protagonist to his resting place, but the meaning of that place is itself conveyed by the poem's ambulatory route. The final stanza reads:

```
g    utsst   rut
th   epil   grim   smet   dby   th   emo   on
tu   r    n    s
u    nse   e    n
t  h   ele   tere   dbe   ll   ygro   anes   cape   s
w   hered   ream   sand
    w   is   hesme   etthe   irga   t   e
```

With long rhyming vowels establishing possible semantic nexuses (one might *escape* through a *gate*, while an unrealized *dream* would remain *unseen*), the concluding quatrain coalesces into the lilting octameter of the final couplet. The full rhyme and metrical regularity of those final lines model a neat formal closure that corroborates the sense of final endings—both to the rhetorical shape of the poem as a whole and to its protagonist's life. This sense of an ending (to borrow Frank Kermode's term) is part of what leads a reader to expect the idiom *met their fate* instead of the odd "met their gate." But the substitution of the rhyming "gate" for the expected *fate* does double-duty. First, the homophone *gait* gathers all those locomotive terms, like "[ ]st rut," to both echo and refigure the displaced "fate" of the earlier instances in the poem in which "f   ate / w   alk   s" and "f   atemu   ll   s" (in the locomotive sense, to "proceed in a desultory manner").[42] Additionally, we might note that the *met* in the final line is prefigured by the abbreviated "[ ]met d[ ]" in the first line of the stanza, which is hard to fully account for but appears as a maimed sort of *meted* ("measured; measured out; apportioned"), both evoking and encapsulating the poem's twined themes of ambulatory pace and poetic pacing.

Second, with the escaping, flatulent groan leaving the body like a last *spiritus afflatus*, the fateful gate recalls the *pearly gates* of the biblical heaven. Moreover, the gate met by dreams at the end of Pritchard's poem suggests the classical *gates of horn and ivory*.[43] From Homer to Virgil and beyond, the image carries through the Western poetic tradition to serve as shorthand for distinguishing false ("wishes") from true (fated) "dreams"—perhaps the very alternatives that "fate mulls" (in the sense of reflective rumination), and precisely what the reader is primed to consider by the rhyming conjunction of *seen* and *dream*. The topic of seeing clearly, or clairvoyance, as we know, was of interest to Pritchard, who titled one of the poems in *The Matrix* "METAGNOMY," the parapsychological term for "the acquisition of information by paranormal means; divination, clairvoyance."[44] Regardless of the metaphysics, and beyond any sense of oneiric assaying, however, the figure of the mythological gates enacts the very sort of pun by which Pritchard substitutes *gate* for *fate* in the first place. The origin of the figure in Homer's Greek hinges on the proximity of the pairs κέρας [horn] and κραίνω [to fulfil], ἐλέφας [ivory] and ἐλεφαίρομαι [to deceive].⁴⁵

Pritchard thus concludes his poem with an allusion to one of the fundamental techniques of his poetics: the slight shift in sound or spelling that transforms one signifier into another, motivating and explaining the narrative description in the process. The poem, indeed, is replete with such mechanisms. For just one illustrative example, the penultimate stanza records "[ ]miss   edhide   s," which evokes both the atmospherics of fog, haze, and concealing mists with which the poem opens (*id est*, the *mist hides*) and the flayed dermis of an earlier "skin stripped" by caustic exhaust and frostbite ("fume brushed exhausts mingle [...] and the skin burns with ice for a scarf"). In both cases, the phrases hinge on the unwritten *muffler*, metonymically related to the automobile exhaust, and explicitly denoting both "a wrap or scarf [...] worn round the neck or throat for warmth" and "something that conceals" or "hides."⁴⁶ These are not isolated instances, and the poem deploys variations on such transitive logic elsewhere, as when the opening "whisper of cats alarms" is followed by "whistled jeers," "whispering hisses," and a "shrill" "screech" where lights "still call."⁴⁷ Against the background of groping "lust," abating "trust," a "cowered rape," and snow that has lost its purity from the sooty automobile exhaust to turn to slush "ridden of spunk," the noises that link "cats" to "call" sum to the implied but unwritten idiom *cat calls*.

Additionally, as we have seen, that cat may activate a pun in the description of the mist-shrouded figure who "walks / in poised pause [paws]." To be sure, those cats (aphaeretic from *hepcat*) may well indicate hipsters paused with a knowing pose, but the appearance in the fog also continues a modernist poetic tradition of figuring low clouds as feline prowlers. Readers may recall Carl Sandburg's atmospherics, patterned in a patter of monosyllabic steps with a *c*- and *f*- chiasmus on either side of the almost palindromic *little* (l-t-t-l) like alternating legs in purposeful linear propulsion: "the fog comes on little cat feet."⁴⁸ More familiar still, T. S. Eliot's famous feline fog "slipped by the terrace" in the opening of "The Love Song of J. Alfred Prufrock."⁴⁹ Whatever the poetic antecedents, and even without the slip from *padded feet* to *footpad*, the poem's description of nocturnal ambulation calques to the idiom *night-walker* (a synonym of *footpad*), perhaps with the nocturnal soundscape—culminating in the still "silence at the last"—recalling William Butler Yeats's lines from "Byzantium": "night's resonance recedes, night-walkers' song / After great cathedral gong."⁵⁰ Furthermore, the night-walker's itinerary down the urban "street," especially in the context of those whistled sexual solicitations, suggests another of the phrase's synonyms in the metonymic *streetwalker*, or prostitute. That street, along a downtrodden locale, would have been known by the allegorical phrase that brings together the final image of Pritchard's poem and its ambulatory setting; "it's really not 'The Bowery,'" one of the residents insisted in a 1960 documentary, "it's 'The Boulevard of Broken Dreams.'"⁵¹ Here, *dreams* itself is broken (into "w hered ream sand") along the street. At the same time, in a formal allegory of the folkloric Sandman, the dreams here leave the residue of sand, lexical particles working their fantasy magic of illusory signification.

With a similar poetics, "t h ele tere dbe ll ygro an" that "es cape s" from the indigested indigent activates a series of parallel networks—some semantic and some paragrammatic—that all return to underscore the theme of mortality. To begin with, the "groan" picks up on the early occurrence of "gripe," when "f atemu ll s / t heni ght' sgripe," in both the sense of complaint and the cause of the complaint: the belly pain caused by colic or gaseous bowels—those "[ ]ran tingpa ins" of the "gu t s" perhaps arising from an impoverished or alcoholic diet, and leading in any case to the idiomatic *gripe of death* or *death-grip*.⁵² Indeed, "groan" and "gripe" are links in the chain of signifiers that precess through the poem from "greed" to "grope" (in the phrases "air gropes," "dark gropes," and "hovelled grope / grope") to "tightened grip" to "grasp." The connotation, indeed, seems to be *grasping* in both the literal sense of what can be desperately clung to and the figurative sense of a "greed" born of drastic need. Both senses relate to the mendicant's search "for a dime," with "gripe" perhaps part of both the rhetorical strategy of solicitation and its motivation. The word, in any case, is a key term in the text; "dime" repeats twice before returning to modify the "dime held fist" that is "clasped" and "held fast." The insistence on *dime*, furthermore, initiates its own proximity to *dim* and the poem's association of *gr*- words with darkness (the foggy air of "dark gropes" and "night's gripe"), all corroborated by the atmospherics and alliteration that connect "hovelled grope" to "fog hovers" and the further antanaclastic hinge of "haunts" that articulates the hovel where "in cooped dim haunts / the edge ridged dark gropes" and the "ghostly figure" (*id est*, one that "haunts") who gropes in the dark and grasps the dime (a coin unlike a nickel, say, which can be distinguished in the dark by its ridged edge). The net of signifiers, in short, although they seem offhandedly paired, is woven fine.

The obscuring atmosphere of fog and the escaping groan both connect to the difficult respiration that characterizes the dying mendicant, who "moans / amid the coffered fumes" of the cars and traffic where "fume brushed exhausts mingle." Those fumes burn the "half open" eyes which are "bleeding" red and "watered," and they also lead to "gruff" "pants / from a throat scorched" and a resultant tussication; the path of the wanderer is "muffled by coughs." Additionally, with that scorched throat burned by the ice that accumulates where a scarf should be ("the skin burns with ice for a scarf"), and recalling that "scarf" is a synonym for *muffler*, the proximity of "muffled" and *muffler* (in the sense of a silencing mechanism on a motor vehicle's exhaust system) may further connect the cause and effect of the automobile exhaust and the exhausted, panting protagonist (a depletion brought home by the "lees" to which the poem's "casque" has been emptied). Regardless, the rhyme between *cough* and *coffered* itself provides a further hinge between "muffled" and "fumes." Ultimately perhaps, following Reed's sense that the poem reflects the legacy of the Middle Passage, one might even catch a hint of *coffle* behind the poem's emphasis on inhibited motion. The ambulating figure in the poem, in any event, both grasps and rasps, and if the fumes are "coffered" in the obsolete eighteenth-century sense of swirling ("to curl up, twist, warp") the dime sought among their dim "haze" might itself be figuratively "coffered" in the tightened grip of the fist, with a punning hint of *chest* in its sense of both a strong box and the anatomical, panting thorax.[53]

The lesson for reading Pritchard's poetry is that what may at first appear to be solecisms, excused by poetic license, often reveal an impeccably reinforced logic. What, for instance—to return to the closing stanza of the poem—does it mean to have the groan escape from a "letered belly"? (Pritchard, as often, uses the archaic Middle English spelling.) On reflection, several discrete associations can be seen to accumulate, forming an underlying logic to the image. To begin with, the sound of air escaping the groaning victim, and (or) the sound of gas escaping the distressed belly, establish an analogue to the last breath forced through the bugle mentioned a few lines earlier: "ab ugles sile nceat t helas t," with the spacing's creation of "helas" ("an exclamation expressing grief, sorrow, etc.; alas!" from the French *hélas*) providing a further parallel to the belly's gripe and "groan."[54] Fanciful readers may even be nudged to imagine the recently distended belly as the perfectly lettered difference between the anagrams *bulge* and *bugle*. At the same time, the proximity of *belly* and *bell* (the flared end of a bugle) reinforces the connection. Further resonances ghost around the pair, like overtones—plausible, but not actually sounded—as when the material of the brass instrument might also describe the respiratory symptoms of the dying character (*brassy*, in medical terminology, like that used by Pritchard's physician father, denotes a certain type of loud, metallic, nonproductive cough associated with subglottic edema or acute laryngotracheitis). Whatever the timbre, the silence following the last bugle call likely indicates "taps," a word that occurs, with some foreshadowing, in the catalogue of the poem's third stanza, with the occurrence of the military verb "enlists" in the poem further corroborating the association. Indeed, recalling the denotations of *agon* as both "combat" and life-and-death struggle, "N OCTUR N" might be considered as a narrative dilation of Pritchard's poem "AGON"; both feature "sprawl" and "dreams" and indigent figures in a wintery commemoration of the dead ("January," in one version of the latter, or "funerary" in the other, to complement the former's "taps").[55] So, having established the prominence of the bugle that plays those taps at the end of "N OCTUR N," we are prepared to recall that the instrument's bell is typically engraved with either the maker's mark or a dedicatory inscription: "a lettered bell[y]" in the most literal sense.[56] In the event, a further overtone would summon the metonymic proximity between the taps-playing instrument and the burial—between the *engraved* and the *grave*. Nonetheless, however strong the poem's associations between bell and belly may be, the text in fact describes only a belly—not a bugle or its bell—as lettered. If taken at face value, then, the phrase would seem to indicate a tattoo (an association reinforced, in the 1960s, by the military and subcultural contexts of the poem). And here, with the image of inked skin, the route from *bell* to *belly* comes unexpectedly full circle with a satisfying explanatory ring. Taps, in the sense of military music, is itself a tattoo: "a signal made, by beat of drum or bugle call."[57] The etymology of the word, in the context of Pritchard's poem, is instructive. As the *Oxford English Dictionary* describes the history:

> In 17th cent. *tap-too*, < Dutch *taptoe* in same sense; < *tap* the tap (of a cask), + *toe* = *doe toe* 'shut'. So Swedish *tapto*, Spanish (1706) *tatu*. Compare German *zapfenstreich*, Low German *tappenslag*, Danish *tappenstreg*, with the first element the same, and second element meaning 'stroke, beat'.
>
> Although Dutch *tap toe* was in military use in our sense in the 17th cent., there is reason to doubt if this was its original use. *Tap toe* = *doe den tap toe* 'put the tap to', 'close or turn off the tap', was apparently already in colloquial use for 'shut up! stop! cease!'; Dr. Kluyver points out, in a play of 1639 from Emden, *Doch hier de tap van toe* = 'but here we shut up', or 'say no more'.[58]

The word thus originates from the silence ("shut up" and "say no more") with which its solemn call to evening lights-out or memorial remembrance will come to be associated and which the poem attributes as its "silence at the last." At the same time, the tap of the cask gestures toward the central figure of "N OCTUR N": "a shattered carcass / of a casque once drunk." Here, the "cars" of the poem's opening return as the first syllable in "carcass," with the following line redistributing the second syllable in a chiasmic play through "casque." But the connection between the two words is further reinforced by a transitive concatenation with the poem's later reference to a casque:

[f]ja gg edpas t s
t heab sence of ash at tere dcasqu e
ab ugles sile nceat t helas t

The insistence on "shattered" does more than merely underscore the irreversibility of the idiomatic *broken body* and allude to the doctrinal Christian metaphor in which "the body is called a vessel, or a case, for the soul" (as John Bunyan explains it).[59] To begin with, the word goes to the heart of the jagged past of the etymology of *casque* itself, which derives from the Spanish word *to shatter*: "< Spanish *casco* 'a caske or burganet, also a head, a pate, a skonce, an earthen pot, sheard or galley cup' (Minsheu), which Diez thinks derived from *cascar* to break into pieces, with the original sense of 'something broken, sherd.'"[60] The casque, in short, contains its telos in its origin, carrying always in advance the shatter of its terminal demise.

Precisely this logic of the "earthen pot" and its linguistic encryption of inevitable demise also animates another poem about a shattered casque (or "cruche cassée"): Francis Ponge's "La Cruche" [The Jug]. Ponge's treatment of the same theme as "N OCTUR N" offers an illuminating comparison, and while the following pages may seem like a excursus taking us far from Pritchard, the route, as we shall discover, leads directly back to *The Matrix* and Pritchard's intellectual, Columbia University milieu. "La Cruche" was composed in early 1948 and published in the artists book *Cinq sapates*, accompanied by etchings by Georges Braque.[61] The work reveals that like Pritchard, Ponge is attuned to the most subtle dynamics between the look and sound of words; the first stanza opens:

Pas d'autre mot qui sonne comme cruche. Grâce à cet u qui s'ouvre en son milieu, cruche est plus creux que creux et l'est à sa façon. C'est un creux entouré d'une terre fragile: rugueuse et fêlable à merci.

[There's no other word that sounds like *cruche*. Thanks to that *u* which opens in its middle, *cruche* is more hollow than *hollow*, and it is, in its way. It's a hollow surrounded by breakable clay: rough and quick to crack.]

Ponge, to be sure, had a graphic imagination; elsewhere, arguing for an understanding of literature as a kind of typography, for instance, he would see the triple *s* in the word *Assyriens* as the stylized tight curls of the beards of warriors depicted in Babylonian bas-reliefs: "Assyriens, d'ailleurs, avec leurs trois sss, c'est comme un peigne passant difficilement dans une toison bouclée. / L'Assyrie ainsi peut-elle encore être dite un encrassement cosmétique de la Syrie" [*Assyrians*, moreover, with those three *sss*, is like a comb struggling through curly wool. / *Assyria*, it could thus be said, is a cosmetic greasing of *Syria*].⁶² The associations, significantly, are not merely visual, but involve a complex transfer from iconicity to thematic association to phonology. Note how in the second sentence the initial syllable of "Assyrie" carries over into "encrassement"—massaged, as it were, into the middle of the word between the paired nasal *en*—as if the eliding power of the phonemes were performing the lubricating action of the hair oil itself: "La lettre *s*, assimilée à une pommade, permet, par agglutination, le glissement de 'la Syrie' à 'L'Assyrie'" [the letter *s*, assimilated to a hair ointment, allows, through its agglutination, the glide from "Syria" to "Assyria"].⁶³ In "La Cruche," similarly, the letter *u* appears as a visually iconic glyph—looking something like the cross-section of the vessel in question—and shapes the sound of the word as well, rounding the speaker's lips slightly more than the diphthong *eu* of *creux*. The production of sound from a hollow, moreover, is precisely what Ponge imagines to be one of the essential aspects of the jug itself, a quality he foreshadows with the echo of sound [*son*] in "façon." The hollowness of the jug affords its sonorousness, turning the vessel into a resonant musical instrument: "cruche vide est sonore / cruche d'abord est vide et s'emplit en chantant" [empty jug sounds / jug first is empty and sings while filling]. Equally, however, the word itself produces musical echoes: *crucher* describes the particular sound of the cromorne, an instrument remembered from the court of Louis XIV, and the organ stop which imitates it.⁶⁴ Ponge—who included an excerpt from the score of the harpsichord cadenza of J. S. Bach's fifth Brandenburg Concerto in his book *Fabrique du pré*, imagining the "very insistent" notes quivering like stalks in a meadow—may have been guided by the fact that *croche* is a musical term as well, denoting an eighth note, or quaver, and whence the verb *crocher*: to engrave musical notes with a burin (musical writing being one way of describing Ponge's project itself).⁶⁵ Additionally, one might note that in the opening description of the jug's material facture, "rugueuse" denotes not only a rough haptic texture, but a rasping sound as well, related to the verb "to roar" [*rugir*]. In the end, the reader is implicitly asked to imagine the percussive music of the jug in another sense as well: the noise of its inevitable shatter. Indeed, immediately after positing the jug's song, Ponge emphasizes the gravitational fall that produces it, as he reiterates what we might call its water music: "de si peu haut que l'eau s'y précipite, cruche d'abord est vide et s'emplit en chantant" [from even the smallest height the water falls, jug first empty and fills singing].

The event of a fall or crash from that frangent gravity would only bring us to multiplied and mutilated versions of the word *cruche* itself; the shards of the broken jug, Ponge imagines, will themselves resemble its original form in a sort of fractal analogue: curved petals that are *crochus* [hooked] (the word, incredibly, has no etymological connection to the English *crock*, which itself denotes both an earthenware jug or similar vessel and also its shattered shards: "a broken piece of earthenware, a potsherd").⁶⁶ As Ponge fantasizes, in the penultimate stanza, those who break a jug will linger, to console themselves, over the mosaic of "des morceaux d'une cruche cassée: notant qu'ils sont convexes ... et même crochus ... pétalliformes" [some pieces of a broken jug, remarking that they are convex, and even crooked, petaliform]. If the image seems strained, bending the description to an implausible point merely to accommodate a single word ("crochus"), we are only returned to the meaning of the jug itself, since *cruche* idiomatically connotes the nonsensical and the silly, in an affectionately demeaning way. The related *crucherie*, for instance, denotes "bêtise, ânerie" [stupidity, nonsense]—although once again the English *crock* (*of shit*), signifying "a lot of nonsense," is a perfect calque with no etymological connection to the French.

Readers reluctant to imagine that Ponge's text would be motivated by such near anagrams are given the protocol for reading in a line that abuts *anse* and *panse* in unmistakable play: the jug, he writes, is "compliqué par une anse; une panse renflée" [complicated by a handle; a swollen belly]. *Panse*, however, not only is an alphabetically extended or graphically swollen version of *anse*, but also denotes the swell of a bell where the clapper strikes, and so the word foreshadows the blow that will shatter the jug with a percussive clatter. That breakage, as foretold by the etymology of *casque* in Pritchard's poem, is the telos of pottery. This fate is the implicit joke in Heinrich von Kleist's comedy *Der zerbrochene Krug* [*The Broken Jug*], in which the eponymous earthenware vessel improbably survives for eons.⁶⁷ Even in the ponderous, mystical metaphysics of Martin Heidegger, the jug—exemplary of thingness—threatens to return to the earth from which it is made:

> Der Töpfer verfertigt den irdenen Krug aus der eigens dafür ausgewählten und zubereiteten Erde. Aus ihr besteht der Krug. Durch das, woraus er besteht, kann er auch auf der Erde stehen, sei es unmittelbar, sei es mittelbar durch Tisch und Bank

> [The potter makes the earthen jug out of earth that he has specially chosen and prepared for it. The jug consists of that earth. By virtue of what the jug consists of, it too can stand on the earth, either immediately or through the mediation of table and bench.]⁶⁸

Emphasizing the affinity—material and gravitational—between the earth and the jug, and the distance between the ground and the jug placed on elevated furniture, Heidegger seems anxious about the precariousness of a fragile object he hopes can stand on its own—a quality he invests with great significance:

> Als Gefäß ist der Krug etwas, das in sich steht. Das Insichstehen kennzeichnet den Krug als etwas Selbständiges. [...] Doch was heißt es, das Fassende stehe in sich? Bestimmt das Insichstehen des Gefäßes den Krug schon als ein Ding? Der Krug steht als Gefäß doch nur, insofern er zu einem Stehen gebracht wurde.
>
> [As a vessel the jug is something self-sustained, something that stands on its own. This standing on its own characterizes the jug as something that is self-supporting, or independent. [...] As a vessel the jug stands on its own as self-supporting. But what does it mean to say the container stands on its own? Does the vessel's self-support alone define the jug as a thing? Clearly the jug stands as a vessel only because it has been brought to a stand.][69]

The passage protests too much about the ability of the vessel to stand, rather than fall, when with the ever-present pull of the earth, ceramics—as Heidegger well knew—do not in fact always remain standing, no matter how carefully placed. Like Ponge, Heidegger focuses our attention on the falling pour [*gießen*] of liquids, under gravity, into the container that seems, by its very existence, to court the same fate.

In Ponge's account, if the tuneful filling of the jug risks overflow, its emptying hazards breakage ("pleine elle peut déborder, vide elle peut casser"), and in the opening line of the seventh stanza, Ponge incorporates the proverb "tant va la cruche à l'eau qu'à la fin elle casse" [the jug goes so often to the water that it ends up breaking], explicating: "Elle périt par usage prolongé. Non par usure: par accident" [It perishes by prolonged use. Not by wearing out: by accident].[70] Ponge thus implicitly counters the wearing away of the jug enacted in the Dada journal *Proverbe*, which carried the subtitle "La simplicité s'appelle Dada" [Simplicity, thy name is Dada!], and in its fifth number simply performed the adage of the jug on itself, wearing away the phrases:

> Tant va la cruche à l'eau qu'à la fin elle se casse.
> Tant va la cruche à l'eau qu'à la fin elle casse.
> Tant va la cruche à l'eau qu'elle casse.
> Tant va la cruche qu'elle casse.
> Tant la cruche qu'elle casse.

Tant qu'elle casse.
Tant
. .⁷¹

For Ponge, in contrast, the only erosion is of the jug's chances of avoiding a fatal impact; he continues: "c'est-à-dire, si l'on préfère, par usure de ses chances de survie" [that is to say, if you like: by wearing out its chances of survival]. Conceivably, Ponge may have struck on the opposition between the jug's two possible fates in an essay by Fyodor Stcherbatskoy on conceptions of time, where the destruction of a jug serves as a figure for competing philosophical positions. Stcherbatskoy writes:

> Les réalistes distinguent deux espèces de destruction: celle dont on a, celle dont on n'a pas conscience. Par la première, on entend, par exemple, la destruction d'une cruche sous l'action d'un coup de marteau. Par la seconde, l'usure graduelle d'une cruche. Cette usure s'opère à chaque moment, sans jamais s'arrêter

> [The realists differentiate two types of destruction: those of which we are aware, and those of which we are inscient. On the one hand, we understand, for example, the destruction of a jug from a hammer blow. On the other hand, the gradual wearing away of a jug. That wearing works continually, without ever stopping.]⁷²

Whatever the source of Ponge's contrast, the juxtaposition of a sudden instant with a ceaseless working over time sets up the pair of linked puns that will—surprisingly—shape "La Cruche." On first reading, Ponge's poem appears to be a straightforward, even earnest, meditation on its ostensible subject. A somewhat clipped grammar, as if merely summarizing the facts, gives way to a more relaxed rhetoric that reinforces the impression of stating the obvious (sentences begin "C'est-à-dire, si l'on préfère," "Ainsi," "Voilà donc," "Certains, il est vrais," "Car," and the questions are similarly rhetorical: "et pourqoi pas?," "Que sais-je?," "Mais n'est pas," "ne pourrait-on le dire"); the tone throughout is of direct, innocuous, unimpassioned description. On reflection, however, attentive readers will note that Ponge chooses a number of words with specifically economic connotations when describing how the jug's fragility requires one to handle it with care, in order to keep it from colliding with other objects: *calculer* [calculate]; *intérêt* [interest]; *éparpille* [scatter]. The latter, for instance, specifically denotes the dispersal of wealth, the irresponsible dissipation of savings, or the circulation of money through different hands.⁷³ Moreover, Ponge leverages the double sense of "interest," as both curiosity and money paid for money lent, elsewhere. In *Le Savon*, he melds the intellectual and financial senses of the word: "Le monde redevient intéressant, à la façon d'un jeu, comme on dit, 'intéresse': quand on décide, vous savez, d'intéresser la partie, enfin de ne plus jouer 'pour rire,' mais pour de vrai, 'pour de l'argent'" [The world becomes interesting, in the manner of a game, as they say, with "vested interest": when you decide, you know, to stake an interest on one side, to no longer play for laughs, but for real, for money].[74] Earlier, he ventriloquizes a skeptical reader's accusation: "vous me direz que je profite ici du crédit que sur mes précédents écrits l'on m'accorde. Que ces déambulations préliminaires n'offrent aucun intérêt" [you tell me that I profit here from the credit which my prior work contracted. That these preliminary ramblings repay no interest].[75] In "La Cruche," accordingly, the jug that shatters will also be "sans intérêt" [without interest] in both senses of the word. On the one hand, the jug is unremarkable, an ordinary, everyday object that is easily replaced ("sa perte ne serait pas un désastre" [to lose it would not be a tragedy]); Ponge insists on the object's cheapness ("bon marché; de valeur médiocre" [cheap, of middling value], "de peu de valeur, bon marché" [of little worth, cheap]), even if its fragility leads one to treat it as something precious ("donc en quelque façon précieuse") while avoiding the collisions that might shatter it. The material of the jug disciplines the bodies that transport it—cradling, sequestering, aware of their peripheral surroundings—as they anticipate the bump or drop that could smash the vessel. On the other hand, the fate of the jug, to shatter rather than to wear away, means that it will avoid "usure," which in French denotes both wearing away ("détérioration par suite d'un long usage") and usury ("profit qu'on retire d'un prêt au-dessus du taux légal ou habituel"). The homonymic mechanism is typical of the way in which "Ponge boucle 'à double tour' les significations—c'est-à-dire multiplie les liens, les resserre et les cache afin de donner au texte sa compacité objective" [Ponge locks down meanings with two turns of the key—that is to say, he multiplies the connections, fastening them and concealing them in order to give the text its objective compactness].[76] Figuratively, *usure* indicates any sort of general surplus; "avec usure, en rendant plus qu'on n'a reçu" [with usury, one makes more than one receives], as the *Littré* defines the use.[77] With a tidy economy, the excess measure of usury obtains in *usure* itself, which illustrates the excess of language—a system that gives more than it receives from a writer's intention or desire—by bringing connotations of cupidity and accumulation back into the orbit of breakage.

Although less salient, the very same poetics also explains more occult networks of vocabulary in Ponge's text. The original version of the proverb at the center of Ponge's argument uses the verb *briser*: "tant va la cruche à l'eau qu'à la fin elle se brise." Indeed, with its greater connotations of vitrinous fragility, accident, and shattering to pieces (rather than cracking or snapping or merely ceasing to function), one would expect Ponge to use *briser* as well. But under the sign of "usure," "se casse" may reveal another nexus at work, registering the gravitational pull of *caisse*: coffer, money box, till—even capital, or a monetary fund, itself, precisely what generates and is distinct from "intérêt." The sublexical poetics that would associate *casse* and *caisse* chimes perfectly with Ponge's compositional methods. As he explicates his poem "L'Huître" [The Oyster], in a conversation with Philippe Sollers:

> Il est evident que si, dans mon texte, se trouvent des mots comme «blanchâtre», «opiniâtre», «verdâtre», ou dieu sait quoi, c'est aussi parce que je suis déterminé par le mot «huître», par le fait qu'il y a la accent circonflexe, sur voyelle (ou diphtongue) t,r,e
>
> [Obviously, if there are words in my text like *blanchâtre* (whiteness), *opinâtre* (obstinate), *verdâtre* (greenish), or god knows what, it is also because I am guided by the word *huître* (oyster), by the fact that it has the circumflex accent on the vowel (or diphthong) followed by the letters *-tre*.][78]

The word *caisse*, moreover, in Ponge's imagination, relates directly to the characteristic of the jug with which his poem begins: its musicality. Elsewhere, Ponge links the architecture of the box to a musical sound very much like the hollow resonating cavity of the jug: "caisse de résonance du verbe français" [the resonant chamber of the French word], a phrase he repeats.[79] Accordingly, Ponge concludes "La Cruche" with a sort of analogic coup de théâtre: "Car tout ce que je viens de dire de la cruche, ne pourrait-on le dire, aussi bien, de paroles?" [Because couldn't everything I have just said about the jug be said, just as well, of words?].

The analogy may not be quite as obvious as Ponge makes it sound, but it would not take much of a stretch to map *la cruche* onto the prevailing ideology of language as a hollow vessel of meaning—a "simple intermédiaire" of everyday utility. Like Ponge's jug, however, the material form of words—the shape of their letters, the formal permutations of their nonmorphemic units—make music; they pattern and sing. In Ponge's argument, the word *cruche* is itself like a jug, but that jug is like any word in turn. As he asserts the circuit in *La fabrique du pré*: "en somme les choses sont, *déjà, autant mots* que choses et, réciproquement, les mots, *déjà*, sont *autant choses que mots*" [in short, things are, already, as much words as things and, reciprocally, words, already, are as much things as words].[80] At moments, as with the word *cruche* itself, the poet can goad the material thingness of language to undertake a certain sort of performativity, to "Faire ce que l'on dit / Dire ce que l'on fait" [do what one says / and say what one does] (as Ponge writes).[81] Words may lack a semantic essence, but Ponge's neo-Cratylism turns that Saussurian structuralism back on itself: however arbitrary the relation of signifer to signified, once the link has been established strange looping and self-reinforcing relays emerge.[82] Such networks are precisely what Ponge's poetics exploits; his writing realizes that in such moments you begin to undermine the foundations of structuralism's classical façade (*vous sapâtes* [you chip away], as he might have written, with a synonym for *creuser*). In this sense, we can begin to understand the title of the volume that first contained "La Cruche": *Cinq Sapates*. *Le sapate*, in French, denotes a "présent considérable, donné sous la forme d'un autre qui l'est beaucoup moins, un citron par exemple, et il y a dedans un gros diamant" [a valuable gift given in the form of another which is much less valuable, such as a lemon which contains within it a large diamond].[83] The word (etymologically unrelated to the verb *saper*, which conjugates to *sapâtes* [perhaps from the Italian *zappare*]) derives from the Spanish *zapatos* [shoes], by analogy to the shoes traditionally put out for Father Christmas to fill with presents. Formed from the familiar, quotidian materials of the alphabet—something even a child can recite—words, like jugs, can convey a music and can overflow with the excessive referential potential of their material form (like the triple *s* of *Assyrians*), giving more than they receive (*usure*).[84] And here we can see the logic of *le sapate*, the mundane container which holds a precious treasure, which, in other words, is a kind of *caisse* [treasure chest]. If we pick the lock (*crocheter*) of Ponge's *cruche* riddle, the *caisse*—quite literally—is broken open to reveal the *casse* [it breaks] within, so that the treasure that results from the breaking is breaking itself, and the strong box becomes its own key. The *caisse* here is a riddle that provides—in the act of its encryption—its own solution.

"Une prose de Ponge," proclaims Michael Riffaterre, "n'est jamais autre chose que l'expansion textuelle d'un mot-noyau. Les caractères formels et sémantiques du texte sont dérivés de ce mot directement ou indirectement" [One of Ponge's texts is always the expansion of a kernel-word. The formal and semantic characters of the text are derived from the word directly or indirectly].[85] Such dilations would come to define poetry itself for Riffaterre, who—elaborating on the hypogrammatic speculation of Ferdinand de Saussure, which I discussed in chapter 1—developed a theory of textual production in which a poetic message is neither directly evident nor explicitly stated; instead, the poem transmits its message through oblique deformations. Like a distant celestial body which cannot be directly observed but the presence of which can be inferred by its gravitational effect on bodies we can see, the kernel-word deforms idiomatic and natural language and "twists the mimetic codes out of shape by substituting its own structure for their structures."[86]

With a delicious coincidence, Riffaterre christened the lexical nucleus around which poems develop as "the matrix," so that Pritchard's poetic mode and the title of the collection that best exhibits that mode align with eponymous perfection. Riffaterre's terminology may come from Samuel R. Levin's use of the word in *Linguistic Structures in Poetry*, but given the fact that Riffaterre and Pritchard were at Columbia University at the same time, the poetry of *The Matrix* may well be the matrix of his "matrix" as a *terme de métier*.[87] Similarly, Pritchard could well have been aware of Ponge through Serge Gavronsky, a Columbia graduate student and Barnard professor in the 1960s, who was interviewing, translating, and promoting the French poet at precisely the same time. Whatever the source of his vocabulary, Riffaterre's most strident formulation posits that "the matrix may be epitomized in one word, in which case the word will not appear in the text."[88] That absent word nonetheless structures the text as the poem rewrites it, substituting other words in order to approach its form and meaning in a series of swerving detours, without ever quite stating the key phrase explicitly: "the poem results from the transformation of the matrix, a minimal and literal sentence, into a longer, complex and nonliteral periphrasis."[89] The poetic text is thus like a torus of variants and deformations—metonyms and ungrammaticalities—accreting about an absent center around which they veer off and slue back in turn.[90] Ponge, describing the object of his own poetics, corroborates this dynamic of attraction and avoidance: "voilà la definition des choses que j'aime: ce sont celles dont je ne parle pas, dont j'ai envie de parler, et dont je n'arrive pas à parler" [here is the definition of things that I love: they are the things I do not speak about, of which I would like to speak, but which I will never come to talk of].[91] Never quite arriving at the point of talking directly about a coffer, for instance, which the economic vocabulary in "La Cruche" suggests he would like to speak about, Ponge constructs his circumvented subject through its very avoidance.

In Pritchard's equally periphrastic text, the coffer plays a similar role. We have seen the network forged between "coffered," "cough," "casque" and "carcass"—in which the terms are related not only by the similarities of their phonemic and graphemic forms but also by the narrative connections of their semantics (the symptomatic cough predicting the body's demise, the body figured as an empty vessel, the onomasiological set of vessels in which both coffers and casques are members, and so on). The two pairs, moreover, point to a further pair of synonyms: *coffin* and *casket*. Having exhumed this matrix of containers for human remains—two kernel-words which the text repeatedly approaches through sounds and semantic associations—the signification of the other containers that haunt the poem come to the fore with explanatory force. To begin with, the military aspect of the alcoholic's demise allegorizes the euphemisms *dead soldier* or *dead marine* to denote an emptied, often shattered, wine or liquor bottle from which the spirits—like the spirit from the carcass—have been drained.[92]

Furthermore, keeping in mind the precarity of the container cautioned by the "shattered casque," we can return to Pritchard's odd title with a new understanding. Although the cityscape evoked by the poem does not suggest the quiet, meditative sense of the musical nocturne, as developed in the nineteenth century by John Field and perfected by Frédéric Chopin, the poem's setting, as a night-piece, is clear enough. But in contrast to *nocturne*, the orthography of the title (*nocturn*) would seem to indicate a group of prayers that was part of the traditional Roman Catholic night office, along with matins and lauds, before its abolition by Pope Paul VI in 1970 (coincidentally, just as *The Matrix* was published). Pritchard was certainly aware of more common liturgical texts and observances. Elsewhere in *The Matrix*, for instance, he makes multiply punning references to the Christian sacrament, where a kind of lexical and linguistic transubstantiation alters the *altar* on which the eucharist is celebrated to an anthimeriac *alter*: "up on an alt e r / b l oo d is b r o k e n / as m eat / is rite"; breaking the word *broken*, the line displaces the bread of the host (leveraged with the idiom *break bread*) which—as in the eucharistic rite—becomes meat.[93] Furthermore, the rite here becomes what is right, in the sense of being fitting or becoming, while the meat becomes meet (itself a synonym of *right*). The idiomatic expression pairing the two words, not coincidentally, is famous from the congregation's response directed by the preface to the eucharistic sacrament in the *Book of Common Prayer*: "it is meet and right" (additionally, the orthography of the Latin word translated by "right"—*iustum*—may explain Pritchard's use of "lust" in this stanza; "l us t re turn s" is the tenor of the metaphor elaborated with the sacramental image). Despite such moments, and the historic synchronicity of the nocturn's expungement, any connection between Catholic prayer and "N O C T U R N" remains unclear, at best, and so the elided *e* works less to make an obvious reference than to edge the word closer to *urn*, or what might be *knocked* (over)—especially by one staggering and stumbling to a sprawl. The funerary urn, further, explains the poem's insistence on the "ashen whims" and "ash face / cashed" (the homophone *cache* perhaps hints at the other homophone hidden with the word), as well as the *ash* that emerges from "ash at tere dcasqu e."[94]

With that casque, taken together with the other containers invoked by the poem, we may even discover the logic of the marked neologism "amberly," whatever its other resonances with warning lights and ambulation, or even the resin known to entomb creatures. An amber, significantly, is also a version of the kinds of container at issue in the poem: "a vessel with one handle" and a synonym of "a pitcher; a cask," as the *Oxford English Dictionary* defines it. The cask ("casque"), of course, emerges in the course of the poem, but that "pitcher," finally, points to the countersignature by which the theme of the poem and its congruent form—a shattered typography in a text about a shattered container—sigillate the work. Pritchard's signature style of idiosyncratic spacing and his deployment of paragraphs are the very methods that would coax *pitcher* and *pritchard* closer together. Even without the retrospective knowledge of Norman Pritchard's own premature, alcoholic demise, the series of analogous vessels in "N OCTUR N"— shattered casque, knocked urn, dead soldier—affirm and attest with a duplicate endorsement.

The Logic of Registration [CHAPTER SIX]

That's not writing, that's typing.
TRUMAN CAPOTE

*Ah my dear, you have to write,
you have to take up typing.*
ONDINE

A hundred pages into *a: a novel*, the book tries to account for itself. As if responding, in medias res, to a reader's objection, one chapter opens:

> No it's a novel that it's being a novel as a matter of fact—vut what do you mean by a novel? uhhhhhh I know it just ... ther's no other brush stroke. 12 hours of Ondine a novel? qou're not going—are you going to put it in a in a book or what make it be one whole book.[1]

Several months and hundreds of pages later, when Ondine (Robert Olivo) again asks, "Do you know what this whole project is?" his companion responds, "Well, it's fairly simple to figure out." "No," Ondine continues, "I mean this whole thing that we're doing, this whole tape. This is called, its gonna be a novel. We're gonna write a novel. It's a novel, It's being transcribed by three girls."[2] Ondine sounds as though he may be protesting a bit too much, and his repeated insistence on the genre of the project, further emphasized in the published book's explanatory subtitle, might be understood as an attempt to establish a ground against which the project as a whole can be better understood (or against which the knowing deviations from the defining conventions of the novel can at least be registered). Regardless of its generic legibility, however, none of the characters could have known quite how unreadable the result of their "whole thing" would be. In the summer of 1965, when the recording for *a* began, the only real precedent for such a work—the kind of "typing" that could take the place of "writing"—was the "Frisco Tape" chapter of Jack Kerouac's *Visions of Cody*.[3]

Despite the similarities, Andy Warhol's book is far less conventional and far more difficult to read than even the most extreme of Kerouac's *Visions*. To begin with, the three transcribers Ondine mentions appear to have worked quickly—speed is all to the point in this amphetamine-fueled work, from theme to inscription—and without the aid of either professional equipment or much experience.[4] The resultant text, not surprisingly, is riddled with transmission errors: misspelled words, incoherently punctuated sentences, and inconsistently or incorrectly identified speakers. Ambient noise or inattentive microphone placement left many words inaudible, while others were intentionally omitted. When Maureen Tucker, the drummer for the Velvet Underground, was enlisted to perform some of the transcription, she refused to type any swear words, leaving blanks instead; as Victor Bockris wryly notes, "there were a lot of blanks."[5] More drastically, complete sides of several tapes appear to be missing entirely, and at least one chapter is severely truncated because its source tape was discarded; in a nice reversal of the book's final line, "Out of the garbage, into The Book," the outraged mother of one of the teenage typists confiscated a tape when she overheard its contents and "threw it in the trash."[6] "It's worse than Henry Miller," as the typist explained her mother's point of view.[7] Finally, Warhol himself complicated matters. When not insisting that all of those errors and irregularities be scrupulously preserved in the published version, he intervened during the production stage, making occasional, capricious alterations and obfuscations of his own. One critic has referred to the results with the understated epithet "reader-unfriendly."[8]

Even when the speakers can be identified and clearly understood, however, the fitful and belated hints about setting leave readers with few of the contextual clues that might help to explain certain utterances or even entire conversations. So, with little discernable narrative, and nothing that resembles a plot, the activity of the book's own construction begins to take center stage. As in the passage quoted above, the project of recording and transcribing is often explicitly at issue, creating something like a book "with the sound of its own making."[9] Even without such pointedly self-reflexive comments, however, many of the conversations register the degree to which they are staged, and the reader is frequently aware that the conversations, like everything else picked up by the microphone, exist in order to end up in a book.[10] This is not to say that all of the conversations are necessarily performed for the tape recorder in the sense that they would not have occurred in its absence, but rather that given the loose parameters of the project—to register a conversational day in the life of Ondine and the *soi-disant* "amphetamine rapture group"—they are performed for the tape recorder in the same way that whatever happens to occur in front of a security camera happens for the camera. The conversations in *a*, whatever form they take, are what the microphone is there to pick up (just as it registers, indiscriminately, all the nonverbal activities of the novel's participants: blowing, biting, smothering, and a range of percussive batteries). As the manuscript reader for Grove Press described it, the novel is "so low-definition as to simply be *there*."[11]

The work thus appears at first glance to be primarily about its unusual mode of composition: an instance, or example, or curiosity.[12] Readers soon realize, however, that the book is as much about the transcriptive and relay mechanisms of the phonograph and telephone as the microphone—about the concatenation of mechanical registrations—and part of its interest lies in the way these discrete media intersect, as one becomes the subject of another, confusing content and form, subject and predicate: "(record: recording)," as the text sums it up concisely at one moment.[13] Above all, the book illustrates the degree to which medial networks frustrate the very communication they permit, and to which noise is the very precondition of any message.[14] This dynamic, as we saw in the introduction, is one of the founding principles of a post-structuralist understanding of language and the operations of the signifier under the laws of its materiality. Tellingly, the prosopopoeia of communicative networks, Mercury himself, appears early in the book. In a unique and anomalous instance of illustration, a line drawing of the god's head follows the end of the chapter marking the first hour of taping.

The drawing prefigures those signs (both advertising and zodiacal) that will fascinate Ondine's companions several hours later, and it will be recalled by one of the legendary episodes of Mare (possibly Arione de Winter), whose "mercury bit" was both irresistibly fascinating and potentially lethal. The pharmakon logic of Mare's mercury, the god in his guise of both trickster and healer, defines the other exploits recounted in the chapter, such as the time she injected everyone in the room with rat poison, resulting not in death but rather in a fantastic high, or the extraordinary hallucinations that followed an awe-inspiring overdose of "200 Seconal."[15] The subsequent two weeks of Mare's barbiturate-induced immobility figures as the inverse of the narrative in which it appears: a single day of amphetamine-amped activity. Indeed, amphetamines—like the tape recorder—are both a subject of the work and its prerequisite, spurring and maintaining the conversations that will return, with a morose delectation, to the Obertrols administered in the opening pages: "I just have to stay awake so I can work all the time—I mean write things."[16] Mercury, of course, was also the god of speed. "By hilaritas: gods; / and by speed in communication," as Ezra Pound had written.[17]

Hopped up, on the go, on the phone: *a* is written, both literally and figuratively, under the sign of Mercury. Announcing the technological, economic, and social networks that will become its focus, the book opens with the sounds of a pay phone clearing its anthropomorphized throat: "Rattle, gurgle, clink, tinkle. / Click, pause, click, ring. / Dial, dial." Long sections of the text that follow are recorded over the phone, and many of those conversations involve talking about talking on the phone: the quality of the connection or cost of the call, interruptions, disconnections, whether to return a call or take a message, and, repeatedly, when to call whom at what number from what phone.[18] Various speakers negotiate answering services, switchboard operators, and directory assistance; they lament an arrest without the customary phone call and extol the privilege of a private line.[19] Moreover, the span of the taping includes the training of a receptionist to answer the phone at the Factory, and for much of the book's first half Ondine is trying to come up with a "studio policy of factory plan regarding the use of the telephone."[20] Recapitulating the early history of telephone advertisements, which were often focused less on selling a particular product than on explaining the proper etiquette for use of the new technology, Ondine's rules illustrate Jonathan Sterne's argument that we ought to "consider media as recurring relations among people, practices, institutions, and machines (rather than simply machines in and of themselves)."[21] In the sixth hour of taping, Ondine finally arrives at something resembling a finished draft:

> One, no phone calls before the hour of 11:00 A.M. Two, use board by the phone for messages and also tools for writing. Three—the ability to let the person who is wanted know without revealing his or her presence to the phone needs. Not to let people who can best be called kibitzers stay longer than 3 minutes on the phone call.[22]

Along with the misplacement of a Maria Callas record, the process of codifying these rules is the closest the book comes to presenting a sustained story. The book, however, will continue to play the telephone game according to other rules, recording interference as well as conversations, and registering the mercurial logic by which channels of communication both convey and distort their messages.[23] As Ondine explains, "The only way to talk is to talk in games, it's just fabulous"; but as Taxine (Edie Sedgwick) qualifies, "Ondine has games that no one understands."[24] For the reader who wants to understand Ondine's game, the problem is not so much a lack of information as an excess. The text is so destabilized by its mode of construction that even the most normative passages can leave the reader unsure of how to resolve its array of potential meanings (or even to know who is speaking and whence those passages arise). For just one example, when Moxanne (Genevieve Charbon) says at one point, "the light screen," the reader cannot determine whether her comment refers to the video equipment that had been delivered earlier that day or the traffic signals seen from the cab the speakers are riding in (i.e., *the light's green*).²⁵ Like the eponymous children's game, the success of which depends both on propagating a sufficient sense of the original message and on the accumulation of errors as it continues to be whispered and misheard, the round of telephone games in *a* foregrounds slippages along the signifier's metonymic chain.²⁶ Those slides are registered at the moment of transcription—with mistypings, phonetic spellings, and even the insertion of the typists' queries and alternative suggestions into the body of the text—but they are already present in the original conversations, which frequently conform to the rules of the telephone game as the social banter plays out.²⁷ At one level, of course, that is simply the language game of communicative language itself. Regardless of their registers or denotations, the sounds and shapes of words evoke other words. And in *a* in particular, the proximity of individual words along the metonymic axis is one of the strongest structuring elements of the otherwise unstructured text.

Most obviously, these structures take the form of either genuine confusion or intentional paronomasia. Misunderstandings are ubiquitous in *a*, with absurd and often inexplicable confusions between "bear" and "there"; "heart sink" and "heart think"; "rat takers" and those who will "take the rap"; *Il Pirata* and "a piranha"; "phallus," "floss," and "frog"— and, more tellingly, between "filmed" and "filled"; "appointments" and "disappointments"; "meeting us" and "meaningless," and so on.²⁸ At other times, the speakers do not seem to be aware of the degree to which they are propelled from one topic to another by such displacements. "Punishing," for instance, seems to lead to "publishing"; "climax" suggests "Max"; a confusion between "kit" and "kid" prefigures "kidding"; and a mention of "steel" reappears as "stealing."²⁹ At one moment, late in a long day of amphetamine overuse, Ondine is unable to complete his sentences and finds himself caught in the proliferating pull of the signifier, skipping with a manic stutter from "Via" to "Vail vile Vial" to "VOIL, I think. Voil Val // I dunno."³⁰ At other points, however, the material proximity of words spurs rather than hobbles or derails the course of conversations. In the sprezzatura repartee of their self-consciously witty conversations, characters frequently follow the suggestions made by the telephone games of language itself. Dialogue moves from "kicks" to "tricks," "hospital" to "hospitality," "Parcival" to "parcel" to "parts." Ondine and Taxine construct a punning name around the paragogic sequence from *split* to *spit* to *shit*.³¹ With a play on "stop" as the punctuation mark of the period, Ondine and Rink (Chuck Wein) coax "groin" into "ground" via several carefully negotiated permutations:

O—Testing   challenge   witness, grointing?
R—Equals.
O—Equals.
R—Groint.
O—Grointo, growing to
R—Growing to a stop.
O—That's, you're using something else there, right.
R—Yeah, ground to a stop ... Testament   challenge   witness, growing to a stop, haltingly it got to identity.
O—You've got to find a way to make it more legible.[32]

Underwriting this exchange is the etymology of "testify," from the Latin *testis*, meaning both a witness and the male reproductive gland. The connection between the two early denotations appears to be either that only males were permitted to take part in certain aspects of Roman legal proceedings or that by swearing to tell the truth one figuratively—and perhaps literally—laid one's balls on the table and on the line. In either case, the history of the word takes on a certain charge in the context of Warhol's drag queen entourage and the pseudonyms Norman Billiard Balls (Norman Holden) and Irving Du Ball (Lester Persky).[33] Ondine, moreover, explains that the witnessing testament of the text's tape recording was itself meant to occur *sub testes*: "I'm supposed to hide it [the microphone] under my balls ... under your balls."[34]

Similarly elided terms also make the logic behind other conversations more legible, as unmentioned middle terms appear to guide or structure entire passages through what we have seen in other chapters here as the transitive property of poetry. "Living," for instance, seems to emerge from the unspoken *lives* conjured by the proximity of the words "lines" and "wives," just as a later conversation appears to move from "schlitz monger" to "shit dog" by way of the absent but implied *mongrel*. At one point, the typist registers her uncertainty about whether she hears "Callas" or "college boards," an indecision that seems mediated less by the alliterative proximity of those words than the rhyme between "boards" and "boredom," a word that happens to occur in the immediately preceding discussion of ennui.[35] For certain passages, the architecture of such bridging is even more extensive and sustained. One entire chapter, for instance, can be understood by tracing the progression of resonance and interference between "mountain," "Mounties," and "mounted." Combined with the misheard "oysters," discarded "orchids," and nonce "orchens" that punctuate the giddy conversation taking place during a downtown cab ride, these terms all once again triangulate the testicles: the cooked *criadillas* or Canadian "mountain oysters."[36]

Recalling the confusion between "punishing" and "publishing," Ondine describes these moves in his linguistic game as "that filthy pun stage" of an amphetamine high, in which speakers work obsessively through linguistic permutations, unable to stop despite the embarrassment that follows.[37] But "stage" also hints at the decidedly theatrical performance of puns and the simultaneous measures of shame and pride—of incognito masking and public exhibitionism—with which personae in *a* assume a range of punning stage names. "Marked by a spirit of theatrical extravagance," the "repertory company of underprivileged agents provocateurs" perform in a debate and elaborate on each other's pseudonyms—Taxine, Mox (Moxi, Moxanne), The Sugar Plum Fairy, Rotten Rita, Irving Du Ball, and so on—speculating about their etymologies and connotations throughout the book.[38] Rechristened to the degree zero of surnames, Billy Linich collapses category and instance (or signified and referent) to appear as simply Billy Name. Ondine insists at one point, perhaps wishfully: "They don't give me, they don't allow me a name. The people I work for don't allow me a name. It's part of the deal."[39] "To work for Warhol," as Wayne Koestenbaum observes, "was to lose one's name."[40] Compounding the screens of disguise and impersonation on display in the text, many of the names in *a* were intentionally altered after its initial transcription. This aliasing adds considerably to the reader's difficulty in following conversations, but even without that editorial intervention, the onomastic fluidity of Warhol's milieu renders names malleable and plastic, suggestively open to the weakest homophonic or graphic associations: "Polk" for "poke"; "Ondine" and "ennui"; "Taxine" and "vaccine."[41] At one point Warhol's own fright-wigged "Drella," a portmanteau of "Dracula" and "Cinderella," ironically suggests "Prell" shampoo.[42] Warhol's pseudonym is further underscored in *a* by the repeated playing of arias from Rossini's *La Cenerentola* (which is to say, in the implied translation: *Cinderella*). His proper nomination is also at issue, and following a confusion between a "whole house" and a "whore house," his name is mistyped as "Warhole."[43] Or not quite proper name: "the whore house" in question "is all the way down avenue A," and the added vowel of "Warhole," in conjunction with the avenue's alphabetic name, reminds the reader of Warhol's given name: Warhola.[44] Indeed, the novel's title, ostentatiously uncapitalized (a convention I have maintained here), completes Warhol's signature, simulated on the cover of the Grove Press edition, as if the terminal letter had floated free of his name, returning, but unreproducible: the small "a" of the Lacanian real—"a lost object (the little bit of the subject lost to the subject, the objet a)."[45] Indeed, with the 1998 reprint of the novel, the *a* makes a doubled, ghostly return as the indication of a registered trademark attached to the photo-reproduced signature: "Andy Warhol®"—the mark mimes the compass of the proper: propriety, property, what is properly one's own.[46]

Before settling on that unsettled *a*, the participants in the taping of the novel considered entitling their book *Maria Callas*, and Callas turns out to be a more central character than even Warhol himself. Indeed, Callas recordings are one of the few consistent themes between the different taping sessions that resulted in *a*, and she is discussed with all the discernment of what Koestenbaum has called "the gay cult of Callas."[47] Always a lightning rod for scandal and controversy, her well-publicized feuds and diva caprice kept "Maria" on a first-name basis with the tabloids at the same time that a series of thrillingly dramatic performances led admirers to crown her La Divina. In the months just prior to the initial taping session in the summer of 1965, "Callasmania" was at its height. Thousands of fans lined up in May for Covent Garden tickets priced at twice the normal cost (the shows were scandalously canceled, save for the one performance attended by the queen), and crowds at the Paris Opéra that March rioted when tickets for *Tosca* became scarce. Accordingly, tickets were strictly rationed to American fans, who camped out weeks early at the Met. Callas had not sung in New York since 1958, and her return was a social event "bigger than opening night," with Jacqueline Kennedy in attendance.[48] In a subsequent society exposé that must have stung Warhol, the same article that featured him as one of "the better-known Outs" named Callas as one of the very few celebrities who was an indisputably secure member of the "in crowd."[49]

Although obviously not chosen as the final title for the book, Callas's name is resonant in the novel, and continues to structure the text in unexpected ways. Like the dropped *a* of *Warhola*, "Callas" disguises its ethnicity: the family name Kalogeropoulos reduced phonetically to Kalos and then transliterated. In the novel, that kind of phonetic transformation allows her name to function as both "callus" and "callous," although the words themselves are never explicitly mentioned. They are, however, circled and approached (in the way that a curve asymptotically approaches a line in calculus, or that a poem, as we saw in the previous chapter, describes its matrix, in Riffaterre's terms). When one character's foot is bothered by a corn, for instance, he exclaims "my callas [...] My callas is hurting me." A pun that might otherwise be taken for a transcription error—or that is produced as part of "the act of transcription" itself—is then corroborated by the interlocutor, who exclaims, "Your calls. He's worried about his callas; it can't even sing."[50] Making light of his companion's pain, the reply is itself decidedly callous and typical of the insensitivity of Warhol's entourage. "They do terrible things and make awful remarks," as Robert Mazzocco describes it, with more praise than condemnation.[51] Veering from casually catty to sadistically cruel, their unguardedly racist and anti-Semitic conversations become increasingly ugly and antagonistic as the effects of the amphetamine increase.[52] Proving the rule with an exception, someone questions Ondine: "How come all of a sudden you're being uhm, sympathetic …?"[53] Deliberately mean and admittedly callous, Ondine spends considerable time searching for the word itself, which is on the tips of his "forked tongue" but never quite within reach.[54] The whole of the fifteenth section, in fact, comprises Ondine's remorseful confessions of insensitivity and his repeated attempts to recall "the word that s frequently applied to the Youth of the Nation." Stumbling toward the word itself, he and Name are unable to summon quite the right term, but they know it means "withOUT EMPATHY" or "unempathetic."[55] Over a hundred pages later, Ondine is still searching for the precise word, which nags him through the end of the novel. The final chapter opens: "I don't KNOW it. The word for—non-empathy."[56]

In the context of these homophones, "Callas" begins to resonate with other words as well. The second side of the tenth tape, for instance, opens with a meditation on Callas's legal name and the appropriately honorific titles that might be appended to it: "la regina del mondo, la superbe di gratcio di Dio.… Maria Menegina Callas, e molto."[57] Woven around this particular discussion, in a kind of conversational counterpoint, are two related concerns: the distortions and repetitions of echoes (nicely enacted at one point by the echoing line "The echo, the echo"); and the ability of the microphone to simultaneously record speaking voices and Callas's singing without distortion. Those questions of medial noise are then immediately transposed from recording to handwriting when Ondine and Rotten Rita (Kenneth Rapp) contrast the orthographically correct and "right" with the secret "rite" of illegible "writing." Bringing all of these themes together, they then debate the legitimacy of the word "calligraful" as a description of the "calligraphic" nature of "Chinese characters."[58] "That's so beautiful," Ondine enthuses a moment later, recalling the basis of their philological speculation: "beautiful," κάλλος, *Callas*.[59] Furthermore, as Ondine's easy step from "calls" to "callas" illustrates, Callas's name also rings with all of the telephone *calls* in *a*.[60] Indeed, the speculation that they "could call the book Maria Callas" follows from the realization that they "could just call her" on the phone, underscoring the way in which both telephones and names involve kinds of calling.[61] More explicitly, Callas is again linked with the telephone when Paul Morrissey declares early in the book that "She sounds like Mother Bell."[62] The text further associates Callas with the telephone through the congruence of "opera" and "operator," but its noisy party line also carries the echo of other conversations, bringing together the telephone, Maria Callas, and amphetamines with the addition of the words "operate" and "operation."[63] To begin with, the drugs in *a* are what allow or prevent one from operating. The Sugar Plum Fairy (Joe Campbell) chooses the word with careful deliberation: "if I take pills, I won't be able to operate for the next few hours."[64] Moreover, the two chief passions of Ondine's opera-queen clique, known around the Factory as "the amphetamine rapture group," were drugs and opera, and the two topics coincide throughout the resonantly titled *a*, which echoes both the high of "a" (then current slang for "amphetamine") and the high A of the soprano.[65] Anticipating a discussion in which "needles" and "needle tracks" are suspended indeterminately between the hypodermic and the phonographic, Rotten Rita at one point quips, "I hope you hit a high C," simultaneously referencing both the piercing finale of the recording they are listening to and the "high" Ondine hopes to achieve from "one cc" of injectable drugs (on the record, Callas has managed, just barely, to will her D into an E-flat at the close of the "mad scene" in *Lucia*).[66]

If that tenuous E-flat does not quite ring true, it is nevertheless an apt reminder of the way in which *a* continues to equate the operatic and the telephonic, personified by Maria Callas and Andy Warhol respectively, through tropes of inaccuracy. Picking up on anxieties about the legitimacy of the project as genuine writing, falsity is a recurrent theme of the novel's conversations, which dwell not only on fraud and forgery but on all manner of illegitimacies, hypocrisies, imitations, and lies. Conversely, the truthful, the real, and the genuine are also all topics of conversation, and their constellation of concerns ultimately returns, through the oxymoron of a "genuine zircon," to the "phoney" gift of the telephone: "he gave me a ring yesterday."[67] In fact, the "phoney" characterizes both the prosthetic voice of the telephone and the ventriloquizing voice that emerges from what Koestenbaum has called the "queen's throat."[68] At the Factory, Ondine and his cast of divas sang along to records played on Name's Harman-Kardon hi-fi, but the fidelity aspired to by that phonographic mechanism is repeatedly betrayed, not only by their accompaniments but by Warhol's portable tape recorder itself, which translates high volume as distortion.[69] Against the verismo graininess of that tape, *a* not only registers Ondine's "fake voice" (the sound waves and seductive singing at the origin of his eponym) and catches him "mimicking in a high affected voice," but it notes the high, affected, male voices attempting to mimic Callas's soprano: those forced, unnatural head voices that are a little false, or "falsetto."[70]

The play of accuracy and discrepancy in the vocal drag of these accompaniments is complicated by the fact that the false note was itself part of the Callas experience—indeed, it was a core part of the authenticity of her vocal signature. By the mid-1960s, Callas's uncertain and unreliable top register, a perennial concern for reviewers, had become less a specific criticism than one of the defining characteristics of her performance, the other side of the coin that purchased her legendary dramatic force. As Harold Schonberg wrote in his review of her 1965 New York *Tosca*: "Miss Callas is operating these days with only the remnants of a voice. Her top, always insecure, now is merely a desperate lunge at high notes." Similarly, a review of her Paris *Tosca* a month before noted that she "appeared to be unsure of her upper register."[71] Problems with register had also, of course, become a hallmark of Warhol's period style and the mode of his painterly production. With the overlapping bleed of paint from misaligned stencils, the signature Warhol silkscreen was characterized above all by its inaccurate registration. As with Callas, these technical errors became a point of interest and almost, on occasion, of pride. Warhol explained, "I wanted to do a 'bad book' just the way I'd done 'bad movies' and 'bad art'"; within the deskilled text of *a* itself, the glaring errors of transmission—ironically often in part because of the undiscriminating registration of recording mechanisms—accrued as the text was filtered through the semi-anonymous and multiply aliased operators of its inscriptive networks, paradoxically becoming the very point at which the text most directly reveals Warhol's own personal signature.[72] The few extant examples of Warhol's personal correspondence anticipate the roughened and idiosyncratic textual surface of *a*. "Almost every sentence in his hand is full of bizarre spelling errors. Clearly, he was dyslexic."[73]

Regardless of the difficulties with her high notes, Callas obviously generated a great deal of excitement among her fans. As Leonard Bernstein famously pronounced, "she was pure electricity."[74] Critics in the 1960s, in fact, would make consistent recourse to that very metaphor, inevitably using electrical terms in place of the vocabulary of heat that had dominated the praise of her singing in the late 1950s, when she (or her voice) was found to be "melting," "liquid," "fiery," "feverish," "hot tempered," and so on. By the mid-1960s, in comparison, Callas was a lightning rod for a different idiom: "her conception of the role was electrical"; her acting was "electrifying"; she was "supercharged"; "on the operatic stage, they [her legion fans] find her electrifying."[75] In *a*, Ondine recalls that when he heard Callas at the Met "she was shocking" and, listening to her voice on record, concludes, "She's lethal."[76] Ondine's assessment of Callas recasts his concern with the potentially lethal electrical apparatus used to produce *a* itself. When someone (possibly Persky, but probably Warhol himself) threatens to throw the microphone and tape player into his bath, Ondine, embodying the elemental water spirit of his eponym, exclaims: "Drella really you must stop with t-t-thing I'm going to electrocute myself—it's electric you know."[77] As Nathan Gluck later quipped, "Andy just likes to shock."[78] Gluck, of course, is characterizing the calculated outrage tirelessly sought by Warhol and his entourage, but "shock" occurs in *a* in its electrical sense as well. Ondine warns at one point, "the current[']s on" and then moves to a description of a "shock room." That room underscores the emphatic exclamations of both "TORTURE" and "CRAZY," with the suggestion of electroshock therapy, but it seems to refer more immediately to some sort of sanctuary in which one can be sequestered for peace and quiet, a special place to which one retreats—or, more darkly, is sent—when one has "talked enough."[79]

A special room for shock and silence had already been figured by Warhol just a few years before in his series of electric-chair paintings, one of which had been the focal point of his show at the Sonnabend Gallery in Paris in 1964.[80] The paintings were first produced (the degree to which one is tempted to write "executed" is a measure of the paintings' self-reflexive mirroring) in 1963, as part of the "Death and Disaster" series inaugurated the previous year. In that context, the chair shares a clear iconic affinity with the series' other images of individual and state violence—police brutality, car wrecks, suicides, a mushroom cloud—and they have an obvious political charge. More specifically, one might note that Warhol took the image from a newspaper article about the execution of Julius and Ethel Rosenberg exactly a decade earlier, a provenance that brings the electric-chair paintings closer to the atomic bomb mushroom cloud that served as the final image in the series.[81] The chair pictured in Warhol's paintings is the apparatus installed in the death chamber at Sing Sing prison. Following renewed debates about the death penalty provoked by California's execution (by gas) of Caryl Chessman in 1960, the state of New York had outlawed the use of the electric chair in 1963.

A later series using the same image would be more tightly cropped, further emphasizing the internal framing of the chair, which sits on a small square mat and is photographed from a perspective that both fits it neatly under the wainscoting border of the back wall and angles it into the small wooden table directly behind it so that the dark wood of the table sets off the overlit back of the chair and the two pieces of furniture seem at first glance part of the same mechanism. But in the wider compass shown in Warhol's original set of paintings from the early 1960s, the gapingly vacant chair—with its drape of slack straps and a sinisterly casual curve to the cable that extends from its feet, head slightly raised at an angle like a snake's—is further blocked by a series of nested frames: the rubber mat balanced above by two pipes hung from a partially dropped ceiling that itself creates a shallow alcove, bordered on either side by flanking doors set in walls that seem to wing out at angles that are hard to reconcile with the pitch of pipes and the horizontal of the ceiling's horizon. The room at Sing Sing extended rather far back, well behind the point from which the photograph was taken, and included a seating area for more than a dozen witnesses and attendants. But against the forward projection of the mat and the opening sweep of the side walls, the photonegative flattening of Warhol's silk-screening cancels that depth and seems to push the chair even closer to the back wall, while the starkly sharp matte shadows of a harsh high contrast further emphasize the evacuated lateral expanse. Even after the viewer has imaginatively reinstated some depth to the image, the small table in the background still seems too much a part of the apparatus to distract from the singular focus on the chair, or to seriously vie for our visual attention. One object in the otherwise empty room, however, repeatedly draws the viewer's eye from the lurid central image: an authoritative institutional sign, hung surprisingly high above the right-hand door, reading "SILENCE." Although it speaks from the wings, calling the viewer away from the center of the canvas, its message seems to reinforce the emptiness of the chair and to underscore the absence of human figures in the tableau (even the implied presence of the photographer is difficult to keep in mind). Captioning the scene in this way, "SILENCE" balances between imperative and description; like the Photostat maps of Robert Smithson's nonsites, the sign returns the viewer to the chair and the similarly sized central panel of the chair back, which itself now seems to hang like a blank, muted sign. The image as a whole thus appears more bluntly straightforward, and indeed blunt address—or perhaps more specifically, the distinctly disciplinary bluntness of institutional address—seems to be the very meaning of the work.[82]

In the hushed silence of that space, however, the whispers play out another round of the telephone game, which requires that any communication will be less clear. Just before embarking on *a*, Warhol had reworked the electric-chair painting in 1964, including it among a series of Thermofax collaborations with Gerard Malanga, whose accompanying poem begins as a caption to Warhol's image and ends by balancing the furniture of that "shock room" with an ominous invocation of electric media:

> The electric chair in a room made silent by signs
> Over the door,
> The flames coming toward us—
> Accidents of some future date,
> We sit on couches, but the sleep
> And ideas persist
> Knowing we gain from it,
> To fall apart again.
> Some simplicities first
> Then nothing—night

The secret, visible late next day. Or next week.
On the telephone. The film.[83]

The final lines of Malanga's poem echo the noir conclusion of George Oppen's *Discrete Series*—"Successive / Happenings / (the telephone)"—updating Oppen's Depression-era poem with the apocalyptic tone of imminent, approaching "flames" and "accidents," which again recalls the nuclear specter of the Cold War and the A-bomb image in the "Disaster" series.[84] Moreover, the last line also reminds us that the electric chair's lineage is inextricably intertwined with electronic media. Specifically, the phonograph and the telephone—those two technologies so prominently on display in *a*—not only share an ancestry that can be traced back to Alexander Bell's "ear phonautograph," but they are also the "sinister counterparts" of their technological stepbrother, Thomas Edison's electric chair.[85] "I like Edison," Warhol enthused. "Oh do I like Edison!" The inveterate telephone conversationalist, who dictated entire books over the phone, may have known that the phonograph originally emerged from Edison's work with the telephone and his desire for a device that could aid transcription by recording a telephone conversation and playing it back more slowly—something that might have helped with the transcription of *a*.[86] From the beginning, moreover, both the phonograph and the telephone were linked with what Jonathan Sterne recognizes as "the peculiar Victorian culture of death" and its attendant spiritualism, an association that carried well into the twentieth century.[87] Accordingly, *a* repeatedly underscores the deathly valence of medial technologies, which themselves constitute something like "a mystery message d'outre tombe."[88] Ondine explains that the voice on the telephone is the voice of "d-e-a-t-h," cryptically elaborating elsewhere: "answer phone, now dead, knalso known as the last ring. I'm what happens when you decide to plug in."[89] Similarly, he equates operatic performance with death, emphasizes the "haunting" quality of an operatic melody, and takes part in a long discussion about a poltergeist.[90] Although their interest in that particular spirit seems to hinge on a belief that "geist" derives from "gas" (summoning the agent of Chessman's execution) and that a "pülter gast" is thus an evil smelling essence—a sort of ghostly flatulence that brings its noxious cloud into the orbit of Mercury (in his guise as the Sunoco mascot) and the novel's various mentions of petroleum, methane, and natural gas—the actual etymology is in fact all to the point: poltergeists (from the German *polt*, "to knock") are loud ghosts, spirits that mark their death by refusing to be silent.[91] The discussion, moreover, brings together the various connotations of medium: spiritual summoner, surrounding fluid, and communicative substrate. Accordingly, in this necrologic context, Ondine's repeated description of a "tin foil tomb" ultimately evokes not only the infamous foil wallpaper of the silver factory "that Billy Name built" but the "resonant tomb" of the phonograph's original tinfoil medium and its thin metal descendant: the electromagnetic tape used to record *a*.[92]

Warhol's novel thus registers the seemingly unshakable cultural trope that has always connected the inscriptive and spiritualist senses of the "medium," a word which also denotes a surrounding atmosphere like the gaseous substances the characters associated with ghosts. But as we have seen, it also connects death and the technological voice through a particular and idiosyncratic logic, triangulating lethal electricity, the telephone, and the phonograph through the figure of Maria Callas. Given that nexus, I want to propose that with Warhol's novel as an intertextual background we might better understand the proper genre of his electric-chair paintings and see them as portraits. I have already noted her association with lethal electricity, but Callas is also identified—both within *a* and in the broader cultural discourse of the time—with silence. On the one hand, Callas not only warrants a reverential silence in *a* ("please don't talk while the record's on"), but the deafening volume at which her records are played frequently silences everything else because "the music's too loud."[93] That "piercing music" breaks into conversation—as when "Opera interrupts"—but it can completely cancel conversation as well.[94] The transcriber of several of the later tapes notes those points at which the conversation is "overcome by opera," "voices [are] drowned out by music," and "music is drowning the voices," or when "Maria Callas and Giuseppe di Stefano are singing the Bnd Act Duet from Rigaletto and are obliterating parts of the conversation."[95] Ultimately, Callas dominates the speakers in *a* as she had once reduced the hapless Kurt Baum to silence with a series of scene-stopping, interpolated E-flats in the Mexico City performances of the early 1950s—some of the very performances, as it happens, to which Ondine and company are listening: "Maria Callas overwhelms any attempt at conversation"; "Maria Callas overwhelms all replies."[96]

At the same time, the threat of Callas's own silence was always imminent. Callas *not* singing had become as much a part of her celebrity as her vocal performances themselves. Her scandalous cancellations, mid-performance walkouts, and professional feuds dramatized the periodic absence of her voice from certain opera houses. Adding to the perpetual drama of whether she would sing, the 1960s brought growing concern about how long she *could* sing. Her seemingly fragile health, debilitating exhaustions, and the increasingly quiet voice to which she was forced to resort in an attempt to manage a declining control over her upper register all seemed to chart an inevitable path toward the total silence of an early retirement. A vocal crisis had led to a hasty, although temporary, retirement in 1959, and as she admitted, "Everyone thought I was finished. The press were writing so frequently that I had lost my voice I got to the point of believing it myself."[97] In an article published in *Time* magazine just days before the taping of *a* began, she spoke of herself in the third person: "Maria Callas has become a lonely world of a woman looking for her voice."[98] When the conversations for Warhol's novel were underway a few months later, Callas had given what were to be her final opera performances, and by the time Ondine finally fell asleep to the hiss of the still-rolling last tape, her retirement from the stage seemed to be an irrevocable fact. When the book was published in 1968, Callas had been silent for years, secluded in her Paris apartment, and it looked as if she would never record again.

Highlighting precisely those tropes that defined contemporaneous discussions of Callas—her distinctive electricity, the contrast between her current silence and the vocal power heard on the great recordings from the 1950s—*a* supplements and reorients Warhol's immediately preceding visual work by inscribing Callas within a network of metonymic associations that extend to the electric-chair paintings as well. The novel, in this way, serves as a lengthy caption to works that otherwise seem to be either hopelessly, impenetrably hermetic or too self-evident to need any gloss at all. Taken together, however, *a* and the electric-chair paintings stand as Warhol's great displaced diptych portrait of Callas, a figure who fits perfectly into his series of coded, elegiac celebrity portraits from the period, all figures of the dead and near dead, all proxies of mourning and loss: Marilyn, Jackie, Liz—even socialite Ethel Scull has her multipanel portrait of photobooth vamping shadowed into a modern memento mori through the ineluctable homophonic slippage of her name. My point, however, is not so much about intertextual hermeneutics as about the way in which history accretes to objects (where history includes the patterns of how we use language and the ways in which its materiality implicates both specific practices and the social relations between its users). That historical accretion is the same mechanism by which the emphatic "SILENCE" and the particular idiomatic force of "chamber" might—in the absence of *a*—shade the electric-chair paintings to look instead like portraits of John Cage, who in the decade prior to Warhol's own taping had become famous for exploring the artistic limits of electromagnetic tape, phonograph cartridges, and durational events.[99] Always best known, of course, for his so-called "silent" piece, *4′33″*, Cage had, in 1961, published *Silence*, which foregrounds one of the many versions of his claim to have experienced an epiphany while isolated in Harvard University's anechoic chamber, an ostensibly silent room in which he could nonetheless hear his circulatory pulse and the high-pitched electrical hum of his nervous system.[100] The Harvard lab is another version of an institutional "shock room," a space constructed under the sign of silence but betrayed by electricity, and a setting further aligned with the room pictured in Warhol's electric-chair paintings by the way in which *chamber* is colloquated idiomatically to both *anechoic* and *execution* (or *death*).[101] Like Picasso's famous portrait of Gertrude Stein, which she slowly grew to resemble, Warhol's electric-chair paintings attract their subjects with an exact but transient verisimilitude. Or perhaps they pose something more like Wittgenstein's dilemma when faced with the aspect-shifting drawing of the Necker cube. In the case of Warhol's re-motivated image, the lens of history brings certain features to the fore, or forces them to recede, even moments later, when we look back.

With the weight of its associations, *a*—the monumental lens of a particular historical record—tips the scales and constructs a perspective capable of switching the aspect, in the Wittgensteinian sense, of the electric-chair paintings. But it also records a moment on the cusp in its own right, a moment between competing attentions and configurations. From the arrival of a professional Norelco slant-track videotape camera in the early pages to the final chapters' record of an early Velvet Underground concert, *a* documents some of the key transitional moments in Warhol's career. But it also memorializes a moment at which the Factory family was disintegrating: Edie drifting away, Ondine about to sober up and settle down with a steady boyfriend and a government job in Brooklyn, Billy Name days away from going deep underground before disappearing entirely. Just before the book's publication, Warhol was pronounced dead. Callas was silent. Which is all precisely why Edison had developed the phonograph in the first place: "for the purpose of preserving the sayings, the voices, and the last words of the dying member of the family."[102] "Poetry is always a dying language," Robert Smithson wrote at exactly the moment *a* was published, but "never a dead language."[103] The novel goes on, as it always has, as it never did. There are thousands of hours of archived tapes boxed in Pittsburgh—unheard, untranscribed, slowly oxidizing.

Ephemerality and debasement, the continual surveillance of everyday life, minor celebrity, affect leveraged into commodity—Warhol's novel offers us a glimpse of social media half a century *avant-la-lettre*. But it also serves as a reminder that the materiality of language extends from single glyphs to the ghost of words summoned by the spell of their alphabetic sequences, and from the substrates of their materializations to the inscriptive relays of those various substrates in rhizomatic concatenations, all the way up to their precarious collective archive and extending to the social relations made legible by the sum of that networked materiality and made newly meaningful in particular historical contexts—including the history of language itself. As we have seen over the course of this book, these are the very conditions under which poetic language thrives, whether in prose or verse or some other form entirely. I hope that my focus on the fine-grained details of a linguistic molecularity and the potential energies that Mina Loy figured as the sublexical "radium of the word" do more than make a case for the individual texts under consideration here. To be sure, I have tried to argue throughout the preceding chapters for the interpretive insights gained by attending—with an insistently and relentlessly radical formalism—to the most minute particulars of linguistic ecologies, and to have demonstrated that such readings require a uniquely local specificity, down to the level of the letter, its placement on a page, and even to the precise mechanisms of how it came to be visible on that page. But I have also tried to demonstrate the portability of such readings, by turning my attention to a series of culturally distinct, stylistically diverse, and even poetically incompatible writers. I hope that other readers will discover the applicability of modes of critical description to yet other instances of works which risk being dismissed as meaningless or illegible in their restive textual opacities—as well as to those, conversely, that might otherwise be too quickly and easily consumed, digested, and summarily absorbed by the metabolizing abstractions of semantics.

Acknowledgments

For their help and support, warm thanks and love to Russell Atkins, Lyuba Basin, Charles Bernstein, Lillian-Yvonne Bertram, Jed Birmingham, Scott Black, John Burroughs, all the baristas at Café Noir, Alex Caldiero, James Davies, Jason Davis, Keegan Finberg, Spenser Goar, Lyn Hejinian, Amanda Hurtado, Peter Inman, the Interlibrary Loan staff at the University of Utah's Marriott Library, Mark Johnson, Branden Joseph, Tom Kryss, Marty Larson-Xu, Jeff Maser, Meredith McGill, Marjorie Perloff, Kevin Pruffer, the two anonymous readers for the University of Chicago Press (from whom I have cribbed in my revisions), Brian Reed, rjs, Mutawaf Shaheed, Danny Snelson, Paul Stephens, Kent Taylor, Jennie Jackson, Barry Weller, and Stephen Woodall.

I am grateful to Alan Thomas, Nan Da, Randy Petilos, Joel Score, and—most especially—Anahid Nersessian for making this book happen.

* * *

A substantially shorter version of chapter 1 was published in *The Work of Genre: Selected Essays from the English Institute*, ed. Meredith McGill (Cambridge: English Institute, 2011); a version of chapter 3 served as the introduction to P. Inman, *Written: 1976–2013* (Manchester: If P Then Q, 2014), © Craig Dworkin 2014; and a version of chapter 6 was published in *Grey Room* 21 (Fall 2005): 46–69, © 2005 Grey Room, Inc., and Massachusetts Institute of Technology.

Notes

Introduction

1. K. Ludwig Pfeiffer, "The Materiality of Communication," in *Materialities of Communication*, ed. Hans Ulrich Gumbrecht and K. Ludwig Pfeiffer, trans. William Whobrey (Stanford, CA: Stanford University Press, 1994), 4.

2. Pfeiffer, "Materiality," 4. Pfeiffer is following Mikkel Borch-Jacobsen's interpretation of Lacan. *Cf.* "les traits essentiels d'un pur jeu du signifiant distinct de tout symbolisme analogique" [the essential features of the pure play of the signifier, distinct from any analogical symbolism] (Philippe Lacoue-Labarthe and Jean-Luc Nancy: *Le titre de la lettre: Une lecture de Lacan* [Paris: Éditions Galilée, 1973], 98; *The Title of the Letter: A Reading of Lacan*, trans. François Raffoul and David Pettigrew [Albany: State University of New York Press, 1992], 95); "une critique purement formaliste qui ne s'intéresait qu'au code, au pur jeu du signifiant, à l'agencement technique d'un texte-objet et négligerait les effets génétiques" (Jacques Derrida, *Positions: Entretiens avec Henri Ronse, Julia Kristeva, Jean-Louis Houdebine, Guy Scarpetta* [Paris: Minuit, 1972], 64).

3. Veronica Forrest-Thomson, *Poetic Artifice: A Theory of Twentieth-Century Poetry* (New York: St. Martin's, 1978), [xi].

4. Gwendolyn Brooks, *Riot* (Detroit: Broadside Press, 1969), 21.

5. Philip A. Greasley, "Gwendolyn Brooks "Afrika,'" *MidAmerica* 13 (Yearbook of the Society for the Study of Midwestern Literature), ed. David D. Anderson (East Lansing, MI: Midwestern Press, 1986), 13; Margot Harper Banks, *Religious Allusion in the Poetry of Gwendolyn Brooks* (Jefferson: McFarland & Company, 2012): 95; Annette Debo, "Reflecting Violence in the Warpland: Gwendolyn Brooks's 'Riot,'" *African American Review* 3.1-2 (Spring-Summer 2005): 149; D. H. Melhem, *Gwendolyn Brooks: Poetry and the Heroic Voice* (Lexington: University Press of Kentucky, 1987), 200. Other readings understand the metaphor to signify "manhood," or the "powerful yet enigmatic remoteness" of a new Black masculinity more generally (George Kent, *A Life of Gwendolyn Brooks* [Lexington: University Press of Kentucky, 1990], 238-39; Jane Hedley, *I Made You to Find Me: The Coming of Age of the Woman Poet and the Politics of Poetic Address* [Columbus: Ohio State University Press, 2009], 141-42).

6. In "Bronzeville Woman in a Red Hat: Hires Out to Mrs. Miles," Brooks ventriloquizes a dehumanizing stream of consciousness, following alliteration to dehumanize the poem's subject: "A lion, really. Poised / To pounce. A puma. A panther. A black / Bear" (*The Bean Eaters* [New York: Harper, 1960]).

7. Gwendolyn Brooks, *Report from Part One* (Detroit: Broadside Press, 1972), 50.

8. *Oxford English Dictionary*, 2nd ed., s.v. "pride"; cited hereafter as *OED*. See, for example, "Black Pride Theme for Dedication Festivities," *Chicago Defender* (30 September 1967); Don L. Lee, *Black Pride* (Detroit: Broadside Press, 1968); Janet Harris and Julius W. Hobson, *Black Pride: A People's Struggle* (New York: McGraw-Hill, 1969). The phrase is widely used in articles throughout *Negro Digest* beginning in 1967.

9. *Velvet*, from the medieval Latin *velvetum*, originates in the classical Latin *villus* [shaggy hair]. *Svelte*, the French adoption of the Italian *svelto*, derives ultimately from the colloquial late Latin *exvellitu* (past participle of "pluck out"). *Veldt* is the Old Dutch form of modern *veld*.

10. See Gwendolyn Brooks, *The Near-Johannesburg Boy and Other Poems* (Chicago: David Co., 1986) and *Winnie* (Chicago: Third World Press, 1988).

11. *Cf.* "Literature is news that STAYS news"—noting that one might equally understand "stays" as *remains* or *arrests* (Ezra Pound, *ABC of Reading* [New York: New Directions, 1960], 29).

12. See Malcolm Beckwith Parkes, "The Influence of the Concepts of Ordinatio and Compilatio on the Development of the Book," in *Scribes, Scripts, and Readers: Studies in the Communication and Presentation, and Dissemination of Medieval Texts* (London: Hambledon Press, 1991), 35–70.

13. Jacques Derrida, *De la grammatologie* (Paris: Minuit, 1967), 136. *Cf.*, in the same text, "le nom propre n'a jamais été possible que par son fonctionnement [...] dans un système de différences" (159).

14. Indeed, the collection *Russell Atkins: On the Life and Work of an American Master* (Warrensburg, MO: Pleiades Press, 2013) is volume 6 in a series titled Unsung Masters.

15. See, for instance, Derek Beaulieu's beautiful transcription of the placement of punctuation on the pages of *a: a novel* (while erasing everything else) (Paris: Éditions Jean Boîte, 2017) and Liz Worth, *No Work Finished Here: Rewriting Andy Warhol* (Toronto: Book*hug, 2015).

16. Andy Warhol, *The Philosophy of Andy Warhol: From A to B and Back Again* (Orlando: Harcourt, 1975), 144. Presented as a neutral description of framing space, the phrase might also be taken as a description of Marcel Duchamp's *Étant donnés: 1° la chute d'eau, 2° le gaz d'éclairage* (Philadelphia Museum of Art).

17. Steve McCaffery, "Diminished Reference and the Model Reader," in *North of Intention: Critical Writings 1973-1986* (Toronto: Nightwood Editions, 1986), 13.

18. Melvin B. Tolson, *Libretto for the Republic of Liberia* (London: Collier, 1953), 66.

19. One might compare Riffaterre's "matrix" with Jacques-Alain Miller's "suture":

le rapport du sujet à la chaîne de son discours; on verra qu'il y figure comme l'élément qui manque, sous l'espèce d'un tenant-lieu. Car, y manquant, il n'en est pas purement et simplement absent. Suture par extension, le rapport en général du manque à la structure dont il est élément en tant qu'il implique position d'un tenant-lieu

[the relation of the subject to the chain of its discourse; we shall see that it figures there as the element which is lacking, in the form of a stand-in. For, while there lacking, it is not purely and simply absent. Suture, by extension—the general relation of lack to the structure—of which it is an element, inasmuch as it implies the position of a taking-the-place-of]

"La suture (Éléments de la logique du signifiant)," *Cahiers pour l'Analyse* 1.3 (January 1966): 39; "Suture (Elements of the Logic of the Signifier)," trans. Jacqueline Rose, in *Concept and Form*, vol. 1, *Key Texts from the Cahiers pour l'Analyse*, ed. Peter Hallward and Knox Peden (London: Verso, 2012): 92–93.

20. Miller, "Suture," 49/101.

21. "Votre métier est infernal. Je n'arrive pas à faire ce que je veux et pourtant, je suis plein d'idées" Quoted in Paul Valéry, *Oeuvres Complètes*, ed. Jean Hytier (Paris: Gallimard, 1960), 1:1324.

22. Valéry, *Oeuvres*, 1:1324.

23. Roman Jakobson, "Yeats' 'Sorrow of Love' through the Years," in *Verbal Art, Verbal Sign, Verbal Time*, ed. Krystyna Pomorska and Stephen Rudy, with Brent Vine (Minneapolis: University of Minnesota Press, 1985), 79. Valéry would rephrase the dictum elsewhere as "si tu veux faire des vers et que tu commences par des pensées, tu commences par la prose" [if you want to make poetry and begin with ideas, you're on your way to prose] (*Oeuvres*, 1:1456). Ezra Pound is only a step away when he admonishes: "don't retell in mediocre verse what has already been done in good prose" and "don't imagine a thing will 'go' in verse just because it's too dull to go in prose" (*Pavannes and Divisions* [New York: Alfred A. Knopf, 1918], 97, 99). On the relation of verse and prose, see chapter 1 below.

24. *Hamlet* II.ii.193.

25. *OED*, s.v. "matter." Cf. "reading matter"; in journalism and job printing the term refers to the main body of the text exclusive of paratexts (such as advertising, masthead, *et cetera*).

26. *Robert Smithson: The Collected Writings*, ed. Jack Flam (Berkeley: University of California Press, 1996), 61. The line is the title of a text Smithson supplied for a 1967 Dwan Gallery exhibition announcement; in 1972 he added a clarifying postscript: "My sense of language is that it is matter and not ideas—i.e., 'printed matter'."

27. Robert Creeley, *A Quick Graph: Collected Notes and Essays* (San Francisco: Four Seasons, 1970), 207, 54.

28. Ludwig Wittgenstein, *Zettel* (Oxford: Basil Blackwell, 1967), §160.

29. Like Wittgenstein, Mukařovský was developing his arguments in direct dialogue with the logical positivism of the Vienna Circle; in Květoslav Chvatík's ratio, Mukařovský is to aesthetics what Wittgenstein is to the philosophy of logic (Květoslav Chvatík, "Jan Mukařovský, Roman Jakobson et le Cercle Linguistique de Prague," *Critique* 43.483–84 [August–September 1987]: 793).

30. Jan Mukařovský, *The Word and Verbal Art: Selected Essays*, Yale Russian and East European Studies, no. 13, trans. John Burbank and Peter Steiner (New Haven, CT: Yale University Press, 1977), 4.

31. Roman Jakobson, "Linguistics and Poetics," in *Language in Literature*, ed. Krystyna Pomorska and Stephen Rudy (Cambridge, MA: Harvard University Press, 1987), 85, 69. Focusing on contingency and the nonsignifying aspects of inscription, David Wellbery arrives at a similar conclusion: "art is the subdomain of semiosis in which the random element intrinsic to all signification is elevated to a constitutive principle" ("The Exteriority of Writing," *Stanford Literature Review* 9.1 [1992]: 22). For a much more nuanced account of the Prague School position, see Anne Jamison, "History in Your Formalism: Why the Prague School Matters," *Western Humanities Review* 63.1 (Winter 2009): 43–55. For a situation of Jakobson within a broad philosophical tradi-

tion, see Steven Cassedy, *Flight from Eden: The Origin of Modern Literary Criticism and Theory* (Berkeley: University of California Press, 1990), 121–32.

32. Roman Jakobson, *Language in Literature* (Cambridge, MA: Harvard University Press, 1987), 378.

33. Viktor Shklovsky, О Теории Прозы (Moscow: Federatzia, 1929): 13; "Art as Technique," *Russian Formalist Criticism: Four Essays*, trans. Lee T. Lemon and Marion J. Reis (Lincoln: University of Nebraska Press, 1965), 12.

34. Jan Mukařovský, *Kapitoly z české poetiky* (Prague: Svobada, 1948), 1:84; *Word and Verbal Art*, 9; emphasis in original. On the changing definition of "material" in the Russian Formalist context from which Jakobson emerged, see Alastair Renfrew, "A Word about Material (Bakhtin and Tynianov)," *Slavonic and East European Review* 84.3 (July 2006): 419–45.

35. Steve McCaffery, "The Death of the Subject: The Implications of Counter-Communication in Recent Language-Centered Writing," $L=A=N=G=U=A=G=E$, supplement no. 1 (June 1980), [2]. Cf. Ron Silliman, "Disappearance of the Word, Appearance of the World," $L=A=N=G=U=A=G=E$, supplement no. 3, "The Politics of Poetry" (October 1981), n.p.

36. Jan Mukařovský, *Studie z estetiky* (Prague: Odeon, 1971), 50; *Aesthetic Function: Norm and Value as Social Facts*, trans. Mark E. Suino, Michigan Slavic Contributions, no. 3 (Ann Arbor: Department of Slavic Languages and Literature, University of Michigan, 1970), 71. Cf. "La langue est encore comparable à une feuille de papier: la pensée est le recto et le son le verso; on ne peut découper le recto sans découper en même temps le verso; de même dans la langue, on ne saurait isoler ni le son de la pensée, ni la pensée du son" (Ferdinand de Saussure, *Cours de linguistique générale*, ed. Rudolf Engler [Wiesbaden: Harrassowitz, 1967], 2:157).

37. Creeley, *Quick Graph*, 54.

38. Creeley says, "I like Wittgenstein, 'the I is what is deeply mysterious'; that sense is fascinating to me" (Bruce Comens, "A Conversation with Robert Creeley," *Review of Contemporary Fiction* 15.3 [Fall 1995]: 35); Creeley, *Quick Graph*, 189 (emphases in original). For considerations of the relation between the writings of the philosopher and the poet, see Peter Quartermain, "Robert Creeley: What Counts," *Boundary 2* 6.3–7.1 (Spring–Autumn 1978): 329–34, and, in the same issue, Linda Wagner, "Creeley's Late Poems: Contexts," 301–8.

39. William Carlos Williams, "Introduction" (to *The Wedge*), in *Selected Essays of William Carlos Williams* (New York: New Directions, 1969), 221.

40. Forrest-Thomson, *Poetic Artifice*, [ix].

41. "FORM IS NEVER MORE THAN AN EXTENSION OF CONTENT," quoted in Charles Olson, "Projective Verse," in *Collected Prose*, ed. Donald Allen and Benjamin Friedlander (Berkeley: University of California Press, 1997), 247; "Now I might say equally, 'Content is never more than an extension of form,'" quoted in Tom Clark, *Robert Creeley and the Genius of the American Common Place* (New York: New Directions, 1993), 142; Charles Bernstein, *A Poetics* (Cambridge, MA: Harvard University Press, 1992), 10.

42. Williams, *Selected*, 256. For a broader consideration of Williams's machine aesthetic, with special attention to Objectivism, see Henry Sayer, "American Vernacular: Objectivism, Precisionism, and the Aesthetics of the Machine," *Twentieth Century Literature* 35.3 (1989): 310–42. I discuss the rhetorical history of textual engines and literary

machines in greater depth elsewhere; see "The Potential Energy of Texts [ΔU = -PΔV]," *Iowa Review* 44.3 (Winter 2014-2015): 133-48.

43. Williams, *Selected*, 256.

44. William Carlos Williams, "The New Poetical Economy: George Oppen's *Discrete Series*," *Poetry* 44 (July 1934): 221.

45. Williams, "New Poetical Economy," 221.

46. Paul de Man, *Allegories of Reading: Figural Language in Rousseau, Nietzsche, Rilke, and Proust* (New Haven, CT: Yale University Press, 1979), 294.

47. Derrida, *De la grammatologie*, 19; *Of Grammatology*, corrected ed., trans. Gayatri Chakravorty Spivak (Baltimore: Johns Hopkins University Press, 1997), 9; emphasis in the original.

48. Wellbery, "Exteriority," 14.

49. Wellbery, "Exteriority," 14.

50. I would emend the phrasing to claim only *just as real*; Claude Lévi-Strauss: *Introduction à l'oeuvre de Marcel Mauss* (Paris: Presses Universitaires de France, 1950), 32.

51. Pfeiffer, "Materiality."

52. Leon S. Roudiez, "Twelve Points from Tel Quel," *L'Esprit Créateur* 14.4 (Winter 1974): 300.

53. Roman Jakobson, "La première lettre de Ferdinand de Saussure sur les anagrammes," *L'Homme* 11.2 (1971): 22.

54. Wellbery, "Foreword," in Friedrich Kittler, *Discourse Networks, 1800/1900* (Stanford, CA: Stanford University Press, 1990), vii; Manfred Frank, *Das Sagbare und das Unsagbare* (Frankfurt: Suhrkamp, 1990), 9. *Cf.* Pfeiffer, "Materiality," 3.

55. Wellbery, "Foreword," xii; *Tractatus* 6.44.

56. Paul de Man, *The Resistance to Theory*, Theory and History of Literature, vol. 33 (Minneapolis: University of Minnesota Press, 1986), 96-97, 96.

57. De Man, *Resistance*, 96, 101. Jean-Claude Milner's sense of linguistics as antinarcissistic because "il est, dans la langue et dans toute locution, quelque chose dont ils [les hommes] ne sont ni maîtres ni responsables" [there is, in language and in every grammatical construction, something which they (people) are neither masters of nor responsible for] (*L'amour de la langue* [Paris: Éditions du Seuil, 1978], 125; *For the Love of Language*, trans. Ann Banfield [New York: St. Martin's Press, 1990], 137).

58. George Oppen, *New Collected Poems*, ed. Michael Davidson (New York: New Directions, 2008), 194.

59. Creeley, *Quick Graph*, 8.

60. Michel Foucault, *L'ordre du discours* (Paris: Gallimard, 1971), 54.

61. Foucault, *L'ordre du discours*, 59, 48.

62. Foucault, *L'ordre du discours*, 61; emphases in original.

63. Foucault, *L'ordre du discours*, 55; emphasis in original.

64. Foucault, *L'ordre du discours*, 60.

65. Pfeiffer, "Materiality," 3-4 *et passim*; Stephen Best and Sharon Marcus, "Surface Reading: An Introduction," *Representations* 108.1 (Fall 2009): 1-21.

66. Best and Marcus, "Surface," 4.

67. See de Man, *Resistance*, 7-15 *passim*.

68. Best and Marcus, "Surface," 11.

69. Best and Marcus, "Surface," 11.

70. Roman Jakobson, "Poetry of Grammar and Grammar of Poetry (Selections)," *Poetics Today* 2.1a (Autumn 1980): 84; emphasis supplied.

71. John Cage, *M: Writings '67–'72* (Middletown, CT: Wesleyan University Press, 1973), 210.

72. Jacques Rancière, "The Politics of Literature," *SubStance* 103 [33.1] (2004): 10. The inverse might also be pursued: "It is only through the radical formalism of a semiological perspective that the operations constitutive of both literature and culture can be held together in what would be, properly speaking, a history of the process of signification" (Jonathan Culler, "Literary History, Allegory, and Semiology," *New Literary History* 7.2 [1976]: 269).

73. Jacques Rancière, *Dissensus: On Politics and Aesthetics*, ed. and trans. Steven Corcoran (London: Continuum, 2010), 202, 153.

74. Jacques Rancière, *Le partage du sensible: Esthétique et politique* (Paris: La Fabrique, 2000), 12.

75. Rancière, *Partage*, 16.

76. Jacques Rancière, *The Politics of Aesthetics*, trans. Gabriel Rockhill (London: Continuum, 2004), 13.

77. *Cf.* Shklovsky's devices of "остранéние" [making strange], understood as "торможении, задержке как об общем законе искусства" [braking and delay as the general law of art] along with the "закон затруднения" [law of difficulty] (Viktor Shklovsky, "Искусство как прием," in *Гамбургский счет: статьи, воспоминания, эссе, 1914–1933* [Moscow: Сов. писатель, 1990], 72).

78. Sara Ahmed, *Queer Phenomenology: Orientations, Objects, Others* (Durham, NC: Duke University Press, 2006), 159–60 *et seq.*, 161. *Cf.* Marcella Schmidt di Friedberg, *Geographies of Disorientation* (Oxon: Routledge, 2018).

79. Alan Ruiz, "Radical Formalism," *Women & Performance: A Journal of Feminist Theory* 26.2–3 (2016): 233.

80. See my *Reading the Illegible* (Evanston, IL: Northwestern University Press, 2003), chap. 1, and *No Medium* (Cambridge, MA: MIT Press, 2013), chap. 1; Paul de Man: *Aesthetic Ideology*, ed. Andrzej Warminski, Theory and History of Literature, vol. 65 (Minneapolis: University of Minnesota Press, 1996), 128.

81. Ahmed, *Queer*, 162; emphasis in original.

82. Ahmed, *Queer*, 171; on the power of description with regard to disorientation devices, see 177.

83. Ahmed, *Queer*, 24.

Chapter One

1. Immanuel Kant, *Gesammelte Schriften* (Berlin: Georg Reimer, 1979), 27:1552.

2. *OED*, s.v. "prosaic."

3. The nearly invisible naturalness of prose suggests the machinations of ideology hard at work (or what Jeffrey Kittay and Wlad Godzich describe as "powerful semiotic mechanisms" [xi]). For one account of the cultural work necessary to secure the prevalence of prose, see their study *The Emergence of Prose* (Minneapolis: University of Minnesota Press, 1987).

4. Kittay and Godzich, *Emergence*, x.

5. Richard Aldington, "A Note on Poetry in Prose," *Chapbook* 22 (April 1921): 18.

6. William Wordsworth, *Lyrical Ballads, with Pastoral, and Other Poems*, 3rd ed. (London: Longman and Rees, 1802), 1:xxiv, note.

7. Wordsworth, *Ballads*, 1:xxiv, note.

8. See, for instances, Pierre Guyotat, *Prostitution* (Paris: Gallimard, 1975) or *Progénitures* (Paris: Gallimard, 2000).

9. W. B. Yeats, ed., *The Oxford Book of Modern Verse: 1892–1935* (Oxford: Clarendon Press, 1936), 1.

10. Walter H. Pater, *Studies in the History of the Renaissance* (London: Macmillan, 1873), 119.

11. Yeats's recognition of Pater's prose-formatted text as already inherently poetic distinguishes his intervention from something like José Garcia Villa's "Adaptations," a set of "experiments in the conversion of prose, through technical manipulation, into poems." "Constructing in verse what originally exists as prose," Garcia Villa took texts from prose genres as sources for found vocabulary. The Adaptations implicitly argue that those sources can be transformed into poetry, not that they are already poetic. Additionally, they do not utilize the inherent qualities of prose; they might have made the same point by ameliorating unpoetic verse. See José Garcia Villa, *Doveglion: Collected Poems* (New York: Penguin, 2008), 147ff.

12. T. S. Eliot, "Prose and Verse," in *The Annotated Waste Land with Eliot's Contemporary Prose*, ed. Lawrence Rainey (New Haven, CT: Yale University Press, 2006), 159.

13. See, for a random instance: "Yeats knew Leonardo from Pater, whose famous description of *La Gioconda* Yeats divided into lines" (Elizabeth Bergmann Loizeaux, *Yeats and the Visual Arts* [Syracuse, NY: Syracuse University Press, 2003], 129). Other scholars describe the text as "chopped up into lines" (Kenneth Clark, introduction to *The Renaissance* [New York: World Publishing, 1961], 16) or "broke into lines" (C. D. Wright, *Cooling Time: An American Poetry Vigil* [Port Townsend, WA: Copper Canyon, 2005], 92), and characterize Yeats as "casting [Pater's] prose into lines" (James Longenbach, *Art of the Poetic Line* [Minneapolis: Graywolf Press, 2008], 103).

14. As Elizabeth Barrett Browning puns, early in *The Book of the Poets*, quoting Chaucer's line from the *Knight's Tale*, "Up rose the sunne, and uprose Emilie," continuing: "and uprose her poet, the first of a line" (Elizabeth Barrett Browning, *Poetical Works* [New York: Dodd, Mead, 1885], 4:310). The intended referent is the genealogical line of kings, but the ghost of "a prose" in the word "uprose" makes Browning's phrase a good reminder that both poetry and prose are printed "of a line."

15. *Princeton Encyclopedia of Poetry and Poetics*, ed. Alex Preminger, enl. ed. (Princeton, NJ: Princeton University Press, 1974), 664.

16. Eve Kosofsky Sedgwick, "Teaching Experimental Critical Writing," in *The Ends of Performance*, ed. Peggy Phelan and Jill Lane (New York: New York University Press, 1998), 111.

17. Meyer Howard Abrams and Geoffrey Galt Harpham, *A Glossary of Literary Terms*, 9th ed. (Boston: Wadsworth Cengage Learning, 2009), 288.

18. However impractical, such books would, of course, not be impossible to print, given resources and expertise; in 1999 Michael Maranda produced an edition of Thomas Carlyle's *History of the French Revolution* as one continuous line printed on a thin strip of paper only one centimeter high but nearly 6.5 kilometers long.

19. Gérard Genette, *The Architext: An Introduction* (Berkeley: University of California Press, 1992), 3.

20. *OED*, s.v. "composition."

21. Ed Folsom, *Whitman Making Books/Books Making Whitman: A Catalog and Commentary* (Iowa City: Obermann Center for Advanced Studies, University of Iowa, 2005), 5.

22. Horace Traubel, *With Walt Whitman in Camden, April 8–September 14, 1889* (Boston: Small and Maynard, 1906), 5:390.

23. Folsom, *Whitman Making Books*, 4.

24. Jorge Luis Borges, *Obras completas*, rev. ed. (Buenos Aires: Emecé Editores, 2005), 1:477; *Labyrinths*, trans. James E. Irby (New York: New Directions, 1964), 39.

25. Borges, *Obras/Labyrinths*, 478/39.

26. Borges, *Obras/Labyrinths*, 480/42.

27. See Ferdinand de Saussure, *Course in General Linguistics*, trans. Roy Harris (Peru, IL: Open Court, 1986), 69ff.

28. Clark Coolidge, *ING* (New York: Angel Hair, 1968), n.p.

29. Edward Foster, "An Interview with Clark Coolidge," *Talisman: A Journal of Contemporary Poetry and Poetics* 3 (Fall 1989): 26.

30. Clark Coolidge, untitled statement, in *Angel Hair Sleeps with a Boy in My Head: The Angel Hair Anthology*, ed. Anne Waldman and Lewis Warsh (New York: Granary Books, 2001), 581. For a discussion of Coolidge's relation to the visual arts, including a reading of "Cabinet Voltaire," see Tom Orange, "Clark Coolidge's Visual Arts Intertexts, 1968–1976," *Fascicle* 2 (Winter 2006-2007), http://www.fascicle.com/issue02/main/issue02_frameset.htm.

31. "The Cabinet is overthrown" is Robert Motherwell's translation of "Le Ministère est renversé" (*Dada Painters and Poets*, 183); the original referent, to be clear, is bureaucratic rather than supellectile (with the reminder that *bureaucratic* itself derives from the name for office furniture [Fr. *bureau*, from OF *burel*, from the baize used to cover writing desks]).

32. Lyn Hejinian, *Writing Is an Aid to Memory* (Berkeley, CA: The Figures, 1978). The book is unpaginated; subsequent citations are to the section number in which a passage appears. A facsimile and searchable electronic version are available at http://english.utah.edu/eclipse/projects/WRITING.

33. Jean Piaget, *Genetic Epistemology*, trans. Eleanor Duckworth (New York: Columbia University Press, 1979), 45; emphases supplied.

34. Piaget, *Genetic Epistemology*, 43; emphases supplied.

35. *The Grand Piano: San Francisco 1975–80: An Experiment in Collective Autobiography*, pt. 3 (Bloomfield Hills, MI: Mode A, 2007), 61. In a previous essay on Hejinian's book, I speculated: "a writerly reading […] may be the original source of this elliptical vocabulary [i.e., the partial words], which could have been generated from a source text in which Hejinian scanned down the left-hand edge of a page of justified and hyphenated prose"; however, unable to discover any conclusive proof at the time, and following protestations by Hejinian herself, I mistakenly concluded that the book merely "gives the uncanny impression of some compositional pattern or system or procedure (Craig Dworkin, "Parting with Description," *American Women Poets in the 21st Century: Where Lyric Meets Language*, ed. Claudia Rankine and Juliana Spahr [Middletown, CT: Wesleyan University Press, 2002], 244–45, 258).

36. *OED*, s.v. "abstract" (v).

37. *OED*, s.v. "abstract" (v).

38. Piaget, *Genetic Epistemology*, 16–17.

39. Perhaps Jerome McGann was not mistaken after all when he referred to *Writing Is an Aid to Memory* as "Lyn Hejinian's excellent *prose* sequence" (emphasis supplied), in *Byron and Romanticism*, ed. James Soderholm, Cambridge Studies in Romanticism (Cambridge: Cambridge University Press, 2002), 230.

40. Hejinian, *Writing*, sec. 7; Leonardo da Vinci, *The Genius of Leonardo da Vinci*, ed. André Chastel, trans. Ellen Callmann (New York: Orion, 1961), 30.

41. Leonardo, *Genius*, 29–30.

42. Leonardo, *Genius*, 30.

43. Hejinian, *Writing*, sec. 13.

44. Leonardo, *Genius*, 214. This angle of reading, bisecting the frame of the page, repeats elsewhere in Hejinian's compositional practice, if less neatly; the line "big things weigh quite thoroughly primitive as that one," from sec. 5, takes its first segment ("big things weigh") from the right-hand side of page 16 of Piaget's *Genetic Epistemology* and its second ("quite thoroughly") from the center of the page lower down, while its last phrase ("primitive as that one") originally falls between the other two, flush to the right margin.

45. Hejinian, *Writing*, sec. 42.

46. Hejinian, *Writing*, secs. 5, 17, 26, 2.

47. Hejinian, *Writing*, sec. 36.

48. Hejinian, *Writing*, sec. 8.

49. *The Book of English Trades and Library of the Useful Arts*, new enl. ed. (London: J. Souter for Richard Phillips, 1818), 56; emphases supplied. The line "great heat to melt on emotional sympathy," for another example of selecting vocabulary from both margins, originates in a column in *Fowler's Modern English Usage* (2nd ed., rev. Sir Ernest Gowers [New York: Oxford University Press, 1965]). On the second column at the top of page 357, where the entry for *melodrama* concludes, Hejinian finds:

> emotional effects of musical accompaniment is obvious, and it is <u>on emotional sympathy</u> that m. still relies.
>
> **melody, harmony.** See HARMONY.
>
> **melted, molten.** *Molten*, apart from its use as a poetic variant of *melted*, is now confined to what needs <u>great heat to melt it</u>.

The first column on the same page is also the source for Hejinian's line "the schoolboy decent to retort"; Fowler illustrates *meiosis* with the examples "the schoolboy *decent/* (=very nice), the retort I'll see you *further* (i.e. in hell) *first* [...]"

50. Hejinian, *Writing*, secs. 14, 23.

51. Hejinian, *Writing*, sec. 26.

52. Hejinian, *Writing*, sec. 21.

53. Hejinian, *Writing*, sec. 23; *Book of English Trades*, 85 (emphases added).

54. Peter Nicholls, "The Poetics of Opacity: Readability and Literary Form," in

Psycho-Politics and Cultural Desires, ed. Jan Campbell and Janet Harbord (London: University College London Press, 1998), 155.

55. See Jan Mukařovský, *Aesthetic Function: Norm and Value as Social Facts*, trans. Mark E. Suino, Michigan Slavic Contributions, no. 3 (Ann Arbor: Department of Slavic Languages and Literature, University of Michigan, 1970), 9-10 *passim*. For an account of the distinction between poetry and prose in terms of poeticity, see Steven Cassedy, *Flight from Eden: The Origin of Modern Literary Criticism and Theory* (Berkeley: University of California Press, 1990), 32 *et seq*. Roman Jakobson, *Language in Literature* (Cambridge, MA: Harvard University Press, 1987).

56. See György Kepes, *Language of Vision* (New York: Paul Theobald, 1944), 36.

57. See, for instances, *Ecstatic Occasions, Expedient Forms: 85 Leading Contemporary Poets Select and Comment on Their Poems*, 2nd ed., ed. David Lehman (Ann Arbor: University of Michigan Press, 1996), 249. *Cf.* David Lehman, "The Orators: An English Study," *Critical Essays on W. H. Auden*, ed. George W. Bahlke (New York: G. K. Hall, 1991), 46; Lee Bartlett, *The Sun Is but a Morning Star: Studies in West Coast Poetry and Poetics* (Albuquerque: University of New Mexico Press, 1989), 173; Stephen Fredman, *Poet's Prose: The Crisis in American Verse*, 2nd ed. (Cambridge: Cambridge University Press, 1990); Margueritte Murphy, *A Tradition of Subversion: The Prose Poem in English from Wilde to Ashbery* (Amherst: University of Massachusetts Press, 1992); Michel Delville, *The American Prose Poem: Poetic Form and the Boundaries of Genre* (Gainesville: University Press of Florida, 1998), 48; Kevin Brophy, *Explorations in Creative Writing* (Melbourne: Melbourne University Press, 2003), 175; Ron Silliman, *The New Sentence* (New York: Roof Books, 1987), 63. Silliman is echoing Williams's opening claim: "the sole precedent I can find for the broken style of my Prologue is Longinus on the sublime, and that one far-fetched."

58. William Carlos Williams, *Imaginations* (New York: New Directions, 1970), 42. Certain passages in Williams's book are italicized to differentiate them with an internal logic; I have not maintained the convention in my quotations.

59. Williams, *Imaginations*, 74, 40, 69, 33, 43, 58. As Williams's poem "The Descent" opens: "The descent beckons / as the ascent beckoned" (*The Desert Music and Other Poems* [New York: Random House, 1954], 3).

60. Williams, *Imaginations*, 45. The grackles triangulate crows and "rows."

61. Williams, *Imaginations*, 32. Compare the figure of the phrase's broken back with the later "you'll break my backbone," arrived at by a pun that draws *my bone* from "*ma bonne*" [my housemaid] (56).

62. Williams, *Imaginations*, 80, 32-33.

63. Williams, *Imaginations*, 16.

64. Williams, *Imaginations*, 36, 37, 77, 78, 37.

65. Williams, *Imaginations*, 33, 55, 61. The gloss to the second part of section XXIV reads:

> Pathology literally speaking is a flower garden. Syphilis covers the body with salmon-red petals. The study of medicine is an inverted sort of horticulture. Over and above all this floats the philosophy of disease which is a stern dance. (77)

Part of the reasoning seems to follow from the etymology of the earlier figure of *Phyllis* [Greek "foliage"], which gestures to a false association with the φίλος [love] at the root of "philosophy" as well as to the anagram of "syphilis." Other passages corroborate: "Coughs go singing on springtime paths across a field; corruption picks strawberries" (57).

66. Williams, *Imaginations*, 37; cf. 55, 44, 52, 71, 20, 25, 31, 39, 62, 81.
67. Williams, *Imaginations*, 14.
68. Williams, *Imaginations*, 17.
69. Williams, *Imaginations*, 33, 67, 66.
70. Williams, *Imaginations*, 44; cf. "the distant range of mountains can be clearly made out" (44).
71. Williams, *Imaginations*, 31, 65, 71.
72. Williams, *Imaginations*, 45, 49, 55.
73. Williams, *Imaginations*, 82, 32, 76.
74. Williams, *Imaginations*, 8.
75. Williams may have been working with the resonance of the word more broadly; the *kora* (etymologically a borrowing from Maninka), meaning a type of stringed instrument made from a gourd, echoes in the figure of a "gourd from a vine," in section XXIII, for instance (75).
76. Williams, *Imaginations*, 55, 79.
77. Williams, *Imaginations*, 67, 71, 8.
78. Williams, *Imaginations*, 49, 47, 80.
79. Williams, *Imaginations*, 65, 73.
80. Williams, *Imaginations*, 75.
81. Julia Kristeva, *La révolution du langage poétique: L'avant-garde à la fin du XIXe siècle: Lautréamont et Mallarmé* (Paris: Seuil, 1974), 23.
82. Kristeva, *Révolution*, 14, 25.
83. Jacques Derrida, *Khôra* (Paris: Galilée, 1993), 95, 52. I retain the different transliterations of the Greek in order to indicate the different emphasis of Derrida's interpretation, which is nonetheless similar to Kristeva's.
84. Derrida, *Khôra*, 45.
85. See Diodorus Siculus, *Library of History*, vol. 3: books 4.59–8, ed. C. H. Oldfather, Loeb Classical Library 340 (Cambridge, MA: Harvard University Press, 1939), 102.
86. Aaron Fogel, "The Nth Muse: The Image of Prose in Prose," *Western Humanities Review* 56.2 (Fall 2002). Fogel's extraordinary essay pioneers the kind of attention to prose that I am trying to sustain here.
87. Robert Hodge, *Literature as Discourse: Textual Strategies in English and History* (Baltimore: Johns Hopkins University Press, 1990), 81.
88. Joseph Roth, *The Radetzky March*, trans. Joachim Neugroschel (Woodstock, NY: Overlook Press, 1995), 60–62.
89. Stephen Crane, *Maggie, A Girl of the Streets (A Story of New York)* (New York: Palgrave, 1999), 167.
90. Crane, *Maggie*, 167. On Crane's relation to the black-and-white visual typography of print, see Jerome McGann, *Black Riders: The Visible Language of Modernism* (Princeton, NJ: Princeton University Press, 1993), 91–94.
91. Eugène Ionesco, *The Hermit*, trans. Richard Seaver (New York: Viking, 1974), 100, 98; *Le solitaire* (Paris: Mercure de France, 1973), 118, 116.
92. Ionesco, *Hermit/Solitaire*, 97–98/115.
93. *OED*, s.v. "coffin."

94. David Antin, "Some Questions about Modernism," n.s., *Occident* 8 (Spring 1974): 14. One might compare Sterne's black page with the ghostly illegibility of the pages in Michael Maranda's *Mikhail Bakhtin: The Bildungsroman and Its Significance in the History of Realism*, part of the artist's "Lost Book Series," which endeavors to "reconstruct books missing from the historical record" (Toronto: Parasitic Ventures, 2007). Maranda tantalizingly blurs the print of the fictitious book so that the words cannot quite be made out, although the full signifying force of prose itself remains: the rhetorical organization of language justified in the service of a critical argument into paragraphs and chapters.

95. William Faulkner, *As I Lay Dying* (New York: Vintage, 1964), 82.

96. Michael Kaufmann, *Textual Bodies: Modernism, Postmodernism, and Print* (Lewisburg, PA: Bucknell University Press, 1994), 36.

97. Faulkner, *As I Lay Dying*, 208-9.

98. Faulkner, *As I Lay Dying*, 92.

99. Faulkner, *As I Lay Dying*, 86, 247; *cf.* 225, 249.

100. Faulkner, *As I Lay Dying*, 241.

101. Similarly, the riddle of the paradoxically filled and empty square may have its solution in the punning connection between *vacant* and *vaca* [cow]. Furthermore, "empty," as the *OED* records, denotes a cow that is not pregnant—an ironic reminder given Dewey Dell's errand in the town at the very moment of the bovine traverse.

102. Ionesco, *Hermit/Solitaire*, 95/112.

103. Ionesco, *Hermit/Solitaire*, 96/113.

104. Ionesco, *Hermit/Solitaire*, 96/113.

105. Wellbery, "Foreword," xii.

106. Andrei Bely, Петербург (Bradda Books: Letchworth, 1967), 15; *Petersburg*, trans. Robert Maguire and John Malmsted (Bloomington: Indiana University Press, 1979), 12.

107. Bely, Петербург/*Petersburg*, 14/10.

108. Lyn Hejinian, *Oxota, A Short Russian Novel* (Great Barrington, MA: The Figures, 1991), 150.

109. Bely, Петербург/*Petersburg*, 14/ 10.

110. Bely, Петербург/*Petersburg*, 14/11-12.

111. Bely, Петербург/*Petersburg*, 14/11-12.

112. Bely, Петербург/*Petersburg*, 14/11-12.

113. Bely, Петербург/*Petersburg*, 14/11-12.

114. Bely, Петербург/*Petersburg*, 457/272, 271.

115. Ionesco, *Hermit/Solitaire*, 98, 99-100, 102/115, 117, 120; Bely, Петербург/*Petersburg*, 457/271-72.

116. Bely, Петербург/*Petersburg*, 457/272.

117. Viktor Shklovsky, *Theory of Prose*, trans. Benjamin Sher (Normal, IL: Dalkey Archive, 1990), 173.

Chapter Two

1. Jacques Derrida, *Sauf le nom* (Paris: Galilée, 1993), 1.

2. Ron Padgett, "Poets and Painters in Paris, 1919-39," *Art News Annual* 34 (1968): 90.

3. John Dos Passos, *The Major Nonfictional Prose*, ed. Donald Pizer (Detroit: Wayne State University Press, 1988), 82.

4. Dos Passos, *Prose*, 83.

5. *The Random House Book of Twentieth-Century French Poetry*, ed. Paul Auster (New York: Random House, 1982), xxxv.

6. Blaise Cendrars, *L'homme foudroyé* (Paris: Denoël, 1946), 188.

7. Cendrars, *Homme foudroyé*, 188.

8. Cendrars's specificity about his tools recalls Tristan Tzara's instructions on how to make a Dadaist poem from a serial: "Prenez un journal. / Prenez des ciseaux" [Take a newspaper. / Take some scissors]. See Tristan Tzara, *Dada manifeste sur l'amour faible et l'amour amer*, section VIII (*La vie des lettres* 4 [Paris: Jacques Povolozky & Cie., April 1921], reprinted in *Oeuvres complètes* [Paris: Flammarion, 1975], 1:382).

9. Henri Morier, *Dictionnaire de Poétique et de Rhétorique* (Paris: Presses Universitaires de France, 1961).

10. Cendrars, *Kodak* (Paris: Stock, Delamain, Boutaelleau, 1924), 43, 13, 32.

11. Carl W. Ackerman, *George Eastman: Founder of Kodak and the Photography Business* (New York: Houghton Mifflin, 1930), 76.

12. *OED*, s.v. "Kodak."

13. Ackerman, *Eastman*, 76.

14. Cendrars mentions several brand names in *Kodak*: "Winchester" rifles (76), "Ford" vehicles and "Bell & Howell" film equipment (77), "Zeiss" field glasses (82), "Canadian Club" whiskey (88), *et cetera*, and he name-checks Kodak cameras twice in the collection, in a series of poems ostensibly about an elephant hunt: "Je garde un homme avec moi pour porter le grand kodak" [I keep one man with me to carry the big Kodak], one line explains, and another specifies, "Je fais rester mes trois hommes sur place chacun braquant son Bell-Howell / Et je m'avance seul avec mon petit kodak sur un terrain où je puis marcher sans bruit" [I have my three men stay put each one aiming his Bell & Howell / I move in alone with my little Kodak to ground where I can walk silently] (77).

15. Cendrars, *Kodak*, 26.

16. Cendrars, *Kodak*, 59.

17. Gustave Le Rouge, "Le Cottage Hanté," in *Le Mystérieux Docteur Cornélius*, vol. 3 (Paris: Union Générale d'Éditions, 1975), 238–39; Cendrars, *Kodak*, 47.

18. Jacques Derrida, *Signéponge* (Paris: Seuil, 1988), 96.

19. George Eastman, "Slow Profits Today, but Sure Profits Tomorrow," *System: The Magazine of Business* 38.4 (October 1920): 711.

20. Quoted in Elizabeth Brayer: *George Eastman: A Biography* (Rochester: University of Rochester, 2006): 63–64.

21. Émile Littré, *Dictionnaire de la langue française*; cited hereafter as *Littré*.

22. *Littré*.

23. Dan Frank, *Bohemian Paris: Picasso, Modigliani, Matisse, and the Birth of Modern Art* (New York: Grove Press, 2001), 208; *cf.* Blaise Cendrars, *Complete Poems*, trans. Ron Padgett (Berkeley: University of California Press, 1992), 367n15.

24. Eleanor M. Garvey, "Resumé: Livres illustrés cubistes et fauves," *Gazette des beaux-arts* 63 (January 1964): 40. *Cf.* Jean Hugues, *50 ans d'édition D.-H. Kahnweiler* (Paris: Galerie Louise Leiris, 1959): n.p.; Riva Castleman, *A Century of Artists Books* (New York: Museum of Modern Art, 1994), 29. The pronouncement is sometimes said

by commentators to be an adage used among printers, but I can find no evidence of its currency.

25. Filippo Tommaso Marinetti, *Distruzione della sintassi: Immaginazione senza fili; parole in libertà* (Milano: Mondadori, 1913).

26. See Marcel Schwob, *Oeuvres complètes*, ed. Pierre Champion, vol. 7, *Mélanges d'histoie littéraire et de linguistique* (Paris: Bernouard, 1928), 85 et seq. *Cf.* vol. 9 (1930); Alice Becker-Ho, *Les Princes du jargon: Un facteur négligé aux origines de l'argot des classes dangereuses* (Paris: Lebovici, 1990); François Villon, *Oeuvres complètes* (Paris: Alphonse Lemerre, 1892), 145 *et seq.*

27. For the status of "Lundi Rue Christine" as cubist collage, see David LeHardy Sweet, *Savage Sight/Constructed Noise: Poetic Adaptations of Painterly Techniques in the French and American Avant-Gardes*, North Carolina Studies in the Romance Languages and Literatures, no. 276 (Chapel Hill: University of North Carolina Press, 2003).

28. See, for examples, "La patronne est poitrinaire"; "Je dois fiche près de 300 francs à ma probloque"; "La serveuserousse a été enlevée par un libraire"; *et cetera*.

29. Although he does not mention these lines, Leroy Breunig argues that "for readers properly attuned the name of the author [i.e., Apollinaire] seems to lurk behind" *-aire* and *-ière* rhymes" ("For a Poetics of the Pseudonym," *Romanic Review* 75.2 [March 1984]: 258).

30. David Sweet, *Savage Sight/Constructed Noise: Poetic Adaptations of Painterly Techniques in the French and American Avant-Gardes* (Chapel Hill: University of North Carolina Department of Romance Languages, 2003), 71.

31. Paul de Man, *The Resistance to Theory*, Theory and History of Literature, vol. 33 (Minneapolis: University of Minnesota Press, 1986), 36; Jean Starobinski, *Les mots sous les mots: Les anagrammes de Ferdinand de Saussure* (Paris: Gallimard, 1971). For a provocative reading of the patronymics of the letter, see Carlo Ossola, "Les 'ossements fossiles' de la lettre chez Mallarmé et Saussure," trans. Nicole Sels, *Critique* 35.391 (1979): 1063-78.

32. Julia Kristeva, Σημειωτική: *Recherches pour une sémanalyse* (Paris: Éditions du Seuil, 1969), 44. For the initial response to the discovery of Saussure's notes, see Ivan Callus, "A Chronological and Annotated Bibliography of Works Referring to Ferdinand de Saussure's Anagram Notebook," *Cahiers Ferdinand de Saussure* 55 (2000): 269-95. I have emphasized the onomastic aspect of Saussure's investigation, but his discoveries were not limited to proper nouns; on the significance of the distinction, see Daniel Heller-Roazen, *Dark Tongues: The Art of Rogues and Riddlers* (Brooklyn: Zone Books, 2013), 120.

33. Hans Robert Jauss, "1912: Threshold to an Epoch. Apollinaire's *Zone* and *Lundi Rue Christine*," *Yale French Studies* 74 (1988): 46.

34. Jauss, "1912," 46.

35. Jauss, "1912," 46.

36. Timothy J. Clark, *Farewell to an Idea: Episodes from a History of Modernism* (New Haven, CT: Yale University Press, 1999), 191, 170, 194.

37. On the gendered institutions behind the authorial signature, see Peggy Kamuf, *Signature Pieces: On the Institution of Authorship* (Ithaca, NY: Cornell University Press, 1988).

38. Jacques Derrida, *Signéponge/Signsponge*, trans. Richard Rand (New York: Columbia University Press, 1984), 95.

39. *OED*, s.v. "signature."

40. Geoffrey Bennington and Jacques Derrida, *Jacques Derrida* (Paris: Seuil, 1991), 101-2; *Jacques Derrida*, trans. Geoffrey Bennington (Chicago: University of Chicago Press, 1993), 105.

41. Derrida, *Signéponge*, 119/118. Cf. Geoffrey Bennington, *Dudding: Des noms de Rousseau* (Paris: Éditions Galilée, 1991), 109 *et seq*. For a more dispersed investigation of the same effects, see Jacques Derrida, *Glas* (Paris: Galilée, 1974). For a similar consideration of antonomasia (with regard to Franz Kafka's writing), see Werner Hamacher, *Premises: Essays on Philosophy and Literature from Kant to Celan* (Stanford, CA: Stanford University Press, 1996), 309-11, 314; cf. 318 *et passim*.

42. Jacques Derrida, *Positions* (Paris: Minuit, 1972), 61.

43. Jacques Derrida, *L'oreille de l'autre: Otobiographies, transferts, traductions* (Montréal: VLB Éditeur, 1982), 105.

44. For the discrimination of the biological lexicon, see L. van der Pijl, *Principles of Dispersal in Higher Plants*, 3rd rev. and expanded ed. (Berlin: Springer-Verlag, 1982), 6-7.

45. The final line reads, "Et comme au coeur du lys le pollen parfumé" ("lys," the careful reader will note, is a homophone of *lis* [you read]). The poem, about Apollinaire's war wound, adds depth to the moments where he identifies military aircraft and bullets as bees: "envolez-vous essaims des avions blonds ainsi que les avettes" in "Chant de l'horizon en Champagne," and in "Chant de l'honneur" Les Balles sing, "de nos ruches d'acier sortons à tire-d'aile / Abeilles"; cf. the "abeille" in "L'Avenir" (*Oeuvres complètes*, 3:284, 1:248,1:304). In *Alcools*, Apollinaire writes of "Le pollen lumineux" (*Oeuvres complètes*, 3:594).

46. Lyn Hejinian, *Writing Is an Aid to Memory* (Great Barrington, MA: The Figures, 1978), n.p.

47. Cf. *Littré*, s.v. "air": "Suite de tons et de notes qui composent un chant. Il se dit aussi du chant et des paroles."

48. Derrida, *Signéponge*, 21/20.

49. On the tradition of encrypting dedicatory names in encomia, see, to begin, François Rigolot, "Ronsard encomiaste: La rhétorique de l'éloge dans les pièces liminaires," *Cahiers Textuel* 1 (1985): 67-82; Jean Starobinski, "Lettres et syllables mobiles: Complément à la lecture des *Cahiers* d'anagrammes de Ferdinand de Saussure," *Littérature* 99 (1995): 7-18; Jacqueline Risset, *L'Anagramme du désir: Essais dur la Délie de Maurice Scève* (Roma: Bulzoni, 1971). On the logical rhetoric of the anagrammatic structure, see François Goyet, "La preuve par l'anagramme: L'anagramme comme lieu propre au genre démonstratif," *Poétique* 46 (1981): 229-46. For the argument that the dedicatory name stands behind the lyric, that there is no "autre amour dans les poèmes d'amour que l'amour du nom" [other love in love poems than love of the name] (38), see Martine Broda, *L'amour du nom: Essai sur le lyrisme et la lyrique amoureuse*, 2nd ed. (Paris: José Corti, 1997), 97-105 *et passim*.

50. Breunig, "Poetics," 260.

51. Gertrude Stein, *Selected Writings of Gertrude Stein*, ed. Carl Van Vechten (New York: Vintage, 1990), 56.

52. The phrase is a stereotype; see, for one example from many, the definition of data in *Encyclopaedia Britannica; or, A Dictionary of Arts, Sciences, and Miscellaneous Literature*, vol. 7 (Edinburgh: Archibald Constable, 1823).

53. See Ulla Dydo, "*Stanzas in Meditation*: The Other Autobiography," *Chicago Review* 35.2 (1985): 12-13 *et passim*.

54. See Susan Gilmore, "Imna, Ova Mongrel, Spy: Anagram and Imposture in the Work of Mina Loy," in *Mina Loy: Woman and Poet*, ed. Maeera Shreiber and Keith Tuma (Orono, ME: National Poetry Foundation, 1998), 302 *et seq.*

55. Amy Lowell, "The New Manner in Modern Poetry," *New Republic* 6.70 (4 March 1916): 124.

56. Gertrude Stein, *A Stein Reader*, ed. Ulla Dydo (Evanston, IL: Northwestern University Press, 1993), 279. Basing her text on Stein's manuscript rather than the typescript and earlier editions, which print "teeth," Dydo restores the verb "teethe."

57. Mina Loy, *The Lost Lunar Baedeker: Poems*, ed. Roger Conover (New York: Farrar, Straus and Giroux, 1996), 94.

58. Quoted in Loy, *Lost*, 203.

59. Loy, *Lost*, 28.

60. Mina Loy, *The Last Lunar Baedeker*, ed. Roger Conover (Highlands, NC: Jargon Society, 1982), xviii.

61. Loy, *Lost*, 36; Gilmore, "Imna," 302n31.

62. Margaret Konkol, "Prototyping Mina Loy's Alphabet," *Feminist Modernist Studies* 1.3 (2018): 295.

63. Loy, *Lost*, 49; Loy reused the ruse when she listed herself on the playbill to Laurence Vail's 1920 *What D'You Want?* as "Imna Oly" (Carolyn Burke, *Becoming Modern: The Life of Mina Loy* [New York: Farrar, Straus and Giroux, 1996], 296–97). On the relation of Loy's strategies to modernist notions of impersonality, see Gilmore, "Imna," 271–317.

64. Loy, *Lost*, 55.

65. Matthew Hofer, "Mina Loy, Giovanni Papini, and the Aesthetics of Irritation," *Paideuma: Modern and Contemporary Poetry and Poetics* 38 (2011): 236.

66. Shreiber reads the figure more generally as "a standard Futurist image of divine authority" (Shreiber and Tuma, *Woman and Poet*, 100), while Blau DuPlessis, in the same volume, reads it as the prosopopoeia of "passion" (50).

67. Loy, *Lost*, 53, 55.

68. Loy, *Lost*, 65, 57.

69. The name for the type of puppet likely comes from the Old French *mariole*, with a dissimilation of the *l* to *n* under the influence of the name *Marian*, the same process that connects the jester's marotte to the Virgin Mary (*OED*, s.v. "marionette" and "marotte"). On the significance of Loy's polyglot poetics, and "the logopoeia that finds satisfaction in discovering the paragrams and puns latent in an given vocabulary," see Marjorie Perloff, "English as a 'Second' Language: Mina Loy's 'Anglo-Mongrels and the Rose,'" *Poetry On and Off the Page: Essays on Emergent Occasions* (Evanston, IL: Northwestern University Press, 1998), 193–207.

70. Loy, *Lost*, 54.

71. Loy, *Lost*, 63. However clearly the fraught topic of fertility recurs throughout the "Songs," the exact referent remains indeterminate or multiple, including infertility, abortion, and parturition. "All modern art," for Loy, "leaves an unlimited latitude for personal response" (Loy, *Lost*, 203). The ambiguities are nicely encapsulated in the line "bossed bellies," where *boss* denotes something both swollen, like a pregnant belly, and bungled or made a mess of ("You're simply bossing up the whole show by philandering with a widow," reads an *OED* example of the word's use in 1903).

72. Loy, *Lost*, 173.

73. Tim Hancock, "'You couldn't make it up': The Love of 'Bare Facts' in Mina Loy's Italian Poems," *English* 54 (Autumn 2005): 186. Hancock argues throughout against the tendency by critics to read "Joannes" as a composite figure, and for seeing the references in "Songs," as I do, pointing directly to Papini. In addition to the bloody butterfly, note the "daily deaths" in XXVII.

74. Loy, *Lost*, 67, 66, 62.

75. Loy, *Lost*, 54, 64, 60, 67.

76. "The prig," at the same time, both refracts the opening figure of the "P[r]ig Cupid" found "rooting erotic garbage" and, in the cant slang sense of "to steal, pilfer," echoes the etymologically precise phrase "prenatal plagiarism," from the Latin *plagiarius* [a "person who abducts a child […], kidnapper, seducer"], and may thus activate a pun on "forager" (Loy, *Lost*, 62) and *forger*. "Flummery," similarly, may further play paronomastically on the Latin *flumen* [river] and the fluvial and riparian images in the "Songs" that range from the "rivers" that "run no fresher / Than a trickle of saliva" to the Arno itself, which reappears in XVI and XXV.

77. See William Evans Burton, *Burton's Comic Songster: A New Collection of Original & Popular Songs* (Pittsburgh: John Kay & Co., 1837), 248. *Cf.* the contemporaneous *Century Dictionary*, s.v. "coxcomb" (*Century Dictionary and Cyclopedia with a New Atlas of the World: A Work of General Reference in All Departments of Knowledge* [New York: Century Company, 1914], 2:1322); *OED*, s.v. "popinjay."

78. Loy, *Lost*, 56.

79. Loy, *Lost*, 46, 47, 46.

80. Loy, *Lost*, 50; Giovanni Papini, "Don Juan's Lament: Melancholic Reflections of the Romantic Hero Who Couldn't Fall in Love," *Vanity Fair* 13.10 (January 1920): 43.

81. Loy, *Lost*, 66, 61, 53.

82. Loy, *Lost*, 53.

83. Loy, *Lost*, 54, 60, 62.

84. Loy, *Lost*, 59, 53.

85. See, for instances among others, Charles Baudelaire's "La Musique" in *Fleurs de mal* (itself an epithet for *weeds*) (*Oeuvres complètes*, ed. F.-F. Gautier [Paris: Gallimard, 1918], 1:136); Max Jacob's "Le coq et la perle" (*Le Cornet à dés* [Paris: Stock, 1923]); and Max Elskamp's "Étoile de la mer" (*La Louange de la vie: 1892–1895* [Paris: Mercure de France, 1898], 109).

86. Loy, *Lost*, 53, 54, 59, 64–65. For a brilliant cartographic orientation of the steps, see Hancock, "You couldn't," 180.

87. See Konkol, "Prototyping," 297–99; Loy, *Lost*, 64.

88. *OED*, s.v. "flummery."

89. Tobias Smollett, *The Expedition of Humphry Clinker* (London: Hutchinson & Company, 1905), 320. *Cf.* "These Sowens (i.e., flummery) being blended together, produce good Yest" (Martin Martin, *A Voyage St. Kilda, The remotest of all the Hebrides; or, Western Isles of Scotland* [London: Griffith, 1749], 59).

90. *OED*, s.v. "sowens."

91. *OED*, s.v. "pap."

92. Suzanne W. Churchill, *The Little Magazine OTHERS and the Renovation of Modern American Poetry* (Hampshire: Ashgate, 2006), 195. On the significance of alliterative patterning and proper names, see Michel Grimaud, "Hermeneutics, Onomastics and Poetics in English and French Literature," *MLN* 92.5 (December 1977): 902 *et passim*.

93. Churchill, *Little Magazine*, 195–96.

94. Loy, *Last*, xviii.

95. Loy, *Lost*, 58, 53, 60, 62, 55, 53, 63, 62, 62, 55.

96. Loy, *Lost*, 58.

97. Loy, *Lost*, 58, 57, 62, 57; *cf.* "irresolvable" (64).

98. Loy, *Lost*, 63, 64, 60, 57, 55–56.

99. *OED*, s.v. "loy."

100. Burke, *Becoming Modern*, 62.

101. Sarah Hayden, *Curious Disciplines: Mina Loy and Avant-Garde Artisthood* (Albuquerque: University of New Mexico Press, 2018), 229.

102. Loy, *Lost*, 68.

103. Loy, *Lost*, 53. In her futurist poem "Human Cylinders," Loy offers another version of producing poetic "litter" with a play of *letters* when she writes, "Among the litter of a sunless afternoon"; without the sun, the *glitter* of sunlight is reduced to "litter." Loy includes the proper diacritic when she uses the word "littérateurs" in "Lions' Jaws" (Loy, *Lost*, 47); its omission here helps nudge the word closer to the English *litter*.

104. "Ladies Aviary," in Loy, *Last*, 44.

105. Loy, *Lost*, 55.

106. On the linguistic aspect of Loy's sexual politics, see Rowan Harris, "Futurism, Fashion, and the Feminine: Forms of Repudiation and Affiliation in the Early Writings of Mina Loy," in *The Salt Companion to Mina Loy*, ed. Rachel Potter and Suzanne Hobson (London: Salt, 2010): 17–46.

107. Shreiber and Tuma, *Woman and Poet*, 105; Churchill, *Little Magazine*, 199; Mary Loeffelholz, *Experimental Lives: Women and Literature, 1900–1945* (Woodbridge, CT: Twayne, 1992), 41; Mary Jane Leach-Rudawski, "The Mongrel Girl of Noman's Land: Sexuality, Feminism, and Motherhood in the Poetry and Prose of Mina Loy" (dissertation, University of Minnesota, 1999), 53; Mark Ford, *A Driftwood Altar: Essays and Reviews* (Oxfordshire: Waywiser, 2005), 129.

108. Gilmore, "Imna," 277.

109. Mabel Dodge Luhan: *Intimate Memories*, vol. 2, *European Experiences* (New York: Harcourt, Brace & Co., 1935), 342.

110. *Cf.* Alex Goody, "Gender, Authority and the Speaking Subject, or: Who Is Mina Loy?," *How2* 1.5 (March 2001). Soon after, she would also adopt Lloyd, the legal name of Arthur Cravan, christened Fabian Avernarius Lloyd, her second husband. *Löwe* [lion] resonates with the title of Loy's "Lions' Jaws," in which the more public reference is likely to *Leonardo* (etymologically from the Latin *leo* [lion]), the title of Papini's journal before he took over *Lacerba*. At the same time, it might also echo Loy's sense of her heritage, evident in "Anglo Mongrels and the Rose" and corroborated in her unpublished "Hush Money," which narrates the paternal power that overshadows Daniel, who is "so enmeshed in his father's words" that he "struggles to escape the lion's den that is his home" (Gilmore, "Imna," 314). On the power of patronymic orthography, relevant also to *Warhola*, as discussed in chapter 6, see Elizabeth Renker, *Strike through the Mask: Herman Melville and the Scene of Writing* (Baltimore: Johns Hopkins University Press, 1996), 15 *et passim*.

111. Burke, *Becoming Modern*, 47; 16.

112. Loy, *Lost*, 58.

113. Loy, *Last*, 157.

114. Quoted in Loy, *Lost*, xii.

115. Loy, *Lost*, 289-90.

116. Loy, *Lost*, 203.

117. On the genre of the questionnaire in modernist little magazines more broadly, see Lori Cole, *Surveying the Avant-Garde: Questions on Modernism, Art, and the Americas in Transatlantic Magazines* (University Park: Penn State University Press, 2019).

118. George Biddle, *The Yes and No of Contemporary Art: An Artist's Evaluation* (Cambridge, MA: Harvard University Press, 1957), 125; Creighton Gilbert, "A Preface to Signatures (with some cases in Venice)," in *Fashioning Identities in Renaissance Art*, ed. Mary Rogers (Hants: Ashgate, 2000), 86.

119. Compare the silhouette of the *Bicycle Wheel* to the sketch Duchamp made of Brancusi's sculpture *Little Girl* (see *Marcel Duchamp: Work and Life/Ephemerides on and about Marcel Duchamp and Rrose Selavy, 1887-1968*, ed. Pontus Hultén [Cambridge, MA: MIT Press, 1993], 27 December 1919).

120. Jennifer Gough-Cooper and Jacques Caumont arrive tentatively at the same reading (Hultén, *Marcel Duchamp*, 4 June 1964). For further links to Roussel via the spokes of the wheel and further links to sculpture, with corroborating dictionary evidence, see Bernard Brunon, *Status of Sculpture* (Lyon: Espace lyonnais d'art contemporain, 1990), 13-14.

121. George Heard Hamilton, "Marcel Duchamp Speaks," *Étant donné: Marcel Duchamp* 4 (2002; recorded 19 January 1959).

122. James Johnson Sweeney, "Interview with Marcel Duchamp," *Bulletin of the Museum of Modern Art* 13.4-5 (1946): 21. *Cf.* Michel Sanouillet and Elmer Peterson, eds., *The Essential Writings of Marcel Duchamp* (London: Thames & Hudson, 1975), 126.

123. Raymond Roussel, *L'étoile au front* (Paris: Jean-Jacques Pauvert, 1963), 34, 85-86.

124. Pierre Cabanne, *Entretiens avec Marcel Duchamp* (Paris: Éditions Pierre Belfond, 1967), 70.

125. Katherine Kuh, *The Artist's Voice: Talks with Seventeen Artists* (New York: Harper & Row, 1962), 88.

126. Quoted in Rudolf Kuenzli, *Marcel Duchamp: Artist of the Century* (Cambridge, MA: MIT Press, 1990), 6.

127. See Dalia Judovitz, *Unpacking Duchamp: Art in Transit* (Berkeley: University of California Press, 1995), 87-88.

128. As Duchamp explained to Arturo Schwartz, the *Bicycle Wheel* "had more to do with chance" than it had to do with found objects (Arturo Schwarz, *The Complete Works of Marcel Duchamp*, 3rd ed. (New York: Delano Greenidge, 1997), 2:588).

129. On the cultural, linguistic, and political transformations that led to the use of the proper name as a signature, which we now regard as natural but which was not always the case, see Béatrice Fraenkel, *La signature: Genèse d'un signe* (Paris: Gallimard, 1992), 98-108 *et seq.*

130. Aimé Césaire, *Soleil cou-coupé* (Paris: K Éditeur, 1948), 31, 24; *The Complete Poetry of Aimé Césaire*, trans. A. James Arnold and Clayton Eshleman (Middletown, CT: Wesleyan University Press, 2017), 347, 335. On the opacity of this poem, see Michel Hausser, "Césaire et l'Hermétisme," *Aimé Césaire; ou, L'athanor d'un alchimiste* (Paris: Éditions L'Harmattan, 1987): 33-52.

131. Greville John Chester, *Transatlantic Sketches in the West Indies, South America,*

Canada, and the United States (London: Smith, Elder & Co., 1869): 19. His observations continue: "They are awfully ugly, but they seem to have the same feelings and ideas as other dogs."

132. René Etiemble, "Sur le Martinique de M. Michel Cournot," *Les Temps Modernes* (February 1950), 1510.

133. Édouard Glissant, *Faulkner, Mississippi* (Paris: Gallimard, 1998), 220; trans. Barbara Lewis and Thomas C. Spear (Chicago: University of Chicago Press, 1999), 160.

134. Aimé Césaire, *Oeuvres complètes*, vol. 1, *Poèmes* (Paris: Désormeaux, 1976), 196; *Complete Poetry*, 623. Césaire's revered and influential teacher, Eugène Revert, was working on a study of the volcano at the time Césaire studied with him (see "La Montagne Pelée et ses éruptions," *Annales de géographie* 225.40 [1931]: 275–91). On the volcano as symbol of imminent political revolt, able to "sweep away the injustices of the past in a cataclysmic moment of renewal," see Eric Preito, "Landscaping Identity in Contemporary Caribbean Literature," in *Francophone Post-Colonial Cultures: Critical Essays*, ed. Kamal Salhi (Oxford: Lexington Books, 2003), 143 *et passim*; *cf.* Hilary Okam, "Aspects of Imagery and Symbolism in the Poetry of Aimé Césaire," *Yale French Studies* 53 (1976): 189. On the volcano's power to triangulate Césaire's own sense of himself, see Vincent Clément, "Latitude and Longitude of the Past: Place, Negritude and French Caribbean Identity in Aimé Césaire's Poetry," *Caribbean Studies* 39.1–2 (December 2011): 178 *et passim*. On the ambivalent reference of Césaire's writing more generally, in which the written word gestures both to concepts and to other typographically related words, see Carrie Noland, *Voices of Negritude in Modernist Print: Aesthetic Subjectivity, Diaspora, and the Lyric Regime* (New York: Columbia University Press, 2015); the discussion of names in chapter 6, "To Inhabit a Wound" is especially relevant to my reading here.

135. Salvador Dalì, *Oui: Méthode paranoïaque-critique, et autres textes* (Paris: Denoël, 1971), 40.

136. See Walter Arensberg, *The Cryptography of Shakespeare* (Los Angeles: Howard Bowen, 1922) and *The Cryptography of Dante* (New York: Knopf, 1921); Tristan Tzara, *Oeuvres complètes*, vol. 6, *Le Secret de Villon*, ed. Henri Béhar (Paris: Flammarion, 1991); Unica Zürn, *Hexentexte* (Berlin: Galerie Springer, 1954). For a thorough study of a foundational figure behind this moment, see Michael Temple, *The Name of the Poet: Onomastics and Anonymity in the Works of Stéphane Mallarmé* (Exeter: University of Exeter Press, 1995), and Werner Hamacher, "History, Teary: Some Remarks on La Jeune Parque," *Yale French Studies* 74 (1988): 89 *et passim*.

Chapter Three

1. Jacques Derrida, "À force de deuil," in *Chaque fois unique, la fin du monde* (Paris: Galilée, 2003), 177.

2. My allusion to the opening line of Rosalind Krauss's "Overcoming the Limits of Matter: On Revising Minimalism" (*American Art of the 1960s*, Studies in Modern Art no. 1, ed. John Elderfield [New York: Museum of Modern Art, 1991], 123–41) is not just to capitalize on her stylistic flair, but to signal some common themes as well: an aesthetic moment in which the time is out of joint; the restiveness of radical abstraction; the importance of distinguishing between seemingly similar formalisms; problems of private

language; and Inman's own reference-points at the intersection between abstract expressionism and '60s sculptural minimalism.

I will return to these topics in more detail, but for now note that Inman's essay on the poetic line traverses *precisely* the same span that Krauss would cover just a few years later. Her essay moves from Frank Stella to the expanding relevance of minimalism. Accordingly, after telegraphically referencing Michael Fried's discussion of Frank Stella in "Three American Painters" with the phrase "deductive structure," Inman concludes by asserting the relevance of minimalist sculpture to his poetics:

> I tend to write in pages • (unlike other people?) not in stories or • poems, though the structural possibilities offered by • one page freq. need following pages to • play off of (aka. I work via • series The pages are, to consciously quote • Sixties minimalists, modular & the modules are • most often one page long […]

P. Inman, "Stein's," in *The Line in Postmodern Poetry*, ed. Robert Frank and Henry Sayre (Urbana: University of Illinois Press, 1988), 204. *Cf.* Michael Fried: "deductive structure concerns the relation of the image to the framing edge" ("Three American Painters: Noland, Olitski, Stella," in *Art and Objecthood: Essays and Reviews* [Chicago: University of Chicago Press, 1998], 249).

3. The Poetry Foundation's "Glossary of Poetic Terms," for instance, states that Language poetry "developed from diverse communities of poets in San Francisco and New York" (accessed 11 August 2011, http://www.poetryfoundation.org/learning/glossary-term/Language%20poetry). Another reference guide narrates, "once again San Francisco and New York served as the twin centers of this new avant-garde [i.e., Language poetry]" (Burton Hatlen, "Foreword," *The Facts on File Companion to American Poetry*, vol. 2, *1900 to the Present* [New York: Facts on File, 2008], xvi); similarly, *The Oxford Dictionary of Literary Terms* defines Language poetry as "an avant-garde movement in American poetry and poetics since the 1970s, with roots in both San Francisco and New York City" (182). Examples could be enumerated at length, but one should note that the same conflation is true in monographs and articles as well as reference books; Grant Matthew Jenkins, for one, argues that Language poets "are bound not only by the time of the 1960s and the places of New York and San Francisco" (*Poetics Obligation: Ethics in Experimental American Poetry after 1945* [Iowa City: University of Iowa Press, 2008], 6). Loss Pequeño Glazier extends the geographical scope beyond the costal binaries but still avoids DC, defining Language poetry as "a loose constellation of experimental writers in New York, San Francisco, and Toronto" (*American Poets since World War II*, 5th series, as *Dictionary of Literary Biography*, vol. 169, ed. Joseph Conte [Detroit: Gale Research, 1996], 14).

More careful commentators, of course, acknowledge the range of the mid-Atlantic distribution. Even though Ron Silliman's *In the American Tree* is bluntly divided between "West" and "East," Silliman specifies that "with only two exceptions, the poets in the west live in the San Francisco Bay area, while the poets in the east are spread out from Ohio to Massachusetts to Virginia" (*In the American Tree: Language, Realism, Poetry*, ed. Ron Silliman [Orono, ME: National Poetry Foundation, 1986], xxii). In 1977, *Roof* magazine included a special forum on Washington (*Roof* 4, ed. James Sherry [New York: Segue, Fall 1977]: 49–80). As that portfolio reveals, Washington was the primal poetic scene not only for Inman, Tina Darragh, Lynne Dreyer, Phyllis Rosenzweig, and Diane Ward, but also for Bruce Andrews, the quintessential "New York" Language poet and coeditor of L=A=N=G=U=A=G=E. Nearby, in Maryland, Kirby Malone and Marshall Reese (editors of Pod books and the magazine *e pod*) and Douglas Messerli (editor of *Là bas* and *Sun & Moon*) were paying close attention to the Dupont Circle scene. Messerli, not coincidentally, was a student of Marjorie Perloff, who taught at the University of Maryland from 1971 to 1976; he introduced her to the work of the Language poets she would go on to champion.

4. Anne Vickery dates the first issue of *Everybody's Ex-Lover* to 1973, edited by Inman, Doug Lang, and Lisa Shea, with Inman as "sole editor for the remaining three issues" of the renamed *EEL* (*Leaving Lines of Gender: A Feminist Genealogy of Language Writing* [Hanover, NH: University Press of New England, 2000], 26–27). I have not seen a copy myself. Edited by Ed Cox, Lee Lally, Michael Lally, and Terrence Winch, Some of Us Press published almost a score of books between 1972 and 1974, the same period during which the Mass Transit open-mic readings took place. That latter collective published five issues of an eponymous magazine between 1973 and 1974; the final issue was edited by Beth Joselow and Inman, whose work appeared in numbers 1 and 4. Mass Transit readings were succeeded by more structured readings at Folio Books (where Doug Lang worked), which ran from 1976 to 1978 (Inman dates its terminus to 1980, although Folio Books closed in 1978; see "*a different table altogether*': P. Inman in Conversation with Roger Farr & Aaron Vidaver," *Documents in Poetics 4* [Vancouver: Thuja Books, 2003], 18).

5. To be punctilious: the cover states the title as *P.Inman U.S.A.*

6. One can instructively compare those name-checked in the poems with the explicit list of influences provided by Inman for the headnote to his entry in Michael Lally's anthology *None of the Above: New Poetries of the USA* (Trumansburg, NY: Crossing Press, 1976): "Lennart Bruce, Rudolph Wurlitzer, Kathy Acker, Julia Vose, Peter Handke, Tom Veitch, Tina Darragh, Doug Lang, Andrei Codrescu, Steve Katz." In a few years, his list has shifted to contemporary art writing (see L=A=N=G=U=A=G=E 7 [1979], n.p.), and in 2000 he "cites Clark Coolidge, Bernadette Mayer, and Aram Saroyan as influences" (Vickery, *Leaving*, 24).

7. *Personal Injury Magazine* 3 (November 1976): 61. The final phrases resonate with an uncredited collage earlier in the magazine, which reproduces part of a *National Enquirer* cover (from 19 November 1974) with an image of "Elvis at 40—Paunchy, Depressed & Living in Fear" (5).

8. Uwe Schneede, *Max Ernst*, trans. R. W. Last (New York: Praeger, 1973), 32.

9. Schneede, *Ernst*, 32.

10. P. Inman, *Platin* (College Park, MD: Sun & Moon, 1979), n.p.

11. For instance (from the *OED*), *ribble*: "to plough [soil, land] by turning earth on to a strip left unploughed between furrows"; *leam*: "a drain or watercourse in fen districts" or "the husk of a nut" or a "light, flame"; *leath*: "cessation, intermission, rest"; *cray*: "chalk"; *et cetera*. Over time, fewer Scots and dialect words appear in the poems, but still with some regularity and with the same indeterminate force (regardless of whether Inman is aware of their denotations). In the following stanza from "acoma" (P. Inman: *Written: 1976-2013* [Manchester: if p then q, 2014], 554), for example, the initial suggestion of shining washed hair, motivated by the structural distribution of individual let-

ters, is complicated by the fact that *hairsh* is a southern Scots dialect version of "hoarse" and *hairst* is Scots dialect for "a grain harvest":

(hairsh
shone ;
(seine;
(ashed;
hairst;
through

A similar destabilization follows from recognizing that "Oshone" and "washed" are words Inman repeats elsewhere, and that the fragmentation of repeated vocabulary, as we shall see, is one of his signature techniques.

12. See Marjorie Perloff, *The Poetics of Indeterminacy: Rimbaud to Cage* (Princeton, NJ: Princeton University Press, 1981).

13. *OED*.

14. Charles Bernstein has made a similar argument about Inman's "Waver," which he reads as an example of the destabilization of form and content and as a reminder that the artifice of poetry is constantly threatened by the naturalizing force of content, just as extreme formal devices threaten to blind us to the content of more artificed writing (Charles Bernstein, "Artifice of Absorption," in *A Poetics* [Cambridge, MA: Harvard University Press, 1992], 16). Despite the similar terms, Bernstein is making a more complicated and broadly applicable argument than I am here when he posits that "a poem composed in the language of artifice & device is not necessarily without content" (14). With a poem like "Waver," he counsels, "an attempt must first be made to elucidate the 'nonsemantic' elements of the poem," and "the devices must be differentiated from the image complex to which they contribute," but then

> this first survey must be dialectically contrasted with how the noted devices might have been used to different ends, what type of overall architecture is constructed by the particular sequence of devices [...], what semantic associations can be attributed to the specific "nonsemantic" elements & which ones are relevant in the particular context of the poems. (15)

15. Jean Toomer, *The Collected Poems of Jean Toomer*, ed. Robert B. Jones and Margery Toomer Latimer (Chapel Hill: University of North Carolina Press, 1988), 15, 16; David Melnick, *PCOET* (San Francisco: G.A.W.K., 1975); Claude Gauvreau, *Œuvres créatrices complètes* (Montréal: Editions Parti Pris, 1977), 1488–98.

Others have seen more similarity between Inman's writing and the заумный язык [beyond-sense language] of Russian Futurism. Douglas Messerli endorses *Red Shift* by stating, "Peter Inman has been one of a few American poets who has helped to bring the 'transrational' poetics of the Russian Futurists into American poetry," and Esteban Pujals Gesali endorses *criss cross* with the claim that "the type of experimentation characterizing his work [...] situates him within the tradition of zaum, the 'transrational' poetry of the Russian futurists Khlebnikov and Kruchenyk." While a history of the poetics of nonstandard words would certainly devote attention to the Futurists and Dadaists, Inman's poems, on close inspection, do not strike me as being very similar to the speculative grammars of Velimir Klebnikov, the permutational sound-play of Aleksei Kruchenykh, or the aggressive impropriety of the dadaist desire to *épater la bourgeoisie*. Though Inman, come to think of it, probably wouldn't mind that either.

16. Aram Saroyan, *Complete Minimal Poems* (Brooklyn: Ugly Duckling Presse, 2008); Robert Grenier, *Sentences* (Cambridge, MA: Whale Cloth, 1978); John Marron, *Oiyeau* (San Francisco: As Is/So & So, 1987).

17. David McFadden, *The Ova Yogas: being a series of poems written in one long strange afternoon* (Toronto: Weed Flower Press, 1972); N. H. Pritchard, *The Matrix* (Garden City, NY: Doubleday, 1970); Bill Bissett, *What Fuckan Theory: a study uv language* (Vancouver: Blewointment Press, 1972), in a new edition edited by Derek Beaulieu and Gregory Betts (Toronto: Bookthug, 2012).

18. See, for examples, Maggie O'Sullivan, *Body of Work* (Hastings: Reality Street, 2006); Gail Sher, *Kuklos* (Providence, RI: Paradigm, 1995) and *La* (Chicago: Rodent Press, 1997).

19. The line "ness. around." (Inman, *Written*, 408) may allude to the second line of Hejinian's poem: "ness seen know it around saying" (Lyn Hejinian, *Writing Is an Aid to Memory* [Great Barrington, MA: The Figures, 1978], n.p.). Inman does use citation on rare occasion (quoting John Berger's definition "money is what time is like" in "Think of One" [as it appears in the eponymous Potes & Poets edition (Elmwood, CT, 1986), 58] and "Less of One" [Inman, *Written*, 183], for instance). See John Berger, *About Looking* (New York: Vintage, 1980), 101.

20. For a reading of the form of "nimr," see Michael Golston, "Mobilizing Forms: Lyric, Scrolling Device, and Assembly Lines in P. Inman's 'nimr,'" in *New Definitions of Lyric: Theory, Technology, and Culture*, ed. Mark Jeffreys (New York: Garland, 1998), 3–15.

For an example of asemantic intrusions from improvisatory expression, consider the hypnagogic language of Jack Kerouac's *Old Angel Midnight* (San Francisco: Grey Fox Press, 1993), which attempts to record the interior linguistic noise generated along the limn of sleep.

21. Inman, *"different table,"* 22–23. Noting that no language can purge itself completely of ideological residue, Inman goes on to qualify: "no matter how defamiliarized, the language in 'Lotioning' does point outside (& despite) itself" (31). Compare this admission with Inman's proposal that writing might "be internally driven, that it be immanently rather than empirically verifiable, productive rather than reproductive of some exterior & logically prior reality" (10–11). Ron Silliman seems to make a similar point when he proclaims, "Inman never divorces meaning from the graphic physicality of the individual letter in a two-dimensional space" ("Realism," *Ironwood* 20 [1982]: 63).

22. P. Inman, "Notes on Slow Writing," *PhillyTalks* 14 (Philadelphia: Kelly Writers House, 1999), n.p.

23. Jeff Derksen, focusing on one term of the dialectic between grammar and inscription in Inman's poetry, has argued that his writing is characterized by its "semantic uselessness (its resistance to meaning) [...]; its rejection of representation; its sheer materiality" ("Culture above the Nation: Globalism, 'Multiculturalism,' and Articulated Locals" [PhD dissertation, University of Calgary, 2000], 226).

24. Inman, "Notes."

25. P. Inman, "Responses to Some Questions," *Aerial* 6/7 (1991): 71.

26. Inman, *PhillyTalks*, 29 November 1999. Transcribed from http://www.writing.upenn.edu/pennsound/x/phillytalks/Philly-Talks-Episode14.html, accessed 10 August 2001.

27. Inman seems to imply something similar when he suggests that "one can take control of language and one can generate a space out of that language rather than being forcefed with a stream of [...] captions." Inman is elaborating on his claim that

> it really is necessary to get away from the continual stream of information and nonspeak that we're being barraged with and sort of try to say, well, there can be a space within an administered whole, to use an Adornian term, to look at the possibility of finding something that could actually create space within that. (*PhillyTalks* transcript)

And elsewhere:

> any unitary word as a point of resistance, an interruption in the ongoing transmission. That which remains single & planted, which doesn't move along the line, which isn't swept along by the trajectory of information & bytes of sensation, of electronic current &/or currency. (Inman, "Notes")

The suspension of attention, a poetics of delay that I am valorizing here, might be read out of Inman's idiosyncratic use of punctuation in sections of *Vel*, *at. least.*, and *amounts. to.* which seems to seek to stop the reader at each and every word. One should compare those similar formal surfaces, for a sense of the differing poetics, with some of the telegraphic experiments submitted for the modernist collection *Readies for Bob Brown's Machine* (Cagnes-sur-Mer: Roving Eye Press, 1931), as well as José Garcia Villa's extraordinary *Volume Two* (New York: New Directions, 1949) and its directly influenced *The Secret Lives of Punctuations, Vol. I* by Eileen R. Tabios (Espoo, Finland: xPress[ed], 2006). In the "Note" to his volume, Garcia Villa explains:

> The reader of the following poems may be perplexed and puzzled at my use of the comma; it is a new, special, and *poetic* use to which I have put it. The commas appear in the poems *functionally*, and thus not for eccentricity [...] the commas are an integral and essential part of the medium: regulating the poem's verbal density and time movement: enabling each word to attain a fuller tonal value, and the line movement to become more measured.

28. Mark Wallace, "Movement beyond the Image: Pattern & Refusal in the Poetry of P. Inman," *Fascicle*, no. 3 (Winter 2006–2007), accessed 12 August 2011.

29. *PhillyTalks* 14 transcript. See his elaboration on that statement at ronsilliman.blogspot.com, posted 7 September 2002.

30. Charles Bernstein, *Parsing* (New York: Asylum's Press, 1976), n.p.

31. Charles Bernstein, "Thank You for Saying Thank You," *Let's Just Say* (Tucson, AZ: Chax, 2003); reprinted in *Girly Man* (Chicago: University of Chicago Press, 2006), 7.

32. Clark Coolidge, *Clark Coolidge* (Lines, 1967), n.p.

33. Clark Coolidge, "Ripping the Graphs," in *Act of Providence* (Cumberland, RI: Combo Books, 2010): 194.

34. Bruce Andrews, "True Flip To," *Give Em Enough Rope* (Los Angeles: Sun & Moon, 1987), 132.

35. Bruce Andrews, "Bieber Line," in *Designated Heartbeat* (London: Salt, 2006), 39.

36. Hejinian, *Writing Is an Aid*.

37. *Bay Poetics*, ed. Stephanie Young (Newton, MA: Faux Press, 2006), 209.

38. "lake. aside.," in *amounts. to.* (Elmwood, CT: Potes and Poets, 2000), 28.

39. P. Inman, *Uneven Development* (Berkeley, CA: Jimmy & Lucy's House of Knowledge, 1982).

40. Marjorie Perloff, *Unoriginal Genius: Poetry by Other Means in the New Century* (Chicago: University of Chicago Press, 2011), 8–9. Perloff defines the style in question in terms that corroborate my assessment of Inman's unassimilable verse: "a poetry of programmatic non-referentiality" in which the foregrounded "syntactic distortion" of abstract language refuses to "'add up' to any sort of coherent, much less transparent statement" (8–9). Inman himself would term this type of writing *anti-narrative*: "narrative triumphs precisely through the consolidation of isolate detail. […] It solidifies" (P. Inman, "One to One," in *The Politics of Poetic Form: Poetry and Public Policy*, ed. Charles Bernstein [New York: Roof, 1990], 223).

41. Viktor Shklovsky, *Bowstring: On the Dissimilarity of the Similar*, trans. Shushan Avagyan (Champaign, IL: Dalkey Archive, 2011), 164, 165. The very models for the artist and the theme of art itself, those "out of place" are, for Shklovsky, "heroes who transgress the ordinary" because they "see differently from those chained by the habitual." With the goal of restructuring the world, the displaced person "exposes the misrecognition of something new" (166, 165).

42. See, for substantiation: "Dust Bowl," presented in the collection *Written* in prose paragraphs, was initially set in blocks of indented verse lines in *Think of One* (Elmwood, CT: Potes & Poets, 1986); "lake, aside." incorporates lines from *Uneven Development* as hemistich parentheticals, just as "stead" "contains language drifted from an uncollected portion of 'Dust Bowl'" (as explained in the copyright-page note to *criss cross* [New York: Roof, 1994]); "Think of One" becomes "Less of One"; "ply" becomes "n.b."; "nimr," as it appears in *Red Shift*, contains lines from a poem by the same title published in *Ironwood*, but both seem completely unrelated to a text under the same title preserved in the Mandeville Special Collections Library, University of California at San Diego (Ron Silliman Papers: 1965-1988, MSS 0075, box 9, folder 31). Further instances of recurrent lines will be adduced below, but for one instance here note that "mang-red hair," from the poem "A Viz" (Inman, *Written*, 96) returns without the hyphen as "mang red hair" in "Decker," a poem that also includes the lines "drew, mang. / figment keeps to hum / off flection," which in turn recall "drew mang off flection" from the poem "nimr." Although it could not have been a direct source, the following coincidence is too delicious to pass over without mention: "The red hair of sea wives is often identified with a reddish brown seaweed that is known in the Barakai language as *mang*" (Patricia Spyer, *The Memory of Trade: Modernity's Entanglements on an Eastern Indonesian Island* [Durham, NC: Duke University Press, 2000], 310).

43. *W*, no. 11, "elf," ed. Ted Byrne (Summer 2005), 4; P. Inman, *now/time* (Milwaukee: Bronze Skull Press, 2006), n.p.

44. P. Inman, "Roscoe Mitchell," *W*, no. 11, 8.

45. Mandeville Collection, Silliman Papers: 1965-1988, MSS 0075.

46. "Language Sampler," ed. Charles Bernstein, *Paris Review* 86 (Winter 1982): n.p.

47. Such dissemination is typical of the general fate of language from the typescript "backbite"; the line "how Stein influenced diabetics," for just one instance of many, returns lineated in "Think of One" (Potes & Poets edition, 42): "how Stein / influenced diabetics."

48. Inman, "Responses," 71.

49. John Bryant, *The Fluid Text: A Theory of Revision and Editing for Book and Screen* (Ann Arbor: University of Michigan Press, 2002), 61.

50. P. Inman, "Plainsong," *Aerial* 6/7 (1991): 65. The Weißbier style of "white beer" suggested by "whited beer" is reinforced by the equation of *Meißen* and *white* via the two lines "meissen / eaction" and "whitecap eaction" (Inman, *Written*, 559, 210).

51. *Raddle Moon* 5 (1987): 76. *Cf.* "prose arrived in fragments" and "What the others had parted to prose / workday arrived another money by. Sand fills the mouth of / plains of footfall between pages" (Inman, *Written*, 259, 366).

One might compare these recurrences with the structure of the Thomas DeLio compositions that take Inman's poems as their texts: *Think on Parch* (1997); *"decker"* (1998); *amounts. to.* (2002); and (to date) *Song: Foxrock near Dublin* (2005). In those works, "a few similar or even identical sonorities (the same chunks of tape, or, better still, the same segment of audio files) are spread across the entire set of works, sometimes literally copied and pasted" (Agostino Di Scipio, "Notes on Digital Silence: Listening to Tom DeLio's Short Tape Works," in *Essays on the Music and Theoretical Writings of Thomas DeLio, Contemporary American Composer*, ed. Thomas Licata [Lewiston, NY: Edwin Mellen Press, 2008], 54). For an introduction to DeLio's use of Inman's texts, see Linda Dusman, "Luminous Presence: Thomas DeLio's *think on parch (four songs for tape)*" (also in Licata, *Essays*, 23–38). The compositions can be heard on *Music/Theatre: New Dimensions* (Centaur Records CRD-2633 [2004]), *Music/Text*, and *Music/Text II* (Capston Records, CPS-8669 [1999] and CPS-8693 [2001]).

52. Compare the poem "stead," with the lines "'passos fixity.' (first / nucif. (glance as Montauk," and Section F of "Dust Bowl": "Montauk miles quiet [...] 'Passos' / fixity," (Inman, *Written*, 280, 202). "Montauk" chimes with the neighboring place-names cited by Inman ("Weehawken," "Setauket," *et alii*), and the reference is presumably to John Dos Passos, perhaps in echo of his memorable passage describing "cars from Montauk" (John Dos Passos, *Manhattan Transfer* [New York: Houghton Mifflin, 1991], 217).

53. Elsewhere, "still" is similarly associated with "finched"; in addition to a line from the poem "glimpse" ("the: one: / pause: that: finched: still" [Inman, *Written*, 349]), the pairing occurs four times over the course of "kilter": "parents from drained rounds the book before a finched still"; "Marne as. finched stills"; "from my skin. / pushed finched still. / torn pages factory"; and "meaning finched. still sentences. calved into. / sentences calved. into tallow" (358, 358, 361, 362).

54. See "Red Shift": "what does steach blood / a white over leverage let into me / lashes rounded none-to-people / skin of one weather following." And the end of "Waver": "steach who / by skin beside." Compare "(a croft. / of beers," from "science fiction," with "Temperature with / beers. Hair croft course," from "Vagabond (1)." (Inman, *Written*, 223, 254, 328, 333.)

55. Inman, *Written*, 54, 614, 618. In the context of the typewriter, with its central revolving platen, the precession of *p-a-i-n* words circle the title of Inman's book *Platin*, as well the authorial name, with which this chapter will conclude: *P. Inman*.

56. Inman, *Written*, 316, 149, 295.

57. Inman, *Written*, 319, 361, 202, 279, 347; but consider also "round but landed [...] imagery" (294).

58. "Blength" appears elsewhere in the poem. *Cf.* "the end of the page the eye could see" (from "subtracted words") and "a page of plot-line / boundaried under" (Inman, *Written*, 351, 315).

59. "Think of One," 364.

60. Inman, *Written*, 354, 529, 80. *Cf.*, to corroborate: "thumb / graze [...] glimpse" (621), with the hint of *gaze* behind "graze."

61. Inman, *Written*, 351, 424, 201, 351. "Fledge," in turn, links back to the edge of a book with "spined fledge" (366), itself perhaps explaining the odd phrase "spinach of a book" as the homophonic *spine-edge* of a book (50; *cf.* 253, 267).

62. Inman, *Written*, 342, 465, 346, 457, repeated at "n.b." (392, 287, 293, 392, 403, 402). *Cf.* "each line minus its breadth" (417).

63. Inman, *Written*, 543 (*cf.* 308, 166); "Think of One" (Potes & Poets edition, 58); Inman, *Written*, 183; *OED*, s.v. "pile."

64. Inman, *Written*, 190, 272, 219. *Cf.* "edges / rubbed off exactly upon her throat" (259).

65. "Skin" and "blood" are linked via "steach," as noted above (note 53). *Cf.* the disarticulating cuts implied in "tattooed on a stack of arm: line rue splits" (Inman, *Written*, 193); "the still pore of an / arm, prose arrived to fragments" (259; but *cf.* 361, 399, 407, 446); "his ridge for parted arm" (333); and "par. ted. arm" (361), as well as the similar set of terms that come under the gravitational pull of *cell*, as the "white cells" of "blood cells" (repeated as "blood [...] cell") (373, 374, 376). But *cf.* 276, 289, 330, 346, 374, *et cetera*: "the tawn stell everything that her pulse. flap / cells on the back of my hand" (289); "celled sifts: / a paper: spread of" (345); "an English: lecture rubbed: into cells" (346); "celled ketchup" (181); *et cetera*.

66. Inman, *Written*, 290, 631, 306, 405, 482.

67. For the example of "burnish" see *A Dictionary of English Etymology*, vol. 3, part 2, ed. Hensleigh Wedgwood (London: Trübner, 1859), 273.

68. *A New and Improved Standard French and English and English and French Dictionary*, ed. A. G. Collot (Philadelphia: C. G. Henderson, 1852).

69. *Century Dictionary and Cyclopedia*, vol. 6 (New York: Century, 1906).

70. Inman, *Written*, 208, 196, 587, 208, 587.

71. Inman, *Written*, 71, 428, 357; but *cf.* 300.

72. Inman, *Written*, 229, 393, 427, 419, 403. *Cf.* "brim [...] glimpsed at a letter's foot"; "lake without brim. a glimpse"; and "under. my. ankles. / in. edges." (616, 363, 564). Through the same process the combination of sound and sense links the lines "blanch ache" (583; *cf.* 666) and "acre whitened" (549) with "bleached" (550). In earlier books, "acreage" recurs with "color" ("each color of acreage" [301; *cf.* color of "acreage vanilla," 690]; "everything as acreage color" (307); "acre colors" (522); "Lake Superior color alike of acreage" (618); and "beached" (367).

73. Inman, *Written*, 299, 293; *cf.* "strain" and "brink" (265).

74. Inman, *Written*, 371; "amagansett #1," uncollected MS (*cf.* "sepa-/ration" on paper [*Written*, 284]); *Written*, 366; "amagansett #1," uncollected MS (*cf. Written*, 369).

75. Inman, *Written*, 189; "sudio w. talk" (529); *cf.* "acoma" (566).

76. Inman, *Written*, 616; *cf.* 692, 694.

77. See Louis Cabri, "Social Address and the Modernist Word in Louis Zukofsky, Bruce Andrews, P. Inman" (PhD dissertation, University of Pennsylvania, 2005), 234 et seq.

78. Inman, *Written*, 56, 63, 72, 77, 85, 87, 73, 74, 108, 114, 129, 158, 236.

79. Inman, "*different table*," 30. Inman elaborates:

> Another writer once introduced me to someone as a "neologist" & I remember being vaguely surprised by that characterization. I didn't see myself as generating snippets of some new linguistic currency. I guess I didn't see the vocabulary as having the kind of permanency you'd need for that kind of project. It seemed like it was more occasional than that; the units fit in where they fit in & then once you left the piece they were gone. You know, they didn't have enough longevity to become units of linguistic currency. (*Ibidem*)

80. Inman, "Responses," 70.

81. Louis Cabri cautions against such a reading ("Social Address," 234-36). One might also note the repeated proximity of *name* and *property* (Inman, *Written*, 195, 198, 245, 275, 674), which triangulates the *proper* name.

82. Inman, *Written*, 196, 511, 333.

83. Inman, *Written*, 227, 198; "subtracted words" (as it appears in *Aerial*); Inman, *Written*, 294, 432, 437, 528.

84. Inman, *Written*, 392; "nimr," Mandeville Collection, Silliman Papers: 1965-1988, MSS 0075; "Think of One" (Potes & Poets edition, 69).

85. *OED*.

86. *Cf.* "longhand" (Inman, *Written*, 534); "longhands" (418); "lettering" (371, 452, 692); "letter.shapes" (426); "handwrites" (451); "needs handwriting" (526); "means 'needs handwriting'" (526); *et cetera*.

87. For "dot," see Inman, *Written*, 213, 248, 305, 315, 328, 340, 366, 367, 369, 371; *cf.* 484. For "blot": 42, 86, 116; for "stubble": 339, 340, 366 (*cf.* 186); for "speck": 352, 371 (*cf.* 187, 245); for "lapse" and "collapse": 47, 50, 187, 190, 192, 221, 328, 341, 611, 716; for "sketch": 315; for "murmur": 315; for "stutter": 450, 480.

88. Inman, *Written*, 462.

89. Inman, *Written*, 86, 366; "Think of One" (Potes & Poets edition, 53); Inman, *Written*, 50.

90. Inman, *Written*, 181, 364, 282.

91. Inman, *Written*, 86. In the original pamphlet publication of *Platin* (College Park: Sun & Moon Press, 1979) the word "blotter," perhaps tellingly, appears as "lotter" (n.p., poem #16).

92. Inman, *Written*, 328; "Think of One" (Potes & Poets edition, 48).

93. *OED*, s.v. "pencil" and "drake."

Chapter Four

1. Walter Lowenfels, "Epitaph for My Punctuation," in *Founds Poems & Others* (New York: Barlenmir House, 1972), 52. By chance, the poem is followed by Lowenfel's "D. A. Levy Poem"; the reason the conjunction is notable will become clear by the end of this chapter.

2. Russell Atkins, "Of," *Free Lance* 7.1 (1963): 23.

3. Contemporaneously, in the contributors notes to one of the journals he edited, Levy described Atkins as the "cleveland hermit [who] shoots poems & sun rays between the toes ... guardian of kinsburry run" (*Marrahwannah Quarterly* 2.2 [1966]: [4]; ellipsis in original).

4. See Newman Ivey White, *American Negro Folk-Songs* (Cambridge, MA: Harvard University Press, 1928), 140–41; White, citing firsthand reports from Alabama in 1915-1916 and South Carolina in 1919, suspects the text's evolution into social and minstrel songs—the very association from which H. T. Burleigh is at pains to distance the song (*Negro Spirituals Arranged for Solo Voice: Oh, Didn't It Rain* [New York: G. Ricordi and Company, 1919]: [1]). See also Howard W. Odum and Guy B. Johnson, *The Negro and His Songs: A Study of Typical Negro Songs in the South* (Chapel Hill: University of North Carolina, 1925), 129; Howard W. Odum, "Religious Folk-Songs of the Southern Negro," *American Journal of Religious Psychology and Education* (Worcester), ed. G. Stanley Hall, vol. 3 (May 1908–July 1909): 350–51. Odum's notion of the "work song" is loaded, since he felt that the authentic informants were itinerants prone to "loafing in general, and working only when compelled to do so" (Howard W. Odum, "Negro Folk-Song and Folk-Poetry," *Journal of American Folklore* 24 [1912]: 259); *cf.* his valuation of the "chain-gang" as an ideal site for gathering data (Howard W. Odum and Guy B. Johnson, *Negro Workaday Songs* [Chapel Hill: University of North Carolina Press, 1926], 6).

5. Odum, "Religious Folk-Songs," 350.

6. Odum, "Religious Folk-Songs," 351.

7. White, *American*, 140; Howard W. Odum and Guy B. Johnson, *The Negro and His Songs: A Study of the Typical Negro Songs in the South* (Chapel Hill: University of North Carolina Press, 1925), 127; *cf.* 129.

8. The quotation comes from the description not of "Spyrytual," but of a roughly contemporaneous (1963) hectograph composed entirely of repeated typewriter quotation marks by Peter Roehr (*Peter Roehr: Avant-Garde Artist of the 1960s: Field Pulsations*, ed. Sarah Hayden and Paul Hegarty [Cologne: Snoeck, 2018], 114).

9. "New Music Roll Issues for March," *Music Trade Review* (27 February 1926), 37.

10. Cameron Williams, "'Really, Music Was the Cause of It': Interview with Russell Atkins, June 2, 2016, at the Grand Pavilion, Cleveland, Ohio," *Jacket2* (3 April 2018), accessed 25 June 2018, https://jacket2.org/interviews/really-music-was-cause-it.

11. As the *Oxford English Dictionary* traces the etymology: "Compare Middle Dutch *spien* (Dutch *spieden*), Middle Low German *spêen*, Middle Swedish *speia*, *speya* (Swedish *speja*), Old Norse *speja*, *spæja*." The look of the word, in its Middle English spelling, with the pair of descenders on the *y*'s, might also establish a visual mannequin for the double downward strokes of the quotation marks that follow.

12. See note 14, below; emphases supplied.

13. See Roberta Martin, "Didn't It Rain," in *Every Time I Feel the Spirit: 101 Best-Loved Psalms, Gospel Hymns, and Spiritual Songs of the African-American Church*, ed. Gwendolyn Sims Warren (New York: Henry Holt, 1997), 114. Warren notes three other published versions of the songs, including one attributed to Lucy Matthews.

14. Following a 1940 recording by the Galilee Singers (Michel Ruppli, *The Decca Labels: The Eastern and Southern Sessions: 1934-1942* [Westport, CT: Greenwood, 1996], 570), the song was best known on record through recordings by Mahalia Jackson, including a performance in the rain on what may be the most famous gospel recording

ever, her performance at the Newport Jazz Festival in 1958 (Mahalia Jackson, *Newport 1958* [Columbia CL1244, 1958]). The song had served as the finale of her modestly titled *The World's Greatest Gospel Singer* (1955); another recording was included on the self-titled *Mahalia* (Kenwood LP-486, 1964) and was issued as a 45-rpm single in 1958 (Columbia 4-41150; cf. 313 755 RF [1962] and CBS 1.134 [1963] and 1607 [1964]), before being the opening track on a 7-inch EP in 1960 (Philips 429 293 BE). A version is included in Jackson's album *Spiritual Gospel*, released the same year as Atkins's *Spyrytual* (CBS 28 014-9, 1966). At the time, Jackson was enough of a cross-over celebrity to attract accusations of selling out, and she was considered "to be the queen of Gospel" (Horace Boyer, Howard Rye, and Barry Kerfeld, "Gospel (2)," *Grove Dictionary of Music*). In the United Kingdom, the song was popularized by a widely viewed BBC broadcast of a concert by Sister Rosetta Tharpe at the Manchester train station on 7 May 1964, splicing its DNA into the history of rock and roll.

15. Quoted in Gloster B. Current, "Black Church Music—How Sweet It Sounds," *The Crisis* 89.9 (November 1982): 22.

16. Russell Atkins, "A Psychovisual Perspective for 'Musical' Composition," *Free Lance* 3.2 (1955): 2; emphasis supplied. See Sandra Jean Graham "Spiritual," in *New Grove Dictionary of American Music*, 2nd ed., ed. Charles Hiroshi Garrett (New York: Oxford University Press, 2013).

17. Cf. "the literary is less an *analogy* for […] music, than an inherent element in his conception of music itself, and a key formal bridge or instigating spur in his compositional process" (Brent Hayes Edwards, *Epistrophies: Jazz and the Literary Imagination* [Cambridge, MA: Harvard University Press, 2017], 93; emphasis in original). Atkins raises the question of these categories in the brief introduction to the Muntu Poets anthology, in which the very question of "whether there is such a thing as 'poetry' or 'music'" depends on the relative decisions of particular groups, including "ethnic groups" (*The Muntu Poets of Cleveland*, 1st rev. ed., ed. Sababa Akili and Mutawaf Shaheed [Cleveland: Uptown Media Ventures, 2016], 5).

18. Edwards, *Epistrophies*, 112.

19. Cameron Williams, "Really," n.p.

20. H. H. Stuckenschmidt, *Twentieth Century Music*, trans. Richard Daveson (New York: McGraw-Hill, 1969), 229. My own summary, which follows, is less certain and more provisional. Atkins's expository style, replete with apodictic definitions, abstraction, and heavy metaphysics, is frequently exacerbated by neologisms, a liberal use of scare quotes, unglossed abbreviations, and an unaccountable reluctance to use articles. Admitting the "convoluted" nature of Atkins's critical essays, Aldon Nielsen cautions readers to remember that their "central wackiness" is the "motivated wackiness" of "serious philosophical musings" (Aldon Lynn Nielsen, *Integral Music: Languages of African American Innovation* [Tuscaloosa: University of Alabama Press, 2004], 6).

21. Atkins, "Psychovisual" (1955), 2. According to the jacket copy for Atkins's *Here in The* (Cleveland: Cleveland State University, 1976), his psychovisualist essay "introduced at the Darmstadt Festival of Avant Garde Music, Germany, 1956, has been widely cited in musical publications." While Hale Smith took some note (Smith's "By Yearning and by Beautiful" is dedicated to "Russell Atkins, whose text stimulated the composition"; and the third movement of his "In Memoriam" sets Atkins's "Elegy"), and Aldon Nielsen valiantly discovers a mention in H. H. Stückenschmidt's 1968 *Twentieth Century Music* (Nielsen does not provide a precise citation, but one assumes the reference

is to Stückenschmidt [see note 20]), and although the jacket blurb claims are reiterated (e.g., Nielsen, *Integral Music*, 2; Kevin Prufer and Michael Dumanis, "Introduction," in *Russell Atkins: On the Life and Work of an Unsung Master* [Warrensburg, MO: Pleiades Press, 2013], 15; Bernard L. Peterson, *Contemporary Black American Playwrights and Their Plays: A Biographical Directory and Dramatic Index* [Westport, CT: Greenwood, 1988], 24; Finding Aid, Russell Atkins Collection, Atlanta University Center Robert W. Woodruff Library Archives Research Center; Leonard Bailey, *Broadside Authors and Artists: An Illustrated Biographical Directory* [Detroit: Broadside Press, 1974], 22), I can find no record of Atkins's participation in any of the most comprehensive music histories (such as Amy C. Beal, *New Music, New Allies: American Experimental Music in West Germany from the Zero Hour to Reunification* [Berkeley: University of California Press, 2006], and Martin Iddon, *New Music at Darmstadt: Nono, Stockhausen, Cage, and Boulez* [Cambridge: Cambridge University Press 2013]), nor in the archives of the Internationales Musikinstitut Darmstadt itself. Nielsen reports on Wolpe's introduction of Atkins's theory (Aldon Lynn Nielsen, "Russell Atkins: 'Heretofore,'" in *Heritage Series of Black Poetry, 1962–1975: A Research Compendium*, ed. Lauri Ramey [Hampshire: Ashgate, 2008], 60; *Integral*, 2) (which derives perhaps from Atkins's own recollection that he "received a letter from a composer, the late Stefan Wolpe, who asked permission to introduce the work during the Festival of Avant-garde Music at Darmstadt, Germany, 1956" ["Russell Atkins," Contemporary Authors Autobiographical Series, vol. 16, ed. Joyce Nakamura (Detroit: Gale Research, 1992): 15]), but the lecture as published contains no mention of Atkins (see "On New (And Not-So-New) Music in America," trans. Austin Clarkson, *Journal of Music Theory* 28.1 [Spring 1984]: 1–45), nor do Wolpe's contemporaneous essays ("Thoughts on Pitch and Some Considerations Connected with It," ed. Austin Clarkson, *Perspectives of New Music* 17.2 [Spring/Summer 1979]: 28–57; "Any Bunch of Notes: A Lecture," ed. Austin Clarkson, *Perspectives of New Music* 21.1–2 [Spring/Summer 1982–Fall/Winter 1983]: 295–310). This is not to diminish Atkins's importance as a theorist, but if nothing else, the claim of being widely cited needs to be understood in the context of the fact that there is no mention of Atkins in the Music Index, the Grove or Oxford music reference collections, the RILM Abstracts of Music Literature, or the Retrospective Index to Music Periodicals.

22. Atkins, "Psychovisual" (1955), 4.
23. Atkins, "Psychovisual" (1955), 5, 6.
24. Atkins, "Psychovisual" (1955), 9.
25. Edwards, *Epistrophies*, 83.
26. Edwards, *Epistrophies*, 82–83.
27. Russell Atkins, *Objects* (Eureka, CA: Hearse, 1961), [17].
28. The first and last example are drawn from Atkins's *A Podium Presentation* (Brooklyn Heights: Poetry Seminar Press, 1960), which also contains "full'd," "somber'd," "vast'd," "vain'd," "exodus'd," "business'd," and "morning'd"; the two other examples are quoted from *Objects 2* (Cleveland: Renegade, 1963), which also features the neologisms "skeletal'd," "drear'd," "amber'd," "insignia'd," "mysterious'd," "foe'd," and "all'd." Further examples could be adduced.
29. Russell Atkins, "Lisbon," *Free Lance* 1 (1953): 28.
30. Physical rising and falling, as with the fall of rain and the rising flood waters implied in "Spyrytual" and its source, recall one of the key themes of Atkins's essays on the phenomenology of music, which seek to defamiliarize conventional metaphors of

verticality in music discourse; why, Atkins provocatively queries, do we not imagine relative frequencies as being further and closer in a field of spatial depth, rather than higher and lower?

31. Abby Arthur Johnson and Ronald Maberry Johnson, *Propaganda and Aesthetics: The Literary Politics of African-American Magazines in the Twentieth Century* (Amherst: University of Massachusetts Press, 1979), 157.

32. In the abbreviated and far more conventional version of the poem that appears in *Heretofore*, the lines read, "the fourth in wrath—the tall flames stagger upon fyr / crashes / straight up / utterly dismal" (Russell Atkins, *Heretofore* [Paul Breman: London, 1968], 11; *cf.* the reprinting in *The Garden Thrives: Twentieth Century African-American Poetry*, ed. Clarence Major [New York: Harper Collins, 1996], 86).

33. On the creation of sand vents, which Atkins describes later in the poem as "ruts," including the particular sand-sloughs recorded in the Iberian peninsula, see Charles Davison, *A Manual of Seismology* (Cambridge: Cambridge University Press, 1921), 111.

34. *Cf.* "And I must say tonight that a riot is the language of the unheard" (Rev. Martin Luther King Jr., "The Other America," speech at Grosse Pointe High School, 14 March 1968).

35. Regennia N. Williams, "Cleveland (Ohio) Riot of 1966," *Encyclopedia of American Race Riots*, vol. 1, *A–M*, ed. Walter C. Rucker and James N. Upton (Westport, CT: Greenwood, 2007), 127. As median family income in Cleveland grew over the half-decade before the riots from $5,935 to $6,895, it shrank from $4,637 to $4,050 in the Hough district, where the unemployment rate was more than double elsewhere in the city.

36. Mark E. Lackritz, "The Hough Riots of 1966" (thesis, Princeton University, 1968), published as Report no. 43 (Cleveland: Regional Church Planning Office, July 1968): 13. For the selectivity of the firebombing, see Paul W. Hanson, "Cleveland's Hough Riots of 1966: Ghettoization and Egalitarian (Re)inscription," *Space and Polity* 18.2 (2014): 163. The damage, at the time, was between one and two million dollars, equivalent to approximately ten million dollars today.

37. Mark Urycki, "The Spark That Set Hough on Fire in July 1966" (WCPN, Cleveland Public Radio, 12 July 2016), accessed 10 April 2018, http://wcpn.ideastream.org/news/the-spark-that-set-hough-on-fire-in-july-1966.

38. Lackritz, "Hough Riots," 15; Olivia Lapeyrolerie, "'No Water for Niggers': The Hough Riots and the Historiography of the Civil Rights Movement," *Cleveland Memory* 28 (2015): 5.

39. Quoted in Hanson, "Hough Riots," 154.

40. *Encyclopedia of Cleveland History*, Case Western Reserve, https://case.edu/ech/articles/h/hough-riots/. For a reading of the Hough riots as "the political emergence of the *demos*" (in Jacques Rancière's sense of the term), see Hanson, "Hough Riots."

41. Genesis 9:11, *cf.* 9:15.

42. Pete Seeger and Paul DuBois Jacobs, *Pete Seeger's Storytelling Book* (New York: Harcourt, 2000), 79. *Cf.* James Baldwin, *The Fire Next Time* (New York: Dial Press, 1963).

43. The iconography of fire and water inflects the imagery of the 1968 film *Uptight!* (directed by Jules Dassin). Shot in part on location in the Hough neighborhood, including takes directly across from the Seventy-Niner tavern, the film includes poet Norman Jordan and other local militants, and the location filming involved altercations and protests by others (see Leatrice W. Emeruwa, "Black Arts and Artists in Cleveland," *Black*

World 22.3 [January 1973]: 25; Christopher Sieving, *Soul Searching: Black-Themed Cinema from the March on Washington to the Rise of Blaxploitation* [Middletown, CT: Wesleyan University Press, 2011], 137). Profits from at least one benefit screening were donated to United Black Artists, the successor to the Muntu Poets (Norman Jordan, "News from Cleveland," *Black Art/Black Culture* (1972), 36). The story, adapted from John Ford's *The Informer* (1935), recounts a fictional dramatization of the strategic differences among African American constituencies in Cleveland following the death of Martin Luther King. Fire, in the form of junk-yard pyres and metal smelting, is presented in the film as an integral part of Cleveland industry, while the city—from the reflectance of its rain-soaked streets to the opacity of rain-streaked windows, in tandem with flooded gutters and steady rains—is awash in precipitous noir atmosphere. The symbolism of liquidity extends to the protagonist's heavy perspiration, ritual face washing, and the currency of blood (donation) in exchange for money to pay for alcohol—and even perhaps to the source-spring surname of the martyred revolutionary Johnny Wells.

44. *465: An Anthology of Cleveland Poets*, ed. D. A. Levy (Cleveland: 7 Flowers Press, 1966): [15]; T. L. Kryss's "prophecy" comes belatedly as it evokes the spirit of Atkins's "Spyrytual": "black fiery wind firewindblack black fire black windfire firewind / blackfirewindblackwindfireblack fierywindwindywindblackfirewindbla" (*Marrahwannah Quarterly* 3.3 [1967]: [32]).

45. Kryss, "prophecy."

46. Mike Golden, ed., *The Buddhist Third Class Junkmail Oracle: The Art and Poetry of D. A. Levy* (New York: Seven Stories Press, 1999), 65.

47. In Levy's words, "The Gate could be what Le Metro once was to New York; a center of communications for poets and concerned beings" ("Poets Read at Gate Friday," *The Cauldron* [Fenn College student newspaper], 29 June 1966, n.p.).

48. Golden, *Buddhist*, 64–65. The other minor present was a fifteen-year-old girl, outwardly Levy's friend, who agreed to secretly tape the proceedings on behalf of the Cleveland police.

49. Russell Atkins, "Lakefront, Cleveland," in Levy, *465*, [5]; "Lake in a Storm," *Silver Cesspool* 3 (1964): [5]; *Whichever* (Cleveland: Free Lance Press, 1978), 3; "Tempest," in *Objects*, [9]; *Whichever*, 8; cf. "Lamps New Lighted," *Objects* 2, [11]; "A Fantasie," in *Heretofore*, 3. Cf. "Trainyard by Night," *Buddhist Thirdclass Junkmail Oracle* 6 (August 1967); "Night and Distant Church," in *Here in The*, 50; "Furious'd Garb," in *Objects*, [7]; "NIGH)Th'CRY,PT," in *Objects*, [10]; "Anxieties," in *Objects* 2, [5]; *Whichever*, 12; "Of Photograph of Flood," in *Objects* 2, [6]. Examples could be multiplied exponentially.

50. Russell Atkins, "A Fantasie," in *Heretofore*,15. Cf. "Four of a Fall," in *Objects*, [5]; "Irritable Song," in *Objects* 2, [15]; "A Storm Shall Break," *Marrahwannah Quarterly* 3.3 (1967).

51. *Marrahwannah Quarterly* 4.1 (1967/1968): [6].

52. T. L. Kryss, [untitled poem], *Marrahwannah Quarterly* 3.4 (1967): [14].

53. Guillaume Apollinaire, *Calligrammes: Poèmes de la paix et la guerre, 1913–1916* (Paris: Mercure de France, 1918), [62].

54. See, among other iterations in various media, Ian Hamilton Finlay, "Wave Rock," *Aspen* 7 (Spring–Summer 1970): n.p.

55. Eugen Gomringer, *Worte sind Schatten* (Reinbeck: Rowohlt, 1969), 39.

56. Ronald Johnson, *Songs of the Earth* (San Francisco: Grabhorn-Hoyem, 1970); Augusto de Campos, *Viva Vaia: Poesia 1949–1979* (São Paulo: Livraria Duas Cidades,

1979); Pedro Xisto, "Autumn," in *Concrete Poetry*, ed. Stephen Bann (London: London Magazine Editions, 1967), 124. For a discussion of the subgenre, with illustrations, see Klaus Peter Dencker, *Optische Poesie: Von den prähistorischen Schriftzeichen bis zu den digitalen Experimenten der Gegenwart* (Berlin: De Gruyter, 2011), 307 *et seq.*

57. Ivo Vroom, "Winden," *Marrahwannah Quarterly* 3.3 (1967): [26].

58. Mary Ellen Solt, *Concrete Poetry: A World View* (Bloomington: Indiana University Press, 1968).

59. Kent Taylor recalls discovering both at Asphodel (private correspondence, 6 June 2018).

60. D. A. Levy, ed., *Poets at The Gate* 1.3 (29 April 1966): [8].

61. *OED*.

62. *OED*, s.v. "hough."

63. *OED*, s.v. "hough."

64. Sarah M. Pourciau, *The Writing of Spirit: Soul, System, and the Roots of Language Science* (New York: Fordham University Press, 2017), 203.

65. Peter Mackridge, *Language and National Identity in Greece, 1766–1976* (Oxford: Oxford University Press, 2006), 306. *Cf.* Richard Clogg: "The Greeks and Their Past," in *Historians as Nation Builders: Central and South-East Europe*, ed. Dennis Deletant and Harry Hanak (London: MacMillan, 1988), 22.

66. Glenn Fleishman, "Typography Wars: Has the Internet Killed Curly Quotes?," *Atlantic* 28 (December 2106). Fleischman discovers that even in contemporary digital publications straight quotation marks have been demoted to less prestigious and professional content within web publications, such as previews and comments, even when printers' quotes are used for features and print versions of the same publication.

67. David Blatner, *Real World QuarkXPress 7* (San Francisco: Peachpit, 2007), 362.

68. Bob LeVitus, *Dr. Macintosh: Tips, Techniques, and Advice for Mastering the Macintosh* (Boston: Addison Wesley, 1989), 276.

69. See Robert Young, "Written Navaho: A Brief History," in *Advances in the Creation and Revision of Writing Systems*, ed. Joshua Fishman (The Hague: Mouton, 1977), 465.

70. Andrew Heisel, "Single Quotes or Double Quotes? It's Really Quite Simple," *Slate* (21 October 2014), http://www.slate.com/blogs/lexicon_valley/2014/10/21/single_quotes_or_double_quotes_it_s_really_quite_simple.html.

71. One anomaly in the evolution of quotation marks is the keyboard for the Xerox Star 8010, which "has curly quotes instead of straight" (Glenn Fleishman, *Not to Put Too Fine a Point on It* [Seattle: Aperiodical, 2017], 37).

72. Code point 7, for instance, in the 7-bit scheme, is devoted to the "Audible bell" of the contemporaneous teletype machine design, while point 13 designated a "Carriage return"; code point 34 is assigned to straight double quotes.

73. C. M. Sperberg McQueen, "Text in the Electronic Age: Textual Study and Text Encoding, with Examples from Medieval Texts," *Literary and Linguistic Computing* 6.1 (1991): 35.

74. The same problems, arising from different sign systems, pertain in Web markup languages, where the mistranslations also persist because the area reserved in ISO-8859-1 by Microsoft for special code points (now designated "Windows-1252") is the default interpretation of the HTML5 standard (https://www.w3.org/TR/2012/CR-html5-20121217/syntax.html#character-encodings-0), and because both MacOS and Windows use the same range (0x80–0xAF).

75. Some versions of Microsoft Word (e.g., 5.1) simply omit the punctuation altogether if users select both the "Smart Quotes" and a font that does not include the glyph.

76. Macintosh and Microsoft operating systems supported a closed curve quote as well, although note that ISO 8859-1, the 8-bit single byte published in 1987, did not provide a character mapped to that form, which would have to wait for 8-bit multibyte encoding standards.

77. *The Unicode Standard* 4.0.0 (Mountain View, CA: Unicode Consortium, 2003), 153.

78. In the most recent revisions proposed to the Unicode technical report, these uses are properly handled by U+02BC (Modified Letter Apostrophe) for the glottal stop and U+02BB (Modified Letter Turned Comma) for the 'okina, with U+3003 as the special ditto mark code and U+2032 as the mathematical prime sign. For some software, U+0022 is available as a contextually selected curled quote.

79. For the politics of Unicode's inclusion of Greek glyph codepoints for precomposed spacing accents, in violation of its principles, see the discussion of the merger compromise between Ελληνικός Οργανισμός Τυποποίησης (ELOT), the Hellenic Organization for Standardization and Unicode ISO Standard 10646 (http://www.opoudjis.net/unicode/gkdiacritics.html). Nick Nicholas has identified the redundant block intended to perform "stealth titlecase treatment of premodifying diacritics" as a legacy of 8-bit encoding practice (http://www.opoudjis.net/unicode/gkdiacritics.html).

80. See *Unicode Standard 9.0* (Mountain View, CA: Unicode Consortium, 2016). "For the Latin script, the Unicode Standard does not distinguish identically appearing diacritical marks with different functions" (http://www.unicode.org/faq/char_combmark.html#11).

81. Nielsen, *Integral Music*, 22.

82. Russell Atkins, "Spyrytual," *Every Goodbye Ain't Gone: An Anthology of Innovative Poetry by African Americans*, ed. Aldon Lynn Nielsen and Lauri Ramey (Tuscaloosa: University of Alabama Press, 2006), 14. In keeping with the difficulty of quoting a poem of quotation marks, this version also introduces some misalignments.

83. As participants understood the name, "*Muntu*: derived from African Zulu culture that means a human being. Sometimes used to mean 'a Black person'" (*Straight Up!*, ed. C. E. Shy [Cleveland: Uptown Media Joint Venture Publishing, 2017], 3). *Cf.* the word's etymons in the Xhosa *umntu* and Zulu *umuntu*.

84. James Robenalt, *Ballots and Bullets: Black Power Politics and Urban Guerrilla Warfare in 1968 Cleveland* (Chicago: Chicago Review, 2018), 176.

85. Akili and Shaheed, *Muntu Poets*, 8, 10, 8. More or less obvious from the context, "miss ann" as "a coded term for any white female" was going out of fashion at just around this time (Clarence Major, *Juba to Jive: A Dictionary of African-American Slang* [New York: Penguin, 1994], 8).

86. Akili and Shaheed, *Muntu Poets*, 23.

87. Akili and Shaheed, *Muntu Poets*, back cover copy.

88. Akili and Shaheed, *Muntu Poets*, 12.

89. D. A. Levy, *Plastic Saxophone Found in an Egyptian Tomb* (Cleveland: Accident Press, 1966).

90. 2 Corinthians 3:6.

91. Don Thomas also figures the thick liquid wet process of the duplicator as excremental: a dripping "dia)rea/lity." (Don Thomas, "noTes from The guTTer / a pre-manifesto statement on concrete poetry," *Marrahwannah Quarterly* 4.2 [1967-1968]: [5]).

92. With some concentration, most of the page can be deciphered; I include a transcription for reference:

for dangerous things

Savonarola died in 1498.The church tries not to talk
about him too much.You probably don't know who Savonarola was.It might be interesting to look him up in
an encyclopedia. It might be very interesting.While
you are there,you might look up Cotton Mather,the [......]ari-
[............] and Joseph McCarthy.Did you notice Cardinal Woolsey
in "A Man For All Seasons"?

sex is very dangerous; not generally
to the participants, especially if
young,but to sterile and regretful
social guardians ..... that fruit
which has withered on the branch
yet refuses to drop off to make way
for a perhaps richer crop.

[LSD] could be dangerous to he who
would not know himself.This generally does not include the young.

[Marijuana?] is not dangerous to anyone, especially the young.

Of great danger to the young is
the unbridled wrath of those myopic,
jaded arbitrators of public sexuality
whose insecure values are shaken by
those who suggest answers which differ from their own. In the name of
protecting youth the not only emas-
culate their own culture, but visit
untold misery upon the lives of that
very youth they claim to protect.

A bad acid trip does far less psychic
damage than the inside of a detention
home and the "gentle" interrogation of
the county prosecutor.

Elsewhere, Levy writes, "i feel like an underground movie / that was burned by Savonarola" (*Suburban Monastery Death Poem* [Cleveland: Zero Editions, 1968], n.p.). In November 1965, *A Man for All Seasons* was performed at the Cuyahoga Community College West (http://images.ulib.csuohio.edu/cdm/singleitem/collection/parma/id/2/rec/2).

93. Aldous Huxley, *The Doors of Perception* (New York: Harper & Row, 1954).

94. The page carries only the shorthand header "BUD/60," perhaps indicating its origins in a 1960 commonplace book by Levy's fellow-traveler Bennett "Bud" Hassink. Earlier issues of the journal included Levy's transcriptions from Hassink's notebooks, one dated "Nov 60" (*Marrahwannah Quarterly* 2.1 [1966]: 27). *Cf.* "Fragment from the notebooks Hassink," *Marrahwannah Quarterly* 1.4 (1965): [12–13]. The contributor's note explains, "over 1,000 of his notebooks in psychedelic scrawl have been discovered in his closet / unfortunately he has totally disappeared" [5]. Hassink, described as "sound organizer & euphoria scribbler—dodging the rollers in and out of the present," had vanished from Cleveland to emerge in Haight-Ashbury, joining the Diggers before moving to Berkeley in the early 1970s. In the dedicatory proem to *ukanhavyrfuckinciti bak*, ed. rjs and T. L. Kryss (Cleveland: Ghost Press, 1967), Levy acknowledges "bud who lived it before it / was hip & forgot it." The same year, Levy included other "Notebook Fragments" from Hassink, also dated 1960, in an anthology of local poets. There, the fragments incorporate unattributed passages from Kenneth Patchen's *First Will and Testament* (New York: Padell, 1948) (Levy, 465, [15–16]); *cf. The Collected Poems of Kenneth Patchen* (New York: New Directions, 1968), 159, 166.

95. Blake's line reads, "This will come to pass by an improvement of sensual enjoyment."

96. See, to begin with, Robert Essick, *William Blake, Printmaker* (Princeton, NJ: Princeton University Press, 1980); Joseph Viscomi, *Blake and the Idea of the Book* (Princeton, NJ: Princeton University Press, 1993); and Michael Phillips, *William Blake: The Creation of the Songs from Manuscript to Illuminated Printing* (Princeton, NJ: Princeton University Press, 2000).

97. For examples of Levy's illegibilities, see the cover for certain copies of *Marrahwannah Quarterly* 4.1 (Winter 1967–1968) and the extended "experiment in destructive writing" of his remarkable *Tibetan Stroboscope* (Cleveland: Ayizan Press, 1968).

98. On the fundamental obscurity of printmaking, where "the marking of the paper occurs in an invisible space," see the inspiring analyses of Jennifer L. Roberts (*Jasper Johns/In Press: The Crosshatch Works and the Logic of Print* [Cambridge, MA: Harvard Art Museums, 2012], 19, and "Backwords: Screen Printing and the Politics of Reversal," in *Corita Kent and the Language of Pop*, ed. Susan Dackerman [Cambridge, MA: Harvard Art Museums, 2015], 67–70).

99. D. A. Levy, "Religious Acid," *Marrahwannah Quarterly* 3.4 (1967): [20].

100. Levy, "Religious Acid," [24].

101. Russell Atkins, "Egocentrical Projection as Object in EP Perspective," in *Phenomena*, 79.

102. Atkins, "Egocentrical Projection," 79.

103. Untitled poem, *Marrahwannah Quarterly* 3.4 (1967): [23].

104. See, for instance, the untitled poems in *Marrahwannah Quarterly* 3.4 (1967): [9–12], especially the poem dedicated "for r.j.s.".

105. Roberts, "Backwords," 61; *Marrahwannah Quarterly* 4.2 (1967): [7]. Note that each poem is animated by an anomalous single glyph extending beyond the border established by its otherwise justified right margin, approximately halfway down the block. In the first instance, a closing parenthesis bends with a curve contrasting with the hooks and angles of the grid; in the second instance, a single oval protrudes from the packed honeycomb.

106. *Marrahwannah Quarterly* 4.1 (1967-1968): [26 et seq.].

107. Francis Ponge, "Végétation," in *Tome Prémier: Douze petits écrits* (Paris: Gallimard: 1965, 101. Atkins recalls, "The printer replaced them [slashes]. And I never did really approve of it, but there wasn't anything I could do about it" (Williams, "Really").

108. The acknowledgments to Levy's *Marrahwannah Quarterly* 2.2 (1966), as it happens, contains one of the earliest recorded instances of *xerox* as a verb ("thanx to ruth & dana for xerox'd chicken soup"). The reference, presumably, is to an instant dry soup mix. Not only are the natures of the various printing processes distinct, but their modes are not always compatible; the posthumous continuation of Levy's last journal pled with its contributors: "PLEASE!!!! Please, please don't send us Xerox copies of artwork or complex concrete stuff. Xerox is impossible for us to reproduce decently and we have nobody with time enough to redo your work so it's dark enough to reproduce" (Angry City Press, *The Buddhist Third Class Junkmail Oracle* 10 [October 1969]: [18]).

109. Thomas, "noTes."

110. Roberts, *Jasper Johns*, 18.

111. In addition to the references above, see D. A. Levy, *Swamp Erie Pipe Dream* (Cleveland, 1967).

112. See, for examples, the last two issues of the "Polluted Lake Series" of pamphlets from Renegade Press, and the "Ohio City Series" from 7 Flowers Press, which—like *Spyrytual*—combine letterpress with stencil duplication, as does Kay Wood's *Greenwood* (Cleveland: 7 Flowers Press, 1966), several issues of *Marrahwanna Quarterly* (1.3 and 1.4 [1965], 4.2 [1967-1968]), and the second number of the *Marrawannah Newsletter* (1967). All mix mimeograph and Ditto, as does the anthology *Three-Oh-Six* [i.e., 306]: *An Anthology of Cleveland Poets*, ed. D. A. Levy (Cleveland: 7 Flowers, 1967). The title, like the earlier *465 Anthology of Cleveland Poets*, indicates the street number of Jim Lowell's Asphodel bookstore, the distributor for Levy's publications, which moved to 306 West Superior from its address at 465 The Arcade (the first indoor shopping mall in America, dating from 1890).

113. With a frugal sourcing of scraps, the same cover stock was used in contemporaneous 7 Flowers editions, such as Kent Taylor's *Late Stations* (Cleveland: 7 Flowers Press, 1966).

114. With a further literalization of terms, one can see the same play of figure and type operating in one of the untitled works from Erica Baum's 1998 *Frick Series*, which enlarges photographs of details from the subject index of the Frick Museum's card catalogue of documentary photographs of its painting collection. Baum focuses on four ditto marks arranged vertically above the *i* in the phrase "Nude figures." The literal index indexes the figured as figures and the type(written) as a type (genre), so that the marks are read as naked (bald, unadorned, direct, unremarked—but also "the nude, as a genre in *Art*") indices of the naked (depicted bodies) (*OED*, s.v. "naked"). With an

understated economy of means, Baum thus offers a wry commentary on the objectification of bodies, the substitutability of individuals under regimes of abstraction, and the indifference of a patriarchal tradition.

115. Jacques Derrida, *Psyche* (Paris: Galilée, 1987), 186.

Chapter Five

1. René Major, *Derrida pour les temps à venir* (Paris: Éditions Stock, 2007), 151.

2. *Liberator* 7.6 (June 1967): 12–13.

3. David Bourdon, in the *Village Voice* (11 January 1965), quoted by Aldo Tambellini, "A Syracuse Rebel in New York," *Captured: A Film & Video History of the Lower East Side*, ed. Clayton Patterson (New York: Seven Stories Press, 2005), 45. *Cf.* another report from the period: "when asked his own definition of poetry, N. H. Pritchard uttered guttural, bestial primitive grunts and groans" (Ishmael Reed, ed., *19 Necromancers from Now* [Garden City, NY: Doubleday, 1970], 257). Others have read these poems as diasporic. Lorenzo Thomas acknowledges that Pritchard "investigated the African underpinnings of 'Black English' before most of us even understood the significance of the term" and argues that "Pritchard's early experiments, which were to lead to a "transrealism" that resembles concrete poetry, resulted in poems written in tampered English in which the combination of sounds approximated vocal styles and tones of African languages" (Lorenzo Thomas, *Extraordinary Measures: Afrocentric Modernism and Twentieth-Century American Poetry* [Tuscaloosa: University of Alabama Press, 2000], 120). Aldon Nielsen speculates that "what Pritchard may hope to chart is the signifying glossolalia of black language as intervention in the world, not just as a recording and recoding of the oral" (Aldon Lynn Nielsen, *Black Chant: Languages of African-American Postmodernism* [Cambridge: Cambridge University Press, 1997], 142).

4. N. H. Pritchard, EECCHHOOEESS (New York: NYU Press, 1971), 28.

5. W. Francis Lucas, untitled note, *Liberator*, 7.6 (June 1967): 12–13.

6. *OED*, s.v. "clish-clash" and "clish-ma-claver."

7. John Ayto and John Simpson, *Oxford Dictionary of Modern Slang* (Oxford: Oxford University Press, 2008).

8. The related noun form denotes small lumps or clods of earth, and specifically "the soil used to fill a grave" (*OED*).

9. Frederic Gomes Cassidy and Robert Brock Le Page, eds., *Dictionary of Jamaican English*, 2nd ed. (Barbados: University of the West Indies Press, 2002).

10. Cassidy and Le Page, *Jamaican English*.

11. Cassidy and Le Page, *Jamaican English*.

12. Stephen E. Henderson, "Worrying the Line: Notes on Black American Poetry," in *The Line in Postmodern Poetry*, ed. Robert Frank and Henry Sayre (Urbana: University of Illinois Press, 1988), 79.

13. Anthony Reed, *Freedom Time: The Poetics and Politics of Black Experimental Writing* (Baltimore: Johns Hopkins University Press, 2014), 142.

14. Helen Clark, untitled review, *Denver Quarterly* 5.1 (Spring 1970): 159. Clark seems most outraged by the economic implications, in which most poetry cannot be sold, being stolen from bookstores instead of legitimately purchased, while Doubleday "finds it profitable" to publish such negligible verse. Ironically, given the eleemosynary

scene and groaning belly featured in the poem from the volume on which this chapter will focus, Clark concludes her review with reference to charity:

> if a meager 500 copies of Mr. Pritchard's magnum opus are sold it would amount to almost $3,000, and all enlightened are aware that this amount, if spent on those very tasteful UNICEF greeting cards, would provide daily protein-rich meals for four months for 1,000 children.

On the cuteness of the avant-garde, see Sianne Ngai, *Our Aesthetic Categories: Zany, Cute, Interesting* (Cambridge, MA: Harvard University Press, 2015), chap. 1.

15. N. H. Pritchard, *The Matrix: Poems, 1960–1970* (Garden City, NY: Doubleday, 1970), 187. Indeed, Pritchard's poem corroborates the hypothesis put forward by the textual history of "Spyrytual": it turns out to be surprisingly difficult to quote quotes. For example, when quoting the poem in a review of the anthology *Every Goodbye Ain't Gone*, where the poem's title is inexplicably revised to a single apostrophe (Norman H. Pritchard, "'" [sic], in *Every Goodbye Ain't Gone: An Anthology of Innovative Poetry by African Americans*, ed. Aldon Lynn Nielsen and Lauri Ramey [Tuscaloosa: University of Alabama Press, 2006], 206), Maria Damon reverses the direction of the marks, transforming Pritchard's closing quotes with a series of open-ended beginnings (*Xcp: Cross-Cultural Poetics* 17 [2007]: 142). In the table of contents to *The Matrix*, to make matters more complicated still, the title of the poem is set as uninflected (i.e., not printers') quotation marks. Pritchard titled other poems ":", "‥", and ".-.-.-."; see Adam David Miller, ed., *Dices or Black Bones: Black Voices of the Seventies* (Boston: Houghton Mifflin, 1970), 67–68.

16. Widely adopted as a book face after the Monotype corporation offered a version in 1923, the clean, generously open and vertical face was first revived by Ivy League presses. A close imitation of Baskerville, cut by Isaac Moore for the Fry Foundry in the late eighteenth century, was used by printing manager Frederic Warde for Princeton University Press publications starting in 1921; contemporaneously, Bruce Rogers advised Harvard University Press to adopt the face, which he sourced from an original font (see Stanley Morison: *A Tally of Types*, ed. Brooke Crutchley [Cambridge: Cambridge University Press, 1973], 84). Alexander Lawson dates Rogers's recommendation to 1919 (*Anatomy of a Typeface* [Boston: Godine, 1990], 192).

A close examination of the page further reveals the words to be individually set; note, for the most obvious instance, how the final "red" in the sixth column is skewed from the baseline.

17. Robert Burns, "Red, Red Rose," in *The Works of Robert Burns in Prose and Verse*, 2nd ed., ed. James Currie (New York: W. W. Borradaile, 1826), 117; Gertrude Stein, *Geography and Plays* (Boston: Four Seas, 1922), 187.

18. Gertrude Stein, *Four in America*, ed. Thornton Wilder (New Haven, CT: Yale University Press, 1947), vi.

19. Stein, *Four in America*, vi.

20. William Carlos Williams, ["the rose is obsolete"], in *Spring & All* (New York: New Directions, 1923), 30.

21. John Lydgate, trans., *The tragedies, gathered by Ihon Bochas, of all such princes as fell from theyr estates throughe the mutability of fortune since the creacion of Adam, vntill*

his time wherin may be seen what vices bring menne to destruccion, wyth notable warninges howe the like may be auoyded (London: Wayland, 1554), n.p.; James Joyce, *Ulysses* (New York: Random House, 1961), 78.

22. Percy Society, *Early English Poetry, Ballads, and Popular Literature of the Middle Ages, Edited from Original Manuscripts and Scarce Sources* (London: Richards, 1840), 2:22.

23. Pritchard, *Matrix*, back cover copy.

24. Reed, *Freedom Time*, 142.

25. Marty Larson-Xu perceptively notes that the very same question is raised by Sol LeWitt's 1962 painting with red squares and white letters (private collection).

26. Nielsen, *Black Chant*, 137.

27. Russell Atkins, *Objects* (Eureka: Hearse, 1961), [14].

28. Miller, *Dices*, 66.

29. Henry George Liddell and Robert Scott, *A Greek-English Lexicon*, 7th ed. (New York: Harper & Brothers, 1889).

30. See David Levinson, "Skid Row in Transition," *Urban Anthropology* 3.1 (Spring 1974): 79–93, and (as editor) *Encyclopedia of Homelessness* (Thousand Oaks, CA: Sage, 2004): 32–35. At the same time, the population of skid-row residents in the Bowery declined over the 1960s, to about a third of what it had been in three decades earlier (Howard Bahr: "The Gradual Disappearance of Skid Row," *Social Problems* 15 [1967]: 41–42) and would drop by almost 50 percent again over the second half of the decade (see Earl Rubington: "The Changing Skid Row Scene," *Quarterly Journal of Studies of Alcohol* 35 [1971]); in addition to a marked increase in African American residents, the population became less seasonal and younger, while the percentage of drug addicts and attendant violent crime increased. These changes, combined with the architectural transformations of urban renewal (including the demolition of the East Side elevated train tracks), gave the palpable sense during the 1960s that the Bowery was undergoing a profound transformation and that its older, more seasonal and communal ethos of a coherent counterculture was on the verge of extinction.

31. With a vocabulary idiomatically associated with epistemological inquiry, anticipating the reader who seeks coherent words by piercing the veil of spaced letters, one line from Pritchard's "Metagnomy" similarly evokes its own visually marked thicket of extrusion and agglutination with the afterimage of *see* and *peer*: "To   s   ee   k / [...] to   pier   c e."

32. Pritchard, *Matrix*, 69.

33. Pritchard, *Matrix*, 55.

34. Lillian-Yvonne Bertram, "'A lance to pierce the possible': Reading N. H. Pritchard," *Harriet the Blog* (May 2015), accessed 14 April 2019, https://www.poetryfoundation.org/harriet/2015/05/a-lance-to-pierce-the-possible-reading-n-h-pritchard/. Because it is often difficult to determine the import of Pritchard's cacography, readers may suspect mere errors, but Paul Stephens argues that such words are likely fragmentary by design; see his important chapter on Pritchard (Paul Stephens, *Absence of Clutter: Minimal Writing as Art and Literature* [Cambridge, MA: MIT Press, 2020]).

35. On "Pritchard's deep spiritualism" and the theosophical aspect of his "transreal" poetics, see Stephens, *Absence*, 111–26.

36. Alex Caldiero, private correspondence, 7 June 2019.

37. Letter to W. H. Low, April 1884, *The Letters of Robert Louis Stevenson*, vol. 2, *1880–1887*, ed. Sidney Colvin (New York: Charles Scribner's Sons, 1911), 209.

38. Norman Pritchard, "Epilogue," in *Matrix*, 75.

39. The poem "PASSAGE," earlier in *The Matrix*, seems to literalize the phrase "middle passage" as a sort of rebus by printing the title down the gutter (the middle) of the recto page (57); see Stephens, *Absence*. The legacy of slavery may also haunt Pritchard's epigraph to *The Matrix*: "words are ancillary to content." Deriving from the diminutive of *ancula*, *ancillary* traces its lineage to a "female slave"; the word was commonly used as the feminine of *servus* (instead of *serva*) (Charles T. Lewis and Charles Short, *Lewis & Short's Latin Dictionary* [Oxford: Clarendon, 1879]).

40. *OED*, s.v. "pass."

41. Reed, *Freedom Time*, 43.

42. *OED*, s.v. "mull."

43. The phrase alludes to Revelation 21:21: "The twelve gates were twelve pearls, each individual gate was of one pearl."

44. *OED*, s.v. "metagnomy."

45. Homer: *The Odyssey*, vol. 2, trans. Arthur T. Murray (Cambridge, MA: Loeb Classical Library, 1919), 19.559–69; Virgil, *Aeneid* 6.893–99. *Cf.* Liddell and Scott, *Lexicon*, s.v. "ἐλεφαίρομαι."

46. *OED*, s.v. "muffler."

47. *Cf.* the "waisted jeers," part pun on *wasted years*, in "Silhouette," which also echoes the dim vision and the focus on gait (the protagonist "shoeless strode") (Pritchard, *Matrix*, 57).

48. Carl Sandburg, "Fog," in *Chicago Poems* (New York: Henry Holt and Company, 1916), 71.

49. T. S. Eliot, "The Love Song of J. Alfred Prufrock," in *Prufrock and Other Observations* (London: Egoist, 1917), 10.

50. See *OED*, s.v. "footpad" and "night-walker." *Cf.* the appositive subtitle of the restoration play, by John Fletcher and James Shirley, *The night-walker; or, The little thief / a comedy as it was presented by Her Majesties servants at the private house in Drury-Lane* (London: Andrew Crook, 1661); William Butler Yeats, "Byzantium," in *The Collected Poems of W. B. Yeats*, ed. Richard Finneran (New York: Scribner, 1996), 248.

51. Dan Halas and Alan Raymond, *How Do You Like the Bowery?* (1964; 16mm film).

52. The "clean free bend of inward ends," in this context, seems to describe the intestinal *innards* that lurks in "inward ends."

53. *OED*, s.v. "coffer."

54. *OED*, s.v. "helas." "Sile," now obsolete except in dialect, adds to the poem's verbs of motion: "to go, pass, move; to glide"; and it anticipates the protagonist's collapse: "to fall or sink (*down*)," "to fall down in a swoon" (*OED*).

55. See *OED*, s.v. "taps." Ultimately, one may even discern a faint echo of the military connotations of "dime," as "a 'tithe' of war," as in Shakespeare's *Troilus & Cressida* (II.ii.18): "Euery tith soule 'mongst many thousand dimes, Hath beene as deere as Hellen."

56. *Cf.* Laurence Libin, *American Musical Instruments in the Metropolitan Museum of Art* (New York: Metropolitan Museum of Art; W. W. Norton, 1985), 80–95 *passim*.

57. *OED*, s.v. "tattoo."

58. *OED*, s.v. "tattoo."

59. John Bunyan, *Doctrinal Discourses* (London: Thomas Ward, 1841), 434. Passages such as "thou shalt dash them [the enemies of God] in pieces like a potter's vessel"

(Psalm 2:9), "we have this treasure in earthen vessels" (2 Corinthians 4:7), and "we are the clay, and you are our potter" (Isaiah 64:8) amplify the earthen origins and fate of humans—dust to dust, per Genesis (2:7).

60. *OED*, s.v. "cask."

61. Francis Ponge, *Cinq Sapates* (Paris: André Tourmon & Cie, 1950).

62. Francis Ponge, "Proclamation et Petit Four," in *Œuvres complètes* (Paris: Gallimard, 1999), 641–42.

63. Ponge, *Œuvres complètes*, 1119n6.

64. As defined in the *Littré*: "Ancien terme de musique. Se disait du son du tuyau d'orgue appelé cromorne" [former musical term denoting the sound of the organ pipe known as a cromorne]. The term is widely defined in specialty dictionaries; see, for instance, "CRUCHER est un terme par lequel on prétend exprimer le son que doit avoir un cromorne. Ainsi l'on dit qu'un cromorne doit *crucher*, qu'un cromorne *cruche bien*" (M. Hamel, *Nouveau manuel complet du facteur d'orgues, ou Traité théorique et practique de l'art de construire les orgues* [Paris: Robert, 1849], 527); "crucher, v. n. Il se dit du son du cromorne" (Antoine de Rivarol, *Dictionnaire classique de la langue française* [Paris: Libraire de L'Université Royale, 1828], 267). The instrument itself, something like a contrabass oboe, is a sort of missing link in the evolution of the oboe: clearly attested to in the historical record but with only tantalizingly vague details that have encouraged a mythological status; see Vincent Robin, "Contrebasse de hautbois, ou cromorne? Éléments de recherche pour l'identification du cromorne français aux XVIIe et XVIIIe siècles" (dissertation, Conservatoire Supérieure, Paris, 1995); Bruce Haynes, *The Eloquent Oboe: A History of the Hautboy, 1640-1760* (Oxford: Oxford University Press, 2001), 38–45 *passim*; James B. Kopp, *The Bassoon* (New Haven, CT: Yale University Press, 2012), 14, 17. *Cf.* David Ponsford, "A Question of Genre: Charpentier's Messe pour plusieurs instruments au lieu des orgues (H513)," in *New Perspectives on Marc-Antoine Charpentier*, ed. Shirley Thompson (London: Routledge, 2016), chap. 5, *passim*. For Ponge's interest in the music of the French baroque, see Patrick Meadows, *Francis Ponge and the Nature of Things: From Ancient Atomism to a Modern Poetics* (Lewisburg: Bucknell University Press, 1997), chap. 3, *passim*.

65. Francis Ponge, *The Making of the Pré*, trans. Lee Fahnestock (Columbia: University of Missouri Press, 1979), 28–29.

66. *Crochu* derives from the Old Norse *krókr* (Swedish *krok*, Danish *krog*) [crook, hook, barb, trident]; unknown elsewhere in Germanic, but apparently belonging to the same ablaut series (*krak-, krôk*), as Old High German *chracho, chracco* [hook]; *cf.* Old Norse *kraki* [boat-hook]. *Crock*, on the other hand, from the Old English *croc*, is "related to Icelandic *krukka* < (Danish *krukke*, Swedish *kruka*) in same sense; and perhaps more remotely to *croh*," a lineage that would link to the French *cruche* through the Old English *cróg, cróh* [small vessel], cognate with Old High German *chruog*, Middle High German *kruoc(g)*, and German *krug*, as well as through an ablaut relation to *crouke/crowke*, via Old English *crúce* [feminine: pot, little pitcher, "urceolus"], a cognate with Old Saxon *krûka* (Middle Dutch *crûke*, Dutch *kruik*, Middle High German *krûche*, dialect German *krauche*). The *OED* demurs: "whether the Celtic words, Middle Irish *crocan*, Gaelic *crogan*, Welsh *crochan* 'pot', are related, is not determined."

67. Heinrich von Kleist, *Der zerbrochene Krug: Ein lustspiel* (Berlin: Realschulbuchhandlung, 1811). *Cf.* the opéra comique by Jean-Frédéric-Auguste Lemière de Corvey, *Les Rivaux de village, ou La cruche cassée* (Paris: Barba, 1820).

68. Martin Heidegger, "Das Ding," in *Vorträge und Aufsätze* (Pfullingen: Neske, 1954), 169; trans. Albert Hofstadter, *Poetry, Language, Thought* (New York: Harper, 2001), 165.

69. Heidegger, "Das Ding"/*Poetry*, 168–69/164–65.

70. Barbara Johnson cites the saying as "La crûche va tellement à l'eau qu'à la fin elle casse," a version I am unable to locate, although the circumflex may reflect the sense of swelling growth (*crû*, from *croire*) in accord with Johnson's understanding of "another meaning of the proverb: pregnancy. 'If she continues to sleep around, she'll end up pregnant'" (Barbara Johnson, *Persons and Things* [Cambridge, MA: Harvard University Press, 2008], 71). This reading would fit with the iconography of paintings such as Jean Baptiste Greuze's 1771 *La cruche cassé* (Louvre) and William-Adolphe Bouguereau's identically titled 1891 canvas (San Francisco Museum of Fine Arts).

71. Paul Eluard, ed., *Proverbe* 5.1 (May 1920), cover; note that in the original layout the poem is rotated so as to be printed horizontally. Belgian Surrealist Louis Scutenaire would recast the adage as a parable: "Tant va la cruche à l'eau qu'à la fin elle en boit" [The jug went to the well so often it eventually drank] (Louis Scutenaire, *Pour Balthazar*, Les Poquettes volantes, vol. 12 [La Louvière: Éditions Daily-Bul, 1967], [leaf 4]).

72. Th. Stcherbatsky [Fyodor Stcherbatskoy], "Le Temps," in *Le théorie de la connaissance et la logique chez le bouddhistes tardifs* (Paris: Libraire Orientaliste Paul Geuthner, 1926), 28; reprinted in *Essays on Time in Buddhism*, Bibliotheca Indo-Buddhica no. 78, ed. H. S. Prasad (Delhi: Sri Satguru, 1991), 457.

73. *Littré*; cf. the adage "Partout la Providence / Veut, en nous protégeant, / Niveler l'abondance, / Éparpiller l'argent" [Providence wants everywhere to protect us by leveling out excess through scattering money] (Pierre Jean de Béranger, "Les Contrebandiers," in *Œuvres complètes* [Paris: Fournier, 1836], 3:76).

74. Francis Ponge, *Le Savon* (Paris: Gallimard, 1967), 123.

75. Ponge, *Savon*, 67.

76. Marcel Spada, *Francis Ponge* (Paris: Seghers, 1979), 48–49.

77. On the metaphoric powers of usury more broadly, see Jacques Derrida, "La mythologie blanche," in *Marges de la philosophie* (Paris: Minuit, 1972), 249 *et seq*.

78. Francis Ponge, *Entretiens de Francis Ponge avec Philippe Sollers* (Paris: Gallimard, 1970), 111.

79. Francis Ponge, *Pour un Malherbe* (Paris: Gallimard, 1965), 180, 189.

80. Francis Ponge, *La fabrique du pré* (Genève: Skira, 1971), 23; emphases in original.

81. Ponge, *Malherbe*, 149.

82. On Ponge's relation to cratylism, see Gérard Genette, *Mimologiques: voyage en Cratylie* (Paris: Seuil, 1976), chap. 16, and Thomas Aron, *L'objet du texte et le texte-objet: La chèvre de Francis Ponge* (Paris: Les Éditeurs Français Réunis, 1980), chap. 9.

83. *Littré*, s.v. "sapte" (one would think even a *small* diamond inside a lemon would qualify).

84. Heidegger, recall, finds the empty capacity of the jug to signify a gift: the mystical beneficence of divine favor ("Das Ding," 170 *passim*).

85. Michael Riffaterre, "Ponge tautologique ou le fonctionnement du texte," in *Francis Ponge: Colloque de Cerisy* 10:18 (Paris: Union Générale d'Éditions, 1977), 66.

86. Michael Riffaterre, *Semiotics of Poetry* (Bloomington: Indiana University Press, 1984), 13.

87. See Samuel R. Levin, *Linguistic Structures in Poetry* (The Hague: Mouton, 1962),

42 *et seq.* Kevin Young makes the same association in his groundbreaking essay on Pritchard: "Signs of Repression: N. H. Pritchard's *The Matrix*," *Harvard Library Bulletin* 3.2 (1992): 36–43.

88. Riffaterre, *Semiotics*, 19. Riffaterre's penchant for totalizing statements ("every text," "tout poème," *et cetera*) should not lead one to dismiss less absolute reformulations of his argument.

89. Riffaterre, *Semiotics*, 19.

90. *Cf.* Riffaterre, *Semiotics*, 13.

91. Francis Ponge, "Tentative Orale," *Méthodes* (Paris: Gallimard, 1961), 245.

92. See *Cassell's Dictionary of Slang*, 2nd ed., ed. Jonathon Green (London: Weidenfeld & Nicolson, 2005), 389. The currency of the terms is corroborated by Martha Rosler's contemporaneous exploration of the language associated with "the Bowery bum" in her photo-text series *The Bowery in Two Inadequate Descriptive Systems*, which offers an interesting rhetorical companion to Pritchard's poem.

93. The implication of the following line's "a cc u ring p aga n / c r u c i fix ion" is less fixed and clear, with the sibilant of *crucifixion* priming both *accusing* and *accursing*, without dislodging the possibility of *occurring*; the only certainty is that the lines are a *crux* ("a difficulty which it torments or troubles one greatly to interpret or explain, a thing that puzzles the ingenuity; as 'a textual crux,'" as the *OED* overclarifies).

94. The urn would also be relevant for the final "silence" of the poem's setting; Philip Schwyzer establishes the association of urns and silence in English literature, from "the 'silent urns' of early modern elegies and funeral sermons" to the "quietness" of Keats's "foster-child of silence" (Philip Schwyzer, "No Joyful Voices: The Silence of the Urns in Browne's Hydriotaphia and Contemporary Archaeology," in *The Palgrave Handbook of Early Modern Literature and Science*, ed. Howard Marchitello and Evelyn Tribble [London: Palgrave, 2017], 301 *et passim*).

Chapter Six

1. Andy Warhol, *a: a novel* (New York: Grove Press, 1968), 100; *cf.* 76, 284. All quotations, including misspellings, appear as in the published text.

2. Warhol, *a*, 357. On the implications of the gendered production, and the ways in which "error, ambiguity, and mistranscription were signs of a process of textual production based not on any individual style or level of proficiency […] but rather on the movement of information through different physical spaces, registers of power, and technological mediations," see Paul Benzon, "Postwar Typewriting Culture, Andy Warhol's Bad Book, and the Standardization of Error," *PMLA* 125.1 (January 2010): 96.

3. See Reva Wolf, *Andy Warhol, Poetry, and Gossip in the 1960s* (Chicago: University of Chicago Press, 1997), 141. In light of Capote's quip about Kerouac's "typing," recall that Warhol was obsessed with Capote; his first exhibit consisted of drawings based on Capote's texts (Wolf, 10–11). See also Victor Bockris, *Warhol: The Biography* (Cambridge, MA: Da Capo, 2003), 91–92. On "mechanogenic writing, a form of writing that was not merely *about* typewriters, but *shaped* by the machine," see Rubén Gallo, *Mexican Modernity: The Avant-Garde and the Technological Revolution* (Cambridge, MA: MIT Press, 2005), 114.

4. Or rather, they seem to have typed quickly and worked slowly. Warhol recalls, "I

had never been around typists before so I didn't know how fast these little girls should be going. But when I think back on it I realize that they probably worked slow on purpose so that they could hang around the Factory more" (Andy Warhol and Pat Hackett, POPism: The Warhol Sixties [New York: Harcourt, 1980], 149). In a discussion of tape recorder technology, Name explains, "there are all these other gadets you can use for it and you can use a typewriter and and stuff like that ... I mean you can put one of those foot pedals on and and work with a foot pedal" (Warhol, *a*, 342). On the cultural context of amphetamines in relation to Warhol, see Juan A. Suárez, "Warhol's 1960s Films, Amphetamine, and Queer Materiality," *Criticism* 56.3 (Summer 2014): 623-52.

5. Bockris, *Warhol*, 557.

6. Warhol, *a*, 451.

7. Warhol, *a*, 314.

8. Gustavus Stadler, "'My Wife': The Tape Recorder and Warhol's Queer Ways of Listening," *Criticism* 56.3 (Summer 2014): 425-56. See Lucy Mulroney, "Editing Andy Warhol," *Grey Room* 46 (Winter 2012), for a more detailed account of the various editorial and design stages of the text.

9. *Cf.* Robert Morris's roughly contemporaneous work for tape, *Box with the Sound of Its Own Making* (1961; Seattle Art Museum).

10. *Cf.* Stéphane Mallarmé: "tout, au monde, existe pour aboutir à un livre" [everything, the whole world, exists in order to end up in a book] ("Le livre: instrument spirituel," in *Oeuvres complètes* [Paris: Gallimard, 1945], 378).

11. Helen R. Lane, quoted in Mulroney, "Editing," 47.

12. Warhol's *a* is not the only book to present the transcript as a literary genre. In addition to Kerouac's *Visions of Cody*, Ed Friedman's *The Telephone Book* (New York: Power Mad Press, 1979) plays out the endgame of New York School poetics by literalizing the basis of Frank O'Hara's "personism": "While I was writing I was realizing that if I wanted to I could use the telephone instead of writing the poem" (Frank O'Hara, *The Collected Poems*, ed. Donald Allen [Berkeley: University of California Press, 1995], 499). Or as Ondine puts it, "We never finished the poem, we just did the telephone" (Warhol, *a*, 250). Kenneth Goldsmith's *Soliloquy* (New York: Granary Books, 2001) extends the duration of Warhol's project and refocuses its scope, transcribing everything the author said for one week. In one revealing and felicitous conversation in *Soliloquy*, Liz Kotz points out the similarity between Goldsmith's project and *a*, although Goldsmith claims not to have known about the precedent. From another tradition, DJ culture has also led to projects such as those by The Spacewürm, *i listen: a document of digital voyeurism* (San Diego: Incommunicado Press, 1999), and Robin Rimbaud, *Warhol's Surfaces* (Erding, Germany: Intermedium CD017, 2003).

13. Warhol, *a*, 103.

14. See Michel Serres, *Le parasite* (Paris: Grasset, 1980).

15. Warhol, *a*, 111, 121, 184, 185, 190-191. Although the conversation seems to suggest otherwise, "200" more likely refers to the dosage than to the number of capsules; 200 mg is the published upper limit of the recommended adult dose for Secobarbitol (sodium quinalbitone). On the logic of the pharmakon, see Jacques Derrida, *Dissemination*, trans. Barbara Johnson (Chicago: University of Chicago Press, 1981), 95.

16. Warhol, *a*, 1-2, 207.

17. Ezra Pound, *The Cantos of Ezra Pound* (New York: New Directions, 1996), 710.

18. For examples, see Warhol, *a*, 235-236.

19. Warhol, *a*, 162.

20. Warhol, *a*, 114.

21. Jonathan Sterne, *The Audible Past: Cultural Origins of Sound Reproduction* (Durham, NC: Duke University Press, 2003), 223.

22. Warhol, *a*, 114.

23. For one insistent registration of "interference" and the noise in the channel, see Warhol, *a*, 203-205.

24. Warhol, *a*, 121.

25. Warhol, *a*, 275.

26. Such moves can be located elsewhere in Warhol's practice. His film *Harlot*, for just one instance, rechristens its subject, Jean Harlow, through the replacement of a single letter. The irreverent play of the title, however, also resonates with the work's filmic mechanism. *Harlot* was Warhol's first sound film and even before the soundtrack's grainy playback begins, the work's title announces a quasi-mechanical, imperfect duplication of sound.

27. Prefiguring the translations from speech to print that will be made by the typists, the book's speakers often spell out words by way of clarification and explanation (Warhol, *a*, 134, 158, 163, 260, 262, 342, *et cetera*); for one registration of the typist's uncertainty, see Warhol, *a*, 310.

28. Warhol, *a*, 27, 166, 211, 285, 313, 360.

29. Warhol, *a*, 254, 252, 244, 50.

30. Warhol, *a*, 433.

31. Warhol, *a*, 126-128, 224, 378, 385.

32. Warhol, *a*, 247; compare the earlier equation of "witness" and "witless" (145).

33. *Cf.* "She's got big balls, I tell ya" (Warhol, *a*, 311).

34. Warhol, *a*, 281.

35. Warhol, *a*, 310; the typist's hesitation is later justified when Rotten Rita (Kenneth Rapp), discussing Callas's early recording of Kundry, associates her with an exquisite boredom: "Parcival is so fuckin dull ... it's fabulous" (Warhol, *a*, 356).

36. Warhol, *a*, 125, 247, chap. 12/1. The Grove Press archives reveal that the words attributed to Ondine in this passage were in fact spoken by Chuck Wein, demonstrating that the work is not a *roman à clef*, and furthermore that the logic of narrative rather than character (or biographic) continuity governs the novel (Mulroney, "Editing," 60-61).

37. Warhol, *a*, 95. Sally Beauman complains: "Because Ondine's brain seems irretrievably addled with amphetamine, most of what he says takes the form of grunts, squeals, and bad puns" (Beauman, review of *a: a novel*, *New York Times* [12 January 1969], 32). As if making a pun on that punning, such actions are in fact known as "punding," a term coined by G. Rylander to describe the compulsive behavior that characterizes the effects of amphetamine overuse. Indeed, between 1964 and 1966, precisely the period in which Warhol was conducting his experiment with the effects of sustained amphetamine use, Rylander was gathering similar data at the Clinic for Forensic Psychiatry in Stockholm, studying the effects of chronic intake of high doses of phenmetrazine. See G. Rylander et al., "Preludin-narkomaner från klinisk och medicinsk-kriminologisk synpunkt," *Svenska Lakartidningen* 63.52 (28 December 1966): 49-73; G. Rylander et al., "Psychoses and the Punding and Choreiform Syndromes in Addiction to Central Stimulant Drugs," *Psychiatria, Neurologia, Neurochirurgia* 75.3 (May-June 1972): 203-212. One might compare the "filthy pun stage" to the psychotic mechanisms described by

Jean-Pierre Brisset, Louis Wolfson, and Raymond Roussel as they were of interest to post-structuralist thinkers; see Gilles Deleuze, *Le schizo et les langues* (Paris: Gallimard, 1970), 5–23; Michel Foucault, preface to *La logique grammaire* (Paris: Tchou, 1970) and *Raymond Roussel* (Paris: Gallimard, 1963).

38. Bockris, *Warhol*, 192; Robert Mazzocco, "a a a a a …," *New York Review of Books* 12.8 (24 April 1969): 34–37, 34.

39. Warhol, *a*, 207.

40. Wayne Koestenbaum, *Andy Warhol* (New York: Viking, 2001), 3.

41. Warhol, *a*, 404; *cf.* 325.

42. Warhol, *a*, 263.

43. Warhol, *a*, 76, 258, 278, 284.

44. Warhol, *a*, 265.

45. Hal Foster, *The Return of the Real* (Cambridge, MA: MIT Press, 1996), 141. For a discussion of the "strange names" of Czechoslovakians, see Warhol, *a*, 73. Additionally, note Warhol's explanation in the first chapter: "I'm not really pop. I'm sort of a little bit 1930 bohemian" (11). Linich claims that the title was an homage to the typographic gimmick of e. e. cummings's signature (Warhol, *a*, 453).

46. For a reading of the implications of the trademark, see Charles Reeve, "Warhol's Death and Assembly-Line Autobiography," *Biography* 34.4 (Fall 2011): 668.

47. Wayne Koestenbaum, *The Queen's Throat: Opera, Homosexuality, and the Mystery of Desire* (New York: Poseidon, 1993), 135. For points at which recordings become the focus of the plot of *a*, such as it is, see 139, 147, 171–172, 357; for the rituals of the cult of Callas, see 59, 241, 309, 369. Howard Klein describes the "blind adulation" that accompanied "irrational and all-consuming dedication" to La Divina (Howard Klein, "Maria Callas's Imperious Carmen," *New York Times* [24 January 1965], X23). Or as Beauman puts it, less sympathetically, "Ondine himself seems to be the silliest of intellectual snobs, boring on for ages about the last exquisite diminuendo in 'Lucia di Lammermoor'" (*Times* review, 32).

48. See Arnold H. Lubasch, "Jubilant Met Crowd Hails Callas Return," *New York Times* (20 March 1965), 17.

49. Sherman L. Morrow, "The In Crowd and the Out Crowd," *New York Times* (18 July 1965), 12–20.

50. Warhol, *a*, 264–265; see also the later mention of "doctor Schooll's corn … corn remedy" and the importance of "the difference between a wen and a wart," as well as additional occurrences of "corn" and the play between "pustural" and "pastoral" (95, 324, 325, 378); Benzon, "Postwar Typewriting," 102.

51. *New York Review of Books* 12.8 (24 April 1969): 36.

52. When Rink complains about the "complete insensibility of the people to what's happening now," he may have meant (or even have said) the proximate "insensitivity" (Warhol, *a*, 162).

53. Warhol, *a*, 347; *cf.* 249. 49, 189, 379.

54. Warhol, *a*, 379.

55. Warhol, *a*, 330.

56. Warhol, *a*, 449.

57. Warhol, *a*, 240.

58. Warhol, *a*, 241, 242; see 238, for an earlier discussion of Chinese scrolls.

59. Warhol, *a*, 74, 244.

60. For a striking example of this echolalic vocabulary, see the passage where "calling," "called," and "calls" appear just before "Callas" (Warhol, *a*, 193). Note also, in particular, "call us" (40, 232).

61. Warhol, *a*, 258.

62. Warhol, *a*, 57.

63. Warhol, *a*, 113, 158-159, 181, 223, 259, 347, 350, *et cetera*. Harold Schonberg describes Callas's performance as "operating," and his assessment was repeated verbatim elsewhere (Schonberg, "Opera: Maria Callas Returns to Met in 'Tosca,'" *New York Times* [20 March 1965], 17; "La Callas," *New York Times* [21 March 1965], E2). Against the continuous chatter of *a*, operators, like loud opera, are one of the few things permitted to break into conversations (see, for instance, Warhol, *a*, 363). "Operation" and "opera" appear together explicitly, as well as with the implicit etymological pun behind "All right Maria, do your work" [Latin *opera*] (Warhol, *a*, 72, 356). The conversation recorded on the first half of the tenth tape focuses emphatically on both the word "operated" and the absence of "operators" (227). Additionally, the operator is called to help find a drugstore (363).

64. Warhol, *a*, 378.

65. Bockris, *Warhol*, 192.

66. Warhol, *a*, 358-362, 370, 371; *cf.* 192, 214, 225, and the "pin holes" at 342. For another discussion of needles, see 360; for another discussion of Callas's high notes, 197. Notice also the equation of opera and "a" in the line "Opera: Aaaaaaaaaaaaah" (383).

67. Warhol, *a*, 52, 59, 99, 123, 174, 285-286, 301, 306, 309, 324-325, 378, 380-383, 427, 438, 450.

68. Koestenbaum, *Queen's Throat*. Warhol proposed a television show to be called *Phoney* and made a related video (1973). For the misspelling in *a*, see Warhol, *a*, 165, 191; correct versions occur at 59, 424, 440.

69. See Warhol, *a*, 368, 372. On the queered sexual connotations of matrimonial "fidelity," with respect to recording technology, see Stadler, "My Wife," 427 *et seq.*

70. Warhol, *a*, 141, 386, 282, 374, 450; for other moments of operatic impersonation, see 104, 238, 253. Speed, once again, is at issue in the fabrication of the falsetto: "Tape speeds up to Munchkin chatter" (390). *Ondine*, from the modern Latin *Undina* of Paracelsus, derives from *unda* [Latin "wave"].

71. Schonberg, "Callas Returns," 17; Jean-Pierre Lenoir, "Paris Welcomes Callas as Tosca," *New York Times* (20 February 1965), 17.

72. Warhol and Hackett, *POPism*, 303. See the discussion with David Bourdon from 1962-1963, in *I'll Be Your Mirror: The Selected Andy Warhol Interviews, Thirty-Seven Conversations with the Pop Master*, ed. Kenneth Goldsmith (New York: Carroll & Graf, 2004), 8-9.

73. Koestenbaum, *Andy Warhol*, 31. As Bockris understates it, "All four [of the typists involved with *a*] shared a disinclination to spell correctly" (Bockris, *Warhol*, 453).

74. Ariana Stassinopoulos, *Maria Callas: The Woman behind the Legend* (New York: Simon & Schuster, 1981), 121. For a mention of Bernstein in *a*, see 64.

75. Schonberg, "Callas Returns," 17; Howard Klein, untitled article, *New York Times* (23 May 1965), X14; "Return of the Prodigal Daughter," *Time* (26 March 1965), 64; unsigned article, *New York Times* (21 March 1965), E2.

76. Warhol, *a*, 59, 253; earlier "Callas" and "ohms" are used in the same sentence (74).

77. Warhol, *a*, 96.

78. Patrick S. Smith, *Andy Warhol's Art and Films*, Studies in the Fine Arts: The AvantGarde, no. 54 (Ann Arbor, MI: UMI Research Press, 1986): 320. Compare similar comments by George Hartman, Gerard Malanga, Henry Geldzahler, and Richard Mazzocco (Patrick S. Smith, *Warhol: Conversations about the Artist* [Ann Arbor, MI: UMI Research Press, 1988], 12, 41, 62, 186; Mazzocco, "a a a a a …," 34).

79. Warhol, *a*, 376; *cf.* 181, 306, 399.

80. Bockris, *Warhol*, 171.

81. "Rosenberg" occurs in *a* in the context of accusations of being "a commie spy" (Warhol, *a*, 151); given the foregrounded transcription of the book, this occurrence reminds one that Ethel was sentenced, in essence, for her typing.

82. The sign is also a reminder that the image comes from a photographic document of a room that was legally beyond descriptive language. After the first state electrocution in New York, expert witnesses attending executions were "required to sign a statement affirming that they would never discuss what they saw in Sing-Sing's death chamber" (Th. Metzger, *Blood and Volts: Edison, Tesla, and the Invention of the Electric Chair* [Brooklyn: Autonomedia, 1996], 171). With all of the ear-splitting opera played in the Factory while these images of silence were being (re)produced, Warhol's deadpan sensibility might well have registered the irony of the chair's location in *Sing Sing*.

83. Transcribed from image.

84. George Oppen, *New Collected Poems*, ed. Michael Davidson (New York: New Directions, 2002), 35. Malanga had corresponded with Oppen in 1963, just after Oppen's return to poetry with *The Materials* (New York: New Directions, 1962). See Mandeville Special Collections Library, University of California at San Diego, MSS 0016, box 7, folder 13.

85. See Sterne, *Audible Past*, chap. 1; Avital Ronell, *The Telephone Book: Technology, Schizophrenia, Electric Speech* (Lincoln: University of Nebraska Press, 1989), 451.

86. Goldsmith, *Mirror*, 69; see Edison's notebook for 17 July 1877, as well as the final entry in his list of uses for the phonograph: "connection with the telephone" (quoted in Sterne, 202).

87. Sterne, *Audible Past*, 301. See also Ronell, *Telephone Book*, 98, 248. For all of its deathly resonance, Edison's phonograph was also underwritten by his love of opera and in particular the bel canto repertoire that Callas reinvigorated. See Allen S. Weiss, *Breathless: Sound Recording, Disembodiment, and the Transformation of Lyrical Nostalgia* (Middletown, CT: Wesleyan University Press, 2002), 95-96.

88. Mazzocco, "a a a a a …," 34.

89. Warhol, *a*, 207, 373; *cf.* 114-115. For the ghostly "spirit" of the telephonic voice in *a*, see 124 and 162.

90. Warhol, *a*, 132-136, 174-175, 265, 384.

91. Warhol, *a*, 144, 270, 384, 389. On the first page of *a*, Ondine connects an exploit in which he dressed up in a sheet and "felt like a ghost" with vocal disturbances: "some of my throat is gone." Mazzocco refers to the characters in *a* as "spook hour hysterics" (Mazzocco, "a a a a a …," 36).

92. Warhol, *a*, 184 (*cf.* 89); Sterne, *Audible Past*, 290, 298.

93. Warhol, *a*, 35, 362, 365; *cf.* 427.

94. Warhol, *a*, 78, 378; *cf.* 382. 91, 332, 353, 357, 383.

95. Warhol, *a*, 374, 389, 254, 353, *et cetera*.

96. Warhol, *a*, 372, 383.

97. Stelios Galatopoulos, *Maria Callas: Sacred Monster* (New York: Simon & Schuster, 1998), 377.

98. "Return of the Prodigal Daughter," *Time* (26 March 1965), 64.

99. Warhol first saw Cage in the summer of 1948, when the latter gave a talk to the Outlines Club at Carnegie Tech (David Revill, *The Roaring Silence: John Cage, a Life* [New York: Arcade, 1992], 94). Many points of personal contact would follow, including Warhol's amorous 1951 correspondence with Tommy Jackson, a printer who, like Cage, was at Black Mountain College (Wolf, *Andy Warhol*, 11). Warhol and Cage would have been most directly connected by way of filmmaker Emile de Antonio, as well as John Cale, and two shared technical collaborators: Billy Klüver worked with both artists in 1966, Ronald Nameth in 1967. "I think John Cage has been very influential," Warhol admitted in 1963, and although some suspicion remains about the authenticity of Warhol's statements in this interview, the point is that the connection was, at the very least, obvious to Gene Swenson (G. R. Swenson, "What Is Pop Art? Answers from 8 Painters, Part I" [1963], reprinted in Goldsmith, *Mirror*, 20). Indeed, Ted Berrigan went so far as to collapse the two in his 1965 "Interview with John Cage," a spurious interview that has Cage ventriloquize Warhol with misattributed quotations lifted from earlier Warhol interviews, including the one with Swenson (Berrigan, *Bean Spasms* [New York: Kulcher, 1967], n.p.). In conversation with Ruth Hirschman in 1963, Warhol would say, "I would grant him [Cage], you know, a lot on purely experimental intellectual 'freeing the other artists' basis" (Goldsmith, *Mirror*, 42). Cage later reciprocated by noting the similarity of their projects (Jean Stein, *Edie: An American Biography* [New York: Alfred A. Knopf, 1982], 235).

100. John Cage, *Silence: Lectures and Writings by John Cage* (Middletown, CT: Wesleyan University Press, 1961), 8. Branden W. Joseph's important notice of the similarity between Cage's account and a passage in Henri Bergson's *Creative Evolution* casts doubt on the veracity of Cage's uncorroborated story (Joseph, "White on White," *Critical Inquiry* 27 [Autumn 2000]: 105–6). Cage most likely simply became aware of his tinnitus.

101. *Chamber* attracts few other words: *music*, significantly given the soundscapes at issue; a related set of disciplinary terms (*judge*, *Senate*, and *torture*); *burial*, in a narrow range of archeological uses; and some specialized scientific *termes de métier*. All other instances are now archaic (*bridal*, *bed-*, *-maid*, *-pot*, *Star*).

102. Theresa M. Collins and Lisa Gitelman, eds., *Thomas Edison and Modern America: An Introduction with Documents* (New York: Palgrave, 2002), 73.

103. Robert Smithson, "A Sedimentation of the Mind: Earth Projects," in *Robert Smithson: The Collected Writings*, ed. Jack Flam (Berkeley: University of California Press, 1996).

Index

Abrams, M. H., 24
abstraction (formal), 4, 5, 11, 28-31, 83, 85, 101, 110, 134, 139, 146, 148-49, 210-11n2
Acker, Kathy, 212n6
Adorno, Theodor, 215n27
affordance, 2, 4, 141
Ahmed, Sarah, 19-20, 196n82
Akili, Sababa, 123
Alberti, Leon Battista, 41
Aldington, Richard, 21, 22
allegory (formal), 6-7, 8, 10-11, 17-18, 19-20, 28, 33-37, 39, 41-42, 44, 45, 50, 53, 58, 72-75, 80, 95, 97, 99-100, 103, 106-7, 109, 126-27, 133, 142, 151, 154-56, 159, 160-68, 178, 230n3, 232n31, 236n93
Anabaptist sects, 98
anagram. *See* paragram
anamorphosis, 11, 75
Andrews, Bruce, 84, 88-89, 212n3
annominatio, 50, 75
Antin, David, 43
antonomasia, 70, 205n41
Apollinaire, Guillaume, 6, 53-68, 74, 76, 115, 204n29, 205n45
Arensberg, Walter, 78
ASCII (American Standard Code for Information Interchange), 210-11
Ashbery, John, 27, 35, 81
Asphodel (bookstore). *See* Lowell, Jim

Atkins, Russell, 4, 5, 7, 101-42, 146, 148-49, 151, 220n3, 221n17, 221n20, 221-22n21, 222n28, 222-23n30, 223n32, 229n107
Auster, Paul, 49

Bach, Johann, 160
Baldessari, John, 34-35
Ball, Hugo, 27, 28, 55
Barrett Browning, Elizabeth, 197n14
Baum, Erica, 229-30n113
Beaulieu, Derek, 192n15, 214n17
Bell, Alexander, 178, 183
Bely, Andrei, 45-47
Benzon, Paul, 236n2
Bergson, Henri, 242n100
Bernstein, Charles, 10, 32, 87-88, 213n14
Bernstein, Leonard, 180, 240n74
Berrigan, Ted, 27, 242n99
Bertram, Lillian-Yvonne, 151-52
Best, Stephen, 14-15
Bissett, Bill, 84
Blake, William, 127-29, 130-31, 133, 228n95
Blau DuPlessis, Rachel, 206n66
Bockris, Victor, 171
Booker, Peter, 1
Bookstaver, May, 67
Borch-Jacobsen, Mikkel, 191n2
Borges, Jorge Luis, 25-26
Bouguereau, William-Adolphe, 235n70
bovines, 44, 98, 103, 202n101

Bowery, 149–50, 156, 158, 232n30, 236n92
Braque, Georges, 159
Breton, 52, 121
Breton, André, 27
Breunig, LeRoy, 204n29
Bridges, Harry, 94
Broda, Martine, 205n49
Brooks, Gwendolyn, 2–3, 7, 15, 191n5, 191n6; cf. 96
Bruce, Lennart, 212n6
Brunon, Bernard, 209n120
Bryant, John, 93
Bunyan, John, 159
Burleigh, H. T., 103, 220n4
Burns, Robert, 148

Cage, John, 5, 16–17, 185–86, 242n99, 242n100
Cale, John, 242n100
Callas, Maria, 173, 175, 177–80, 184–86, 238n35, 239n47, 240n60, 240n63, 240n66, 241n87
Callus, Ivan, 204n32
calque, 25, 50, 70, 73, 155, 161, 200n65
Capote, Truman, 170, 236n3
Carco, Francis, 67
Carlyle, Thomas, 197n18
Carmines, Al, 143
Cassedy, Steven, 193–94n31, 200n55
Caumont, Jacques, 209n120
Cendrars, Blaise, 6, 48–53, 203n8, 203n14
Césaire, Aimé, 77–78, 209n130, 210n134
chance, 4, 6, 12, 14, 24, 28, 30, 34, 35, 36, 47, 57, 58, 64, 65, 74, 77, 119, 193n31, 209n128, 219n91, 219n1
Chaucer, Geoffrey, 104
Chester, Greville John, 76, 209–10n131
Churchill, Suzanne, 72
Chvatík, Květoslav, 193n29
Clark, Helen, 146, 150–51, 230–31n14
Clark, T. J., 59, 61
Clément, Vincent, 210n134
Codrescu, Andrei, 212n6
coffin, 43–44, 167–68
Cole, Lori, 209n117
collage, 31, 50, 56–58, 80, 127, 203n8, 204n27, 212n7

Columbia University, 143, 159, 167
communicative function, 1, 8–11, 16, 19–20, 22, 34, 76, 84–86, 186–87, 200n55
Conceptual writing, 32
concrete poetry, 5, 6, 43, 105–6, 112–18, 137–42, 143, 148, 161, 224–25n56, 227n91, 230n3
Coolidge, Clark, 26–28, 29, 31, 47, 80, 81, 84, 88, 198n30, 212n6
coquille, 53–55, 76
Cortázar, Julio, 80
Cournot, Michel, 76
Crane, Stephen, 42, 44, 201n90
Cravan, Arthur, 208n110
Creeley, Robert, 8, 10, 13, 19, 194n38, 194n41
critical description, 15–16, 18, 53, 86, 187, 196n82, *et passim*
cromorne, 160, 234n64
Culler, Jonathan, 196n72
Cummings, E. E., 146, 239n45
Curie, Marie, 68

Dada, 27–28, 55, 80, 83, 162, 198n31, 203n8, 210n136, 213–14n15
Dalì, Salvador, 78
Damon, Maria, 231n15
D'Annunzio, Gabriele, 70
Dante Alighieri, 78
Darragh, Tina, 211–12n3, 212n6
da Silva, Linda Molina, 54–55
Dassin, Jules, 223–24n43
de Antonio, Emile, 242n99
de Campos, Augusto, 115
de Campos, Haroldo, 22
de Corvey, Jean-Frédéric-Auguste Lemière, 234n67
Degas, Edgar, 7
Delaunay, Robert, 59–61
Delaunay, Sonia, 48, 59, 76
DeLio, Thomas, 217n51
de Man, Paul, 11, 13, 15
Dencker, Klaus Peter, 225n56
Derain, André, 53–55
Derksen, Jeff, 214n23
Derrida, Jacques, 4, 6, 11–12, 39, 48, 52, 62–65, 72, 77, 79, 142, 191n2, 192n13,

205n41, 235n77, 237n15. *See also* signature
Dessoir, Max, 1
DiPalma, Ray, 83
disorientation, 4, 7, 9, 19, 20, 34, 43, 82–83, 87, 91, 105, 107, 108, 133, 187, 196n77, 196n82, 214n21, 216n41, 222–23n30
Ditto (machine). *See* duplicator
Dodge, Mabel, 74
Dorsey, Thomas, 104
Dos Passos, John, 48, 94, 206n52
Dossi, Dosso, 75
Dreyer, Lynne, 212n3
Duchamp, Marcel, 75–77, 192n16, 209n119, 209n120, 209n128
duplicator, 5, 103, 111, 112, 123, 124–27, 131, 134, 137–41, 227n91, 229n108, 229n112
Dusman, Linda, 217n51
Dydo, Ulla, 67, 206n56

Eastman, George, 51–53
Edison, Thomas, 183, 186, 241n86, 241n87
Edwards, Brent Hayes, 105–6, 221n17
Eliot, T. S., 23, 155
Ellington, Duke, 105
Ernst, Max, 80
Etiemble, René, 76
etymology, 3, 11, 31, 50, 51–53, 70, 71, 72–73, 78, 94, 96, 98, 100, 104, 118–19, 123, 137, 143, 145, 146, 150, 153, 154–55, 157, 158–59, 161, 166, 175, 179, 183, 192n9, 198n31, 200–201n65, 206n69, 207n76, 208n110, 220n11, 226n83, 233n39, 234n66, 236n93, 240n70
Evans, Ahmed, 5, 123

F. A. O. Schwarz, 68
Faulkner, William, 43–44, 45, 202n101, 210n133
Finlay, Ian Hamilton, 115, 118
Fluxus, 143
Fogel, Aaron, 39, 201n86
Folsom, Ed, 25
Forrest-Thomson, Veronica, 1–2, 10, 20

Foucault, Michel, 13–15, 76
Fraenkel, Béatrice, 209n129
Fried, Michael, 211n2
Friedman, Joel, 111–12
Futurisms, 9, 54–55, 68–70, 73, 74, 83, 87, 143, 193n29, 193–94n31, 194n34, 206n66, 208n103, 208n106, 208n110, 213–14n15

Gappmayr, Heinz, 115
García Lorca, Federico, 80
Garcia Villa, José, 197n11, 215n27
Gauvreau, Claude, 83
Gavronsky, Serge, 167
Geismar, Maxwell, 148
Genette, Gérard, 235n82
genre, 21–22, 28, 29, 31, 34, 35, 39, 47, 49, 50, 74, 94, 105, 115, 127, 137, 141–42, 170, 184, 197n11, 205n49, 209n117, 225n56, 229–30n114, 234n64, 237n12
Gilbert, Creighton, 75
Gilmore, Susan, 206n63
Glazier, Loss Pequeño, 211n3
Glissant, Édouard, 76
Gluck, Nathan, 180–81
glyph, 1–12, 52, 55, 57–58, 68, 75, 98, 99, 100, 103–9, 112, 115, 120–22, 126, 127, 134, 137–42, 143, 146–47, 152, 160, 161, 176–77, 178, 186, 218n72, 219n86, 226n75, 226n76, 226n78, 226n79, 226n80, 229n105, 229n107, 229–30n114, 231n15
Godzich, Wlad, 21, 196n3
Goldsmith, Kenneth, 237n12
Golston, Michael, 214n20
Gomringer, Eugen, 115
Gough-Cooper, Jennifer, 209n120
Goyet, François, 205n49
Grenier, Robert, 84
Greuze, Jean-Baptiste, 235n70
Grimaud, Michel, 207n92
Grögerová, Bohumila, 115
Guyotat, Pierre, 22

Hall, Jon, 123
Hamacher, Werner, 205n41, 210n136
Hampton, Fred, 3

Hancock, Tim, 69–70, 207n73
Handke, Peter, 212n6
hapax legomenon. *See* neologism
Hassink, Bennett (Bud), 228n94
Hausser, Michel, 209n130
Hayden, Robert, 101
Hayden, Sarah, 73, 220n8
Hedley, Jane, 191n5
Heidegger, Martin, 161–62, 235n84
Hejinian, Lyn, 3–4, 7, 28–34, 39, 45, 47, 65, 84, 89–90, 198n35, 199n39, 199n44, 199n49, 214n19
Heller-Roazen, Daniel, 204n32
Henderson, Stephen, 146
Hiršal, Josef, 115
Hodge, Robert, 39, 41
Hofer, Matthew, 69
Holbein, Hans, 75
Holland, Joyce. *See* Morice, Dave
Holmes, David, 118
Homer, 154–55
homophones, 37, 51, 65, 67, 71, 76–77, 94, 148, 154, 168, 176, 178, 185, 200n61, 205n45, 218n61, 233n47, 240n60
Hughes, Langston, 150
Huxley, Aldous, 127–30

Inman, Peter, 4, 6, 7, 79–100, 210–11n2, 212n6, 212–13n11, 213n14, 213–14n15, 214n19, 214n21, 214n23, 215n27, 216n40, 217n51, 217n55, 219n79
Ionesco, Eugène, 42–43, 44–45, 46

Jackson, Mahalia, 101, 104–5, 220–21n14
Jackson, Tommy, 242n99
Jacob, Max, 54, 67, 207n85
Jakobson, Roman, 7, 9, 13, 16, 119, 193–94n31, 194n34
Jamison, Anne, 193n31
Jauss, Hans Robert, 58–59
Jenkins, Grant Matthew, 211n3
Johns, Jasper, 149, 228n98
Johnson, Abby and Ronald, 108
Johnson, Barbara, 235n70
Johnson, Ronald, 115
Johnson, Samuel, 71

Jordan, Norman, 223–24n43
Joseph, Branden, 242n100
Joyce, James, 148

Kahnweiler, Daniel-Henry, 53–54, 59–61
Kakridis, Ioannis, 120
Kamuf, Peggy, 204n37
Kant, Immanuel, 21
Katz, Steve, 212n6
Kaufmann, Michael, 43
Kennedy, Jacqueline (Onassis), 177, 185
Kent, George, 181n5
Kepes, György, 35
Kermode, Frank, 154
Kerouac, Jack, 81, 170, 214n20, 236n3, 237n12
khôra, 38–39, 44, 201n75
King, Martin Luther, Jr., 110, 223n34, 224n43
Kittay, Jeffrey, 21, 196n3
Klüver, Billy, 242n10
Kodak, 48–49, 51–53, 203n14. *See also* Eastman, George
Koestenbaum, Wayne, 176, 177, 179
Kostelanetz, Richard, 143
Kotz, Liz, 237n12
Krauss, Rosalind, 210–11n2
Kristeva, Julia, 12, 15, 38–39, 57
Kryss, T. L., 112–18, 134–35, 224n44

Lacan, Jacques, 176, 191n2
Lally, Michael, 212n3, 212n6
Lang, Doug, 212n4, 212n6
Language poetry, 6, 79, 84, 87, 90, 92, 211–12n3
Larson-Xu, Marty, 232n25
Leonardo da Vinci, 23, 31–33
Le Rouge, Gustave, 49–52
letter (alphabetic). *See* glyph
letterpress, 5, 24, 26, 42–44, 54, 140–41, 229, 231n16
Levin, Samuel R., 167
Lévi-Strauss, Claude, 12, 195n50
Levy, D. A., 101, 111–12, 115–18, 123–42, 219n1, 220n3, 224n97, 227–28n92, 228n94, 228n97, 229n108, 229n112
LeWitt, Sol, 232n25

Index   247

lineation, 1, 4, 6, 21-28, 29-35, 36-38, 39, 41, 44, 45-46, 57, 59, 81, 91, 123-24, 127, 130, 148, 154, 168, 197n13, 197n14, 199n44, 199n49, 211n2, 214n20, 215n27, 217n51, 218n62, 218n65
lion, 2-3, 74, 191n6
Living Theatre, 143
Livy, Titus, 58
Lotto, Lorenzo, 75
Lowell, Amy, 67
Lowell, Jim, 5, 118, 123, 131, 225n59, 229n112
Lowenfels, Walter, 101, 219n1
Loy, Mina, 6, 7, 68-75, 187, 206n63, 206n71, 207n76, 208n103, 208n110
Lucas, Charles, 110
Lydgate, John, 148
lyric, 6, 8, 21, 22-23, 24-26, 28, 30-34, 36, 37, 39, 40, 47, 48, 54, 56, 57, 58, 65, 70-75, 84, 85, 91, 94, 103, 106, 108, 111, 122, 127, 148, 154, 187, 239n50. *See also* genre

macaronics, 38, 51, 67, 69, 73, 75, 99
machines, 1, 3, 10-11, 14, 16, 19, 43, 48-49, 56, 76-77, 103, 111, 112, 120-21, 124-26, 137, 141, 143, 157, 172, 173, 179, 180, 181, 183, 187, 194-95n42, 203n14, 225n72, 236n3, 238n26. *See also* medium
Major, René, 143
Malanga, Gerard, 182-83, 241n84
Mallarmé, Stéphane, 7-8, 9, 76, 101, 210n136, 237n10
Malone, Kirby, 212n3
Mantler, Michael, 81
Maranda, Michael, 197n18, 202n94
Marcus, Sharon, 14-15
Marinetti, Filippo Tommaso, 55, 68, 69, 71
Marron, John, 84
Marx, Karl, 94, 98
materiality, 1-16, 24, 35, 44-45, 75, 86, 105, 142, 185-87, 242n23. *See also* typography
Mayer, Bernadette, 212n6
McCaffery, Steve, 9
McFadden, David, 84

McGann, Jerome, 199n39
medium, 5, 15-16, 85, 105, 183-84, 120, 125-27, 137, 141-42, 143, 172-73, 178, 179, 182-83, 184, 185-86, 217n51, 236n2, 236-37n4, 240n68. *See also* paper
meiosis, 199n49
Melnick, David, 83, 84, 97
Melville, Herman, 29, 208n110
Mercury, 172, 183
Messerli, Douglas, 212n3, 213n15
Microsoft Word, 141, 225n74, 226n75
Miller, Adam David, 149
Miller, Henry, 171
Miller, Jacques-Alain, 6-7, 192-93n19
Milner, Jean-Claude, 195n57
Milton, John, 76
mimeograph. *See* duplicator
mimesis, 18, 31, 42, 48-50, 84-86, 133-34, 214n23, 241n82
Mitchell, Roscoe, 84, 91-92
Monotype, 25-26, 231n16
Morice, Dave, 83
Morier, Henri, 50
Morrison, Van, 101
Morrissey, Paul, 178
Motherwell, Robert, 27-28, 80, 198n31
Mozart, Wolfgang, 70, 72
Mukařovský, Jan, 8-10, 34, 36, 39, 193n29, 200n55
Muntu workshop, 5, 123-24, 221n17, 223-24n43, 226n83

names, 4, 6, 38, 48-79, 94, 98-100, 152, 169, 176-77, 203n14, 204n29, 204n31, 204n32, 204n37, 205n41, 205n49, 207n92, 208n110, 209n110, 209n129, 212n5, 217n55, 219n81, 239n45, 241n86, 241n87. *See also* signature
neologism, 82-84, 98, 143, 152, 169, 175, 213n15, 219n79, 221n20
Ngai, Sianne, 231n14
Nicholas, Nick, 226n79
Nicholls, Peter, 34
Nielsen, Aldon Lynn, 104, 122, 149, 220n20, 221-22n21, 226n82, 230n3, 231n15

Noland, Carrie, 210n134
nom de plume, 50, 51, 53, 58, 66, 68, 74, 98–99, 212n5, 217n55. *See also* names
novel, 2, 5, 8, 16, 25, 31, 38, 39, 40–47, 48–50, 53, 76, 83–84, 107, 158, 170, 171–72, 177, 184, 216n40, 218n58, 238n36, 238n47, 248n36. *See also* genre

Odum, Howard, 101–2, 103, 220n4
O'Hara, Frank, 27, 237n12
opacity. *See* transparency
opera, 1, 174, 176, 177, 178–81, 183, 184–85, 234n67, 238n35, 239n47, 240n63, 240n66, 240n70, 241n82, 241n87. *See also* Callas, Maria
Oppen, George, 13, 183, 241n84
Orange, Tom, 198n30
Ossola, Carlo, 204n31
O'Sullivan, Maggie, 84

panther. *See* lion
paper, iv, 8, 9, 15, 22, 30, 41, 44, 72, 96–99, 105, 124, 125–27, 139, 141, 197n18, 203n8, 211n2, 217n53, 219n91, 229n113, 233n39, 239n58
Papini, Giovanni, 68–72, 208n110
paragram, 3, 6, 12, 13, 15, 19, 48, 53, 54, 55, 57–59, 63, 64, 65, 68–69, 70, 71, 73, 74, 75, 76, 78, 82, 94, 95, 96, 97, 98, 99, 154–55, 156, 157, 158, 159, 161, 166, 174, 175, 200–201n65, 204n31, 204n32, 205n49, 209n69, 210n136, 238n26, *et passim*
Pater, Walter, 22–24, 39
Perloff, Marjorie, 82, 90, 206n69, 212n3, 216n40
Pfeiffer, Ludwig, 1, 14, 191n2
Phillips, Tom, 34
phonograph, 143, 172, 173, 179, 183–86, 241n86, 241n87
Piaget, Jean, 4, 29–30, 199n44
Picasso, Pablo, 59–63, 66, 186
Plato, 38
politics, 1, 5–6, 15–20, 79, 84–86, 94, 101, 110, 118, 121, 123, 181, 208n106, 209n129, 210n134, 226n79. *See also* radical formalism

pollen, 65, 72, 205n45
Pollock, Jackson, 98
Ponge, Francis, 63, 137, 159–67, 234n64, 235n82
Pound, Ezra, 22, 172, 192n11, 193n23
Preito, Eric, 210n134
Princeton Encyclopedia of Poetry and Poetics, 24
Pritchard, Norman (N. H.), 4, 6–7, 10, 84, 143–69, 230n3, 230–31n14, 232n31, 232n34, 232n35, 233n39, 236n92
prose, 4–5, 21–47, 48–49, 53, 59, 81, 84, 90, 91, 94, 105, 130, 166, 186–87, 193n23, 196n3, 197n11, 197n14, 198n35, 199n39, 200n55, 201n86, 202n94, 216n42, 217n51, 218n65
prosopopoeia, 6, 172, 206n66

Quartermain, Peter, 194n38
queer, 19–20, 36, 148, 240n69. *See also* disorientation

radical formalism, 11, 17, 19, 187, 196n72. *See also* politics
Rancière, Jacques, 17–19, 223n40
Reed, Anthony, 146, 148–49, 153
Reese, Marshall, 212n3
referential fallacy, 9
Renfrew, Alastair, 194n34
Renker, Elizabeth, 208n110
Riffaterre, Michael, 6, 37, 58, 166–67, 177, 192n19, 236n88
Rigolot, François, 205n49
Rilke, Rainer Maria, 80
Rimbaud, Arthur, 76, 80
Risset, Jacqueline, 205n49
rjs, 131, 132, 228n104
Roberts, Jennifer, 134, 137, 228n98
Roehr, Peter, 220n8
Rosenzweig, Phyllis, 212n3
Rosler, Martha, 236n92
Roth, Joseph, 40–42, 44, 45, 47
Roussel, Raymond, 75–77, 209n120, 238–39n37
rules, 14–15, 28, 32, 39, 40, 58, 111, 172, 173–74, 178, 181, 196n77, 241n82

Salmon, André, 67
Sandburg, Carl, 155
Sappol, Michael, 80
Saroyan, Aram, 84, 212n6
Saussure, Ferdinand de, 6, 9, 12–13, 16, 26, 52, 57–58, 63–64, 166, 194n36, 204n32, 205n49
Sayer, Henry, 194n42
Schneede, Uwe, 80
Schwob, Marcel, 55
Schwyzer, Philip, 236n94
Scots, 82, 97, 145, 212–13n11
screen printing, 5, 131, 134, 136–37, 139–42, 180, 182, 228n98; *cf.* 173–74
Scutenaire, Louis, 235n71
sdělovací funkce. *See* communicative function
Sedgwick, Eve Kosofsky, 24
Seeger, Pete, 111
Shakespeare, William, 8, 9, 18, 78, 127, 233n55
Shea, Lisa, 212n4
Sher, Gail, 84
Shklovsky, Viktor, 9, 26, 47, 91, 196n77, 216n41
Shreiber, Maeera, 206n66
signature, 6, 49–51, 57–58, 61–65, 67, 73, 75–77, 98–100, 169, 176–77, 204n37, 209n129, 239n45. *See also* names
silkscreen. *See* screen printing
Silliman, Ron, 35, 83, 87, 90–91, 200n57, 211n3, 214n21
Smith, Hale, 221n20
Smithson, Robert, 8, 182, 186, 193n26
Smollett, Tobias, 71
Soffici, Ardengo, 55
Sollers, Philippe, 165
Solt, Mary Ellen, 118
spectral, 105, 119, 124, 126, 137, 142, 152–54, 156, 168, 176, 183–84, 186, 232n35, 241n89, 241n91
Sperberg-McQueen, C. M., 121
Starobinski, Jean, 205n49
Stcherbatskoy, Fyodor, 163
Stein, Gertrude, 3, 6, 21, 22, 35, 65–68, 75–76, 80, 148, 153, 186, 206n56, 211n2, 217n47

Stella, Frank, 211n2
Stephens, Paul, 232n34, 232n35, 233n39
Sterne, Jonathan, 173, 186
Sterne, Laurence, 43, 202n94
Stevenson, Robert Louis, 153
stumbling, 35, 97–98, 107, 151, 152–53, 154, 157, 164
substrate. *See* medium
Suckling, John, 127
surface reading, 14–15
Surrealism, 17, 27, 75, 79, 80–81, 235n71
Sweet, David, 57

Tabios, Eileen, 215n27
telephone, 172–74, 177, 178–79, 182–84, 237n12, 240n60, 240n68, 241n86
teletype, 121, 225n72
Temple, Michael, 210n136
testes, 175, 176, 238n32, 238n33
Tharpe, Sister Rosetta, 221n14
Thomas, Don, 134, 136, 137, 227n91
Thomas, Lorenzo, 230n3
Toklas, Alice B., 66, 67
Tolson, Melvin, 6
Toomer, Jean, 83
transitive property, 7, 94, 96–97, 155, 158–59, 175, 217n50
transparency, 7, 9, 13, 16, 20, 31–47, 86, 98, 99, 133–34, 187, 209n130, 214n14, 214n23, 216n40, 224n43, 228n97, 228n98, 229n108, 230n3
trobar clus, 82
Tucker, Maureen, 171
typewriter, 5, 94, 100, 120–21, 122, 124–26, 134, 137, 139, 141, 152, 170, 171, 174, 175, 217n55, 220n8, 236n2, 236n3, 236–37n4, 238n27, 241n81
typography, 4–6, 8, 21–46, 50–51, 53–55, 72, 73, 76, 84, 93, 95–100, 101–43, 146–50, 151, 153, 159–60, 169, 176–77, 187, 193n25, 193n26, 197n14, 197n18, 201n90, 210n134, 225n66, 231n16, 235n71. *See also* materiality
Tzara, Tristan, 78, 80, 203n8

Umbra (workshop), 143
Unicode, 121–22, 226n78, 226n79

Valéry, Paul, 7, 26, 193n21, 193n23
Vallejo, César, 80
Veitch, Tom, 212n6
Velvet Underground, 171, 186
Villon, François, 55, 78
von Kleist, Heinrich, 161
Vose, Julia, 212n6
Vroom, Ivo, 115

Wagner, Linda, 194n38
Wallace, Mark, 87
Ward, Diane, 212n3
Warhol, Andy, 4–5, 6, 7, 34, 131, 149, 170–87, 192n16, 208n110, 236n2, 236n3, 236–37n4, 237n12, 238n26, 238n35, 238n36, 238–39n37, 239n45, 241n82, 242n99
Weiner, Norbert, 11
Wellbery, David, 13, 193n31
White, Newman, 220n4
Whitman, Walt, 24–25
Wilhelm (Kaiser), 66–68
Williams, Cameron, 105
Williams, William Carlos, 10, 11, 15, 16, 19, 35–38, 124, 194n42, 200n57, 200n59, 200n61, 201n75
windows, 9, 37, 40–44, 45, 56–57, 59, 66, 76, 103, 105, 133–34, 224n43
Wirth, Eric, 93
Wittgenstein, Ludwig, 8, 10, 13, 149, 186, 193n29, 194n38
Wolpe, Stefan, 222n21
Wordsworth, William, 21–22
Worth, Liz, 192n15
Wurlitzer, Rudolph, 212n6

Xerox (machine). *See* duplicator
Xisto, Pedro, 115

Yeats, William Butler, 22–24, 39, 155, 197n11, 197n13
Young, Kevin, 236n87

Zürn, Unica, 78

www.ingramcontent.com/pod-product-compliance
Lightning Source LLC
Chambersburg PA
CBHW051354290426
44108CB00015B/2002